WHEN IN DOUBT, CHECK HIM OUT

A WOMAN'S SURVIVAL GUIDE

Joseph Culligan
Licensed Private Investigator

NATIONAL ASSOCIATION OF INVESTIGATIVE SPECIALISTS
HALL OF FAME MEMBER

JODERE
GROUP

Jodere Group, Inc.
San Diego, California

When in Doubt, Check Him Out

Jodere Group, Inc.
San Diego, CA 92191

Please note that all government agencies, including driving and motor vehicle records departments, are constantly changing policies insofar as what access to records and files will be accorded the public.

Library of Congress Catalog Card Number: 2001029321
ISBN: 1-58872-001-2
Printed in the United States of America

Library of Congress Cataloging-in-Publication Data

Culligan, Joseph J.
    When in doubt, check him out : a woman's survival guide / Joseph J. Culligan.
        p. cm.
    ISBN 1-58872-001-2 (tradepaper)
    1. Public records--United States--Research--Handbooks, manuals, etc. 2. Biography--Research--Methodology--Handbooks, manuals, etc. 3. Investigations--Handbooks, manuals, etc. I. Title.
    JK2445.P82 C85 2001
    001.4'2--dc21

                                                        2001029321

Neither the author nor the publisher assumes any responsibility for the use or misuse of information and sources contained in this book.

*This book is dedicated
to all who come through their own crisis
and hell and go on to lend a hand
of support and guidance to others.*

CONTENTS

PREFACE

In addition to a fiancé or prospective mate, remember that the sources in this book are those that can be used to check any person's or company's background. You may want to check out a prospective business partner, a nanny, a future employee, or that roofer who's fixing your house who you have more and more doubts about by the minute.

Please read the following excerpt from the Preface I wrote over seven years ago:

> *The following two sobering statistics are from the Committee on the Judiciary, United States Senate, 102nd Congress chaired by Joseph R. Biden, Jr.:*
>
> *"Almost 4 years ago, the Surgeon General of the United States warned that violence was the No. 1 public health risk to adult women in the United States. Unfortunately, four years later, it still remains the leading cause of injuries to women ages 15–44, more common than **automobile accidents, muggings, and cancer deaths combined.**"*
>
> *"We live in a country with three times as many animal shelters as battered women's shelters."*

Well, there you have it. I had that published over 2,100 days ago. Even though 37 states have anti-stalking laws, domestic abuse prosecution is aggressively pursued (and no longer given a wink and a nod by disinterested prosecutors), and women's groups offer support more than ever before—the problem that women (and some men, also) face is just as deadly and daunting. If the public would just use some background checks on people they know in business or in their personal lives, then so much needless abuse—mental, physical, and financial—could be avoided.

I hope the above will set the tone for this book. The information that is provided in just one chapter can possibly save you from the physical or mental abuse of a potential mate who has a history of violence and dishonesty. When you read the information contained in divorce files found in Chapter 2, I am sure you will agree this book is a good place to start in order to prevent involvement with that wrong "Mr. Right."

Imagine how many of the readers of this book will be able to save themselves grief and heartache by simply using telephone numbers and Web addresses on pages 7-26 though 7-28 and finding out that your boyfriend and future son-in-law had been an inmate . . . or by checking his driving record to discover drunken driving charges . . . or by reviewing his divorce record to discover that he had abused his wife . . . or by checking with the sources in the Child Enforcement chapter to see that he owes child support.

In this book, I will show you methods to use to find an individual's Social Security Number and how to use a company (used by law enforcement, governments, private investigators, and attorneys) to run a background check on that number so you will be able to see what addresses he has called "home" in past years. You will read about the valuable types of court records, licenses, and reports that will enable you to know a little more about your "friend."

The point is very simple. Because you are reading this book, you are now in the frame of mind to save yourself years of financial woes or physical and mental abuse by being aggressive and finding out **who he really is.** After you read *"The Trouble with Boyfriends"* article at the end of Chapter 6, you will get a jolt that will give you the impetus to take charge and investigate.

Let me know about your success using this book. You may wish to share your story with others via magazines and television so they can learn just how easy and inexpensive a little investigation can be. In some cases, it may even prove to be lifesaving. I may be contacted by visiting: **www.josephculligan.com.**

❧ ❧ ❧

Driving &
Automobile Records

I s his address of the past and present what he says it is? Does he have a valid license? Does he have an excessive amount of traffic tickets? Are the tickets for speeding, reckless or drunken driving? If he was arrested for drunken driving charges, does the police report reflect the date of birth, place of birth, and place of employment **that your "friend" had told you about?** Does he own the vehicles that he says he owns? Are they registered at an address that **may be that of a girlfriend or a wife?** Does he co-own vehicles with someone else? Is he being sued for accidents that may cause a liability, which may become **your liability** upon exchanging marriage vows?

We will find out how to learn about this information and more in this chapter. This chapter illustrates the different responses from the states regarding their policies regarding the release of licenses and registrations. Please keep in mind that the states change their rules insofar as fees, and what they will and will not release to the public. To do your background profile on your "friend" properly and professionally, you should write to the state and ask what the present fees are. Ask if there are any restrictions for release, and **has the state instituted a policy of informing the subject that their driver's license record was pulled.**

When writing to request a copy of the subject's driving record, include the date of birth. If you do not have an exact date of birth for the subject, write and ask for an alphabetical search.

Here is a sample letter requesting a driving record when you do not have a date of birth:

Date
Jane Doe
123 Anywhere Drive
Anytown, New York 12345

Dear Commissioner of Motor Vehicles:
    Kindly send me the driving record of Robert Hamilton. I am sorry that I do not have a date of birth, but please do an alphabetical search for the year of 1943. Find a check attached for the appropriate fee. I am also submitting an additional check for $15. This will cover any additional costs should there be more than one Robert Hamilton.
    If your search reveals that there are numerous Robert Hamiltons, please advise me and I will decide on what course of action I wish to pursue.

Sincerely,
Jane Doe

The above letter does wonders. If the driving record division writes to you and says there are many individuals who have your subject's name with that year of birth, you will want to write back and give the area of the state in which the subject resides. If you receive several driving records and do not know which is your subject, don't despair. **Driving records may contain some or all of the following, which will assist you in determining which of the licensees is your subject:**

Address	**Social Security Number**
Height	**Date of Birth**
Weight	**Dates and Locations of Accidents**
Hair Color	**Dates and Locations of Traffic Tickets**
Eye Color	**Restrictions, i.e., Eyeglasses**

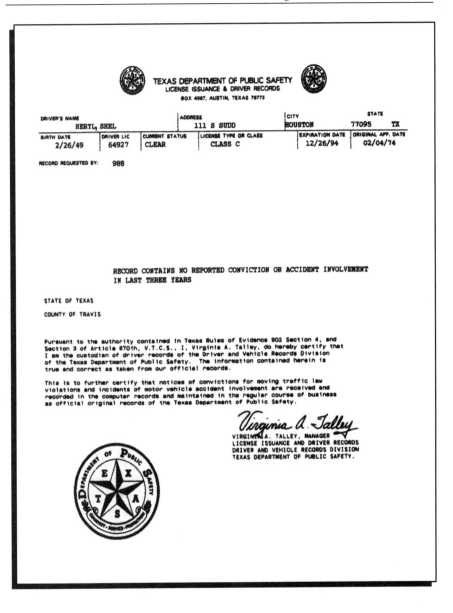

This typical response for a driving record illustrates that this individual has a clear driving record for the past three years. It is important to note that the original application date was 2/4/74, when this person was 25 years old. You will want to check further and find out where he had been licensed previously. **Is it believable that your "friend" was 25 years old when he first became licensed?** You may check out the addresses that he lived at through the years by running his Social Security Number for old addresses or by checking voter's registration records.

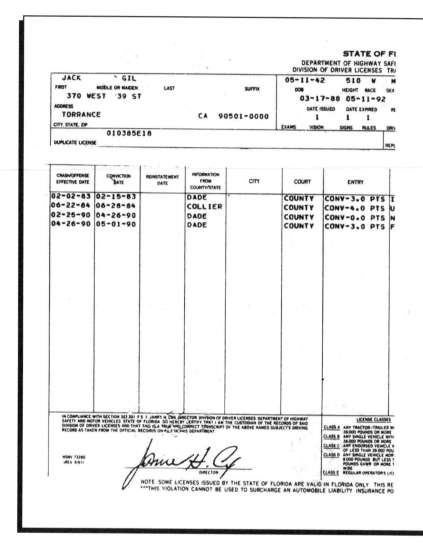

This license indicates what counties the tickets were issued in. You may want to review Chapter 5, which will give you much guidance on how to look up records of an individual on the county level. Even though Dade County is obviously the predominant county on this license, you will want to check Collier County, also. Was he just passing through Collier County, or did he have living arrangements on or about June 22, 1984? This individual's license was originally issued in 1972, but you will note that a California address appears. Check out this address if you did not know about it. **Why would this person need to keep an address in another state?** Also note the wide span of years in which the traffic tickets were issued. Was he shuffling back and forth between the states during this period? And if so, why?

FLORIDA
SAFETY AND MOTOR VEHICLES
TRANSCRIPT OF DRIVER RECORD

M	283-08-7645		10-06-92		0600	
SEX	SOCIAL SECURITY NUMBER		SEARCH DATE		REQUESTOR	
		DRIVER EDUCATION				
		G400-423-42-17				
RESTRICTIONS	ENDORSEMENTS	FLORIDA DRIVER LICENSE NUMBER		PRIOR STATE AND DRIVER LICENSE NUMBER		
0	0 0	05-31-72		84LCEL	031788W	
DRIVING	MOTORCYCLE	DATE ORIG DL ISSUED	CDL ISSUE DATE	PREVIOUS BATCH	CURRENT BATCH	

REPLACEMENT LICENSE

DESCRIPTION	R E P O R M	C E T A G	C R A S H	D I S P	A C T I O N	DOCKET OR TICKET NUMBER	DEPT. USE ONLY BATCH
IMPROPER TURN					1	98KQ	309
UNLAWFUL SPEED 071/55					1	7479	422
NO/IMPROPER CHILD RESTRAINT DEVICE					1	2991	012
FAIL TO OBEY TRAF INSTR SIGN/DEVICE					1	2365	013

SSES

	RESTRICTIONS		REPRESENTATIVE CODES	CITATION/CRASH CODE
LER WITH A GVWR OF	A CORRECTIVE LENSES	M HAND CONTROLS OR PEDAL EXTENSION	C REPRESENTED BY COUNSEL	C INDICATES CITATION ISSUED
MORE	B OUTSIDE REARVIEW MIRROR	N LEFT FOOT ACCELERATOR	W COUNSEL WAIVED	A INDICATES CRASH
E WITH A GVWR OF	C BUSINESS PURPOSES	P PROBATION—INTERLOCK DEVICE		
MORE	D EMPLOYMENT PURPOSES	R RESTRICTED	DISPOSITION CODES	ACTION CODES
IICLE WITH A GVWR	E DAYLIGHT DRIVING ONLY	S OTHER RESTRICTIONS		
20 POUNDS	F AUTOMATIC TRANSMISSION	X MEDICAL ALERT BRACELET	1 GUILTY	D DEPARTMENT ACTION
E MORE THAN	H 1 1/2 TON SINGLE UNIT VEHICLE	1 VEHICLES W/O AIR BRAKES	2 ESTREATURE	C COURT ACTION
LESS THAN 26,000	I DIRECTIONAL SIGNALS	2 CDL INTRASTATE ONLY	3 FORFEITURE	
MORE THAN 80 INCHES	J HEARING AID	3 CDL BUS ONLY	4 ADJUDGED DELINQUENT	
	K GRIP ON STEERING WHEEL	4 CMV < 26,000 LBS GVWR	5 ADJUDICATION WITHHELD	
FS LICENSE	L SEAT CUSHION	5 NO TRACTOR/TRAILERS		

IS RESULTS FROM APPLICANT RETAINING A VALID LICENSE FROM ANOTHER JURISDICTION
:E POLICY F S 626.9701

This driving record lists numerous tickets but of importance is the violation for **"improper child restraint device."** This may lead you to children that your "friend" has not told you about. At the very least, you will want him to take the proper precautions with your child. Take note that the Social Security Number appears, which will be of tremendous assistance. Note the speeding, improper turn, and failure-to-obey traffic signs or device violations. You will want to order copies of these tickets. Was he driving an automobile he owned, or was it a vehicle that was **owned by a wife, girlfriend, or business associate you know nothing about?** Check to see if he had taken out a loan for an automobile. I have explained elsewhere what procedures to follow to order the registration of a vehicle once you obtain the plate number, which, of course, is listed on the traffic ticket.

MISSOURI DEPARTMENT OF REVENUE DRIVERS LICENSE BUREAU P. O. BOX 200 JEFFERSON CITY, MO 65105-0200	MISSOURI DRIVER RECORD	ISD FORM 3201	

PAGE   1

CUSTOMER NUMBER	DRIVER		LICENSE NUMBERS
	NAME James R. Rogers	CLASSIFIED	
	ADDRESS 1265 Thornwood Street	GENERATED	
713	CITY : Joplin STATE : MO ZIP : 64865	PREVIOUS :	

PERSONAL DATA	LICENSE INFORMATION	ENDORSEMENTS	RESTRICTIONS
BIRTH : 06/24/29	CLASS : F	NO ENDORSEMENTS	A-ADEQUATE GLASSES
SEX : M	EXPIRES : 06/19/94		
EYES : BROWN	SEQ NO : 120217000		
HEIGHT : 510	ISSUED : 06/21/91		
WEIGHT : 150	TYPE : NEW		

DRIVER STATUS		PERMIT INFORMATION
MO STATUS :		CLASS :
CDL STATUS :		EXPIRES :
LICENSE DENIAL : B		SEQ NO :
CLERK CODE :		ISSUED :
		ENDORSEMENTS :
MESSAGE		RESTRICTIONS :

THIS IS A TRUE AND ACCURATE COPY AS OF : 01/12/93

TRAILER	DEPARTMENT/ LOCATION	DATE			ACTIVITY	ACT	ACC OR REIN	VIOL TYPE CASE	CASE NO OR VIOLATION DESCRIPTION	CDL C/H	FILE NUMBER	DAYS PTS
		MO	DA	YR								
1	SURRENDER	06	19	91	FL TO MO						G65392829	

Note that the above driving license was issued on 6/21/91 and that the individual previously had a license in Florida. You would want to order a Florida driving record, and if that license indicates that the person, who was born in 1929, was older than 18 when they applied in Florida, you would follow the paper trail to another state for an earlier license. James R. Rogers is required to wear glasses when driving, is 5'10" tall, weighs 150 pounds, and has brown eyes. Check this description with what you know about your "friend." **Remember that the driving license is the most commonly used instrument when assuming another person's identity.**

NEIL GOLDSCHMIDT
GOVERNOR

OFFICE OF THE GOVERNOR
STATE CAPITOL
SALEM, OREGON 97310-0370
TELEPHONE: 378-3111

Thank you for sending me a copy of your letter to Karl Kruege regarding a request for Driver License/ID Card Application History.

Mr. Kruege tells me he has apologized for the misunderstanding. He also explained that the Motor Vehicles Division no longer has Ronald Ezell's original driver license application.

We take pride in the service we provide and hope to do better next time.

Sincerely,

Neil Goldschmidt
Governor

NG:cm

cc: Karl Krueger

I noted previously that if you do not have an exact date of birth, you will want **to ask for an alphabetical search.** Sometimes you will get a clerk who will send you a letter stating that they need an exact date of birth. The above letter is a response I had from a letter I wrote to the governor complaining that a clerk would not search for a driving record by name only. There is no reason that you should be denied a search if the name you request a license for does not come up with a thousand duplicates, which would be the case for a John Smith.

DRIVER'S LICENSES

ALABAMA
Driver's Licenses
State of Alabama
P.O. Box 1471–H
Montgomery, Alabama 36192

ALASKA
Driver's Licenses
State of Alaska
P.O. Box 20020–E
Juneau, Alaska 99802

ARIZONA
Driver's Licenses
State of Arizona
P.O. Box 2100–L
Phoenix, Arizona 85001

ARKANSAS
Driver's Licenses
State of Arkansas
P.O. Box 1271–L
Little Rock, Arkansas 72203

CALIFORNIA
Driver's Licenses
State of California
P.O. Box 944231–O
Sacramento, California 94244

COLORADO
Driver's Licenses
State of Colorado
140 West 6th Avenue
Denver, Colorado 80204

CONNECTICUT
Driver's Licenses
State of Connecticut
60 State Street
Wethersfield, Connecticut 06109

DELAWARE
Driver's Licenses
State of Delaware
P.O. Box 698–R
Dover, Delaware 19903

DISTRICT OF COLUMBIA
Driver's Licenses
District of Columbia
301 C Street, N.W.
Washington, DC 20001

FLORIDA
Driver's Licenses
State of Florida
Neil Kirkman Building
Tallahassee, Florida 32399

GEORGIA
Driver's Licenses
State of Georgia
P.O. Box 1456–E
Atlanta, Georgia 30371

HAWAII
Driver's Licenses
State of Hawaii
530 South King Street
Honolulu, Hawaii 96813

IDAHO
Driver's Licenses
State of Idaho
P.O. Box 7129–I
Boise, Idaho 83707

ILLINOIS
Driver's Licenses
State of Illinois
2701 South Dirksen Parkway
Springfield, Illinois 62723

INDIANA

Driver's Licenses
State of Indiana
State Office Building
Indianapolis, Indiana 46204

IOWA

Driver's Licenses
State of Iowa
100 Euclid Avenue
Des Moines, Iowa 50306

KANSAS

Driver's Licenses
State of Kansas
Docking Office Building
Topeka, Kansas 66626

KENTUCKY

Driver's Licenses
State of Kentucky
State Office Building
Frankfort, Kentucky 40622

LOUISIANA

Driver's Licenses
State of Louisiana
P.O. Box 64886–D
Baton Rouge, Louisiana 70896

MAINE

Driver's Licenses
State of Maine
State House, Room 29
Augusta, Maine 04333

MARYLAND

Driver's Licenses
State of Maryland
6601 Ritchie Highway, N.E. Room 211
Glen Burnie, Maryland 21062

MASSACHUSETTS

Driver's Licenses
Commonwealth of Massachusetts
100 Nashua Street
Boston, Massachusetts 02114

MICHIGAN

Driver's Licenses
State of Michigan
7064 Crowner Drive
Lansing, Michigan 48918

MINNESOTA

Driver's Licenses
State of Minnesota
Transportation Building, Room 108
St. Paul, Minnesota 55155

MISSISSIPPI

Driver's Licenses
State of Mississippi
P.O. Box 958–J
Jackson, Mississippi 39205

MISSOURI

Driver's Licenses
State of Missouri
P.O. Box 200–O
Jefferson City, Missouri 65105

MONTANA

Driver's Licenses
State of Montana
303 North Roberts
Helena, Montana 59620

NEBRASKA

Driver's Licenses
State of Nebraska
301 Centennial Mall South
Lincoln, Nebraska 68509

NEVADA

Driver's Licenses
State of Nevada
555 Wright Way
Carson City, Nevada 89711

NEW HAMPSHIRE

Driver's Licenses
State of New Hampshire
10 Hazen Drive
Concord, New Hampshire 03305

NEW JERSEY
Driver's Licenses
State of New Jersey
25 South Montgomery Street
Trenton, New Jersey 08666

NEW MEXICO
Driver's Licenses
State of New Mexico
P.O. Box 1028–E
Santa Fe, New Mexico 87504

NEW YORK
Driver's Licenses
State of New York
Empire State Plaza
Albany, New York 12228

NORTH CAROLINA
Driver's Licenses
State of North Carolina
1100 New Bern Avenue
Raleigh, North Carolina 27697

NORTH DAKOTA
Driver's Licenses
State of North Dakota
Capitol Grounds
Bismarck, North Dakota 58505

OHIO
Driver's Licenses
State of Ohio
P.O. Box 7167–Y
Columbus, Ohio 43266

OKLAHOMA
Driver's Licenses
State of Oklahoma
P.O. Box 11415–C
Oklahoma City, Oklahoma 73136

OREGON
Driver's Licenses
State of Oregon
1905 Lana Avenue, N.E.
Salem, Oregon 97314

PENNSYLVANIA
Driver's Licenses
State of Pennsylvania
P.O. Box 8695–O
Harrisburg, Pennsylvania 17105

PUERTO RICO
Driver's Licenses
Commonwealth of Puerto Rico
P.O. Box 41243–L
Santurce, Puerto Rico 00940

RHODE ISLAND
Driver's Licenses
State of Rhode Island
345 Harris Avenue
Providence, Rhode Island 02909

SOUTH CAROLINA
Driver's Licenses
State of South Carolina
P.O. Box 1498–U
Columbia, South Carolina 29216

SOUTH DAKOTA
Driver's Licenses
State of South Dakota
118 West Capitol Avenue
Pierre, South Dakota 57501

TENNESSEE
Driver's Licenses
State of Tennessee
P.O. Box 945–C
Nashville, Tennessee 37202

TEXAS
Driver's Licenses
State of Texas
P.O. Box 4087–C
Austin, Texas 78773

UTAH
Driver's Licenses
State of Utah
1095 Motor Avenue
Salt Lake City, Utah 84116

VERMONT

Driver's Licenses
State of Vermont
120 State Street
Montpelier, Vermont 05603

VIRGINIA

Driver's Licenses
State of Virginia
2300 West Broad Street
Richmond, Virginia 23269

WASHINGTON

Driver's Licenses
State of Washington
211 12th Avenue, S.E.
Olympia, Washington 98504

WEST VIRGINIA

Driver's Licenses
State of West Virginia
1800 Washington Street, East
Charleston, West Virginia 25317

WISCONSIN

Driver's Licenses
State of Wisconsin
P.O. Box 7918
Madison, Wisconsin 53707

WYOMING

Driver's Licenses
State of Wyoming
122 West 25th Street
Cheyenne, Wyoming 82002

STATE OF NEVADA

EXECUTIVE CHAMBER
Carson City, Nevada 89710

BOB MILLER
Acting Governor

TELEPHONE
(702) 885-5670

Thank you for your recent letter regarding record information for the State of Nevada. Below are answers to your specific questions regarding the accessing of drivers license and vehicle registration/title records through the Nevada Motor Vehicle Record Section.

1. A driving record can be manually accessed by name only; however if multiple listings appear for the name searched, a "no match" will be reported. A positive identifier is always advisable, i.e., drivers license number, social security number, or date of birth.

2. The current charge is $3.00 for a driving record.

3. The standard record includes a three year history. Law enforcement officials and the courts have access to the entire file of an individual.

4. Requests for driving records should be submitted to:

    Department of Motor Vehicles & Public Safety
    Record Section
    555 Wright Way
    Carson City, Nevada 89711-0250

5. Requests for records submitted in letter form are acceptable.

6. An individual's drivers license file will drop off the system after ten years with no action on the license.

You can see that driving records can be retrieved by name only. Most states will accept a request for records by way of a letter and not a preprinted form. If a person had any traffic violations, the license file would be extended ten years, and **a drunken driving charge would keep the record on file indefinitely.** Your request for driving records will, of course, always be fulfilled more promptly when you give as much information as possible. Many driving records will contain the Social Security Number. I cannot stress strongly enough how important it is to run past addresses using this number. Your subject may not have been ultracareful to hide certain addresses four or five years ago since he did not think you would be checking those addresses today.

7. A reason is mandatory from an individual requesting drivers license or registration records. A reason of "simple curiosity" is not acceptable and the request for information would be denied. NRS 481.063 states, that the Department may deny any private use of the files if it is believed that the information may be used for an illegal purpose or is an unwarranted invasion of a person's privacy.

8. Vehicle registrations can be accessed by name only. However, multiple listings will result in a "no match" if an address is not provided by the requesting party.

9. Registration records are public record.

10. A printout of a current registration is $3.00. Requests should be sent to the same address as used for drivers license requests.

The information above was obtained through the Nevada Department of Motor Vehicles and Public Safety. If you have additional questions, you may wish to contact Mr. Wayne Teglia, Director, Department of Motor Vehicles and Public Safety, 555 Wright Way, Carson City, Nevada 89711.

Again, than you for writing. Please contact my office if I can be of further assistance.

Sincerely,

BOB MILLER
Governor

BM/lw

In most states, vehicle registrations can be accessed by name only. This is important because your "friend" may not have given you his exact date of birth during your relationship. He may have simply wanted to shave a few years off his age, but he may also **have wanted to thwart any future background checks on himself.** So if you get a "no match" when using the exact date of birth on your subject, then make another request for a search by name only. Many responses from governors will include a certain official's name. In this letter, it was Wayne Teglia, and as you can see, he is the Director of Motor Vehicles.

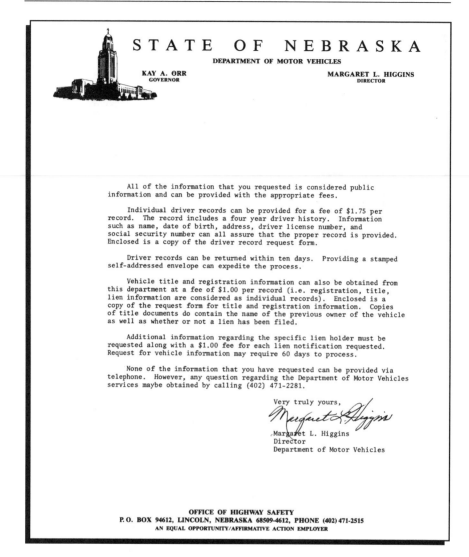

STATE OF NEBRASKA

DEPARTMENT OF MOTOR VEHICLES

KAY A. ORR
GOVERNOR

MARGARET L. HIGGINS
DIRECTOR

All of the information that you requested is considered public information and can be provided with the appropriate fees.

Individual driver records can be provided for a fee of $1.75 per record. The record includes a four year driver history. Information such as name, date of birth, address, driver license number, and social security number can all assure that the proper record is provided. Enclosed is a copy of the driver record request form.

Driver records can be returned within ten days. Providing a stamped self-addressed envelope can expedite the process.

Vehicle title and registration information can also be obtained from this department at a fee of $1.00 per record (i.e. registration, title, lien information are considered as individual records). Enclosed is a copy of the request form for title and registration information. Copies of title documents do contain the name of the previous owner of the vehicle as well as whether or not a lien has been filed.

Additional information regarding the specific lien holder must be requested along with a $1.00 fee for each lien notification requested. Request for vehicle information may require 60 days to process.

None of the information that you have requested can be provided via telephone. However, any question regarding the Department of Motor Vehicles services maybe obtained by calling (402) 471-2281.

Very truly yours,

Margaret L. Higgins
Director
Department of Motor Vehicles

OFFICE OF HIGHWAY SAFETY
P. O. BOX 94612, LINCOLN, NEBRASKA 68509-4612, PHONE (402) 471-2515
AN EQUAL OPPORTUNITY/AFFIRMATIVE ACTION EMPLOYER

A self-addressed stamped envelope will assist the motor vehicle departments in giving you a more prompt response. Also note that, in most states, title documents will indicate previous owners. Did your "friend" receive his automobile from **a business partner, girlfriend, or ex-wife** in a divorce settlement or from an inheritance? You may, at the very least, have the name of another person who could provide you with background information on your subject. Most states will not give you information over the telephone, but as you can see from the above letter, they will answer inquiries. This may save you the task of letter writing in some cases where all you had was a simple question about fees or what restrictions the state has regarding release of records.

JOHN ASHCROFT
GOVERNOR

DUANE BENTON
DIRECTOR OF REVENUE

MISSOURI DEPARTMENT OF REVENUE
DIVISION OF MOTOR VEHICLE AND DRIVERS LICENSING
POST OFFICE BOX 629
JEFFERSON CITY, MISSOURI 65105-0629

JOHN A. LUCKS
DIRECTOR
DIVISION OF MOTOR VEHICLE
AND DRIVERS LICENSING

The Missouri Motor Vehicle Bureau's records may be obtained by owner's name and year, make, vehicle identification number, title number or license plate number of the vehicle in question. The date of birth of a vehicle owner is not required to obtain titling and registration records.

The Missouri Motor Vehicle Bureau will accept a written request from the general public for information from the files with an initial fee of $4.00. An additional $4.00 charge per copy is required for each non-computer-generated document. The written request and fee should be submitted to: Motor Vehicle Bureau, P.O. Box 100, Jefferson City, Missouri 65105-0100.

The Missouri Drivers License Bureau may complete a driver record search by name only; however, there is no guarantee that the record found is the individual in question since there are many individuals with the same name. A drivers license record may also be obtained by an individual's date of birth or social security number and a Missouri drivers license number or address at the time of application.

The length of time drivers license information is maintained on file depends on the type of activity entered on an individual's driving record. Less serious convictions, suspensions, revocations, denials, etc., are maintained on an individual's driving record for five years. More serious convictions, suspensions, revocations, denials, etc., can remain on an individual's driving record permanently even if he/she moves to another state or allows his/her drivers license to expire. An individual's driver record is deleted at the next scheduled purge, if his/her drivers license has expired over seven months and no other activity exists.

Most states will keep a driving record on file **permanently** if the person had any suspensions, revocations, etc. This policy is very useful when doing your background profile because you may need to look up the address your "friend" had 20 years ago in a particular state, even though he had moved to another state. If you do see a drunken driving charge on your subject's driving record, then you will want to write to the jurisdiction noted to order a complete copy of the arrest file. Also, once again, you will note that there is no date of birth required in most states for obtaining a vehicle registration.

STATE OF GEORGIA

OFFICE OF THE GOVERNOR

ATLANTA 30334

Joe Frank Harris
GOVERNOR

This is in response to your recent letter requesting drivers license and title information for the State of Georgia.

Copies of your letter have been forwarded to Colonel Curtis D. Earp, Jr., Commissioner of the Department of Public Safety, for answers to your drivers license inquiries; and, to Honorable Marcus Collins, Commissioner of the Department of Revenue, for the title information. You should be hearing from someone in these departments soon.

With kindest regards, I remain

Sincerely,

Joe Frank Harris

JFH/hd

cc: Colonel Curtis D. Earp, Jr.
    Commissioner Marcus Collins

When I do not receive a prompt response from motor vehicle departments, I write to the governor of a state. You will, no doubt, on occasion have a response from a clerk that is unsatisfactory when requesting records. Write to the governor, attaching a copy of the response you are unhappy about. You can see that the replies sent from governors' offices are of much assistance. Take note of the names the governor is sending copies to.

STATE OF MAINE
OFFICE OF THE GOVERNOR
AUGUSTA, MAINE
04333

JOHN R. McKERNAN, JR.
GOVERNOR

Thank you for your letter requesting information on the access of driving records and vehicle registrations in Maine.

These matters are handled by the Division of Motor Vehicle, which comes under the jurisdiction of the Secretary of State. Therefore, I have taken the liberty of forwarding your letter to the Office of the Secretary of State for their response.

Thank you, again, for writing, and best wishes for the holidays.

Sincerely,

John R. McKernan, Jr.
Governor

JRM/kmb

cc: G. William Diamond, Secretary of State

The above letter is a response from the governor of Maine and was of much assistance. In this case, I could not wait for a long period of time for the response to an inquiry, as Christmas was approaching and the mails would be slow. The governor's letter to G. William Diamond effected an immediate response to my request. The turnaround time for a response from a governor's office is usually faster than any other department in state government.

The following is a list of addresses for the governors. As you can see from the previous two pages and throughout the book, using the office of the governor will assure you of a prompt and complete response for your inquiry.

STATE GOVERNORS

ALABAMA

http://www.governor.state.al.us
Governor's Office
State House
Montgomery, Alabama 36130

ALASKA

http://www.gov.state.ak.us
Governor's Office
State Capitol
P.O. Box 110001
Juneau, Alaska 99811-0001

ARIZONA

http://www.governor.state.az.us
Governor's Office
State House
Phoenix, Arizona 85007

ARKANSAS

http://www.state.ar.us/governor
Governor's Office
State Capitol
Little Rock, Arkansas 72201

CALIFORNIA

http://www.state.ca.us/s/governor
Governor's Office
State Capitol
First Floor
Sacramento, California 95814

COLORADO

http://www.state.co.us/gov_dir/gover-nor_office.html
Governor's Office
State Capitol
Denver, Colorado 80203-1792

CONNECTICUT

http://www.state.ct.us/governor/
Governor's Office
State Capitol
210 State Capitol Avenue
Hartford, Connecticut 06106

DELAWARE

http://www.state.de.us/governor/index.htm
Governor's Office
Legislative Hall
Dover, Delaware 19901

FLORIDA

http://fcn.state.fl.us/eog
Governor's Office
State Capitol, PL05
Tallahassee, Florida 32399-0001

GEORGIA

http://www.ganet.org/governor
Governor's Office
State Capitol
Atlanta, Georgia 30334

HAWAII

http://gov.state.hi.us
Governor's Office
State Capitol
Honolulu, Hawaii 96813

IDAHO

http://www2.state.id.us/gov/govhmpg.htm
Governor's Office
State Capitol
Boise, Idaho 83720

ILLINOIS

http://www.state.il.us/gov
Governor's Office
State Capitol
Springfield, Illinois 62706

INDIANA

http://www.state.in.us/gov
Governor's Office
State Capitol
Indianapolis, Indiana 46204

IOWA

http://www.state.ia.us/government/-
governor
Governor's Office
State Capitol
Des Moines, Iowa 50319

KANSAS

http://www.ink.org/public/governor/-
main.html
Governor's Office
State Capitol
2nd Floor
Topeka, Kansas 66612-1590

KENTUCKY

http://www.state.ky.us/agencies/gov/-
govmenu6.htm
Governor's Office
State Capitol
700 Capitol Avenue
Frankfort, Kentucky 40601

LOUISIANA

http://www.gov.state.la.us
Governor's Office
P.O. Box 94004
Baton Rouge, Louisiana 70804-9004

MAINE

http://www.state.me.us/governor/gov-
home.htm
Governor's Office
State House, Station 1
Augusta, Maine 04333

MARYLAND

http://www.gov.state.md.us
Governor's Office
State House
Annapolis, Maryland 21401

MASSACHUSETTS

http://www.magnet.state.ma.us/gov
Governor's Office
State House, Room 360
Boston, Massachusetts 02133

MICHIGAN

http://www.migov.state.mi.us/migov.html
Governor's Office
P.O. Box 30013
Lansing, Michigan 48909

MINNESOTA

http://www.governor.state.mn.us
Governor's Office
130 State Capitol
St. Paul, Minnesota 55155

MISSISSIPPI

http://www.govoff.state.ms.us
Governor's Office
P.O. Box 139
Jackson, Mississippi 39205

MISSOURI

http://www.gov.state.mo.us/index.htm
Governor's Office
P.O. Box 720
Jefferson City, Missouri 65102

MONTANA

http://www.state.mt.us/governor/-
governor.htm
Governor's Office
State Capitol
Helena, Montana 59620

NEBRASKA

http://gov.nol.org
Governor's Office
State Capitol
Lincoln, Nebraska 68509

NEVADA

http://www.state.nv.us/gov/gov.htm
Governor's Office
State Capitol
Carson City, Nevada 89710

NEW HAMPSHIRE

http://www.state.nh.us/governor/index.html
Governor's Office
State House
Concord, New Hampshire 03301

NEW JERSEY

http://www.state.nj.us/governor/officeo.htm
Governor's Office
State House
CN 001
Trenton, New Jersey 08625

NEW MEXICO

http://www.governor.state.nm.us
Governor's Office
State Capitol
Santa Fe, New Mexico 87503

NEW YORK

http://www.state.ny.us/governor
Governor's Office
State Capitol
Albany, New York 12224

NORTH CAROLINA

http://www.governor.state.nc.us
Governor's Office
State Capitol
Raleigh, North Carolina 27603

NORTH DAKOTA

http://www.health.state.nd.us/gov
Governor's Office
State Capitol
600 E. Boulevard
Bismarck, North Dakota 58505-0001

OHIO

http://www.state.oh.us/gov
Governor's Office
77 South High Street
30th Floor
Columbus, Ohio 43366-0601

OKLAHOMA

http://www.state.ok.us/~governor
Governor's Office
State Capitol, Room 212
Oklahoma City, Oklahoma 73105

OREGON

http://www.governor.state.or.us/-
governor.html
Governor's Office
Office of the Governor
State Capitol
Salem, Oregon 97310

PENNSYLVANIA

http://www.state.pa.us/PA_Exec/Gover-
nor/overview.html
Governor's Office
225 Main Capitol Building
Harrisburg, Pennsylvania 17120

RHODE ISLAND

http://www.governor.state.ri.us
Governor's Office
State House
Providence, Rhode Island 02903

SOUTH CAROLINA

http://www.state.sc.us/governor
Governor's Office
P.O. Box 11369
Columbia, South Carolina 29211

SOUTH DAKOTA

http://www.state.sd.us/governor/-
governor.htm
Governor's Office
500 East Capitol
Pierre, South Dakota 57501

TENNESSEE

http://www.state.tn.us
Governor's Office
State Capitol
Nashville, Tennessee 37243-0001

TEXAS

http://www.governor.state.tx.us
Governor's Office
P.O. Box 12428, Capitol Station
Austin, Texas 78711

UTAH

http://www.governor.state.ut.us
Governor's Office
210 State Capitol
Salt Lake City, Utah 84114

VERMONT

http://www.cit.state.vt.us/governor/in-
dex.htm
Governor's Office
109 State Street
Montpelier, Vermont 05609

VIRGINIA

http://www.state.va.us/governor
Governor's Office
State Capitol
Richmond, Virginia 23219

WASHINGTON

http://www.governor.wa.gov
Governor's Office
Legislative Building
Olympia, Washington 98504

WEST VIRGINIA

http://www.state.wv.us/governor
Governor's Office
State Capitol
Charleston, West Virginia 25305

WISCONSIN

http://www.wisgov.state.wi.us
Governor's Office
State Capitol
P.O. Box 7863
Madison, Wisconsin 53707

WYOMING

Governor's Office
http://www.state.wy.us/governor/gover-
nor_home.html
State Capitol
Cheyenne, Wyoming 82002

If your subject appears to be a person who will not give proper information on any licenses or other documents, then traffic tickets will be of assistance. If your subject's driving record indicates traffic violations, take note of the jurisdiction or location that issued the ticket. Write to that authority and request a photocopy of the ticket.

On the ticket will be the make, model, and license number of the vehicle the subject was driving when stopped for the citation.

You will want to write to the motor vehicle registration department, supplying the license plate number of the vehicle. Many times the registration that you receive with the vehicle will indicate ownership of a person other than your subject, such as a wife, girlfriend, phony company name used as a front, or possibly another name used by your subject. **Also note that the telephone number of your "friend" may be on the ticket along with his date of birth and home address. Is this the personal information as you know it? Does the address that was on the ticket from several years ago seem correct?**

After you have the subject's driving record and address, you may discover that the address is not the current one. Of course, there are many ways to receive a person's new address, but you may want to write to the appropriate motor vehicle department. Armed with the subject's date of birth from the driving record, request a list of all motor vehicles listed in the subject's name. You will also be surprised that your subject may have vehicles listed in his name and his **spouse's** name, a spouse you never knew existed.

Motor vehicle registrations are important to request, since a driver's license may be **renewed as infrequently as every eight years** in some states, whereas automobile registrations are **renewed every year**. Of course, this gives you a more current address to check out.

Here is a sample of a letter:

Date
Jane Doe
123 Anywhere Drive
Anytown, New York 12345

Dear Commissioner of Motor Vehicles:
   Kindly send me the motor vehicle information for vehicles owned by: Robert Hamilton, Date of Birth: 03/04/43. Please find a check attached to cover the costs of the requested registration information for up to five vehicles. If there are more than five vehicles, please contact me, and I will be glad to remit the amount requested.

Sincerely,
Jane Doe

Fees were not included in this chapter because most of the states will adjust prices within the next 24 months. Write to the states for a current price structure. Please note that all government agencies, including driving and motor vehicle records departments, are constantly changing policies insofar as what access to records and files will be accorded the public. There may be a federal law in the near future that will restrict driving record information in all states.

For instance, a marriage record is public record in Dade County, Florida, whereas a marriage record is NOT public in any of the five boroughs of New York City. A driving record is NOT public record in California, but in most other states, it is. If the driving record is not available to you, then use the myriad of other sources in this book to check him out, such as divorce records, voter registration, property records, hunting and fishing licenses, etc.

In many states, you can order a microfilm copy of your subject's application for a driver's license. Even though it may be difficult to read, you will be able to compare the signature of the applicant with your "friend" so you can make sure **that somebody hasn't changed identities.** The microfilm copy will also have an address that may not show up in any other record. In the following example, the address is over20 years old. Check out the address using the means shown in other chapters in this book, making use of property records, voters registration, mortgages, lawsuits, etc.

State of Florida
DEPARTMENT OF
HIGHWAY SAFETY AND MOTOR VEHICLES
FRED O. DICKINSON, III
Interim Executive Director

LAWTON CHILES
Governor
JIM SMITH
Secretary of State
BOB BUTTERWORTH
Attorney General
GERALD LEWIS
Comptroller
TOM GALLAGHER
Treasurer
BOB CRAWFORD
Commissioner of Agriculture
BETTY CASTOR
Commissioner of Education

RE: Luis Angel Santa

In reply to your recent inquiry, the certified copy of the application is enclosed.

Further correspondence regarding this inquiry should be directed to the Division of Driver Licenses, Kirkman Building, Tallahassee, Florida 32399-0575, or call (904) 487-2369.

Sincerely,

ALAN COCHRANE, Chief
Bureau of Records
Public Request Sub-Section

REGISTRATION AND TITLES

ALABAMA
http://www.ador.state.al.us/motorvehi-cle/MVD_MAIN.html
Department of Motor Vehicles
State of Alabama
P.O. Box 104–I
Montgomery, Alabama 36101

ALASKA
http://www.state.ak.us/local/akpages/AD MIN/dmv/dmvhome.htm
Department of Motor Vehicles
State of Alaska
5700 Todor Road
Anchorage, Alaska 99507

ARIZONA
http://www.dot.state.az.us/MVD/mvd.htm
Department of Motor Vehicles
State of Arizona
1801 West Jefferson Street
Phoenix, Arizona 85001

ARKANSAS
http://www.ark.org/revenue/motorv.mvfaq .html
Department of Motor Vehicles
State of Arkansas
P.O. 1272–I
Little Rock, Arkansas 72203

CALIFORNIA
http://www.dmv.ca.gov
Department of Motor Vehicles
State of California
P.O. Box 932328–S
Sacramento, California 94232

COLORADO
http://www.state.co.us/gov_dir/rev-enue_dir/MV_dir/mv.html
Department of Motor Vehicles
State of Colorado
140 West 6th Street
Denver, Colorado 80204

CONNECTICUT
http://dmvct.org
Department of Motor Vehicles
State of Connecticut
60 State Street
Wethersfield, Connecticut 06109

DELAWARE
http://www.state.de.us/pubsafe/index.htm
Department of Motor Vehicles
State of Delaware
State Office Building
Dover, Delaware 19903

DISTRICT OF COLUMBIA
http://www.washingtondc.gov/
Department of Motor Vehicles
District of Columbia
301 C Street
Washington, DC 20001

FLORIDA
http://www.hsmv.state.fl.us
Department of Motor Vehicles
State of Florida
2900 Apalachee Parkkway
Tallahassee, Florida 32399

GEORGIA
http://www.state.ga.us/
Department of Motor Vehicles
State of Georgia
104 Trinity Washington Building
Atlanta, Georgia 30334

HAWAII
http://www.hawaii.gov/index/transporta-tion.htm
Department of Motor Vehicles
State of Hawaii
896 Punchbowl Street
Honolulu, Hawaii 96813

IDAHO

http://www.state.id.us/itd/overorg.htm#mvb
Department of Motor Vehicles
State of Idaho
P.O. Box 34–G
Boise, Idaho 83731

ILLINOIS

http://www.sos.state.il.us:80/depts/drivers/mot_info.html
Department of Motor Vehicles
State of Illinois
Centennial Government Building
Springfield, Illinois 62756

INDIANA

http://www.state.in.us/bmv
Department of Motor Vehicles
State of Indiana
State Office Building, Room 416
Indianapolis, Indiana 46204

IOWA

http://www.state.ia.us/government/dot/-index.html
Department of Motor Vehicles
State of Iowa
Park Fair Mall, Box 9204
Des Moines, Iowa 50306

KANSAS

http://www.ink.org/public/kdor/dmv/
Department of Motor Vehicles
State of Kansas
P.O. Box 12021-L
Topeka, Kansas 66616

KENTUCKY

http://www.kytc.state.ky.us
Department of Motor Vehicles
State of Kentucky
State Building, Room 204
Frankfort, Kentucky 40622

LOUISIANA

http://www.dps.state.la.us/omv/home.html
Department of Motor Vehicles
State of Louisiana
P.O. Box 64886–A
Baton Rouge, Louisiana 70896

MAINE

http://www.state.me.us/sos/bmv/bmv.htm
Department of Motor Vehicles
State of Maine
State Building
Augusta, Maine 04333

MARYLAND

http://mva.state.md.us
Department of Motor Vehicles
State of Maryland
6601 Ritchie Highway, N.E.
Glen Burnie, Maryland 21062

MASSACHUSETTS

http://www.state.ma.us/rmv/index.htm
Department of Motor Vehicles
Commonwealth of Massachusetts
100 Nashua Street, Room 100
Boston, Massachusetts 02114

MICHIGAN

http://www.sos.state.mi.us/dv/index.html
Department of Motor Vehicles
State of Michigan
Mutual Government Building
Lansing, Michigan 48918

MINNESOTA

http://www.dps.state.mn.us/dvs/index.html
Department of Motor Vehicles
State of Minnesota
Transportation Building, Room 159
St. Paul, Minnesota 55155

MISSISSIPPI

http://www.mmvc.state.ms.us
Department of Motor Vehicles
State of Mississippi
P.O. Box 1140–D
Jackson, Mississippi 39205

MISSOURI

http://www.dor.state.mo.us
Department of Motor Vehicles
State of Missouri
P.O. Box 100–T
Jefferson City, Missouri 65105

MONTANA

http://www.doj.state.mt.us/mvd/index.htm
Department of Motor Vehicles
State of Montana
925 Main Street
Deer Lodge, Montana 59722

NEBRASKA

http://www.nol.org/home/DMV/
Department of Motor Vehicles
State of Nebraska
P.O. Box 94789–O
Lincoln, Nebraska 68509

NEVADA

http://www.state.nv.us/dmv_ps
Department of Motor Vehicles
State of Nevada
State Building
Carson City, Nevada 89111

NEW HAMPSHIRE

http://www.state.nh.us/dot/
Department of Motor Vehicles
State of New Hampshire
James H. Hayes Building
Concord, New Hampshire 03305

NEW JERSEY

http://www.state.nj.us/mvs
Department of Motor Vehicles
State of New Jersey
135 East State Street
Trenton, New Jersey 08666

NEW MEXICO

http://www.state.nm.us/tax/mvd/mvd_-home.htm
Department of Motor Vehicles
State of New Mexico
P.O. Box 1028–B
Santa Fe, New Mexico 87504

NEW YORK

http://www.nydmv.state.ny.us
Department of Motor Vehicles
State of New York
State Office Building North
Albany, New York 12228

NORTH CAROLINA

http://www.dmv.dot.state.nc.us
Department of Motor Vehicles
State of North Carolina
1100 New Bern Avenue, Room 124
Raleigh, North Carolina 27697

NORTH DAKOTA

http://www.state.nd.us/dot
Department of Motor Vehicles
State of North Dakota
806 East Boulevard
Bismarck, North Dakota 58505

OHIO

http://www.dot.state.oh.us/
Department of Motor Vehicles
State of Ohio
P.O. Box 16520
Columbus, Ohio 43266

OKLAHOMA

http://www.oktax.state.ok.us/oktax/-motorveh.html
Department of Motor Vehicles
State of Oklahoma
409 Northeast 28 Street
Oklahoma City, Oklahoma 73105

OREGON

http://www.odot.state.or.us/dmv/index.htm
Department of Motor Vehicles
State of Oregon
1905 Lana Avenue, NE
Salem, Oregon 97314

PENNSYLVANIA

http://www.dmv.state.pa.us/home/index1.asp
Department of Motor Vehicles
Commonwealth of Pennsylvania
P.O. Box 8691-W
Harrisburg, Pennsylvania 17105

PUERTO RICO

http://www.dtop.gov.pr/english/DISCO/Di
schome.htm
Department of Motor Vehicles
Commonwealth of Puerto Rico
P.O. Box 41269-I
Santurce, Puerto Rico 00940

RHODE ISLAND

http://www.dmv.state.ri.us
Department of Motor Vehicles
State of Rhode Island
State Office Building
Providence, Rhode Island 02903

SOUTH CAROLINA

http://www.state.sc.us/dps/dmv
Department of Motor Vehicles
State of South Carolina
P.O. Box 1498–T
Columbia, South Carolina 29216

SOUTH DAKOTA

http://www.state.sd.us/state/executive/rev-
enue/motorvcl.htm
Department of Motor Vehicles
State of South Dakota
118 West Capitol Avenue
Pierre, South Dakota 57501

TENNESSEE

http://www.state.tn.us/safety
Department of Motor Vehicles
State of Tennessee
500 Deaderick Street
Nashville, Tennessee 37242

TEXAS

http://www.dot.state.tx.us/insdtdot/orgchart/
vtr/vtr.htm
Department of Motor Vehicles
State of Texas
5805 North Lamar Boulevard
Austin, Texas 78773

UTAH

http://www.dmv-utah.com
Department of Motor Vehicles
State of Utah
1095 Motor Avenue
Salt Lake City, Utah 84116

VERMONT

http://www.aot.state.vt.us/dmv/dmvhp.htm
Department of Motor Vehicles
State of Vermont
120 State Street
Montpelier, Vermont 05603

VIRGINIA

http://www.dmv.state.va.us
Department of Motor Vehicles
State of Virginia
P.O. Box 27412–H
Richmond, Virginia 23269

WASHINGTON

http://www.wa.gov/dol/main.htm
Department of Motor Vehicles
State of Washington
P.O. Box 9909–H
Olympia, Washington 98504

WEST VIRGINIA

http://www.state.wv.us/dmv
Department of Motor Vehicles
State of West Virginia
State Office Building
Charleston, West Virginia 25305

WISCONSIN

http://www.dot.state.wi.us/dmv/dmv.html
Department of Motor Vehicles
State of Wisconsin
4802 Sheboygan Avenue
Madison, Wisconsin 53707

WYOMING

http://wydotweb.state.wy.us/
Department of Motor Vehicles
State of Wyoming
122 West 25th Street
Cheyenne, Wyoming 82002

DRIVING RECORDS, REGISTRATIONS, AND TITLES—CANADA

ALBERTA

Department of Motor Vehicles
10365 97th Street
Edmonton, Alberta T5J 3W7

BRITISH COLUMBIA

Department of Motor Vehicles
2631 Douglas Street
Victoria, British Columbia V8T 5A3

MANITOBA

Department of Motor Vehicles
1075 Portage Avenue
Winnipeg, Manitoba R3G 0S1

NEW BRUNSWICK

Department of Motor Vehicles
P.O. Box 6000–A
Fredericton, New Brunswick E3B 5H1

NEWFOUNDLAND

Department of Motor Vehicles
P.O. Box 8710–Y
Saint John's, Newfoundland A1B 4J5

NORTHWEST TERRITORIES

Department of Motor Vehicles
P.O. Box 1320–H
Yellowknife, Northwest Territories,
X1A 2L9

NOVA SCOTIA

Department of Motor Vehicles
P.O. Box 54–O
Halifax, Nova Scotia B3J 2L4

ONTARIO

Department of Motor Vehicles
2680 Keele Street
Downsview, Ontario M3M 3E6

PRINCE EDWARD ISLAND

Department of Motor Vehicles
P.O. Box 2000-U
Charlottetown, Prince Edward Island,
C1A 7N8

QUEBEC

Department of Motor Vehicles
1037 de la Chevrotiere Street
Quebec, Quebec G1R 4Y7

SASKACHEWAN

Department of Motor Vehicles
2260 11th Avenue
Regina, Saskatchewan S4P 2N7

YUKON

Department of Motor Vehicles
P.O. Box 2703–S
Whitehorse, Yukon Y1A 2C6

Now that you have the registration information, you may want to do additional research. Every state keeps a record of all transactions regarding the sale of a motor vehicle because of the need to ensure continuity of odometer readings and to prove that the records followed a specific sequence in case the validity of a vehicle identification number is questioned or in the event of tampering.

You may want to request a "body file" or "vehicle history" of a particular motor vehicle of the subject. You will receive a packet that may occasionally include up to 30 pages. The photocopies will include paperwork with the subject's signature. This may help you to compare what you have on record as positive proof that you have a relationship with a person who is **really who he claims to be.**

You will also see that the history of the motor vehicle will indicate what previous addresses were contained on the yearly registrations. You may need these addresses so that you can contact the current occupants and inquire discreetly about what your subject may have discussed during the transaction insofar as employment, a spouse, children, and other personal information.

The information will indicate the name and address of the previous owner. This individual may have known the subject and may be able to provide you with more information. Even if the previous owner did not know the subject, ask the individual if, during casual conversation as the sale of the vehicle was being consummated, there was any mention of employment or other personal information, such as spouse, children, and domestic problems. If you recall the last time you bought or sold a vehicle, look how much information you and the other person exchanged just by chatting.

If you write and request the file on a vehicle that the subject does not own anymore, this may also provide new information. The packet of information you will receive about the sold vehicle will indicate the new owner's address. **Your subject may have sold the vehicle to this person because the subject needed money, was leaving the state and wanted to sell an extra vehicle, wanted the money from the sale so that they could buy a new vehicle, or pay for medical expenses for a wife or child.** The point is, the subject, like all of us, had to explain to the buyer why the vehicle was being sold. There will be many possibilities for new information regarding your subject, and little nuances regarding his lifestyle way back when.

Here is a sample letter to order a "body file" or "vehicle history":

Date
Jane Doe
123 Anywhere Drive
Anytown, New York 12345
Telephone Number: 212-558-1234

Dear Tag Department:
Kindly send the complete vehicle history of the following vehicle:

Title number: 74651201
Vehicle Identification Number: 2398UTG670KR453H6

I have attached a check for $8.00. If this is not sufficient, please contact me and I will remit the requested amount.

Sincerely,
Jane Doe

State of Florida
DEPARTMENT OF
HIGHWAY SAFETY AND MOTOR VEHICLES

LEONARD R. MELLON
Executive Director
Neil Kirkman Building, Tallahassee, Florida 32399-0500

BOB MARTINEZ
Governor
JIM SMITH
Secretary of State
BOB BUTTERWORTH
Attorney General
GERALD LEWIS
Comptroller
BILL GUNTER
Treasurer
DOYLE CONNER
Commissioner of Agriculture
BETTY CASTOR
Commissioner of Education

```
        If you wish to request copies of a complete body file, you
need to ask for a complete title history.  If you only wish to
receive copies of a certain date, you need to ask for copies of
that actual date, or state exactly what you want a copy of.

        Copies are $1.00, per page.  You may reach our Photo-Copy
Section at (904) 488-3838, for further information.

        If I can be of further assistance, please do not hesitate to
contact me.

                        Sincerely,


                        Willie Mae Lamar, Chief
                        Bureau of Title-Lien Services
                        Division of Motor Vehicles
```

You may also get lien information when ordering the "body file." This will let you know where his banking relationships were. The lender, with complete address, is listed. You will note that the microfilm copies are usually of poor quality because these type of documents are reproduced from microfilm. Remember to note the address on the title. Do you positively know who lived at this address years ago?

BOB MARTINEZ
Governor
JIM SMITH
Secretary of State
BOB BUTTERWORTH
Attorney General
GERALD LEWIS
Comptroller
BILL GUNTER
Treasurer
DOYLE CONNER
Commissioner of Agriculture
BETTY CASTOR
Commissioner of Education

State of Florida
DEPARTMENT OF
HIGHWAY SAFETY AND MOTOR VEHICLES

LEONARD R. MELLON
Executive Director
Neil Kirkman Building, Tallahassee, Florida 32399-0500

.CERTIFICATION

I, Charles J. Brantley, Director, Division of Motor Vehicles of the State of Florida hereby certify that I am the Custodian of Motor Vehicle Records of this Department and that a search has been made pertaining to:

A 1981 DATS 2-Door
VIN # 1HZ06S2BX4105
TITLE # 212831

Attached hereto are copies of the records of the aforesaid vehicle which are the exact copies of the microfilm records of the vehicle as shown by the files in this office. This file consist of 38 pages.

ACCIDENT REPORTS

If your subject's driving record indicates an accident, you will want to order a copy of the accident report. This report will, of course, contain much information such as addresses, vehicles involved in the accident, location of accident, etc., but primarily what I use this report for is to find out about the other party in the accident or other people in the automobile, such as **a wife, children, or girlfriend, etc.**

If the accident report indicates that your subject was at fault and there was damage to the vehicles and injuries, your subject may have been sued or will be facing a court date in the near future. You will need the other party's information because you will want to search the public records for a suit filed by this party. The address of this other party is important because they may file suit where they reside, which may not necessarily be in the same court jurisdiction where the accident occurred or where your subject lives. You will want to know if your subject is exposed to a large liability that may become **your** liability after marriage.

Pay particular attention to the subpoena the subject was served and the address at which they were served. If any damages were awarded that exceeded the subject's insurance coverage, there will be numerous records indicating the liens and attachments that have been filed. You may be able to glean numerous addresses for the subject by reviewing these public records.

If your subject was not at fault, then they may have filed suit. You will want to review the files of any litigation. You can be assured that any address listed for your subject will be accurate because the subject had filed this suit with the intent of collecting damages and, of course, a correct address would have been supplied by the subject so he would be able to collect any damages. This "correct" address may lead you to a spouse.

You may order the accident report from the jurisdiction that is noted on the driving record. The following list of state police agencies is included in this chapter since the state will usually have a copy of every accident involving damage and injuries. If the jurisdiction on the accident report is unclear, the state police will be able to either provide you a copy of the accident report or will evaluate the accident location from the information on the driving record and advise you exactly where to make your inquiry so you will be able to pull all the files.

STATE POLICE AGENCIES

ALABAMA

Alabama Department of Public Safety
State of Alabama
P.O. Box 1511
Montgomery, Alabama 36192

ALASKA

Department of Public Safety
State of Alaska
P.O. Box N
Juneau, Alaska 99811

ARIZONA

Department of Public Safety
State of Arizona
2102 West Encanto Boulevard
Phoenix, Arizona 85005

ARKANSAS

Department of Public Safety
State of Arkansas
Three Natural Resources Drive
Little Rock, Arkansas 72215

CALIFORNIA

State Department of Justice
State of California
P.O. Box 944255
Sacramento, California 94244

COLORADO

Colorado Bureau of Investigation
State of Colorado
690 Kipling Street
Lakewood, Colorado 80215

CONNECTICUT

State Police Department
State of Connecticut
294 Colony Street
Meriden, Connecticut 06450

DELAWARE

Delaware State Police Department
State of Delaware
P.O. Box 430
Dover, Delaware 19903

DISTRICT OF COLUMBIA

Department of Public Safety
District of Columbia
P.O. Box 1606
Washington, DC 20013

FLORIDA

Department of Law Enforcement
State of Florida
P.O. Box 1489
Tallahassee, Florida 32302

GEORGIA

Department of State Police
State of Georgia
P.O. Box 370748
Decatur, Georgia 30037

HAWAII

Department of Public Safety
State of Hawaii
465 South King Street
Honolulu, Hawaii 96813

IDAHO

Department of State Police
State of Idaho
6083 Clinton Street
Boise, Idaho 83704

ILLINOIS

Department of State Police
State of Illinois
260 North Chicago Street
Joliet, Illinois 60431

INDIANA

Indiana State Police
State of Indiana
100 North Senate Avenue
Indianapolis, Indiana 46204

IOWA

Department of Public Safety
State of Iowa
Wallace State Office Building
Des Moines, Iowa 50319

KANSAS

Kansas Bureau of Public Safety
State of Kansas
1620 Southwest Tyler
Topeka, Kansas 66612

KENTUCKY

Kentucky State Police
State of Kentucky
1250 Louisville Road
Frankfort, Kentucky 40601

LOUISIANA

Department of Public Safety
State of Louisiana
P.O. Box 66614
Baton Rouge, Louisiana 70896

MAINE

Maine State Police
State of Maine
36 Hospital Street
Augusta, Maine 04330

MARYLAND

Maryland State Police
State of Maryland
1201 Reisterstown Road
Pikesville, Maryland 21208

MASSACHUSETTS

Department of Public Safety
Commonwealth of Massachusetts
One Ashburton Place
Boston, Massachusetts 02108

MICHIGAN

Department of State Police
State of Michigan
714 South Harrison Road
East Lansing, Michigan 48823

MINNESOTA

Department of Public Safety
State of Minnesota
1246 University Avenue
St. Paul, Minnesota 55104

MISSISSIPPI

Department of Public Safety
State of Mississippi
P.O. Box 958
Jackson, Mississippi 39205

MISSOURI

Department of Public Safety
State of Missouri
1510 East Elm Street
Jefferson City, Missouri 65102

MONTANA

Department of State Police
State of Montana
303 North Roberts
Helena, Montana 59620

NEBRASKA

Nebraska State Police
State of Nebraska
P.O. Box 94907
Lincoln, Nebraska 68509

NEVADA

Department of Public Safety
State of Nevada
555 Wright Way
Carson City, Nevada 89711

NEW HAMPSHIRE

New Hampshire State Police
State of New Hampshire
10 Hazen Drive
Concord, New Hampshire 03305

NEW JERSEY

New Jersey State Police
State of New Jersey
P.O. Box 7068
West Trenton, New Jersey 08628

NEW MEXICO

Department of Public Safety
State of New Mexico
P.O. Box 1628
Santa Fe, New Mexico 87504

NEW YORK

New York State Police
State of New York
Executive Park Tower
Albany, New York 12203

NORTH CAROLINA

Department of Public Safety
State of North Carolina
407 Blount Street
Raleigh, North Carolina 27602

NORTH DAKOTA

North Dakota Bureau of Investigation
State of North Dakota
P.O. Box 1054
Bismarck, North Dakota 58502

OHIO

Department of Investigations
State of Ohio
P.O. Box 365
London, Ohio 43140

OKLAHOMA

Department of Public Safety
State of Oklahoma
P.O. Box 11497
Oklahoma City, Oklahoma 73136

OREGON

Oregon State Police
State of Oregon
3772 Portland Road
Salem, Oregon 97310

PENNSYLVANIA

Pennsylvania State Police
Commonwealth of Pennsylvania
1800 Elmerton Avenue
Harrisburg, Pennsylvania 17110

RHODE ISLAND

Department of Public Safety
State of Rhode Island
72 Pine Street
Providence, Rhode Island 02903

SOUTH CAROLINA

Department of Law Enforcement
State of South Carolina
P.O. Box 21398
Columbia, South Carolina 29221

SOUTH DAKOTA

Division of Criminal Investigation
State of South Dakota
500 East Capitol Avenue
Pierre, South Dakota 57501

TENNESSEE

Department of Public Safety
State of Tennessee
1150 Foster Avenue
Nashville, Tennessee 37224

TEXAS

Texas State Police
State of Texas
P.O. Box 4143
Austin, Texas 78765

UTAH

Department of Public Safety
State of Utah
4501 South 2700 West Avenue
Salt Lake City, Utah 84119

VERMONT

Vermont State Police
State of Vermont
103 South Main Street
Waterbury, Vermont 05676

VIRGINIA

State Police of Virginia
State of Virginia
P.O. Box 27272
Richmond, Virginia 23261

WASHINGTON

Washington State Police
State of Washington
P.O. Box 2527
Olympia, Washington 98504

WEST VIRGINIA

West Virginia State Police
State of West Virginia
725 Jefferson Road
South Charleston, West Virginia 25309

WISCONSIN

Wisconsin Law Enforcement Bureau
State of Wisconsin
P.O. Box 2718
Madison, Wisconsin 53701

WYOMING

Criminal Investigation Bureau
State of Wyoming
316 West 22nd Street
Cheyenne, Wyoming 85002

❧ ❧ ❧

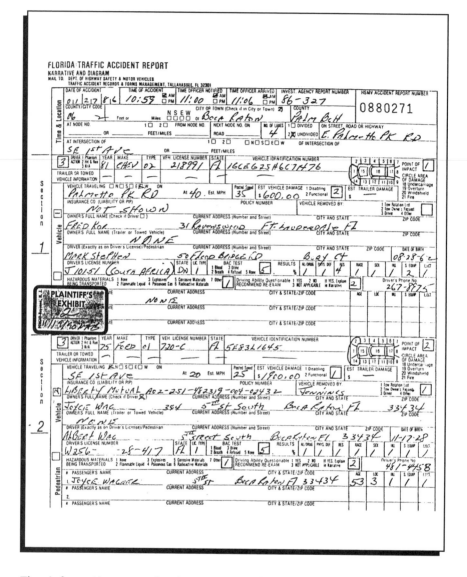

The information contained on an accident report may include home addresses, telephone numbers, names of insurance companies, etc. Remember that the reproduction of these reports may be difficult to read, but you will be able to learn much information about your "friend." Review the information about the other party involved in the accident. You may want to contact them if you feel that they may be able to provide some new insight regarding your subject.

☐ COMPLAINT AFFIDAVIT   ☐ ARREST FORM

SHADED FIELDS MUST BE ANSWERED IF DEFENDANT **NOT** IN CUSTODY

ARREST NO. _____   OBTS NO. _____

FILING AGENT	OFFENSE REPORT	LOCAL I.D. NO.	FDLE	FBI	SS NO.
B.S.O DIST	92-4-192				

DEFENDANT'S LAST NAME		FIRST	MIDDLE	SUF	ALIAS/STREET NAME		CITIZENSHIP
LIVAN		TIMOTHY	P.				

RC.	SEX	HGT.	EYES	HAIR	WGT.	COMP.	AGE	D.O.B.	BIRTHPLACE	SCARS, MARKS, TT	
WHT	MALE	5'1	HAZEL	BRN	174	M	23	2-27-68	CHICAGO	NONE VISIBLE	

PERMANENT ADDRESS				LOCAL ADDRESS	
12 SW 7 ST	LAUDERDALE FL				

RESIDENCE TYPE:	(1) CITY	(2) COUNTY	(3) FLORIDA	(4) OUT-OF-STATE	PLACE OF EMPLOYMENT	LENGTH
					C.P.A, ACCOUNT, COHER, FXC	4yr

HOW LONG DEFENDANT IN BROWARD COUNTY	BREATHALYZER BY/CCN	READING	PLACE OF ARREST	DATE/TIME ARRESTED	ARRESTING OFFICER(S) CCN
	REFUSED		2400 BLK OF N S7	04/26/92 0444	677

OFFICER INJURED	UNIT	ZONE	BEAT	SHIFT	UNIT TRANSPORTING PRISONER	TRANSPORTING OFFICER/CCN	PICK-UP TIME-	DRUG TYPE
Y ☐ N ☒	492	407	- A	93		677	TIME ARRIVED AT BSO	NA

TYPE	B-BARBITURATE	H-HALLUCINOGEN	P-PARAPHERNALIA/	U-UNKNOWN	ACTIVITY	ACTIVITY	S-SELL	A-SMUGGLE	M-MANUFACTURE	K-DISPENSE/	Z-OTHER	INDICATION OF	Y N UK
N-NA	C-COCAINE	M-MARIJUANA	EQUIPMENT	Z-OTHER	N	N-NA	B-BUY	D-DELIVER	PRODUCE/	DISTRIBUTE		ALCOHOL INFLUENCE	☒ ☐
A-AMPHETAMINE	E-HEROIN	O-OPIUM	S-SYNTHETIC			P-POSSESS	T-TRAFFIC	E-USE	CULTIVATE			DRUG INFLUENCE	☐ ☐ ☒

ATTACH DEFENDANT'S PHOTO

DEFENDANT'S VEHICLE-MAKE **VOLK** TYPE **4D** YEAR **87** COLOR **BLU** VIN. NO. **IVWFA0175HV**

VEHICLE TOWED TO **MACS** TAG NO. **SFS** OTHER IDENTIFIERS OR REMARKS _____

VEHICLE INVOLVED IN AN ACCIDENT

NAME OF VICTIM (IF CORPORATION, EXACT LEGAL NAME AND STATE OF INCORP.)	ADDRESS	PHONE #
STATE OF FLA		

COUNT NO.	OFFENSES CHARGED	CITATION #, IF APPLICABLE	F.S.# OR CAPIAS/WARRANT #
1	DRIVING WHILE UNDER THE INFLUENCE OF AN ALCOHOLIC BEVERAGE	494 WBX	31	193
		IMPLIED CONSENT WAS READ TO SUBJECT / PRIOR TO ...	

MOBILE

CENTRAL FILE

PROBABLE CAUSE AFFIDAVIT

Before me this date personally appeared **DEP. C. LASZ** who being first duly sworn deposes and says that on **26** day **APRIL** , 19 **92** at **2400 BLK OF NSR   LAUDLKS** (crime location) the above named defendant committed the above offenses charged and the facts showing probable cause to believe same are as follows:

I CONTACTED SUSPECT AT NW 24 ST /AND N.S.7, SUSPECT HAD BEEN

You will be able to ascertain from the narrative on the arrest record what type of **conduct** your subject exhibited during the arrest. Note that the breathalizer test was refused. Place of employment, home address, date of birth, place of birth, and other important information is reflected. Does all this personal information seem to be what was told to you by your "friend"? You will note that this subject's vehicle was involved in an accident. Check into this case very carefully, and investigate on the county level to see if a lawsuit was brought against this subject. **If there was a lawsuit, what was the disposition? Does the subject have to make payments? If so, for how long and how much?**

INVOLVED IN AN ACCIDENT. WHILE RECEIVING HIS INFORMATION ABOUT THE ACCIDENT I COULD SMELL A STRONG ODOR OF AN ALCOHOLIC BEVERAGE EMITTING FROM HIS BREATH, HIS EYES WERE VERY RED AND GLOSSY. AFTER E.M.S HAD CHECKED HIM AND HE SIGNED THE MEDICAL RELEASE FORM. I ADVISED SUSPECT THAT I WAS NOW INVESTIGATING HIM FOR DRIVING UNDER THE INFLUENCE. SUSPECT ADVISED ME HE HAD A FEW DRINKS EARLIER. SUSPECT FAILED THREE ATTEMPTS ON REPEATING THE ALPHABET. AFTER HIS THIRD ATTEMPT HE BECAME ANGRY HE BEGAN YELLING AT ME AND THROWING HIS HANDS UP AS I GAVE HIM INSTRUCTIONS ON THE WALK AND TURN TEST HE ADVISED ME HE WOULD NOT CONTINUE TESTING. I THEN TRANSPORTED HIM TO THE D.U.I TESTING UNIT WHERE HE ALSO REFUSED ALL TESTING DURING THE VIDEO TAPE.

THERE ARE NO KNOWN INJURIES IN THIS ACCIDENT AND DRIVER OF SECOND VEHICLE FLED SCENE BEFORE MY ARRIVAL.

The narrative indicates that the subject started yelling at the officer. This may give you an indication about how he **will react to you in the future** after a "few drinks." His level of cooperation in refusing any testing may be another warning sign to you. This subject was so intoxicated that he failed on three attempts to repeat the alphabet. If he can be this intoxicated and get into an automobile and drive, will he be responsible enough in the future to not chauffeur you or your children in this condition? Was this an isolated incident when your subject drove while intoxicated? Make thorough inquiries in every state in which he resided for other drunken driving charges. Investigate any other accidents that have the potential of a lawsuit being initiated against your "friend."

6. OFFENSE		7. LOCATION NUMBER	STREET	APT	8 KIND OF PROPERTY RECOVERED / MIS:
Police Assist					
9. DATE AND TIME OCCURRED		10 DAY OF WEEK		11. VALUE	DATE AND TIME REPORTED
09/10/92	1834	Thur			09/10/92

52 NARRATIVE: Include description of evidence obtained and desposition, detailed description of property taken, general resume of crime, etc. Describe additional suspects and/or witnesses, and number and charge. List person reporting crime, and person discovering crime. Explain all affirmative answers to question blocks

Compl. LIVAN, TIM P.

Subj — LIVAN, JULIE

Responded ref welfare check — Compl. concerned that above subject, ex-wife, and two children have been unable to be reached by phone. Contact made with subject, all are ok. Subject apparently does not wish to speak to Complainant and stated that she considers police involvement an intrusion of her privacy. Dispatch notified of contact and will advise. Compl.

Police reports sometimes contain revealing information. After the subject was arrested, he became concerned that he could not reach his ex-wife and two children by telephone. **Did you know about them?** The narrative indicates that the ex-wife did not want contact with the subject. You may want to consider reviewing the divorce file of this couple because this may not have been an amiable divorce, considering the ex-wife does not want to help the subject who is incarcerated. The term "welfare check" does not mean public assistance, but is a standard term used by law enforcement officials. It means that police check to see if next of kin are aware that their loved one was arrested so they will not worry that something else happened. Also, since, in this case, the breadwinner of the family may have been incarcerated, the police may want to make sure that, perhaps, children were not left home unattended or that the family is not going hungry.

NOTES

Divorce, Marriage, Birth & Death Records

DIVORCE RECORDS

Divorce records are filed in the county where the divorce took place. Write or visit the County hall of records, and, with only a name (date of birth not required), you will be able to have access to the file. A review of a divorce file may yield information that will give you a clearer picture of your subject. The following is some of the information contained in divorce files and related documents.

Name of spouse
Names and dates of birth of children
Date and place of marriage
Marital property and disbursement of assets
What health and life insurances are required to be
    provided to the wife and/or children
Allegations of physical and/or mental abuse
Mention of restraining orders against your subject
Names of any girlfriends named in the divorce
Credit card numbers and balances
Stocks, tax returns, and other financial information
Amount of alimony to be paid and duration of payments
Amount of child support
Allegations of child abuse

You can readily see what importance the above information may have to you. The name of the spouse will permit you to contact the individual if you choose. The names and ages of the children may not be exactly what you were told.

The date and place of marriage will give you another document to review. A section on what information is contained in marriage records will be in this chapter.

Houses, land, automobiles, boats, and other marital assets will be listed. It is important to see what your subject retained after the divorce proceedings. Have you been told by your subject of what he will keep? More important is the matter of payments on marital property. **Will your "friend" be required to make the house payments?**

The divorce file will contain a list of vehicles owned by the couple and will include the vehicle identification number (VIN) in many instances. See which vehicle your subject took possession of. Even if this case is years old, the VIN will never change on a vehicle, so you may want to order a *body history* on the vehicle (Chapter 1). If your subject does not own the vehicle anymore, you will be able to see all the documentation that will include the name of the person who purchased it. You may then contact that individual and he/she may be able to provide information about your subject.

Be careful to read the file thoroughly because you will want to know if there are any vacation homes. Will this property still be jointly owned? **Perhaps your subject will have received the extra home as part of the settlement and has not told you about it.**

Your subject may be required to keep health insurance for the wife and/or children for a specified period of time. What will this cost? Does the file state what amount the life insurance policy must be for? If your subject is required to have life insurance policies for others, what effect will this have when your future husband requests additional life insurance naming you as beneficiary? Will the life insurance company allow this new amount of life insurance on your subject? Remember, the life insurance naming the children as beneficiary is required by court order to be in force but a policy that names you as a beneficiary is not. What are the costs of the health and life insurance policies? **The premiums on these policies may have to be paid for as long as 18 years.**

Did your subject physically or mentally abuse his wife? The divorce file will note any allegations if this was a basis for the divorce. If he was an abuser, then you will have to determine if your subject was going through a difficult period in his life and that **he is now a changed man.** Did your subject tell you he was accused of wife beating? If he didn't, then now may be an excellent time to query him on his behavior that is spelled out in the divorce files.

If the wife had requested a restraining order and one was, in fact, issued, then you may want to get a copy of the restraining order by accessing the records at the County hall of records. See how long the order will be in effect. If there is no ending date, it may be advisable to discuss this with your "friend." The reason for this is to make clear to him that if he does make contact with his ex-wife and exceeds the parameters spelled out in the order, he may be subject to arrest. If you intend on sharing a future together, you will have a vested interest in keeping your subject from making inappropriate contact with the former spouse in times where he may be upset with some of her actions.

If a girlfriend of your subject was a contributing factor in the marital breakdown, she may be named. Who is she? What relationship did she have with your subject? Does she live locally? Is the relationship over? Are any children a product of this affair? **Is she in any position to make any claims against your subject in the way of a palimony claim?** Use the chapters found elsewhere in this book to look into her background in the same way you are checking into your subject's life.

Divorce files will contain credit card numbers and the balances as of the date of filing. Is your subject required to pay the balances? Are they joint accounts? If your subject does not ensure that the ex-wife keep just the credit cards in her name, **he will continue to be liable for any charges under a joint account.**

Tax returns, stock ownership, and other financial information may be contained in the divorce file you review. Are the amounts on the returns consistent with the figures your subject told you about? How will the stocks and bonds be split up? Will the wife continue to get the dividends paid by the portfolios? You may also get a better picture of what kind of investor your subject is. If he had losses that you are not comfortable with, you may want to ask him to restrict his stock market investing when you marry. The money he plays with after marriage will be yours and the losses will be yours also.

The divorce files will state how much alimony your subject will be required to pay his former wife. **How long will he make the payments?** Until the children reach 18? When she remarries? Until she reaches 62 and is eligible for Social Security? Until she learns a new vocation and is able to support herself?

The amount of child support will be listed in the file. Look at the ages of the children and you will see the length of time the child support will continue. If the children are infants, you are looking at 18 years of child support payments. You will want to know if the child support payments constitute over 50 percent of the cost of raising the child. The importance of this is due to the tax consequences. If your subject does not contribute to over 50 percent of the cost of the upbringing, then he will not be able to claim the children on the tax returns, thus creating a bigger tax liability for you and your future mate.

Any allegations of child abuse will be noted in the divorce files. I have not included allegations of child abuse in the examples of documents I have selected in this chapter. The allegations I have read in many files are just too graphic, and I am sure you agree, that for the purpose of this book, it was not necessary to spell out what abuses can be committed upon children. If you do find child abuse allegations, then you may want to retrieve any police reports that were filed, if available.

❧ ❧ ❧

In Re: The Marriage of   Family Division
Judith H. Roberly   Case No: 92-41963 FC119
Petitioner, Husband,
VS
Harold L. Roberly   Petition for
                                Dissolution of Marriage
Respondent, Wife.

Comes Now, the Petitioner, Husband, Harold L. Roberly by and
through his undersigned attorney and files this his Petition for
Dissolution of Marriage and avers:

    1.   This is an action for dissolution of Marriage and other
related relief.
    2.   That the husband has been a bona fide resident of the State
of Florida for more than six months prior to the filing of this
Petition.
    3.   That the parties were married to each other on March 20,
1979 in Paramus, New Jersey, and continued to cohabitate together
until separation in July of 1991.
    4.   That there have been two children born during the term of
the marriage, to-wit: Mary Sue Roberly born March 15, 1986 and
James Arthur Roberly born July 18, 1988. That there shall be shared
parental responsibility pursuant to Florida Statute 61.13(2)B. That
it would be in the best interest of the parties minor children for
the Wife to provide the primary residence home.
    That there is presently an Order for Support in Union County,
State of New Jersey, specifically Docket No. FD 6-231-92U Reference
No. CC 8732. That said Order requires the Petitioner, Husband to
pay the sum of two hundred fifty-two dollars ($252.00) per month,
per child as child support, as and for the benefit of the parties
minor children.
    5.   That The Husband presently has health insurance for the
benefit of the parties minor children. The Husband agrees to
maintain said insurance benefits for the parties minor children
until they attain the age of eighteen or becomes otherwise
emancipated and further agrees to provide the Wife with any and all
necessary forms and documentation with regards to said insurance.
    6.   That the Husband has a life insurance policy on himself in
the amount of fifty thousand dollars ($50,000.00), naming the
parties minor children as beneficiaries. That the life insurance
policy shall be held in trust by the Wife for the parties minor
children.

This petition, filed by your subject, may not be a full account of the facts of
the case. On the next page, the wife disputes certain statements. This document, which can be found in the county records section, shows you the
state the subject resided in. The names of the children are listed, along with
their dates of birth. You will be able to see what amount of child support
your subject must pay. Beware that your "friend" is required to maintain health
insurance for the children until they reach the age of 18. Will this policy be
paid by his employer, or will a separate policy be needed to satisfy this require-
ment, which may lead to an expense of thousands of dollars a year? **This
expense may reduce the amount of money your subject will have to contribute to your household funds once you are married.**

7. That the husband, who has repeatedly physically beat, over the past several years, his wife to such a severe degree that three separate hospitalizations were required and has agreed that he mentally abused his wife in unison with his girlfriend, Maria Alvaria, will cease and desist from any further transgressions.

8. That the Husband and Wife jointly owned and sold real property in California in which federal incomes taxes may be due. That equity and justice suggest that the parties be equally responsible for any federal income tax due on same.

9. That the Husband has a private pension plan. That the Wife is not entitled to any interest in same. That this pension plan shall be the property of the Husband sole title and sole possession.

10. That the parties have settled all their joint debts and obligations. The Wife has a Citibank Mastercard, specifically account number 6231 1882 8263 4122. That the Husband agrees to pay the sum of one thousand one hundred forty-seven dollars and ninety cents)$1,147.90) towards this obligation of the Wife.

11. That the Wife's maiden name of "JUDITH H. CLARMONT" be restored to her for legal use.

12. That there are irreconcilable differences between the parties and the marriage is irretrievable broken.

13. That the Husband will pay the Wife ($1,050.00) a month alimony until Wife receives Social Security payments at the age of 62 or remarries.

14. That the Husband will convey to the Wife ownership of marital home, free and clear of any mortgage or encumbrances. That property being located at 826 Mountain Drive, Paramus, New Jersey.

15. That the Husband will convey to the Wife ownership of jointly owned automobile, free of encumbrances, that being a 1989 Ford Mustang, License Tag 821-FRG, Vehicle Identification Number, R321G6713VRJ89067.

Were you aware of the charge of wife beating that is involved? Who was Maria? Does she still have an involvement with your subject? How much do you know about the property that your "friend" sold, and exactly how much federal tax is still owed, if any? Will you be able to automatically be included in the pension plan that your subject has, and what are the amounts his pension plan will yield? Is the credit card mentioned still listed as a joint account with his former spouse? Is the amount of monthly alimony of $1,050 the figure he told you about? Get a copy of the former spouse's license or check into her voter's registration record to ascertain her exact age so you will be able to determine just how many more years he will be required to pay this monthly allotment to her. Your "friend's" monthly contribution to your future joint funds will be reduced by the alimony amount, and, of course, simple math will tell you whether or not you will be put into financial hardship for years to come.

RE: CASE NUMBER 92-419

Attention: Honorable James Harris

This written response is filed regarding the amended petition for dissolution or marriage case #92-41963 FC 119. I am the defendant/respondent named in the case, Judith H. Roberly. I reside in New Jersey and am financially unable to retain a Florida attorney. My attorney is not admitted to practice law in the state of Florida and, therefore, is unable to represent me in this matter.

Since my children and I will continue to reside in New Jersey, difficulty would arise if required to litigate issues concerning visitation and child care in Florida. Dissolution of marriage is agreed upon and desired. However, I do not agree with several provisions in the petition as explained below:

Paragraph #3 is incorrect. Mr. Roberly and I were married on May 20, 1979. We lived separately from June, 1990 through February, 1991.

Paragraph #4 - Attached is a copy of the signed court order granting custody of Mary Sue Roberly and James Arthur Roberly on November 14, 1991 to their mother.

Paragraph #5 - No provision is made sharing the childrens' uninsured medical and dental expenses 50% as verbally agreed upon by the two parties.

Paragraph #6 - No provision is made verifying the existence of this life insurance policy. No provision is made for disability insurance.

Paragraph #8 - The parties have not amicably divided their jointly-owned personal property.

Paragraph #9 - The "private" pension plan is a military pension plan. The wife does have an interest in same, not for herself but for her children.

No provisions are made for the children's day care expenses, frequency of visitation, and college education.

I respectfully request that you grant the dissolution of this marriage with the provision that the above stated items are taken into consideration and addressed accordingly.

Many issues have not been resolved, as is clearly illustrated by this letter that the wife wrote to the judge. Paragraph 4 indicates that your subject does not have custody of the children. Will your subject have years of expenses ahead in fighting for custody if he chooses to challenge the court order? Will your subject have to pay for a disability policy that is alluded to in Paragraph 6? The property settlement has not been resolved as indicated in Paragraph 8, **which may lead to an expensive round of litigation.** This litigation may adversely affect your pocketbook if it continues into your marriage, because money will be sapped from your joint money reserves once you are married to the subject. Since no provisions have been made for day-care expenses and college education, it may be wise to query your subject on this. What will the estimated costs be, and from where will these funds come?

In Re: The Marriage of   Family Division
Ruth Caufeld   Case No: 93-68113-A
Petitioner, Wife,
and   WIFE S VERIFICATION PETITION
FOR
Morton Caufeld   DISSOLUTION OF MARRIAGE
Respondent, Husband.   OTHER RELIEF

The wife, having been duly sworn, deposes and states as follows:

1.   ACTION FOR DISSOLUTION. This is an action for dissolution of marriage.

2.   RESIDENCE. The wife has been a resident of Miami, Dade County, Florida for more than six (6) months prior to filing this petition.

3.   VENUE. The parties last resided together as husband and wife in Dade County, Florida; which was their last marital domicile.

4.   MARRIAGE. The parties were married to one another on August 18, 1967 in Israel.

5.   MARRIAGE IRRETRIEVABLY BROKEN. The marriage between the parties is irretrievably broken and the husband departed form the marital domicile on or about July 1, 1991.

6.   SWORN STATEMENT FOR SERVICE BY PUBLICATION. The husband is over the age of eighteen (18), not in the military service of the United States of America or of any of its allies, and has been absent from the State of Florida for more than sixty (60) days next preceding the making of this sworn statement.

This document indicates that your subject was married in Israel in 1967. Did you know he lived in another country years ago? You will note that July 1, 1991, was the final date that your subject had lived with his wife. When did you meet the subject? Was he living with his wife when you first met, but indicated he had left his wife years before? If he was not living with you after July 1, 1991, then **where was he living before, and did he have any roommates?** Section 6 is a standard statement in all divorce documents. If your subject had been in the military service, the rules of service of a subpoena for divorce would have had to be served differently. With the case number that is indicated, you will be able to follow all the filings, pleadings, and other petitions in this case.

7. HUSBAND S CURRENT ADDRESS. There is no person in the State of Florida upon whom service of process would bind the Husband. The Wife has made diligent inquiry and search and has discovered that the current residence or mailing address as designated by the Husband is:

8216 JERUSALEM AVENUE
BAT-YA, ISRAEL

8. NO JOINT PROPERTY AND NO MINOR CHILDREN. The parties do not own any joint real property or personal property. The last child of the parties will reach majority age (18 years) on May 24, 1992 and, consequently, the Wife is not requesting Child support from the Husband.

9. MUTUAL RESTRAINING ORDER. The Husband has made threats of severe bodily harm and permanent injury to the Wife should she attempt to obtain a dissolution of their marriage. The Wife believes that absent the issuance of a Restraining Order the Husband will inflict severe and permanent injury upon her.

10. RESTORATION OF MAIDEN NAME. The Wife wishes to have her maiden name of Kaplan restored to her and to henceforth be legally known as Ruth Aronstein.

WHEREFORE, The wife prays for the rendition of a Final Judgement of Dissolution of Marriage awarding her the relief request hereinabove and or the issuance of a Mutual Restraining Order.

Your subject had an Israel address when paperwork was to be served. Was he with you in the states and had simply tried to thwart the subpoena? Is this the honesty you are looking for in a mate? Someday, he may be clever with **you** if you have an occasion to sue him. The wife is not claiming child support, but were you told of this child who reaches 18 years old on May 24, 1992. **This is a person that may have a claim on your "friend's" estate should he die after you get married.** This document indicates that the wife has a real concern for her safety. Was this just legal posturing, or does your subject have periods where he may exhibit violent rages? Did the wife successfully have the restraining order issued? Is your subject the type of person who may violate this order and possibly face arrest? This document will also give you the wife's maiden name. I continue to suggest throughout this book that contacting a former spouse is one avenue to carefully consider because she may have much to tell you if the divorce was not on amicable terms.

Texas Department of Health

| Robert Bernstein, M.D., F.A.C.P.
Commissioner | 1100 West 49th Street
Austin, Texas 78756-3191
(512) 458-7111 | Robert A. MacLean, M.D.
Deputy Commissioner
Professional Services

Hermas L. Miller
Deputy Commissioner
Management and Administration |

                                    Re: Divorce Inquiry
                                             McCall, Janet
                                             1968 to Present
                                             Texas

Dear Sir or Madam:

    This office has received your request of recent date relating
to the issuance of a divorce decree to the above-named person.

    We have made a thorough search of the alphabetic indexes of
this office relating to reports of divorce or annulment of
marriage and find under our number 035 1-70 a report indicating
that a divorce was granted to William T. McCall and Janet Sharon
Robinson Hall on September 5, 1982 in Harrison County, Texas.

    To obtain a certified copy of the divorce decree, you must
contact Ms. Betty Cawood, District Clerk, Harrison County,
Marshall, Texas 75670.

    If we may be of further assistance, please do not hesitate to
write to the above address or call this office at (512) 458-7386.

                                    Sincerely yours,

                                    Donna D. Greathouse
                                    Branch Manager
                                    Certifications Branch
                                    Bureau of Vital Statistics

Write to the appropriate state agency to check divorces for the entire state if you do not find a divorce on file in the county records. Request for divorce file searches are honored by most states. Annulments are also part of the search conducted as indicated by the above letter. Once you have a file number, you may write to the county where it is filed. In this instance, they searched by alphabetical index because I did not have a date of birth for either of the parties.

MARRIAGE RECORDS

Marriage records will provide the following information about the bride and groom:

Name
Address
Date of birth
Place of birth
Previous marriage status (married or never married)
Last marriage ended by: (death, divorce, or annulment)
Number of previous marriages
If divorced, where
Name of person performing the ceremony
Signatures of bride and groom
Names of the witnesses

There are a myriad uses for the information gleaned from the marriage record. If you do not know if your subject is married, order a search conducted for a span of several years. If you do locate a marriage record, then review the certificate for the above-noted information. If there is a divorce indicated, you may want to order of copy of the divorce file. The witnesses and person who performed the ceremony may be contacted. They may know obscure details about your subject.

You will need to contact each jurisdiction regarding the release of all records including marriage. Some governments severely restrict the release of records, and a perfect example could be New York City. They release a copy of marriage information only to the bride and groom, whereas all areas in the State of Florida consider this to be a public record. I do not hinge a background investigation on just one document. If you cannot get any particular document, including a marriage certificate, then continue by checking all other types of records. I check property records, voter's registrations, divorce records, driving records, Social Security Number updates, and a myriad of other records if I cannot get marriage records released. You will be able to retrieve information that is contained in a marriage record by just going another route.

```
                              MARRIAGE
FILE NUMBER   LOC   BOOK PAGE    DATE      NAME
-------------------------------------------------------------------
92-  4629     05    355  340   03/19/92  SOTOLONGO, JUAN
92-  242      24    353 2349   01/25/92  SOTOLONGO, MAYRA
93-  1984     21    360  886   02/05/93  SOTOLONGO, ORLINDA
92-  6097     26    355 1952   04/13/92  SOTOLONGO, RENE CARLOS
92-  5704     21    356  260   04/08/92  SOTOLONGO, SALY M
92-  6192     05    356 1803   04/30/92  SOTOLONGO, SERGIO JR
92- 18734     21    359 1821   11/27/92  SOTOLONGO, YORDANKA
92-  1486     05    354  287   01/04/92  SOTOMAYOR, EDNA E
93-  1293     05           NTRT           SOTOMAYOR, IVETE
93-  3601     05    360 2437   03/02/93  SOTOMAYOR, PEDRO ANTONIO
93-  3877     21           NTRT           SOTUYO, ERASMO
92- 13938     05    358 1235   08/19/92  SOUFFRANC, LAURETTE
92-  428      26    353 2315   01/09/92  SOULES, ADAM J
92- 21168     05    359 3638   12/22/92  SOULOUQUE, ROSE M
92- 19510     26    359 2032   11/25/92  SOURIAC, DAPHNEE G
92- 18021     26    359  492   11/03/92  SOUSA, GRACIELA
92- 12521     23    358  154   07/30/92  SOUTH, DARREN GARY
92-  1433     23    354  363   01/08/92  SOUTH, GEORGE DE CORDOVA
92-  9730     21    357  589   06/27/92  SOUTHERN, DAWN A
92- 19168     05    359 1619   11/20/92  SOUTHERS, RONALD E
92- 11814     21    357 2154   07/18/92  SOUTO, DELARAY
92- 14110     05    358 2989   08/19/92  SOUTO, FRANK J
92- 19206     23    359 2005   11/28/92  SOUVERAIN, RONALD
92-  3626     24    354 2496   03/02/92  SOUZA, ERICA A
92- 19775     05    359 4732   12/05/92  SOUZA, LUIS J
93-  2285     24    360 1605   02/10/93  SOVIERO, ROBERTO PEPPINO
93-  1511     24    360 1679   01/29/93  SOWARDS, TAMMY L
92-  7722     21    356  714   05/16/92  SOWERS, DAVID M
92-  2302     26    354 2115   02/01/92  SOWERS, JANALYN K
92-  4703     05    355  712   03/20/92  SOWERS, WILLIAM B
92-  8444     24    356 1489   05/23/92  SOYKA, MARK
93-  693      21    360  350   01/18/93  SOZA, DINORAH DEL C
93-  3305     21    360 2212   02/25/93  SOZA, ELDER ANTONIO
93-  1761     05    360  684   02/03/93  SOZA, LUIS ALBERTO
92- 14130     26    358 1386   08/21/92  SOZOS, PETE
92-  5441     23    356   58   04/02/92  SPADAVECCHIA, ANGELA M
92-  630      21    353 2961   01/25/92  SPAGNOLA, WILLIAM D
92-  6449     24    355 2520   04/26/92  SPAKMAN, ANNA
92- 19165     21    359 1618   11/27/92  SPALDING, EDWARD CUDAHY
92- 11836     26    357 2525   07/01/92  SPALDING, PAUL WILLIAM
92-  1960     26    354 1069   02/14/92  SPAN, ARTHUR LEE
92-  551      05    353 2414   01/13/92  SPANDONARI, MIRIAM G
92-  8915     05    356 2489   05/13/92  SPANIOLI, JOHN M
93-  836      23    360  407   01/22/93  SPANN, OTIS
92-  9056     20    357 2081   05/04/92  SPANN, PRISCILLA A
92- 16118     26    358 3241   10/02/92  SPANN, SUREATHA
92- 11945     26    357 2193   07/16/92  SPANN, WILLIAM (JR)
93-  1073     24    360  737   01/22/93  SPARIOSU, MARIN
92-  4123     05    354 2173   03/10/92  SPARKES, ERIC F
93-  3588     24           NTRT           SPARKES, KARL ROBIN
92-  6979     26    355 2909   04/27/92  SPARKS, ANA M
```

This is a microfiche copy of the register from the county records section that contains all marriages performed, and the names are listed in alphabetical order. Marriage indexes are usually broken down by dates of marriage. The above record reflects mornings with application dates for 1992–1993. The column that indicates the book and page number will enable you to request a copy of the marriage application and certificate. The next page is the other half of this document.

DOB	NAME	DOB	APPLIC. DATE
021726	MUNOZ, MARIA E	021533	03/19/92
081060	VALDES-MALDONADO, REYNALDO	031469	01/07/92
042547	HERNANDEZ, RODOLFO	100148	02/05/93
092670	MONROY, SINIA PATRICIA	090170	04/13/92
060273	ALVAREZ, IHOVANY	050873	04/06/92
103065	TORAYA, AMPARO	112963	04/15/92
102575	VIANA, SAMUEL	020576	11/16/92
062951	GASCON, DANIEL	050758	01/30/92
112471	MORAN, LUIS F	081169	01/26/93
100850	GALVEZ, MIRTA	061544	03/02/93
082131	VILLAFANE, DAISY RUBIELA	102544	03/05/93
011062	ALTIDOR, EDDY	010361	08/19/92
091359	MONHOLLEN, TANYA L	090369	01/09/92
090871	JOUBERT, VLADIMIR	030664	12/22/92
122570	CINEAS, JOSEPH EDOUARD	112469	11/25/92
102047	PUENTES, ENRIQUE	010839	11/03/92
011665	HOLT, LORRAINE	121256	07/27/92
033166	MASTERS, ANTOINETTE M	102866	01/29/92
070768	PEARCE, JEFFREY W	091867	06/10/92
042444	TAYLOR, BETTY G	022251	11/20/92
112171	GARCIA, JUAN JOSE	092470	07/15/92
101768	GARCIA, LISSETTE B	120969	08/21/92
040761	BELAIR, ETHEL	062669	11/20/92
011469	ALEXANDER, PAUL L	050658	03/02/92
021052	LLOPIS-MARTELL, VIRGINIA E	111760	12/02/92
052058	GUILLEN, ROSALBA ARLENY	020867	02/10/93
021876	MARTINEZ, MANUEL VALDIMIR, III	062073	01/29/93
060943	WHAN, MIRIAM D	051642	05/08/92
033066	NEBRAT, STEPHEN G	122765	02/12/92
012051	SEIDEL, PATRICIA M	122759	03/19/92
120243	STEINLE, GABRIELE E	061661	05/20/92
071667	CASTILLO, FABRICIO	060165	01/15/93
031172	YABER, ALICIA EILEEN	120570	02/25/93
120244	GIRALDO, NELLY	020145	02/03/93
052648	TRANI, IRENE	061643	08/21/92
022972	HARRIS, MICHAEL B	092263	04/01/92
081068	GABLE, LORI L	022268	01/14/92
101667	BABCHIN, YEVGENY	060562	04/17/92
020549	CAPONE, ANGELA	070360	11/20/92
091067	OXLEY, CARYN MICHELLE	010571	07/15/92
081359	FLETCHER, ALFREDA D	042861	02/07/92
061067	GOMEZ, ANGEL	073058	01/13/92
072759	MORALES, MARITZA	032862	05/28/92
062668	RHODES, SONYA D	013173	01/19/93
100261	DINGLE, DAVID	091558	05/29/92
022274	SIMPSON, WELLINGTON G	101173	10/02/92
011749	ROUX, ASIA L	010459	07/16/92
072368	ELMADY, SUYAPA BARAHA	122761	01/22/93
111662	BERMUDEZ, MARIA G	040962	03/10/92
120658	TIEZ, MARIANNE	032060	03/02/93
040256	LOZADA, GUILLERMO FELIX	120753	04/27/92

There is much information that can be learned from just reviewing a marriage index. You can see from this index that the date of birth of the bride and groom are listed. Also you will be able to obtain the maiden name of the wife. This important information on the wife will enable you to start a background profile on this individual if you wish.

Ohio Departments Building
Room G-20
65 South Front Street
Columbus, Ohio 43266-0333

We conducted a special search of the statewide indexes for the years 1964 through 1976 and we were unable to locate the marriage certificate for Eloise Moran.

We conducted a special search of the statewide indexes for the years 1964 through 1979 and located 6 divorces in the names of Eloise Moran Howard and Eloise Moran Harris and Trego.

To determine whether or not any of those divorce certificates are for the Eloise Moran Howard or Eloise Moran Harris you are interested in, it will be necessary for you to review the certificates.

To obtain uncertified copies of the 6 divorce certificates, return this letter with a $3.60 check or money order.

We have deposited $18.00 of your remittance to cover the cost of searching the files. A $12.00 refund check will be mailed.

Sincerely,

Mrs. Barbara Dawson, Supervisor
Division of Vital Statistics

BD/go

If I cannot find a marriage record on the county level, then I will write to the state registry to ask for a search. If you are not sure of the year of marriage or where the marriage took place, you may want to request that a number of years be reviewed. I had the years 1964–1976 searched since there was no evidence of marriage in the entire state. I also checked some of the surrounding states of Ohio. I had searches done on divorces because a divorce would have indicated where the marriage had taken place.

BIRTH RECORDS

Birth Records will usually contain the following information:

Complete name
Subject's exact date of birth
Place of birth
Name of the father and mother
Age of the father and mother
Occupation of the father and mother
Mother's maiden name
Address of the father and mother
Place of birth of the father and mother

Complete name: You will want an exact name when checking the motor vehicle records, and a good source to verify that name would be a birth certificate. A middle name is of importance because many individuals use a middle name prominently later on. For example: G. Gordon Liddy, J. Edgar Hoover, F. Scott Fitzgerald, H. Norman Schwartzkopf.

Subject's exact date of birth: If you did not have the exact date of birth of your subject, you would have ordered a search for a particular year or a span of several years to find the birth certificate. Now that you have the birth record, you have the exact date of birth.

Place of birth: There is much research that can be done when you are aware of the place of birth of your subject. You may want to search for other relatives at the city of birth.

Name of father and mother: From the birth record, you now have the complete name of the father and mother. If you feel that the subject's parents may be alive, then you can conduct a search of the motor vehicle records for their location. They may be able to provide information. You are the only one who can decide if it is appropriate in your situation to contact his parents if he has made the decision for you not to meet them. I have included much of the sections on contacting the parents and siblings of your "friend" for the benefit of my readers who are mothers-in-laws.

Age of the father and mother: Birth records will usually contain the age but not the exact date of birth of the parents. The age of the parents at the time of birth of the subject will give you an approximate year of birth.

Occupation of the father and mother: The occupations, professions, or trades of both parents are listed on the birth certificate. If you have a problem finding the parents of the subject, you may want to check trade associations and unions if the parents had occupations that required participation or membership in an organization. The occupation listing may list physician, attorney, barber, taxi driver, certified public accountant, or any of a myriad of professions that necessitate licensing that generate records that are public information. You will want to inquire if the parent is still licensed or order a record from the archives if many years have passed. Again, contacting a parent of the subject is another avenue you will want to evaluate.

Mother's maiden name: The mother's name is of importance because this will be one of the only records you will be able to retrieve to access the mother's maiden name from. You may want to conduct a search for the family of the mother and question them on your subject who, of course, is their relative.

Address of father and mother: The address of the parents at the time of birth may be different from the place of birth of your subject. You may want to check property records. The family may still own the residence or, as has happened before, the subject may own property through an inheritance. If you discover that the property the address matches was a rental by the parents, you may want to inquire through the real estate records who owned the property then, and who owns the property now. An inquiry to the owner may provide information as to the whereabouts of the parents.

Place of birth of the father and mother: You may need to contact the parents in certain cases because your subject has misled you. Remember that the parents may be divorced and together with the fact that many years may have passed, a place of birth of either parent will yield a starting point for a search for each parent.

Contact with the family will provide information that could not have been developed independently. The contact with the family is an excellent method of research that many do not utilize because their location at the present time seems hopeless to ascertain. But as you see from the birth record, you have enough information regarding the parents to conduct a search for them.

You can see that the information that is contained in a birth certificate will give you much information in one document. I now not only have the exact spelling of the subject's name, but the names of the parents, the mother's maiden name, their age, their occupations, and even the home address. Because of the widespread misuse of birth certificates to create new identities, you may find the release of these documents becoming more and more restricted.

The birth certificate of your subject would be one avenue to explore in your search for information. You may also want to contact the physician listed

NEW YORK STATE DEPARTMENT OF HEALTH
OFFICE OF VITAL STATISTICS
ALBANY

CERTIFICATE OF BIRTH REGISTRATION

This is to certify that a birth certificate has been filed for

Joseph J. Culligan

Born on August 20, 1946 _____ White Plains, New York
_____ P.O.B. White Plains
Son
Daughter of F. Cornelius Culligan Age: 22 Occupation: Policeman *and*
_____ P.O.B. Irvington, New York
Felicia Patricia Colucci Age: 21 Occupation: Housewife
Home Address: 36 County Centre Road, White Plains
Date filed August 23, 1946 _____ J.E. Jansen
LOCAL REGISTRAR

THIS CERTIFICATE IS EVIDENCE OF AGE, PARENTAGE AND PLACE OF BIRTH AND SHOULD BE CAREFULLY PRESERVED.
When the child is vaccinated against smallpox and inoculated against diphtheria or any other disease, ask the physician or clinic to fill in the spaces below.

Date   Physician or Clinic

Vaccinated against smallpox_____
Inoculated against diphtheria_____
Inoculated against whooping cough_____

on the birth record for additional information about the location of your subject's family.

As noted in other chapters, you will be requesting death certificates on persons other than your subject. The reason for this is in order to do a background profile on a subject that has not left much of a paper trail, the best way to get information is to locate the subject's family and make inquiries. Every death record will have a physician's name certifying the cause of death. Many times the family physician will be the official who attests to the cause of death. This physician may be of some assistance in locating family members. In certain instances, the family will give you information about your "friend," especially if you are trying to locate him because he has already taken money or valuables from you.

DEATH RECORDS

Death records provide the following:

A person's complete name
Date of death
Date of birth

Social Security Number of the deceased
Place of birth of the deceased
Occupation of the deceased
Place of death
Cause of death
Name of the father and mother of the deceased
Mother's maiden name
Name and address of cemetery or crematory
Name of physician that certified cause of death

Death records are of value because you may want to order a search to be conducted on the parent or a relative of your subject. From the death record, you will be able to have enough information to possibly contact persons who know your subject.

Step one was to order a sweep done on several years if you do not know when a parent or sibling died. Now that you have the death record, you will see that there are several avenues to explore. You may want to contact the funeral home listed on the death record. The funeral home maintains records in hard copy form. On record will be the person responsible for making and paying for the arrangement of internment. Many times, as you can imagine, this person may be the brother or sister of your subject who, perhaps, is **unaware of you.**

Cause of death is important because one of the most successful methods of locating relatives of your subject is through autopsy records. Check to see if a parent, sibling, or relative has died. If the cause of death is homicide, automobile accident, industrial accident, etc., an autopsy is performed. In many locales, the autopsy is public record. The routine entries in the files will provide very specific information. The medical examiner makes notes regarding who was contacted to make arrangements for disposition of the body. The full names, telephone numbers, and addresses of relatives are entered on the record. If you wish, ask them about your subject.

If you do not have an autopsy to review, you may want to contact the probate court. If the parent of the subject died without a will (intestate), there will be a wealth of information in the probate court files. Information in the file will contain the names, addresses, and amounts of monies of each of the persons who are recognized by the court as heirs.

Women and their special needs caused by physical and mental abuse to them and their loved ones are now getting the attention deserved.

St. Petersburg Times

Battered wife is set free

By Diane Rado
Times Staff Writer

TALLAHASSEE - Convicted murderer Kimberly Bliss Soubielle, symbol of a movement to shine light on spouse abuse, was granted clemency Wednesday and freed from prison.

Six years ago, she shot her husband Pierre Soubielle six times in the back, reloaded her gun and shot him again. She said he had abused her and their young daughter.

Wednesday, she walked out of the Pine Hills Community Correctional Center near Orlando a free woman—the first prisoner released under new state policies on clemency for abused women.

"I am in shock and I'm elated. The road to freedom has been a long one," Soubielle said after she was released. "We cannot forget the others who are still in jail who should not be. I'm glad to be free, but the work must go on."

Gov. Lawton Chiles and four of Florida six Cabinet members believed she was abused for years by the man she killed. They commuted her 15-year sentence to the five years that she had served.

Her release was in large measure due to a visit Education Commissioner Betty Castor paid to Soubielle in prison after she made her appeal for clemency. Castor said she wanted to satisfy herself that Soubielle truly was an abuse victim, not a cold-hearted killer taking advantage of the new clemency system.

"We spent quite a while with her," Castor said of the prison visit. "She was a very serious, intelligent woman who obviously was the victim of abuse."

Soubielle was remorseful about her husband's death, Castor

said, but she also talked about the fear she felt for her daughter, who, Soubielle said, was being sexually abused by her husband.

The governor said it was not an easy call, but Castor's findings helped persuade him to grant clemency.

"Our decision is not a justification for homicide," Chiles said when he announced the decision Wednesday.

"This action is a recognition that battering of women is a tragic reality that affects women in every walk of life," he said. "And the circumstances in this particular case indicate that it certainly played a considerable role in the actions of Kimberly Soubielle."

Soubielle, 27, said she had suffered four years of physical and sexual abuse before she shot her husband in 1987 in their Casselberry home. She said she was driven to the act after discovering that he had abused their 2-year-old daughter.

Soubielle's was the first case considered under the state's new clemency policies on Battered Woman Syndrome cases.

Under the procedures, women who say they were driven to kill because of abuse by their husbands,ex-husbands, boyfriends, live-in lovers or family members related by blood or marriage can apply for clemency and be considered by special panels with expertise in the area of battered women.

Law enforcement officials questioned whether Soubielle really was an abused woman; they said she already had received mercy when a jury convinced her of second-, rather than first-degree murder.

It was the jury's verdict that persuaded Secretary of State Jim Smith to disagree with the rest of the Cabinet. He opposed clemency.

"They really set a precedent that will be difficult to live with," Smith said. He noted that the jury in Soubielle's case rejected the notion that abuse caused her to kill.

"I believe very strongly in the jury system," Smith said. "That is not the purpose of clemency, to second-guess the jury system."

Attorney General Bob Butterworth also was not willing to second-guess the jury on the abuse issue, but he signed off on the clemency for different reasons, according to Deputy Attorney General Peter Antonacci.

"His view of it was that she's been a good prisoner, a model prisoner, and she has served sufficient time given the circumstances of the case," said Antonacci.

Soubielle had a tentative

release date from prison of July 2, 1996, said documents distributed by the governor's office, and she has been on a program that allows her to work as a paralegal at an Orlando law firm.

As a condition of clemency, Soubielle will be on probation and must get counseling and therapy for herself and her 8-year-old daughter, Allison.

Agreeing with Chiles to grant clemency were Castor, Agriculture Commissioner Bob Crawford, Comptroller Gerald Lewis and Insurance Commissioner Tom Gallagher. It takes the governor, and at least three Cabinet members to grant clemency.

Representatives from women's groups joined Chiles and the Cabinet at the clemency announcement, and applauded the decision.

"This sends a tremendous message nationally," said Candy Slaughter, chairwoman of the Women in Prison Committee of the Florida Coalition Against Domestic Violence.

Slaughter's group was formed in the fall of 1990, and began a campaign to increase awareness about abused women. The group tried to educate Cabinet members about the issue of battered women and encourage people to write in support of Soubielle.

She said three other battered women convicted of murder will go before the clemency panel in June.

—Information from the Associated Press was used in this report.

(Reprinted by permission, the *St. Petersburg Times*)

NOTES

Social Security Administration

The Social Security Administration permits the public to check the Social Security Death files to see if a death has occurred for anyone that has died since 1962. Later in this chapter, I will discuss what value knowing the location of death of an individual will have to your **background check on your subject.**

Most of you are aware that a Social Security Number is of great use in finding someone and checking someone's past history and background for addresses. This chapter will contain a source you will be able to use to run Social Security Numbers to obtain an address of an individual. Pages 3-3 and 3-4 will show you that you can find the Social Security Number of your subject by looking through public records such as a summons and a child support order.

AREA NUMBERS

Social Security Numbers are presently assigned to individuals within the first two years of birth. Numbers were assigned before 1977 when a person applied, which was usually at approximately, the age of thirteen.

The first three numbers reflect the state the applicant resided in when they made an application to the Social Security Administration. If your subject says he has always lived in New York but has a Social Security Number that starts with 570, then you may want to intensify your background check to include the state represented by the three digit preface.

001–003	New Hampshire	516–517	Montana
004–007	Maine	518–519	Idaho
008–009	Vermont	520	Wyoming
010–034	Massachusetts	521–524	Colorado
035–039	Rhode Island	525	New Mexico
040–049	Connecticut	526–527	Arizona
050–134	New York	528–529	Utah
135–158	New Jersey	530	Nevada
159–211	Pennsylvania	531–539	Washington
212–220	Maryland	540–544	Oregon
221–222	Delaware	545–573	California
223–231	Virginia	574	Alaska
232–236	West Virginia	575–576	Hawaii
237–246	North Carolina	577–579	District of Columbia
247–251	South Carolina	580	Virgin Islands
252–260	Georgia	581–584	Puerto Rico
261–267	Florida	585	New Mexico
268–302	Ohio	586	Guam, American Samoa
303–317	Indiana		
318–361	Illinois	587–588	Mississippi
362–386	Michigan	589–595	Florida
387–399	Wisconsin	596–599	Puerto Rico
400–407	Kentucky	600–601	Arizona
408–415	Tennessee	602–626	California
416–424	Alabama	627–645	Texas
425–428	Mississippi	646–647	Utah
429–432	Arkansas	648–649	New Mexico
433–439	Louisiana	650–699	Unassigned—for future use
440–448	Oklahoma		
449–467	Texas	700–728	Railroad workers through 1963 then, discontinued
468–477	Minnesota		
478–485	Iowa		
486–500	Missouri	729–799	Unassigned— for future use
501–502	North Dakota		
503–504	South Dakota	800–999	Not valid Social Security Numbers
505-508	Nebraska		
509–515	Kansas		

**Department of Health
and Rehabilitative
Services, Office of
Child Support
Enforcement, ex. rel.**

Marian H. Antonis   **Family Division**

S.S.N.#: 063-21-9864   **Case Number: 92-434**

    Petitioner,

vs.

Harrison Giannotti

S.S.N.#: 098-42-6731   PATERNITY
    Respondent.

COMES NOW, State Attorney, requests the Respondent/Defendant to produce the following to the undersigned Counsel on or before the sate of hearing in the above cause:

  1. Copies of your Federal Income Tax returns for the past two (2) years.

  2. Copies of the most recent W-2 withholding tax statement.

  3. All business records, or income records for the past two (2) years, including your last six (6) pay stubs.

  4. All information regarding savings accounts, checking accounts, certificates of deposit, saving bonds, stocks held by you and all other income and resources.

  5. Completed financial statement.

  6. Verification of health insurance for non-receipt of health insurance of company plan.

  7. If unemployed:

    (a) Unemployment compensation registration card
       OR
    (b) Doctor's statement of inability to work.

  8. Copies of all receipts of child support payments.

  9. Bring copies of last credit card statements.

Not only will the Social Security Number of an individual show up on a paternity suit, but look at all the other information the respondent was ordered to bring in. If your "friend" was ever named in a paternity suit, then you will have **access to tax returns, business records, savings and checking account information, a full financial statement, etc.** All of these items can be found when you review the entire file. Take special care to see what charges are on his credit card statement, because the information may reveal vacations, dinners, or a high-living style that he does not share with you.

CIVIL DIVISION	CIVIL ACTION SUMMONS Personal Service on a Natural Person (En Espanol al Dorso) (Francais Au Verso)	CASE NUMBER 92-635
PLAINTIFF(S) LINDA ELLIS	VS. DEFENDANT(S) MARVIN BARN 327-98-8852	CLOCK IN

To Defendant(s): MARVIN BARN   Address: 176 NW 36 Ave
FT. LAUDERDALE, FL. 33311

A lawsuit has been filed against you. You have 20 calendar days after this summons is served on you to file a written response to the attached Complaint with the clerk of this court. A phone call will not protect you; your written response, including the case number given above and the names of the parties, must be filed if you want the Court to hear your side of the case. If you do not file your response on time, you may lose the case, and your wages, money and property may thereafter be taken without further warning from the Court. There are other legal requirements. You may want to call an attorney right away. If you do not know an attorney you may call an attorney referral service or a legal aid office (listed in the phone book).

IV-D ORIGINAL PROCESS

If you choose to file a written response yourself, at the same time you file your written response the Court, located at:

Clerk of Courts

Additional Court locations are printed on the back of this form.

You must also mail or take a copy of your written responses to the "Plaintiff/Plaintiff's Attorney" named below.

Subpoenas and Summons will have the Social Security Number next to the name. The reason for this is, of course, to assure the process server that he has the correct person when he serves the civil action. The home address of the defendant will also appear. **Is this the address that you knew nothing about?** Also, you may want to contact the plaintiff to see if she has any information that can give you a clearer picture of your "friend." After all, this person, in all probability, is not on good terms with your subject. If this was a summons for a paternity suit, you may want to find out the disposition of the case by looking through the file, assuming that the plaintiff you contacted didn't give you enough background on your subject.

I use a company in Miami that is in the same business area I am located in to run Social Security Number Address Update Reports, Criminal Record Searches, and Death Master File Reports for me. It is the Research Is Company. This firm does not advertise, as its clients are investigative firms and governments, and they keep their telephone number unlisted. However, orders are accepted from the public for the items mentioned here. In fact, you may have seen Pam Casey of Northern California who was reunited with her sister after 42 years on *The Maury Povich Show*. She, along with three other families on that particular program, had used the Research Is Company.

Research Is Company
Box 1636
Miami, Florida 33152

SOCIAL SECURITY NUMBER ADDRESS UPDATE REPORT

Research Is Company provides Social Security Number Address Update Reports. If you have gleaned your subject's Social Security Number from research, you may submit a request for a list of addresses used by that number

Addresses that the subject had used for any dealings with certain businesses, governments, credit card companies, and other entities may be given. This system is perfectly legal because no credit information is given. The Research Is Company charges a fee of $64 and is the only company I know of that will not charge a fee if the computer search fails to return at least one address.

The past few years have brought many investigations that have resulted in the arrests of individuals who had "connections" with persons who worked for the Internal Revenue Service or the Social Security Administration. These individuals had apparently paid money so that they could obtain the Social Security Numbers of people. We cannot stress how important it is that you do not get a subject's Social Security Number by paying a government worker. The federal government considers the person paying money for the Social Security Number of another person guilty of bribery, and prosecutions are handled very aggressively.

Remember, Social Security Numbers can be obtained legally from many sources that are considered public records such as, in many instances, marriage records, divorce records, voter's registration records, driver's licenses in some states, mortgage documents on file in the County Clerk's office, corporate documents on file in the state capitol, fictitious names or DBAs, hunting license applications, fishing license applications, subpoenas, pet licenses, bankruptcy records, FCC license applications, accident applications, arrest records, federal and state tax liens on file in the County Clerk's office, in the documents of lawsuits, worker's compensation files in some states, occupational license applications, etc. **Research Is Company will do the research, if you wish, for you and give you the Social Security Number of your subject for $264.00. If they do not provide you with the Social Security Number of your subject, then your money will be refunded. You may prefer to spend the money, but if you have the time, try the many methods that are mentioned here. Getting someone's Social Security Number is just a matter of time and some researching.**

After running a Social Security Number Address Update Report so many readers will find that their "friend" had addresses he had **forgotten** about. There is no problem that he forgot, but who did the address belong to? A girlfriend? A wife? A mail drop? A prison?

STATEWIDE CRIMINAL CHECKS

The Research Is Company will run a statewide criminal check on your subject for $304.00. If they do not find any record on your subject, the fee will be $95.00, and $209.00 will be refunded to you. Research Is Company will return the results of their investigation to you in approximately 21 days, but they have an expedited service for an additional $125.00 and will mail you the results by overnight mail 48 hours after receiving your order, provided the fee is paid by money order. They cannot do expedited service with personal checks. Each additional state after the first one will be only $140.00, and the fee for no record will be $70.00.

Research Is Company has always done these searches for their clients, but since being listed in books and other publications, they have received so many requests that they have decided to offer their services to the public. Please do not be disappointed if your search comes back with no record, because you can be assured that a complete and comprehensive search is done and the information is only what the state has. **Guarantee:** Research Is Company will refund the money you paid for a statewide criminal check if you ever find that the person had a criminal record in the state they had checked for you and Research Is Company had said there was not a record.

FIRST NAME AND DATE-OF-BIRTH SEARCH

Give Research Is Company a person's first name and date of birth, and they will give you the names of all the people in the United States who have that first name and date of birth. We just did an "impossible" missing persons case for television where we found the twin of a person, and all they had was the date of birth and first name. This is a great search technique that resolves many cases when nothing else will work. Research Is Company will not charge any fee if there are no hits and if they do not give you at least one name with the first name and date of birth you submitted.

This first name and date-of-birth technique has helped so many people when doing adoption searches because many times the new parents keep the first name of the child. Or if the child is several months old or older, it is often difficult to change the first name. Also, men who want to find their childhood sweetheart use this particular search because they know the name and remember the birthday of the female. Research Is Company charges $354.00 for this service. Try other avenues of searching first, but if there is no other way of finding someone, then you may want to consider using the first name and date-of-birth search.

If there are over 100 people with the same date of birth and first name, then Research Is Company makes a nominal charge of $2.00 for each group of 50 names over the first 100 people because there are names such as John that will return numerous results of people with a particular date of birth. A good suggestion for you (if your request is for a common first name) is to pick a state or several states to be run.

If all else fails, Research Is Company will find the person you're looking for, for $324.00 on a *no-trace/no-charge* basis. They will refund your money if your subject cannot be found within 14 days of receiving your check.

ACTIVE MILITARY PERSONNEL SEARCH

When you want to check to see if your "**friend**" really is in the military, then you may want to use the active military personnel search. Just send the Research Is Company the name of your subject, and they will search to see if your subject is currently in the military. You do not need to provide the branch of service. If you look at the following list of names that was run on John Anderson, you will see that this list can sometimes spot a name for you that is not that usual, such as John Campbell Anderson. You will see that at the time this list was run, he was stationed in zip code 92134. You then know there are many records you can run that may lead you to an off-base housing unit he may reside in. He may even be listed in the telephone directory. **The important thing is that you may have a child-support order or a legal debt that has to be paid, and now you can contact the branch of service he is in to assist you in your debt collection.** Or he may be just an old friend and you can ask the branch of military (which you just narrowed down by this search) to forward a message to him. Sometimes you may have several people with the exact same name, such as John M. Anderson. In this case, you will try to contact both individuals to see which is your subject. Research Is Company's fee for this service is $174.00, and they send the results to you in seven days after receiving your order.

Anderson, John D—Air Force—is stationed in AK 99506
Anderson, John Michael—Army—is stationed in AL 36362
Anderson, John Lewis—Army Guard—is stationed in AL 35611
Anderson, John Dale—Army Reserve—is stationed in AL 35205
Anderson, John E—Air Force—is stationed in AZ 85707
Anderson, John H —Marine Reserve—is stationed in AZ 85009
Anderson, John T—Air Force Reserve—is stationed in AZ 85309
Anderson, John Campbell—Navy—is stationed in CA 92134
Anderson, John F—Air Force Reserve—is stationed in CA 92518
Anderson, John Fitzgerald—Navy Reserve—is stationed in CA 90731
Anderson, John M—Air Force Reserve—is stationed in CA 94535
Anderson, John M—Air Force—is stationed in CA 94535
Anderson, John Miller—Army—is stationed in CA 95813
Anderson, John R—Air Force—is stationed in CA 93524
Anderson, John W—Air Force Guard—is stationed in CA 94545

SOCIAL SECURITY DEATH MASTER FILE

There is no quicker or more precise method for ascertaining someone's death. It has been a great tool to use for the past several years. Here are the various ways the Master Death File can be accessed:

1. **By name only**
2. **By name and date of birth**
3. **By Social Security Number**
4. **By name and date of death**
5. **By first name only with date of birth**

The total number of persons listed in the Master Death File is currently at 62 million. The list includes all deaths since 1962, the year this system was automated.

Several companies have bought the magnetic tapes that the Social Security Administration makes available for sale that contain the Master Death File. They have spent $32,000 to convert the tapes over to computer disks and the quarterly updates cost $1,700.

The most important use of the Death Master File is to quickly, and with a minimum of information, find a death record of a parent of your subject. If I believe that a parent of the subject has died, I will request that a Death Master File record be run on their name. Even though you will usually not have the date of birth, Social Security Number, or even the place of death of the parent, a search can be conducted. Of course, a name like John Smith will not yield good results because of the long list that will be produced, but if you have the year of birth, then the field can be narrowed down considerably.

The Social Security Administration will not accept any requests for Death Master File searches. Research Is Company charges $34 for each name search. This fee covers a list of up to 100 duplicate names returned for each name submitted that you request. The fee for over 100 duplicate names is $30 per hundred.

When I review the Death Master File record of a parent, I look for the zip code that states the place of death. I will order a death certificate and then contact the funeral home that is listed. The funeral home's records will indicate the next of kin. The home address and telephone number of the spouse or other family member will be contained in the funeral home's records. These close relatives may be queried about your subject if you find this desirable. **The questions you ask now, especially if your subject had neglected to tell you about these family members, may save you much grief.**

Since you now have the place of death of the parent, you may want to contact the probate court of jurisdiction. If the parent had died intestate (no will), there will be a file that contains much information, including the names and addresses of all persons that were paid monies by the probate court for the estate.

Because your subject was an offspring, they will be entitled to part of the estate. The subject's address will be listed along with the **amount of money they received and any property given to your subject will be noted.**

Your "friend" may be receiving an annuity from a relative's estate. This annuity check may be paid to him biweekly, monthly, or yearly. When you review the probate file, pay particular attention to the address he is having the checks sent to. The address may be a bank that puts the check directly into a mutual fund or other type of investment you may not have been told about. These annuities will be part of the marital estate after you are married.

THE INFORMATION THAT IS CONTAINED
ON THE MASTER DEATH FILE IS AS FOLLOWS:

St Soc Sec Num Last Name First Name Birth Date Death Date Resi Zip1 Zip2

St: This indicates what state the subject lived in when they applied for a Social Security Number.

Soc Sec Num: Social Security Number

Last Name: The name that the death benefits list as account holder

First Name: Walt would be Walter, Larry would be Lawrence, and Bob would be Robert—if this is the formal name used by the decedent when they applied for their Social Security Number. A name of Harry could very well be Harry instead of Harold—if this is what was written on the original application.

Birth Date: The full birth date is usually printed on the Master Death File.

Death Date: The exact day is sometimes missing, but the month and year are usually displayed.

Resi: This stands for residence and indicates in which state the death occurred.

Zip1: The zip code in which the death occurred

Zip2: The zip code where the lump sum payment was mailed to

The following sample records of well-known persons will be used to illustrate different information that may or may not appear on the Death Master Record.

St	Soc Sec Num	Last Name	First Name	Birth Date	Death Date	Resi	Zip1	Zip2
MD	215-09-2405	Disney	Walter	03/21/1878	08/00/1967	(MD)	21228	
IL	342-10-3698	Disney	Walter	10/17/1890	05/00/1973	(IL)	61734	
DC	577-07-8270	Disney	Walter	05/31/1894	01/00/1979	(MD)	61734	
NY	110-12-1395	Disney	Walter	08/14/1897	10/00/1980	(FL)	33062	
KY	402-07-4149	Disney	Walter	09/09/1899	06/00/1983	(KY)	40906	
* CA	562-10-0296	Disney	Walter	12/05/1901	*12/00/1966	( )	00000	
TN	413-09-3359	Disney	Walter	03/20/1908	10/00/1972	(TN)	37311	
VA	228-10-8454	Disney	Walter	09/24/1912	03/00/1978	(KY)	40391	24277
KY	401-24-1418	Disney	Walter	09/11/1921	03/00/1972	(KY)	40272	
TN	408-76-5315	Disney	Walter	04/20/1947	09/00/1985	(TN)	37714	

20782 MD Hyattsville........	37311 TN Cleveland............	40906 KY Barbourville.....
21228 MD Baltimore............	37714 TN Caryville.............	61734 IL Delavan................
24277 VA Pennington Gap	40272 KY Louisville..........	
38062 FL Pompano Beach	40391 KY Winchester........	

The above list contains all the Walter Disneys that have died since 1962. When you have a record that does not indicate a place of death, then look at the beginning of the record. The Social Security Number of the highlighted Walter Disney shows that this individual applied for his number in California. This would be where you would start a search for a will that will show the distribution of assets. **If this was the father of your subject, in this hypothetical sample, his will would be a good record to review to see if your "friend" received a large inheritance.**

St	Soc Sec Num	Last Name	First Name	Birth Date	Death Date	Resi	Zip1	Zip2
KY	402-03-2297	Truman	Harry	10/16/1884	10/00/1966	(KY)	41015	
* MO	448-40-6969	Truman	Harry	05/08/1884	*12/00/72	(MO)	64050	
PA	170-03-8745	Truman	Harry	05/15/1866	03/00/1973	(PA)	15223	
MI	386-01-1149	Truman	Harry	08/08/1887	07/00/1963	(MI)	00000	
KY	402-20-8745	Truman	Harry	01/27/1890	03/00/1978	(KY)	40205	
WA	535-20-8745	Truman	Harry	10/30/1896	05/00/1980	(WA)	98611	98532
PA	178-05-8291	Truman	Harry	07/04/1897	10/00/1965	(PA)	00000	
MI	367-26-8037	Truman	Harry	03/12/1901	11/00/1978	(OH)	43023	
AZ	527-01-2253	Truman	Harry	02/17/1905	02/00/1968	(CA)	95258	
NY	119-26-6047	Truman	Harry	08/19/1905	02/00/1985	(IN)	47130	

15223 PA Pittsburgh........... 47130 IN Jeffersonville..... 95258 CA Woodbridge........
40205 KY Louisville........... 49415 MI Fruitport............. 98532 WA Chehalis.............
41015 KY Covington........... 64050 MO Independence... 98611 WA Castle Rock........
43023 OH Granville........... 92646 CA Huntington Beach..

St	Soc Sec Num	Last Name	First Name	Birth Date	Death Date	Resi	Zip1	Zip2
* MO	495-50-5300	Truman	Bess	02/13/1885	*10/00/1982	(MO)	64050	
WV	234-80-3101	Truman	Bessie	04/18/1889	12/30/1989	(WV)	25276	
IN	305-70-2063	Truman	Bessie	08/07/1889	09/00/1983	(IN)	46806	
OR	542-22-6633	Truman	Bessie	01/15/1893	07/00/1976	(OR)	97034	
OK	445-32-1574	Truman	Bessie	10/05/1936	11/00/1969	(OK)	73502	

27276 WV Spencer..................... 64050 MO Independence.......... 97034 OR Lake Oswego............
46806 IN Fort Wayne............. 73502 OK Lawtow......................

The two Truman Master Death Records were ordered by name only. There are numerous decedents with the name Harry Truman, but if you knew that the person you were searching for was from Missouri, then you would have isolated the focus of your search easily.

You will notice that there is only one Bess Truman who has died since 1962. In this case, you did not need to know what area the person was from.

St	Soc Sec Num	Last Name	First Name	Birth Date	Death Date	Resi	Zip1	Zip2
CA	563-66-4692	Astaire	Ann	12/22/1878	07/00/1975	(CA)	91202	
* CA	568-05-4206	Astaire	Fred	05/10/1899	*06/00/1987	(CA)	90213	
ME	004-12-2305	Astaire	Theodore	08/12/1913	09/00/1979	(CT)	06503	06511

06503 CT New Haven..........	90213 CA Beverly Hills.....	
06511 CT New Haven...........	91202 CA Glendale	

The above record for the last name Astaire will show that certain names will not produce a lengthy list that will make your search that much easier. Since 1962, only three people with the name Astaire have died.

St	Soc Sec Num	Last Name	First Name	Birth Date	Death Date	Resi	Zip1	Zip2
TN	408-50-1182	Presley	Earl	07/09/1930	03/00/1985	(TN)	38555	
GA	256-48-7374	Presley	Earl	05/08/1936	02/00/1987	(GA)	31904	
MS	428-58-7758	Presley	Eddie	05/25/1934	05/00/1983	(MS)	39501	
WV	232-58-9834	Presley	Edward	01/11/1930	03/00/1983	( )	24830	
AL	424-52-7031	Presley	Edward	07/22/1937	03/00/1980	(AL)	36256	
TN	409-64-5512	Presley	Elmer	08/06/1940	09/22/1990	( )	38134	
* TN	409-52-2002	Presley	Elvis	01/08/1935	*08/16/1977	( )	38116	
MS	425-11-0453	Presley	Elvis	10/24/1957	04/00/1987	(MS)	38858	
TX	455-46-8412	Presley	Ernest	12/24/1930	03/00/1979	( )	76179	

25830 WV Elbert.................	38116 TN Memphis................	38858 MS Nettleton............
31904 GA Columbus............	38134 TN Memphis..............	39501 MS Gulfport ....
36256 AL Daviston..............	38555 TN Crossville..........	76179 TX Saginaw...............

The above record is a result of a request for all persons with the last name Presley and the first name containing the letter *E* as the first letter. You will notice that in this case, the highlighted Presley does not show a place of death under Zip Code 1, but Zip Code 2 indicates where the lump sum Social Security was sent. For each space on a death master file record, there may be no information entered. You can see that there are several death date, Resi, Zip1, and Zip 2 spaces that have no information.

☙ ☙ ☙

NOTES

Child Support Enforcement

C all the appropriate state office listed in this chapter and ask if your subject is wanted for failure to pay child support. You probably would be surprised by how many times a man that seems to be A-OK in every way owes child support. You want to know because you will want to do the right thing and would not want young children given anything less than what they have coming from your subject. Also, if you marry your subject, there may be a knock on the door in the middle of the night and your subject will be arrested, which may possibly jeopardize his livelihood, besides all the other consequences including embarrassment. Remember, after you are married you will also be **liable for any debts** of your husband. Back payments may run into the tens of thousands of dollars.

Even though some of the following is not pertaining to checking out your "new friend," I think it is important because the readers of this book are predominantly female and **may have a friend that could use this information or even need the following for themselves.**

Many readers of this book will be able to use the government to conduct a search for them. If an individual has a child support order against a subject, with minimum information (the subject's name and Social Security Number), the Federal Parent Locator Service can search for a current address in the records of the Department of Defense, the National Personnel Records Center, the Social Security Administration, and the Veterans Administration.

The Federal Parent Locator Service is a service operated by the Office of Child Support Enforcement within the purview of the United States Department of Health and Human Services to assist the individual states in locating persons for the purpose of obtaining child support payments. This agency is also used in cases of parental kidnaping related to custody and visitation cases.

The first step in seeking the location of a subject that has an obligation to pay child support is to contact your state's Child Support Enforcement office. They will first use the State Parent Locator Service. This service will check the records of other state agencies such as motor vehicle registration, unemployment insurance, state income tax, and correctional facilities. If the subject has moved to another state, the above noted Federal Parent Support Service will be contacted.

The Internal Revenue Service, in conjunction with State and Federal Child enforcement agencies, will disclose information from the tax return of the subject to the child support office which will be of assistance in finding the subject and **determining the subject's financial condition.**

Besides salary garnishment, other items that may be seized from the subject are lottery winnings, automobiles, boats, land, and any monies in banks here or abroad.

Before reading the rest of this chapter that includes important addresses and telephone numbers of Child Enforcement Departments, you may want to review the following statistics and facts supplied by The United States Department of Commerce, Economics and Statistics Administration in their latest press release.

- The child support award rate for unmarried women was **19 percent.** The award rate for married women was **76 percent.**

- A higher percentage of fathers with **joint custody** pay the child support due **(91.3 percent)** than fathers who have visitation privileges **(78.3 percent)** and those without visitation or joint custody provisions **(42.1 percent).**

- The poverty rate for all women with children from absent fathers was **32 percent**.

- Over **55 percent** of absent fathers resided in the same state as their children in 1990; an additional **29.5 percent** of absent fathers lived in another state. The residence of the remaining **15.5 percent** of absent fathers was either overseas or unknown.

- Women with four or more years of college were **more likely** to be awarded payments than women with less than a college education.

- Younger women with children from absent fathers were much more likely to have family incomes below the poverty level than their older counterparts. The poverty rate for women under 30 **(48.4 percent)** was about double that of women over 30 **(24.3 percent).**

- The number of women living with children whose father was absent from the home is **10,345,000** as of spring 1990, an increase of **44 percent** in little more than a decade. Approximately 17 million children with absent fathers lived in these households. At present **33 percent** of all children are born to **unmarried mothers.**

- Health-care benefits were included in the child support awards of 43 percent of mothers; however, **only two thirds of the absent fathers required to do so actually provided them.**

The following are the addresses and telephone numbers of the State Child Support Enforcement Departments:

ALABAMA

http://www.dhr.state.al.us/csed/
Department of Human Resources
Child Support Enforcement
50 Ripley Street
Montgomery, Alabama 36130-1801
(334) 242-9300
FAX: (334) 242-0606

ALASKA

http://www.csed.state.ak.us/
Child Support Enforcement Division
550 West 7th Avenue, Suite 310
Anchorage, Alaska 99501-6699
(907) 269-6900 or (800) 478-33000
FAX: (907) 269-6650

ARIZONA

http://www.de.state.az.us/links/dcse/
index.html
Division of Child Support Enforcement
P.O. Box 40458
Phoenix, Arizona 85067
(602) 252-4045 or (800) 882-4151
FAX: (602) 248-3126

ARKANSAS

http://www.state.ar.us/dfa/childsupport/
index.html
Office of Child Support Enforcement
P.O. Box 8133
Little Rock, Arkansas 72203
Street Address: 712 West Third Street
Little Rock, Arkansas 72201
(501) 682-8398 or (800) 264-2445
FAX: (501) 682-6002

CALIFORNIA

http://www.childsup.cahwnet.gov/-
Default.htm
Office of Child Support
Department of Child Support Services
(DCSS)
P.O. Box 944245
Sacramento, California 94244-2450
(916) 654-1532 or (800) 777-2515
FAX: (916) 657-3791

COLORADO

http://www.childsupport.state.co.us
Department of Human Services
Colorado Child Support Enforcement
1200 Federal Boulevard
Denver, Colorado 80204-3221
(720) 944-3666
FAX: (720) 944-3096

CONNECTICUT

http://www.dss.state.ct.us/svcs/csupp.htm
Department of Social Services
Bureau of Child Support Enforcement
25 Sigourney Street
Hartford, Connecticut 06106-5033
(860) 424-5251 or (800) 228-5437
FAX: (860) 951-2996

DELAWARE

http://www.state.de.us/dhss/irm/dcse/
dcsehome.htm
Division of Child Support Enforcement
Delaware Health and Social Services
1901 North Dupont Hwy., Biggs Bldg.
New Castle, Delaware 19720
(302) 577-4863, 577-4800
FAX: (302) 577-4783

DISTRICT OF COLUMBIA

http://www.csed.dcgov.org
Office of Paternity and
Child Support Enforcement
Department of Human Services
800 9th Street, S.W, 2nd Floor
Washington, DC 20024-2485
(202) 645-7500

FLORIDA

http://sun6.dms.state.fl.us/dor/childsupport
Child Support Enforcement Program
Department of Revenue
2410 Allen Road
Tallahassee, Florida 32312
(800) 622-5437
FAX: (850) 413-9011

GEORGIA

http://www.div.dhr.state.ga.us/dfcs_cse/
Child Support Enforcement
2812 Spring Road, Suite 150
Atlanta, Georgia 30339
(770) 434-4901
FAX: (770) 434-2551

GUAM

Department of Law
Child Support Enforcement Office
238 Archbishop F.C. Flores, 7th Floor
Agana, Guam 96910
(671) 475-3360

HAWAII

http://kumu.icsd.hawaii.gov/csea/csea.htm
Child Support Enforcement Agency
Department of Attorney General
601 Kamokila Boulevard, Suite 251
Kapolei, Hawaii 96707
(808) 587-4250 or (888) 317-9081
FAX: (808) 692-7001

IDAHO

http://www2.state.id.us/dhw/hwgd_-www/contentlist.html#child
Bureau of Child Support Services
Department of Health and Welfare
1720 Westgate Drive
Boise, Idaho 83704
(208) 334-0750
FAX: (208) 334-0759

ILLINOIS

http://www.state.il.us/dpa/html/cs_programs.htm
Child Support Enforcement Division
Illinois Department of Public Aid
32 West Randolph Street
Room 900
Chicago, Illinois 60601-3405
(800) 447-4278 or (800) 374-3346
FAX: (312) 793-1961

INDIANA

http://www.state.in.us/fssa/HTML/PROGRAMS/DFCSupport.html
Child Support Office
129 East Market St., Suite 100
Indianapolis, Indiana 46204
(317) 327-1800
FAX: (317) 327-1801

IOWA

http://www.dhs.state.ia.us/HomePages/DHS/csrunit.htm
Bureau of Collections
Department of Human Services
Hoover Building, 5th Floor
Des Moines, Iowa 50319
(515) 281-5580 or (888) 229-9223
FAX: (515) 281-8854

KANSAS

http://www.state.ks.us/
Child Support Enforcement Program
Department of Social
& Rehabilitation Services
415 S.W. Eighth St.
Topeka, Kansas 66603
(785) 296-3237
FAX: (785) 296-5206

KENTUCKY

http://www.law.state.ky.us/childsupport/Default.htm
Division of Child Support Enforcement
P.O. Box 1040
Frankfurt, Kentucky 40602-1040
(502) 564-5390 or (800) 248-1163
FAX: (502) 564-4035

LOUISIANA

http://www.dss.state.la.us/
Support Enforcement Services
530 Lakeland Avenue
Baton Rouge, Louisiana 70804
(225) 342-4780
FAX: (225) 342-7397

MAINE

http://www.state.me.us/dhs/main/bfi.htm
Bureau of Family Independence
Department of Human Services
11 State House Station—Whitten Road
Augusta, Maine 04333
(207) 287-2826
FAX: (207) 287-5096

MARYLAND

http://www.dhr.state.md.us/csea/index.htm
Child Support Enforcement
Administration
Department of Human Resources
311 West Saratoga Street
Baltimore, Maryland 21201
(800) 332-6347 or (800) 234-1528
FAX: (410) 333-8992

MASSACHUSETTS

http://www.state.ma.us/cse/cse.htm
Child Support Enforcement Division
Department of Revenue
51 Sleeper Street
Boston, Massachusetts 02205-9492
(617) 626-2300 or (800) 332-2733
FAX: (617) 626-2330

MICHIGAN

Michigan Family Independence
1200 6th St.
Detroit, Michigan 48226
(313) 256-1028
FAX: (313) 256-1095

MINNESOTA

http://www.dhs.state.mn.us/ecs/Program/csed.htm
Office of Child Support Enforcement
Department of Human Services
444 Lafayette Road
St. Paul, Minnesota 55155-3846
(651) 282-5272
FAX: (612) 297-4450

MISSISSIPPI

http://www.mdhs.state.ms.us/cse.html
Division of Child Support Enforcement
Department of Human Services
939 N. President
Jackson, Mississippi 39202
(601) 359-4861
FAX: (601) 359-4415

MISSOURI

http://www.dss.state.mo.us/cse/cse.htm
Department of Social Services
Division of Child Support Enforcement
P.O. Box 2320
Jefferson City, Missouri 65102-2320
(573) 751-4301
FAX: (573) 751-8450

MONTANA

http://www.state.mt.us/
Child Support Enforcement Division
Department of Public Health and
Human Services
P.O. Box 202943
Helena, Montana 59620
(406) 442-7278

NEBRASKA

http://www.hhs.state.ne.us/cse/cseindex.htm
Child Support Enforcement Office
Department of Health
and Human Services
P.O. Box 94728
Lincoln, Nebraska 68509-4728
(402) 479-5555 or (800) 831-4573
FAX: (402) 479-5543

NEVADA

http://www.state.nv.us/ag/agpub/chldsupp.htm
Child Support Enforcement Program
Nevada State Welfare Division
2527 North Carson Street
Carson City, Nevada 89706-0113
(775) 687-4744
FAX: (775) 684-8026

NEW HAMPSHIRE

http://www.dhhs.state.nh.us
Office of Child Support
Division of Human Services
Health and Human Services Building
129 Pleasant St.
Concord, New Hampshire 03301-3857
(603) 271-4427
FAX: (603) 271-4787

NEW JERSEY

http://www.njchildsupport.org
Division of Family Development
Bureau of Child Support
and Paternity Programs
Quakersbridge Plaza, Bldg 6
P.O. Box 716
Trenton, New Jersey 08625-0716
(609) 588-2915 or (877) 655-4371
FAX: (609) 588-2064

NEW MEXICO

http://www.state.nm.us/
Child Support Enforcement Bureau
Department of Human Services
P.O. Box 25109
Santa Fe, New Mexico 87504
Street Address: 2025 S. Pacheco
Santa Fe, New Mexico 87504
(505) 476-7040
FAX: (505) 827-7285

NEW YORK

http://www.dfa.state.ny.us/csms
Division of Child Support Enforcement
NY State Office of Temporary Assistance
40 N. Pearl Street
Albany, New York 12243
(518) 474-9081
FAX: (518) 486-3127

NORTH CAROLINA

http://www.dhhs.state.nc.us/dss/cse/cse_
mission.htm
Child Support Enforcement Office
Department of Human Resources
Courthouse, Suite 819
Raleigh, North Carolina 27602
(919) 856-6630 or (800) 992-9457
FAX: (919) 856-5714

NORTH DAKOTA

http://discovernd.com/government/agen-
cies.html
Department of Human Services
Child Support Enforcement Agency
P.O. Box 7190
Bismarck, North Dakota 58507-7190
(701) 328-3582
FAX: (701) 328-6575

OHIO

http://www.state.oh.us/odhs/ocs
Office of Family Assistance and Child
Support Enforcement
Department of Human Services
899 East Broad Street–4th Floor
Columbus, Ohio 43205-1190
(614) 644-9000 or (800) 686-1568
FAX: (614) 644-6674

OKLAHOMA

http://www.okdhs.org/ichildsupport
Child Support Enforcement Division
Department of Human Services
P.O. Box 53552
Oklahoma City, Oklahoma 73152
Street Address: 2409 N. Kelley Avenue
Annex Building
Oklahoma City, Oklahoma 73111
(405) 522-5871
FAX: (405) 522-2753

OREGON

http://www.afs.hr.state.or.us/rss/child-
supp.html
Recovery Services Section
Adult and Family Services Division
Department of Human Resources
500 Summer Street N.E., 2nd Floor
Salem, Oregon 97310-1013
(503) 945-5601
FAX: (503) 373-7032

PENNSYLVANIA

http://www.pachildsupport.com
Bureau of Child Support Enforcement
Department of Public Welfare
Office of Income Maintenance
Health & Welfare Building, Room 432
Harrisburg, Pennsylvania 17105-2675
(717) 787-1894
FAX: (717) 787-6765

PUERTO RICO

Child Support Enforcement
Department of Social Services
P.O. Box 3349
San Juan, Puerto Rico 00902-3349
Street Address: Majagua Street, Bldg 2
Wing 4, 2nd Floor
Rio Pedras, Puerto Rico 00903-9938
(787) 767-1500
FAX: (787) 282-7411

RHODE ISLAND

http://www.state.ri.us/
Child Support Enforcement
Division of Administration
Division of Taxation
77 Dorrance Street
Providence, Rhode Island 02903
(401) 222-2847
FAX: (401) 277-6674

SOUTH CAROLINA

http://www.state.sc.us/dss/csed
Department of Social Services
Child Support Enforcement Division
P.O. Box 1469
Columbia, South Carolina 29202-1469
(800) 768-5858

SOUTH DAKOTA

http://www.state.sd.us/
Office of Child Support Enforcement
Department of Social Services
700 Governor's Drive, Suite 84
Pierre, South Dakota 57501-2291
(605) 773-3641
FAX: (605) 773-7295

TENNESSEE

http://www.state.tn.us/humanserv
Child Support Services
Department of Human Services
Citizens Plaza Building–12th Floor
400 Deadrick Street
Nashville, Tennessee 37248-7400
(615) 313-4880
FAX: (615) 532-2791

TEXAS

http://www.oag.state.tx.us
Office of the Attorney General
Child Support Division
P.O. Box 12017-K
Austin, Texas 78711-2017
(512) 460-6000
FAX: (512) 479-6478

UTAH

http://www.ors.state.ut.us
Bureau of Child Support Services
Department of Human Services
515 E. 100 South
Salt Lake City, Utah 84145-0011
(801) 536-8500 or (800) 662-8525 /
(800) 257-9156
Fax: (801) 536-8509

VERMONT

http://www.ocs.state.vt.us
Office of Child Support
103 South Main Street
Waterbury, Vermont 05671-1901
(802) 479-4204 or (800) 786-3214
FAX: (802) 479-4225

VIRGIN ISLANDS

Paternity and Child Support Division
Department of Justice
GERS Building, 2nd Floor
48B-50C Krondprans Gade
St. Thomas, Virgin Islands 00802
(809) 775-3070
FAX: (809) 774-3808

VIRGINIA

http://www.dss.state.va.us/division/-
childsupp
Division of Child Support Enforcement
Department of Social Services
730 East Broad Street
Richmond, Virginia 23219
(800) 468-8894, FAX: (804) 692-1405

WASHINGTON

http://www.wa.gov
Division of Child Support
Department of Social Health Services
P.O. Box 9162
Olympia, Washington 98504-9162
Street Address: 712 Pear St. S.E.
Olympia, Washington 98504
(800) 737-0617 or (800) 442-5437
FAX: (360) 586-3274

WEST VIRGINIA

http://www.wvdhhr.org/bcse
Bureau of Child Support Enforcement
Department of Health &
Human Resources
350 Capitol Street, Room 147
Charleston, West Virginia 25301-3703
(800) 249-3778

WISCONSIN

http://www.dwd.state.wi.us/bcs/
Bureau of Child Support
Division of Economic Support
P.O. Box 7935-E
Madison, Wisconsin 53707-7935
Street Address: 1 West Wilson Street,
Room 382
Madison, Wisconsin 53707
(608) 266-9909, FAX: (608) 267-2824

WYOMING

http://dfsweb.state.wy.us/
Child Support Enforcement Program
Department of Family Services
2300 Capital Avenue
Hathaway Building, room 361
Cheyenne, Wyoming 82002-0170
(307) 777-6948, FAX: (307) 777-3693

REGIONAL OFFICES
OF CHILD SUPPORT ENFORCEMENT

REGION I

Connecticut, Maine, Massachusetts,
New Hampshire, Rhode Island,
Vermont

OCSE Program Manager
Administration for
Children and Families
John F. Kennedy Federal Building
Room 2000
Boston, Massachusetts 02203
(617) 565-2478

REGION II

New York, New Jersey, Puerto Rico,
Virgin Islands

OCSE Program Manager
Administration for
Children and Families
Federal Building, Room 4114
26 Federal Plaza
New York, New York 10278
(212) 341-0900
FAX: (212) 264-4881

REGION III

Delaware, Maryland, Pennsylvania,
Virginia, West Virginia,
District of Columbia

OCSE Program Manager
Administration
for Children and Families
150 South Independence Mall
West, Suite 864
Philadelphia, Pennsylvania 19106-
3499
(215) 861-4054

REGION IV

Alabama, Florida, Georgia, Kentucky, Mississippi, North Carolina,
South Carolina, Tennessee

OCSE Program Manager
Administration for
Children and Families
Atlanta Federal Center
61 Forsyth Street S.W., Suite 4M60
Atlanta, Georgia 30303-8909
(404) 562-2900
FAX: (404) 562-2981

REGION V

Illinois, Indiana, Michigan, Minnesota, Ohio, Wisconsin

OCSE Program Manager
Administration for
Children and Families
233 N. Michigan Avenue, Suite 400
Chicago, Illinois 60601-5519
(312) 353-4237
FAX: (312) 886-5373

REGION VI

Arkansas, Louisiana, New Mexico,
Oklahoma, Texas

OCSE Program Manager
Administration for
Children and Families
1301 Young Street, Room 914
(ACF-3)
Dallas, Texas 75202
(214) 767-3749

REGION VII

Iowa, Kansas, Missouri, Nebraska
OCSE Program Manager
Administration for
Children and Families
601 East 12th Street, Room 276
Federal Building, Suite 276
Kansas City, Missouri 64106
(816) 426-3584
FAX: (816) 426-2888

REGION VIII

**Colorado, Montana, North Dakota,
South Dakota, Utah, Wyoming**
OCSE Program Manager
Administration for
Children and Families
Federal Office Building
1961 Stout Street, Room 325
Denver, Colorado 80294-3538
(303) 844-3100

REGION IX

**Arizona, California, Hawaii, Nevada,
Guam**
OCSE Program Manager
Administration for
Children and Families
50 United Nations Plaza, Room 450
San Francisco, California 94012
(415) 437-8400
FAX: (415) 437-8444

REGION X

Alaska, Idaho, Oregon, Washington
OCSE Program Manager
Administration for
Children and Families
2201 Sixth Avenue
Seattle, Washington 98121
(206) 615-2547
FAX: (206) 615-2574

State of Florida, Department
of Health and Rehabilitative
Services, Child Support
Enforcement, on behalf of:
MARY LANSER
SUSAN LANSER
by and through AGNES LANSER
As Custodian
Petitioner,

FAMILY DIVISION

CASE NUMBER: **93-281**

vs.

EDWARD LANSER
Respondent,
SSN: 271-68-8012

PETITION TO ESTABLISH CHILD SUPPORT AND FOR OTHER RELIEF

COMES NOW the Plaintiff, Department of Health and Rehabilitative
Services, et. al., by and through the undersigned attorney, and files
this Petition for Child Support and other Relief, and as grounds states
as follows:

   1. This is an action to establish child support and for other relief
for the dependent child(ren):

      MARY LANSER BORN ON MARCH 25th 1985 in NYACK, NEW YORK
      SUSAN LANSER BORN ON AUGUST 17th 1983 in NYACK, NEW YORK

   2. This Court has personal jurisdiction of the Defendant in that the
Defendant is currently or was preceding commencement of this action a
resident.

   3. AGNES LANSER and the child(ren) reside in MONROE COUNTY, Florida.

   4. Defendant is legally responsible parent of the child(ren).

   5. The child(ren) needs and has needed since birth, support from the
Defendant who has had the ability to provide support.

   6. The Defendant is over 18 years of age and is not a member of the
Armed Forces of the United States or its allies.

   7. The Department has incurred administrative costs, fees for legal
services and court costs in this action which Defendant is able to pay.

   8. The child(ren) is or had been a beneficiary of Public Assistance
or is otherwise eligible for services of the Department pursuant to
Chapter 409, F.S.

   9. The participation of the Department and the representation of the
undersigned attorney are limited in scope as set forth in s. 409.2564
(5), F.S.

If your friend was named in a "Petition to establish child support and for
other relief," you will be able to ascertain the names and dates of birth of
the children. This will be of importance to you because your subject will be
paying this child support until the children are 18. That is assuming none
of the children are retarded or handicapped to the point of not being able
to support themselves when they are over 18 because if this is the case, then
support will be mandatory permanently. You may want to consider what
priorities your "friend" has because you now know from the above petition
that the children have been on welfare as indicated in number eight. The
defendant will also have to pay costs and fees associated with this action.

child may participate. The parties further agree that, if either of them has knowledge of any illness or accident or other circumstances affecting the child's health and general welfare, the Husband or the Wife, as the case may be, shall promptly notify the other of such circumstances. The party who is notified shall have immediate access to the minor child notwithstanding where the child may be.

10. **CHILD SUPPORT.** Commencing in the month of December, 1992, the Husband will pay the sum of $130.00 per month for the support of the minor child. The parties have calculated the said child support payments based on their present income, which is as follows: The Wife represents that she has a net income of $962.75 per month. The Husband represents that he has a net monthly income of $438.66 per month. Under the existing Child Support Guidelines, child support should total $311.00 per month. The Wife has the obligation to contribute 70% of the guidelines amount and the Husband has the obligation to contribute 30% of said guidelines amount. Therefore, the Husband's child support obligations is $94.50. However, the parties agree that the Husband will continue to contribute the sum of $130.00 per month for child support. As additional child support the Husband agrees to contribute the sum of $70.00 towards the medical expenses of the minor child not covered by insurance. Therefore, the total child support that the Husband will pay monthly shall be $200.00, payable on the 1st of each month.

The parties acknowledge that the Husband is presently underemployed, and that the amount of child support contributed by the Husband does not well cover the expenses incurred by the minor

-7-

OFF. REC BK)
15758 PG 0647

Many cases do not have the original copy available, and the copy may have been reduced to microfiche. The clerk at the county office of records will assist you in locating the records. Note number 10 of this document. You will see that the total this husband will be paying is $200 a month. Also, you will note that the subject has a gross income of $438.66 a month. Is this the amount of money your subject claims he earns? That's less than $110 a week. The child support he will have to pay is **almost half of the gross monthly income.** That leaves the subject with $238.66 a month of disposable income. **Is this enough to set up housekeeping for life with him?**

Dec. 24 1992 COURTHOUSE TOWER
DATE MICROFILMED LOCATION
DEPUTY CLERK, CIRCUIT COURT
CAMERA OPERATOR

_86 - 314_, case number

ARREARS

X The Obligor is in arrears in court ordered payments in the amount of

$ _7,607.29_ as of _5/13/92_ .

___ The amount of arrears is in dispute or undetermined.

___ The amount of arrears and/or payment is reserved.

X Interest has accrued on the support arrearage at the statutory rate. The issue of the amount of interest due on the arrearage is reserved.

ISSUE OF CONTEMPT

___ NOT-CONTEMPT - The Obligor is found not in willful contempt.

___ CONTEMPT - The Obligor is found in willful contempt because:

___ The Obligor presently has and previously has had the ability to comply with the Court's Order, in whole or in part, but has willfully failed and refused to do so and the Obligor has the present ability to pay the purge set forth below.
___ The Obligor failed to appear before the Court, after having been properly noticed to do so.

X A WRIT OF BODILY ATTACHMENT be entered and the Obligor brought before the Court for sentencing. Bond to be set in the amount of $ _500.00_ .

___ The Motion for Contempt is [] DENIED [] WITHDRAWN.

___ Adjudication on the issue of Contempt is: [] WITHHELD [] RESERVED.

PAYMENT

X The Obligor shall continue to timely pay $ _25.00_ per _week_, for child support;

X the Obligor shall pay the additional sum of $ _5.00_ per _week_, toward the child support arrears established herein, commencing with the next regularly scheduled payment,

___ plus the Clerk's fees of $_____ per _____,

X For a Total of $ _30.00_ per _week_. Payment shall be made payable to the CENTRAL DEPOSITORY who shall forward all monies to the State of Florida, Department of HRS, for disbursement to: ___ Obligee (L/NA) ___ the Initiating State (U) X the State of Florida. (L/PA)

COSTS

___ COSTS are [] RESERVED [] DENIED.

___ The Obligor, upon the entry of the Order on this Report, shall pay:
___ Court costs in the amount of $_____ within _____ days.
___ Attorney fees/administrative costs in the amount of $_____ within _____ days.
X Fees/Costs are payable to The Department of HRS. & The State Attorney's Ofc. 100 S. Biscayne Blvd. Suite 3100 Miami, FL 33131.

58 PG 1496

This document from the county records indicates that this individual is in arrears for **$7,607.29.** Also note that a writ of bodily attachment has been issued. That is another way of saying that there is a **warrant outstanding for his arrest.** You may want to ask your "friend" to show you paperwork proving he has resolved the writ. You will see that, at $5 extra a week to pay towards the arrears, **it will take 1521 weeks to satisfy this debt—which is over 29 years.**

	HRS			
DEPARTMENT OF HEALTH AND REHABILITATIVE SERVICES				

CASE NO: _93 - 434_

ADELAIDA ABRE)
)
)
)
)
SSN: _____)
V.)
RIGARDO D. ABRE)
)
SSN: _____)

CHILD SUPPORT
GUIDELINES
WORKSHEET

		A. MOTHER	B. LEGAL OR ALLEGED FATHER
1. GROSS INCOME -	Actual		
	Imputed	736.66	736.66
2. TOTAL DEDUCTIONS -	Actual		
	Imputed	60.67	60.67
3. NET INCOME - (Subtract 2 from 1)	Actual		
	Imputed	675.99	675.99
4. COMBINED AVAILABLE INCOME (Add 3A and 3B		1,351.98	
5. EACH PARENT'S MATHEMATICAL SHARE OF SUPPORT (Divide 3A by 4 and 3B by 4)		50%.	50%.
6. MINIMUM SUPPORT NEED (Table A)		769.00	
7. CHILD DAY CARE		00. —	
8. TOTAL SUPPORT NEED (Add 6 and 7)		769. —	
9. Monthly Child Support Obligation of Each (Multiply 8 by 5A and 8 by 5B)		384.50 mo	88.73 P/wk. 384. 50 mo.

This is another record that you will be able to obtain from the files of the divorce of child support petition. This gives you a document to see exactly what obligation your "friend" has. The father has a gross income of $736.66. He has regular deductions of $60.67, which brings the net income to $675.99. After the deduction of $384.50 for child support, the father's net is $291.49. Are you aware that **you will have to supplement this man's income if you marry him?**

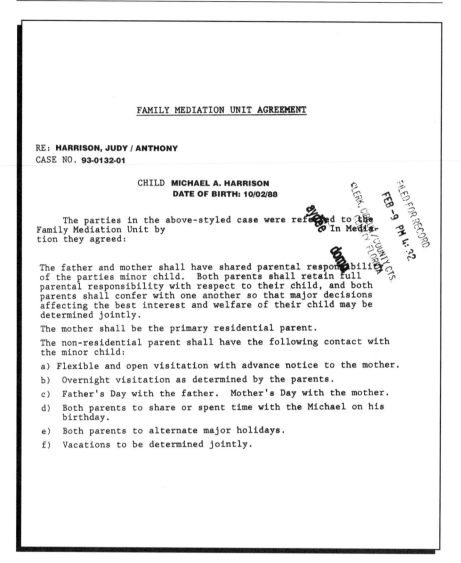

FAMILY MEDIATION UNIT AGREEMENT

RE: **HARRISON, JUDY / ANTHONY**
CASE NO. **93-0132-01**

CHILD　**MICHAEL A. HARRISON**
DATE OF BIRTH: 10/02/88

The parties in the above-styled case were referred to the Family Mediation Unit by _____ In Mediation they agreed:

The father and mother shall have shared parental responsibility of the parties minor child. Both parents shall retain full parental responsibility with respect to their child, and both parents shall confer with one another so that major decisions affecting the best interest and welfare of their child may be determined jointly.

The mother shall be the primary residential parent.

The non-residential parent shall have the following contact with the minor child:

a) Flexible and open visitation with advance notice to the mother.

b) Overnight visitation as determined by the parents.

c) Father's Day with the father. Mother's Day with the mother.

d) Both parents to share or spent time with the Michael on his birthday.

e) Both parents to alternate major holidays.

f) Vacations to be determined jointly.

Since their inception, Family Mediation Unit Agreements have helped to define exactly what the custody and visitation rights will be. You will note that the father will have certain times he will have his son's company. Even though you may have been aware of this child and that you want your "friend" to spend time with his son, **were you told about these specific times as shown above?** Will those times integrate well with your obligations and schedules? Since the agreement states "vacations will be determined jointly," do you feel that the vacation periods of the ex-wife, your future spouse, and you can be coordinated to such a complete agreement so that there will be no scheduling conflicts?

County Records

There are a myriad of public records that can be accessed on the county level. The following is a list of the types of records you will find that contain information about your subject:

Assumption Agreement	**Certificate of Organization**
Abstract	**Certificate of Title**
Affidavit	**Change of Name**
Agreement	**Condominium Rider**
Agreement for Deed	**Corporation**
Agreement Not To Encumber	**Cost Judgment**
Amended Judgment	**Declaration of Trust**
Assignment	**Deed**
Assignment of Judgment	**Discharge**
Assignment of Lien	**Disclaimer**
Assignment of Mortgage	**Dismissal**
Assignment of Proprietary Lease	**Divorce**
Breach of Agreement	**Easement**
Breach of Contract	**Easement Deed**
Breach of Lease	**Eminent Domain**
Certificate	**Estate Tax Closing Letter**
Certificate of Additional Tax	**Estate Tax Lien**
Certificate of Approval	**Fictitious Name**
Certificate of Merger	**Foreclosure of Chattel Mortgage**

Guardianship
Incompetency
Incorporation
Involuntary Bankruptcy
Judgment
Lease
Levy
Lien
Modification Agreement
Mortgage Modification Agreement
Name Restoration
Nontaxable Certificate or Receipt
Notice of Federal Tax Lien
Notice of Lis Pendens
Notice of Tax Lien (State)
Partial Release of Lien
Personal Representative's Deed
Power of Attorney
Public Defender's Claim
Quit Claim Deed
Restrictions (Covenants)
Receipt of Advance

Release of Estate Tax
Release of Federal Tax Lien
Release of Lien (Mechanic's Lien)
Resolution
Restoration of Incompetency
Restored Corporation
Revocation of Power of Attorney
Satisfaction of Final Decree
Satisfaction of Judgment
Satisfaction of Release of Lien
Satisfaction of Release of
    Mortgage
Satisfaction of Tax Executions
Separation
Support Agreement
Tax Warrant
Title Opinion
Trust Agreement
Trustee Resignation
Voluntary Bankruptcy
Warranty Deed
Writ of Garnishment

You may search for any of the above records with just the name of your subject. You will note that the list contains public documents that range from **Federal and State** tax liens to writs of garnishment.

VOTER'S REGISTRATION

Voter's registration information is available upon written request. Write to the county you believe your subject may have been or is registered in.

The example shown on the next page will clearly illustrate how easy it is to ascertain the subject's date of birth and old home address. In this case, the only information I had was that the subject named Lub lived in Baldwin, New York, at one time. I was not supplied a first name. I wrote to the Board of Elections of the county of jurisdiction for Baldwin. I sent a nominal fee of $3 because this is the average cost of requesting a voter's registration record.

I requested that I be sent the voter's registration information of every person named Lub in Baldwin. In this case, I was fortunate that my request was for an unusual name.

The response I was sent stated that the potential subject, Lub, did not live in Baldwin and had moved in 1985. The potential subject's new address was 140 Larch Street, Wantagh, New York, and included the date of birth of the potential subject. Since I was aware that my subject had been in a serious accident on a certain date and at a certain location, I ordered this potential subject's driving record. The accident date and location that I had been supplied with matched with what was listed on the driving record.

To be able to write one letter and be provided with a full name for the subject makes this one of the best background profile techniques. If your subject has an **unlisted telephone number** and it is on his voter's registration information, then you can consider it available to you as part of a public record.

Sinita Walker, President
Republican Commissioner

John W. Matthews, Secretary
Democratic Commissioner

BOARD OF ELECTIONS
ADMINISTRATION BUILDING
400 COUNTY SEAT DRIVE
MINEOLA, L.I., NEW YORK 11501
(516) 535-2411

July 24, 1991

RE: Lub

To Whom It May Concern:

A letter was received in this office requesting information on the above mentioned, possibly residing in Baldwin, New York.

A search of our official records shows that there was a Kathleen J. Lub who moved out of Baldwin in 1985 and now resides from 140 Larch Street, Wantagh, New York.

Her date of birth is 9/30/56.

Enclosed, is your receipt for research fee. Thank you.

Very truly yours,

Edward Ahit /et ___ Rep. Member

___ Dem. Member
Record Access Officers

EH/NAS: lt
enc.

Commissioners
MICHAEL J. HAMBLET
Chairman
ARNETTE R. HUBBARD
Secretary
CHRIS ROBLING

LANCE GOUGH
Executive Director

BOARD OF ELECTION COMMISSIONERS
CHICAGO, ILLINOIS 60602
ROOM 308 CITY HALL
(312) 269-7900
FAX NO. (312) 263-3649

August 6, 1992

We have checked our current active and inactive registrations on
John W. Galbrea   and could not find any record of him.

We also checked the 1984-5-6-7-8-89 micro-films and his name was not
listed. Thank you.

Sincerely yours,

Donna R. Schuth

Donna R. Schuth
Ass't Mgr. Records Processing
Registration & F/M Div.

DRS:va

The voter's registration department in most locales will search a number of years for your subject. In this letter, you will note that the search was conducted back to 1984. If the subject did have a voter's registration file that was valid even ten years ago, this would be an excellent way to see what addresses he had listed.

```
ALTERNATE REGISTRATION FORM          PLEASE PRINT          CHECK ALL THAT APPLY:
Please see instructions at left.                            □ This is a new registration in this county.
                                                           This is a change of □ Name ☑ Address ☑ Telephone □ Party
```

	Month	Day	Year	Female □		Democratic □
221-06-3784	2	4	51	Male ☑	821-0367	Republican ☑
Soc. Sec. No. (If available)	Birth Date			Gender	Telephone	Party

NAME: DEREK HUDSON

COMPLETE ALL YOU KNOW

ADDRESS: 8123 Holland Street Apt. 7
House number & street (or rural route) plus apartment & box number

COUNTY NAME: Linn

SCHOOL DISTRICT: C.R.Community

Edmonton, Ohio 44132
City, State, and Zip Code

CITY (if inside limits) Cedar Rapids

PREVIOUS REGISTRATION INFORMATION: I was previously registered to vote in

Edward County

TOWNSHIP (If outside city):

SECTION NUMBER (If outside city):

My name then was Daryl Hudsen

I certify that I am a citizen of the United States, that I am or will be an eligible elector at any election at which I attempt to vote and that all of the information I have given upon this voter registration form is true. I authorize cancellation of any prior registration to vote in this or any other jurisdiction and my eligibility to vote in any jurisdiction where voter registration is not required. I am aware that fraudulently registering, or attempting to do so, is an aggravated misdemeanor under Iowa law.

FOR OFFICE USE ONLY

Registration date: _____

Codes: _____

Signature _____ Date _____

Form 2E (Rev. 88) CFN-337-5005 CPF-66929

The Social Security Number on the voter's registration card will usually be a valid one. Individuals will frequently write their Social Security Number on government forms and change one number, but because most people are not aware that the voter's registration card is public information, they will write the correct number down. You will note that the telephone number is listed on the card whether it is an unlisted telephone number or not.

On the top right of the above card, two spaces are checked. The address and telephone have been changed so you now have the very latest information. Make sure when you order the voter's registration that a special request is made for any "alternate" registration forms such as the above one.

Also, pay particular attention to any name changes. You can see that this individual changed the spelling of his first name from "Daryl" to "Derek," and that the last name was changed from "Hudsen" to "Hudson." Couple this with the fact that the name will change with the new address and may indicate that this individual may be making it more difficult for people to find him. **The question is why!**

COUNTY OF LOS ANGELES
REGISTRAR-RECORDER/COUNTY CLERK
5557 FERGUSON DRIVE — P.O. BOX 30450, LOS ANGELES, CALIFORNIA 90030-0450 / (213) 721-1100

CHARLES WEISSBURD
REGISTRAR-RECORDER/COUNTY CLERK

VOTER REGISTRATION/SEARCH

FEE: $5.00   DATE OF SEARCH: 02/03/93

As you requested, a search of the voter registration records in the County of Los Angeles was made and the following information was found.

Name: _____ Charles L. Maur _____

Registered Address: _____ 49 Kisk Av. _____

_____ Hacienda Heights, CA.   91745

Date of Registration: July 22, 1974   ☐ Active   ☑ Canceled

Other Data Requested: _____

☐ No record found (year(s) if applicable) _____

☐ No record found with birthdate of _____

☐ Found _____ voter(s) with the same name

☐ Found _____ voter(s) with a middle name or initial

☐ Found _____ voter(s) without a middle name or initial

Additional information required for search:

☐ Full Name (middle name/initial) _____

☐ Address: _____

_____

☐ Date of Birth: _____   ☐ Birthplace: _____

Additional fee of $_____ required for:

☐ _____ Voter registration search(es)

☐ _____ Year search for other than current information

Clerk's initials

In this case, the search was conducted back to 1974. You will note that the voter's registration card was cancelled. This is good news because it indicates there was a card issued and that card will contain the information you are seeking. If you send for voter's registration information and no record is found with birth date indicated, then you will want to make another request using the exact birth date.

OCCUPATIONAL LICENSES

Many counties require that a person who has any type of independent business apply for an occupational or vendor's license. These records are usually filed three ways: subject's name, address, or company name.

You may want to request that a search be done by address or company name if you have this information. The subject may not be listed if you order the search to be conducted by name because the subject could have changed their name by just a few letters or assumed a whole new identity. When accessing by address or company name, you will be able to evaluate if **any of the principals of the company fit the profile of whom you believe your subject to be.**

PET LICENSES

Persons that arrange many details of their lives to avoid being found will overlook the fact that the license they had issued for their pet is public record. Write to the county you believe your subject resides in for a list of all pet licenses issued in your subject's name, and you may find that the license is listed in the **spouse's name,** which may be a name you were never aware of. The telephone number listed on the license application may be unlisted, but it is public information if your subject chose to put it on the public record.

POWER OF ATTORNEY

Pay special attention to any filing that involves your subject that is listed as Power of Attorney. You will want to know the person's name that your subject gave Power of Attorney to. If you are having difficulty in finding anything under your subject's name, this may be the reason. Persons that are trying to avoid detection will often give Power of Attorney to a family member or close friend. That person will then conduct all business transactions on behalf of your subject, thus giving the subject the benefit of not having their name listed in public records. **You may not have the benefit of certain monies, properties, and valuables because your subject has chosen not to tell you about them.**

ASSET CHECKS

Remember, you may wish to conduct an asset check to determine if **any property exists that you do not know about.** You may use the addresses in this manual to check for ownership of automobiles, trucks, motorcycles, recreational vehicles, boats, aircraft, real estate, etc.

FICTITIOUS NAMES

Your subject may own a business but did not want to incorporate. Your subject would be required to apply for a fictitious name if they wanted to open a business account at a bank. Your subject could have a house painting, landscaping, accounting, hot-dog vending cart or any type of business, and they will have filed a fictitious name with the county. The application on file will **provide you with home and business addresses that may be new to you.** Look for the Social Security Number of your subject.

Write to the county asking that a search be conducted. Provide the subject's full name and the years you want searched.

APPLICATION FOR
REGISTRATION OF FICTITIOUS NAME

Section 1

1. Investments Unlimited
   Fictitious Name to be Registered

2. 5686 36th Street
   Mailing Address of Business
   White Plains,   32801

3. County of _____ Westchester

4. City of _White Plains_, Florida _32801_
5. FEI Number: _____   *Zip Code*

This space for office use only

Section 2

A. Owner(s) of Fictitious Name If Individual(s) (use additional sheets if necessary):

1. Rogers, Harold
   Last   First   M.I.
   15672 Emeet Street
   Address
   Orlando, Florida   32801
   City   State   Zip Code
   SS# _251-28-2982_

2. Hadesty, Nancy
   Last   First   M.I.
   15672 Emeet Street
   Address
   Orlando, Florida   32801
   City   State   Zip Code
   SS# _325-78-2789_

B. Owner(s) of Fictitious Name If Corporation(s) (use additional sheets if necessary):

1. N/A
   Corporate Name

   Address

   City   State   Zip Code
   Corporate Document Number: _____
   FEI Number: _____
   ☐ Applied for   ☐ Not Applicable

2. N/A
   Corporate Name

   Address

   City   State   Zip Code
   Corporate Document Number: _____
   FEI Number: _____
   ☐ Applied for   ☐ Not Applicable

Section 3

I (we) the undersigned, being the sole (all the) party(ies) owning interest in the above fictitious name, certify that the information indicated on this form is true and accurate. I (we) further certify that the fictitious name shown in Section 1 of this form has been advertised at least once in a newspaper as defined in chapter 50, Florida Statutes, in the county where the applicant's principal place of business is located. I (we) understand that the signature(s) below shall have the same legal effect as if made under oath. (At Least One Signature Required)

Harold H. Rgn
Signature of Owner   Date
Phone Number: _407-982-9276_

Nancy Hardesty
Signature of Owner   Date
Phone Number: _407-982-9276_

TAX COLLECTOR/PROPERTY APPRAISER

The tax collector will have an alphabetical listing of all persons that paid property tax. Request that a search be conducted, and specify the years. The tax collector maintains records that go back in time longer than any other record. The necessity of title companies to trace a complete history of property ownership is the reason these records are maintained for perpetuity. Remember, if your subject had a telephone listed on the property records, then it becomes part of the public record. **Do you know about this address?**

Property may be owned by your subject, and a review of the tax bill may show that the address it is being sent to is out of state or in another country. The land may also be in the name of a **spouse** from two or three marriages ago. Your subject may still be paying the mortgage as part of **a settlement you did not know about.**

SMALL CLAIMS COURT

If a search of county records reveals that your subject had a case filed in small claims court, you will want to order the complete file. The file will contain the address of the subject, any witnesses the subject subpoenaed to court, and details about the court case. You may want to review the subpoena the subject was served if the subject had been a defendant in the case. The subpoena will have noted the address the subject had been served at. If the subject has been sneaky about his whereabouts, but was found by a process server, then you will want to pay special attention to this address because it may be different from the listed home address and may be the home of a **girlfriend** or **spouse**.

When an individual or company has a case decided in their favor in Small Claims Court, they are entitled to file a lien against any property that the defendant owns, if the damages are not paid and this will become of liability of **yours**.

The plaintiff, in many instances, is made aware of the ownership of property by the defendant through a questionnaire that the judge, at the request of the plaintiff, ordered the defendant to answer. The questions ask about property ownership, stocks, bank account locations, **wives, children,** etc. You may review this questionnaire, which is part of the court file. You will be able to glean much information about your subject.

Alton B. "Bud" Parker
Property Appraiser
Hillsborough County, Florida

Room 273B
Hillsborough County Courthouse
Tampa, Florida 33602
Telephone (813) 272-6100

Re: 27 Alafia Ridge Road
Riverview, Fl 33569   Date: May 16, 1988

Dear Sir/Madam:

   This is in response to your recent inquiry for property ownership information.

   Our records indicate the following:

No property assessed to _____

_____

Address/legal description furnished is assessed under

Folio Number(s) _____
                    and general history of home
Ownership/legal/assessment printout enclosed. Please remit your check
in the amount of $_____ made payable to "Hillsborough County
Property Appraiser".

Homestead exemption in the name of _____

_____

198__ assessment is _____

Other information: We charge $.25¢ per screen print-
out plus $3.00 postage & handling

_____

_____

_____

   If we can be of further assistance, please let us know.

                    Sincerely,

                    ALTON "BUD" PARKER
                    PROPERTY APPRAISER

                    Anita Menendez

                    Anita Menendez
                    Manager, Customer Service Dept.

Not only did I receive the current ownership of this house, but I was given a general history of the property. The printout that was sent to me had the complete layout of the home along with names of the previous owners with the dates of sale and the amounts paid. I also received the name of the bank that held the mortgage. Of interest to you will be the amount of monthly mortgage your subject pays. Did he overextend himself financially to buy his dream house? **Does he own it in his name only? Is the house in his name at all?**

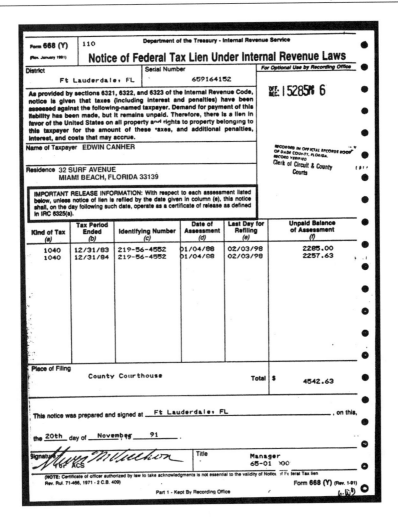

Form 668 (Y) 110
(Rev. January 1991)

Department of the Treasury - Internal Revenue Service

Notice of Federal Tax Lien Under Internal Revenue Laws

District	Serial Number	For Optional Use by Recording Office
Ft Lauderdale, FL	659164152	

As provided by sections 6321, 6322, and 6323 of the Internal Revenue Code, notice is given that taxes (including interest and penalties) have been assessed against the following-named taxpayer. Demand for payment of this liability has been made, but it remains unpaid. Therefore, there is a lien in favor of the United States on all property and rights to property belonging to this taxpayer for the amount of these taxes, and additional penalties, interest, and costs that may accrue.

OFF. REC. 15285% 6

Name of Taxpayer EDWIN CANHER

RECORDED IN OFFICIAL RECORDS BOOK OF DADE COUNTY, FLORIDA.
RECORD VERIFIED
Clerk of Circuit & County Courts

Residence 32 SURF AVENUE
MIAMI BEACH, FLORIDA 33139

IMPORTANT RELEASE INFORMATION: With respect to each assessment listed below, unless notice of lien is refiled by the date given in column (e), this notice shall, on the day following such date, operate as a certificate of release as defined in IRC 6325(a).

Kind of Tax (a)	Tax Period Ended (b)	Identifying Number (c)	Date of Assessment (d)	Last Day for Refiling (e)	Unpaid Balance of Assessment (f)
1040	12/31/83	219-56-4552	01/04/88	02/03/98	2285.00
1040	12/31/84	219-56-4552	01/04/88	02/03/98	2257.63

Place of Filing			
County Courthouse		Total $	4542.63

This notice was prepared and signed at ___Ft Lauderdale, FL___ , on this,

the __20th__ day of __November__ __91__ .

Signature _____ (for) ACS | Title | Manager
65-01)00

(NOTE: Certificate of officer authorized by law to take acknowledgments is not essential to the validity of Notice of Federal Tax Lien
Rev. Rul. 71-466, 1971 - 2 C.B. 409)

Part 1 - Kept By Recording Office

Form 668 (Y) (Rev. 1-91)

This document was retrieved simply by looking up the individual's last name at the county hall of records. You will see that your subject may have a Federal Tax Lien. Column A will note what this lien is for, and in this case it is for underpaying tax due on the form 1040, which, of course, is personal income tax. The dates in column B indicate the years 1983 and 1984. Column C gives the subject's Social Security Number, which you can be assured is the correct number. Column D shows the date that the lien was accessed. Column E indicates when the individual can file again to pay the monies due. Column F shows what amounts the government feels it was owed. Were you told about this Federal Tax Lien by your subject? This money will have to be paid and cannot be absolved through bankruptcy. **Interest and penalties will accrue, and these may be an obligation you will have to help pay off for your "friend."**

NOV 25, 1991 COURTHOUSE TOWER
DATE MICROFILMED   LOCATION
CAMERA OPERATOR
DEPUTY CLERK, CIRCUIT COURT

9 1R4 13352 1991 NOV 25 15:45

Form **668(Z)**   30   Department of the Treasury - Internal Revenue Service

(Rev. April 1984)

Certificate of Release of Federal Tax Lien

District	Serial Number	For Optional Use by Recording Office
Ft Lauderdale, FL	659150902	

I certify that as to the following-named taxpayer, the requirements of section 6325 (a) of the Internal Revenue Code have been satisfied for the taxes listed below and for all statutory additions. Therefore, the lien provided by Code section 6321 for these taxes and additions has been released. The proper officer in the office where the notice of internal revenue tax lien was filed on ___September 19___, 19 _91_, is authorized to note the books to show the release of this lien for these taxes and additions.

OFF.
REC. 15285%

Name of Taxpayer JOSEPH M. SAR

RECORDED IN OFFICIAL PFCORDS BOOK
OF DADE COUNTY, FLORIDA.
RECORD VERIFIED
Clerk of Circuit & County
Courts

Residence   150   S.W. 89TH COURT
MIAMI, FL 33176

COURT RECORDING INFORMATION:

Liber	Page	UCC No.	Serial No.
15196	2573	n/a	91r3299

Kind of Tax (a)	Tax Period Ended (b)	Identifying Number (c)	Date of Assessment (d)	Last Day for Refiling (e)	Unpaid Balance of Assessment (f)
941	03/31/89	74-2392365	09/03/90	10/03/00	2897.58
941	06/30/89	74-2392365	09/03/90	10/03/00	2885.50
941	09/30/89	74-2392365	09/03/90	10/03/00	2874.32
941	12/31/89	74-2392365	09/03/90	10/03/00	2666.28
940	12/31/89	74-2392365	09/03/90	10/03/00	83.62

Place of Filing

County Courthouse

Total $ 11407.30

This certificate was prepared and signed at___F. Lauderdale, FL___, on this,

the _20th_ day of_November_, 19_91_

Signature   Title

Chief, SPf

(NOTE: Certificate of officer authorized by law to take acknowledgements is not essential to the validity of Certificate of Release of Federal Tax Lien Rev. Rul. 71-466, 1971-2 C.B. 409)

Form 668(Z) (Rev. 4-84)

You may be able to find a release of a lien when you are at the county records department. This Certificate of Release of Federal Tax Lien will **assure you that the subject has fulfilled his obligations insofar as the federal portion of their taxes is concerned**, but there are city, county and state taxes that may have gone unpaid. You will want to search for these records.

1990 AUG 28 PM 1:46   90R31

OFF. REC: 14679PG349   IN THE COUNTY COURT IN AND

CASE NO.: 90-096 . PR05

BELL TELEPHONE
AND TELEGRAPH COMPANY,

        Plaintiff,

v.

    STENIO LAFRA

        Defendant.

FINAL JUDGMENT UPON DEFAULT
FLORIDA BAR   13567

EVELYN ACOSTA

THIS CAUSE came on for pre-trial and the defendant failing to appear and the Court having entered a Default, the plaintiff having proved the material allegations of its Statement of Claim; the Court having reviewed the file and affidavit filed herein and having found that said defendant is justly indebted to plaintiff in the sum of $ 717.71 ; and the Court being otherwise fully advised in the premises, it is hereby

ORDERED AND ADJUDGED that:

1. A Final Judgment Upon Default is entered against defendant Stenio Lafrance

2. Plaintiff shall recover from defendant Stenio Lafrance _____ the following sums:

    a. principal amount due $ 608.50
    b. interest $ 53.21
    c. filing fee $ 42.00
    d. service of process $ 14.00
    e. other $ 0.00
    Total amount of final judgment $ 717.71

for which let execution issue.

.OFF. REC BK]
14616PG0766

RECORDED
JUL 09 1990
Clerk of Circuit
& County Courts

You will be able to retrieve any judgments against your subject by searching the county records. In the above case, you will have the plaintiff's name, amount owed, and any penalties by searching the county records. You will be able to retrieve many documents, such as the above, that will give the framework to develop a complete background profile of your subject. Was this amount to the telephone company a misunderstanding or **part of a pattern of debts owed by your subject?**

DATE MICROFILMED   LOCATION   DEPUTY CLERK, CIRCUIT COURT

☐ IN THE CIRCUIT COURT OF THE ELEVENTH JUDICIAL CIRCUIT IN AND FOR DADE COUNTY, FLORIDA.
☐ IN THE COUNTY COURT IN AND FOR DADE COUNTY, FLORIDA

DIVISION		CASE NUMBER
☐ CIVIL ☐ OTHER	FINAL JUDGMENT FOR REMOVAL OF TENANT	92-3271-CC24

PLAINTIFF(S)	VS. DEFENDANT(S)	CLOCK IN
MIGUEL ONTIVE	MANUELA GONZ. AND OTHERS	

This action was heard before the Court on Plaintiff's Complaint for Removal of Tenant(s). On the evidence presented

IT IS ADJUDGED

1. That a final judgment be entered in favor of the Plaintiff(s) MIGUEL ONTIVE.

and against the Defendant(s) MANUELA GONZ   AND OTHERS

for possession of the premises located at and

known as 635 8TH STREET APT. #9 MIAMI BEACH, FL 33139

ORDERED in Dade County, Florida, this ___16___ day of _December_, 19_92_

_____
JUDGE

RECORDED
DEC 23 1992
Clerk of Circuit
& County Courts

OFF. REC BK
15758 PG 05

In the final judgement for removal that is available at the county record hall, you will be able to see what costs, if any, are assessed against your subject. You will be able to find out all the details of the lawsuit by using the case number listed and ordering the complete file. **Are there any more debts that your subject owes that he has failed to tell you about?**

ORIGINAL

FEE TICKET

MICHAEL J. FLYNN

COUNTY CLERK COOK COUNTY, ILLINOIS
NOTARY PUBLIC DEPARTMENT

No. 42055   Chicago, Ill., _6-7-_ 194_5_

Cash Paid By _____

NUMBER				
	Recording Notary Public Commission	@	.25¢	
	" Physician's License	@	1.00	
	" "	@	.25¢	
	" Private Detective	@	1.00	
	Lodging House Affidavits			
	Approving Bonds	@	2.00	
	Certified Copies of Instruments (Each 100 Words)	@	.15¢	
	Annual Statements Per Page	@	.10¢	
	Certificates Under Seal	@	.35¢	
	Justice of Peace } Certificate Police Magistrate }	@	.25¢	
	Registering School Bonds	@	.50¢	
	Certificate of Magistracy	@	.25¢	
	78792-111197			✓
			TOTAL	

If you find an old receipt such as the one above when you are helping your subject go through his paperwork, you may want to save it. You will note that there are numbers at the bottom of the receipt. You can send these numbers to the county clerk's office and see **what documents your subject was looking at.** This receipt is from 1945. The document numbers that are listed may go to any number of documents including adoption, mental competency hearings, tax liens, property ownership, etc.

PENDING LITIGATION

If you have information that your subject had been at fault in an automobile accident, then you will want to find out in what county the accident occurred. Write to that county once a month, and eventually a suit may be filed, naming your subject as the defendant. If an action is filed, you will want to order the file. As noted previously, check the file for the address that your subject was served at. **Paternity** suits, judgments, tax liens, and foreclosures are some actions that may not be listed now, but are public records you may be able to anticipate the filing of.

BAR ASSOCIATIONS

The following list of Bar Associations will be of assistance because you will retrieve records such as divorce, foreclosures, paternity suits, small claims court actions, support agreements, tax liens, and other legal instruments that have an attorney's name on them. Many of the records will be decades old. You can contact the Bar Association, and they will give you the current address and telephone number of the attorney. It is important to note that you will be seeking the attorney of a spouse or someone who has sued your subject, and, of course, you would have learned this name from the aforementioned records. This attorney may be able to provide information unknown to you about your subject.

BAR ASSOCIATIONS

ALABAMA

http://www.alabar.org
Alabama State Bar
P.O. Box 671
Montgomery, Alabama 36101
(205) 269-1515

ALASKA

http://www.alaskabar.org
Alaska Bar Association
P.O. Box 279
Anchorage, Alaska 99510
(907) 272-7496

ARIZONA

http://www.azbar.org
State Bar of Arizona
234 North Central
Phoenix, Arizona 85004
(602) 252-4804

ARKANSAS

http://www.arkbar.com/
Arkansas Bar Association
400 West Markham
Little Rock, Arkansas 72201
(501) 375-4605

CALIFORNIA

http://www.calbar.org
State Bar of California
555 Franklin Street
San Francisco, California 94102
(415) 561-8200

COLORADO

http://www.cobar.org/
Colorado Bar Association
250 West 14th Street
Denver, Colorado 80204
(303) 629-6873

CONNECTICUT

http://www.ctbar.org
Connecticut Bar Association
15 Lewis Street
Hartford, Connecticut 06103
(203) 249-9141

DELAWARE

http://www.dsba.org
Delaware State Bar Association
820 North French Street
Wilmington, Delaware 19801
(302) 658-5278

DISTRICT OF COLUMBIA

http://www.dcbar.org
The District of Columbia Bar
1426 H Street NW
Washington, DC 20005
(202) 638-1500

FLORIDA

http://www.flabar.org/
The Florida Bar Association
650 Apalachee Parkway
Tallahassee, Florida 32301
(904) 561-5600

GEORGIA

http://www.gabar.org/
State Bar of Georgia
84 Peachtree Street
Atlanta, Georgia 30303
(404) 522-6255

HAWAII

http://www.hsba.org/
Hawaii State Bar
820 Mililani
Honolulu, Hawaii 96813
(808) 537-1868

IDAHO

http://www.state.id.us/isb
Idaho State Bar
P.O. Box 895
Boise, Idaho 83701
(208) 342-8958

ILLINOIS

http://www.illinoisbar.org
Illinois Bar Center
424 South 2nd Street
Springfield, Illinois 62701
(217) 525-1760

INDIANA

http://www.ai.org/isba
Indiana State Bar Association
230 Eat Ohio Street
Indianapolis, Indiana 42604
(317) 639-5465

IOWA

http://www.iowabar.org
Iowa State Bar Association
1101 Fleming Building
Des Moines, Iowa 50309
(515) 243-3179

KANSAS

http://www.ksbar.org
Kansas Bar Association
P.O. Box 1037
Topeka, Kansas 66601
(913) 234-5696

KENTUCKY

http://www.kybar.org
Kentucky Bar Association
West Main at Kentucky River
Frankfort, Kentucky 40601
(502) 564-3795

LOUISIANA

http://www.lsba.org
Louisiana State Bar Association
210 O'Keefe Avenue
New Orleans, Louisiana 70112
(504) 566-1600

MAINE

http://www.mainebar.org
Maine State Bar Association
P.O. Box 788
August, Maine 04330
(207) 622-7523

MARYLAND

http://www.msba.org/
Maryland State Bar Association
207 East Redwood Street
Baltimore, Maryland 21202
(301) 685-7878

MASSACHUSETTS

http://www.massbar.org/
Massachusetts Bar Association
One Center Plaza
Boston, Massachusetts 02108
(617) 523-4529

MICHIGAN

http://www.michbar.org/
State Bar of Michigan
306 Townsend Street
Lansing, Michigan 48933
(517) 372-9030

MINNESOTA

http://www.mnbar.org
Minnesota State Bar Association
430 Marquette Avenue
Minneapolis, Minnesota 55402
(612) 335-1183

MISSISSIPPI

http://www.msbar.org/
Mississippi State Bar
P.O. Box 2168
Jackson, Mississippi 39205
(601) 948-4471

MISSOURI

http://www.mobar.org/
The Missouri Bar
P.O. Box 119
Jefferson City, Missouri 65102
(314) 635-4128

MONTANA

http://www.montanabar.org/
State Bar of Montana
P.O. Box 4669
Helena, Montana 59604
(406) 442-7660

NEBRASKA

http://www.nebar.com
Nebraska State Bar Association
206 South 13th Street
Lincoln, Nebraska 65808
(402) 475-7091

NEVADA

http://www.nvbar.org/
State Bar of Nevada
834 Willow Street
Reno, Nevada 89501
(702) 329-4100

NEW HAMPSHIRE

http://www.nhbar.org/
New Hampshire Bar Association
18 Centre Street
Concord, New Hampshire 03301
(603) 224-6942

NEW JERSEY

http://www.cjnj.org/html/the_nj_-
bartender.html
New Jersey State Bar Association
172 West State Street
Trenton, New Jersey 08608
(609) 394-1101

NEW MEXICO

http://www.nmbar.org/
State Bar of New Mexico
P.O. Box 25883
Albuquerque, New Mexico 87125
(505) 842-6132

NEW YORK

http://www.nysba.org
New York State Bar Association
One Elk Street
Albany, New York 12207
(518) 463-3200

NORTH CAROLINA

http://www.barlinc.org
North Carolina State Bar
P.O. Box 25908
Raleigh, North Carolina 27611
(919) 828-4620

NORTH DAKOTA

http://www.sdbar.org/
State Bar Association of North Dakota
P.O. Box 2136
Bismarck, North Dakota 58502
(701) 255-1404

OHIO

http://www.ohiobar.org/
Ohio State Bar Association
33 West 11th Avenue
Columbus, Ohio 42301
(614) 421-2121

OKLAHOMA

http://www.okbar.org/publicinfo/admissions/
Oklahoma Bar Association
P.O. Box 53036
Oklahoma City, Oklahoma 73152
(405) 524-2365

OREGON

http://www.osbar.org/
Oregon State Bar
1776 S.W. Madison
Portland, Oregon 97205
(503) 224-4280

PENNSYLVANIA

http://www.pabar.org/
Pennsylvania Bar Association
P.O. Box 186
Harrisburg, Pennsylvania 17108
(717) 238-6715

PUERTO RICO

http://home.microjuris.com/federalbar/
Bar Association of Puerto Rico
Box 1900
San Juan, Puerto Rico 00903
(809) 721-3358

RHODE ISLAND

http://www.ribar.com/
Rhode Island Bar Association
1804 Industrial Bank Building
Providence, Rhode Island 02903
(401) 421-5740

SOUTH CAROLINA

http://www.scbar.org/
South Carolina Bar Association
P.O. Box 11039
Columbia, South Carolina 29211
(803) 799-6653

SOUTH DAKOTA

http://www.sdbar.org/
State Bar of South Dakota
222 East Capitol
Pierre, South Dakota 57501
(605) 224-7554

TENNESSEE

http://www.tba.org/
Tennessee Bar Association
3622 West End Avenue
Nashville, Tennessee 37205
(615) 383-7421

TEXAS

http://www.texasbar.com/start.htm
State Bar of Texas
P.O. Box 12487
Austin, Texas 78711
(512) 475-4200

UTAH

http://www.utahbar.org/
Utah State Bar
425 East First South
Salt Lake City, Utah 84111
(801) 531-9077

VERMONT
http://www.vtbar.org/
Vermont Bar Association
P.O. Box 100
Montpelier, Vermont 05602
(802) 223-2020

VIRGINIA
http://www.vba.org/
Virginia State Bar
700 East Main Street
Richmond, Virginia 23219
(804) 786-2061

WASHINGTON
http://www.wsba.org/
Washington State Bar Association
505 Madison
Seattle, Washington 98104
(206) 622-6054

WEST VIRGINIA
http://www.wvbar.org/
West Virginia State Bar
2006 Kanawha Boulevard
Charleston, West Virginia 25311
(304) 346-8414

WISCONSIN
http://www.wisbar.org/
State Bar of Wisconsin
P.O. Box 7158
Madison, Wisconsin 53707
(608) 257-3838

WYOMING
http://www.wyomingbar.org/
Wyoming State Bar
P.O. Box 109
Cheyenne, Wyoming 82003
(307) 632-9061

Call the Bureau of Prisons at (202) 307-3126 and they will advise you on how to check to see if your "friend" has ever been an inmate of the Federal Prison System. You will not even need a Social Security Number or date of birth if there aren't two inmates with the same name. You will be told what prisons someone has been in, what the length of their sentence was, and what they were convicted of. A charge of stock fraud, drug trafficking, kidnaping, and interstate transportation of weapons are among the hundreds of different crimes that put people into federal prison. **Isn't it worth the call to check out your "friend," son-in-law, employer, or someone else in your life you may have a doubt about?**

For state and local criminal charges, you will have to check county records. These records are usually public information. The court keeps an alphabetical listing by defendant's name and the charge, disposition, and pending status, if any. Some states will permit you to check on the state level for any record that was reported to them by the county. Check with the governor's office and question the current policy insofar as release of criminal records. The list of county mailing addresses are contained in the appendix.

One of the best techniques I have found to find out about the lifestyle of your subject is to run an "incident report" check on any addresses he has lived at. Almost all police agencies on the local level keep reports about any incidents that have occurred at a certain address.

You can submit the address to the police agencies of jurisdiction, and they will usually give you a printout of all police responses to the address for the past three years. Responses to a particular home address will reveal police dispatches even for minor incidents such as noise complaints from neighbors or serious complaints such as assault and battery reports.

When I investigated the Kennedy-Smith rape case for the media, I retrieved information about certain individuals involved in this case. The background profiles I developed were significantly enhanced by requesting incident reports on each of the addresses the individuals had resided at. The incident reports yielded newsworthy investigative pieces shown on television that you have certainly viewed.

I have reprinted replies received from governors. I have mentioned elsewhere in this book that writing to the governor of a state is the quickest way to get a response to a question about state government. The addresses and their telephone numbers are listed in Chapter 1.

STATE OF ARKANSAS
OFFICE OF THE GOVERNOR
State Capitol
Little Rock 72201

Bill Clinton
Governor

July 25, 1988

Dear Joseph:

Thank you for writing me concerning information about acquiring a criminal history check.

I asked Colonel Tommy Goodwin, Director of the Arkansas State Police to review your reequest and respond to it. He has provided my office with a copy of his letter.

Again, Thank you for writing. I hope this information will be of some assistance to you. If you have any further questions please feel free to contact Colonel Goodwin at P. O. Box 5901, Little Rock, AR 72215.

Sincerely,

Bill Cllinton

BC:vm

I wrote to Bill Clinton when he was governor, and you can see what a thorough response I received. The governor wrote to the Director of the State Police on my behalf, waited for the response, and then forwarded me the above letter and Director Goodwin's letter to me. The misspelling of the word "reequest" and the name "Clinton" is the way I received this letter, almost like a Dan Quayle mistake.

[XX] IN THE CIRCUIT COURT OF THE TWELFTH JUDICIAL CIRCUIT IN AND FOR SARASOTA COUNTY, FLORIDA

[ ] IN THE COUNTY COURT IN AND FOR SARASOTA COUNTY, FLORIDA

REQUEST TO SEARCH RECORDS/
CERTIFICATE OF CLERK

TO THE CLERK OF THE CIRCUIT AND COUNTY COURT:

Please make due and diligent search among the records filed and recorded in your office for the record, pleading, document, paper or instrument of writing required of authorized to be made, filed or recorded in your office described as:

Requestor:_____   RE:Paul Rube

Address:_____

_____

(___) I certify that after due and diligent search thereof, I fail to find the above requested record among the records filed or recorded in this office.

(XXXX) I certify that, after due and diligent search thereof, I find the record, pleading, document, paper or instrument of writing filed or recorded in this office as described below:

71-294-F   Possession of Marijuana   6-7-71 Adj. w/held
                                                2 years probation

MICROFILM COPY

| KAREN E. RUSHING CLERK OF COURTS | BY: _____ DEPUTY CLERK | DATE 3-15-91 (COURT SEAL) |

I wrote to a county in western Florida for this information. They researched their records for a span of over two decades to get this information for me. The most important information is the file number. With this number, you can retrieve the entire file so that **you may review the exact facts of the case and what your subject's involvement really was.** After reading the file, you may ask him for his position insofar as the arrest. The above arrest, by the way, was a real charge against an actor that appeared in children's television programs and movies.

DEPARTMENT OF PUBLIC SAFETY
36 HOSPITAL STREET ● AUGUSTA, MAINE 04330

Your recent letter inquiring as to Criminal History Record information has been referred to this office for reply.

The State Bureau of Identification, which is located within the Bureau of Maine State Police, is the legally mandated central repository of Criminal History Record Information for the State of Maine. These files are a consolidation of records from all jurisdictions within the state.

In accordance with the provisions of Title 16 M.R.S.A., C. 3, sub. c. VIII, §615, any person may obtain adult conviction data relative to another person for any purpose. This record consists of a brief history which provides the contributor of the information, charge, date of offense and the disposition.

Inquiries should be submitted in writing clearly identifying the following:

1. Purpose of request.

2. Full name of person inquired upon, including any names previously used.

3. Date of birth.

There is a $7 processing fee which must accompany each request. A check should be made out to Treasurer, State of Maine.

The turn-around time for a **no record** response is two to three days. Inquiries that match with a record require four to six weeks to complete the process.

There are no provisions for expedited service.

I trust that this information is responsive to your request.

Sincerely,

JOHN R. ATWOOD
Commissioner

JRA/sw

County records, as I have mentioned, are the most open records to check for an arrest, but you may want to write to the State Police department (see Chapter 1 for addresses) for their policy regarding releasing arrest information. As you can see, Maine is one of many states that maintains a very clear and open policy for releasing records.

STATE OF MINNESOTA
OFFICE OF THE GOVERNOR

ST. PAUL 55155

RUDY PERPICH
GOVERNOR

Thank you for your recent letter regarding your request for information on FDLE. I appreciate your time and interest in writing to me about this matter.

I have instructed my staff to forward your letter to the Department of Public Safety for review and consideration. The agency will respond directly to you in about two weeks, and will notify my office when that occurs.

In order for state government to run efficiently, we must be responsive to the opinions and needs of our citizens. To that end, I want to assure you I will take your comments into consideration. Once again, thank you for writing.

Sincerely,

RUDY PERPICH
Governor

Here is another governor's letter where you will see that a response was prepared for me regarding the policy of releasing arrest records. The response I received stated that the State of Minnesota does not permit release of records. With this information, I took the most logical course, which was to check the county my subject resided in. Surrounding counties were also checked for arrest records.

STATE OF WISCONSIN
DEPARTMENT OF JUSTICE

DONALD J. HANAWAY
ATTORNEY GENERAL

Mark E. Musolf
Deputy Attorney General

Michael W. Stead
Executive Assistant

Division of Law Enforcement Services
John W. Killian, Administrator

Crime Information Bureau
Robert L. McGrath, Director

Justice Building
P.O. Box 2718
Madison, WI 53701-2718
608/266-7314

I am writing in response to your letter to the Governor's Office dated June 20, 1988 regarding Wisconsin's Criminal Records access policy. The Crime Information Bureau (CIB) of the Wisconsin Department of Justice is the Central Repository for Identification information for the state. State Statute's 165.83 and 165.84 require Wisconsin agencies to forward fingerprint cards to the CIB for all felony arrests and for certain enumerated misdemeanors. Criminal records relating to adults are considered public information and can be accessed when minimum required data is provided accompanied by the appropriate fee.

Enclosed please find a letter explaining the procedure for requesting a record and the form Wisconsin uses for that purpose. Please feel free to reproduce this form as needed. Records are released only through the mail and the current processing time is three (3) to five (5) working days after receipt of the request. The Crime Information Bureau files contain arrest information from all jurisdictions in the state. The record released will list the arrest date, arresting and contributing agencies, charge(s), disposition (if available), name and date of birth used at time of arrest, and the sex and race of the arrested person..

Should you have additional questions or need more information please contact Michael Roberts, Supervisor of the Identification Section at (608) 266-7314. On behalf of the Crime Information Bureau, I remain

Sincerely

Robert L. McGrath
Director
Crime Information Bureau

RLM/smy

CC: Mr. Charles Hoslet
Legal Assistant
(Governor's Office)

Enclosure

I use arrest records of subjects to verify information they have given. In the above letter, it is indicated that the name and date of birth are included in the record. But you will want to probe further because in the file will be the name, address, and telephone number of a next of kin. **Was this next of kin a wife or girlfriend you know nothing about?**

The bigamist in this article was married five times in the same county. He also had a divorce and a restraining order. These records could have been retrieved by doing some basic research (in most jurisdictions).

St. Petersburg Times

Accused Bigamist Married 6 Times

James William Perry, 31, started marrying in 1981. Before landing in Jail Sunday, he married five more women without divorcing the first, officials say.

By Rick Gershman
Times Correspondent

NEW PORT RICHEY - Theresa Perry got the news after her husband, Jim, received a call from a woman named Kim.

Theresa asked her husband who Kim was.

His reply: "That's my wife."

That's how Theresa Perry discovered her husband was a bigamist. But she didn't know the half of it. Not until three months ago, anyway, when she contacted the Pasco County Sheriff's Office.

James William Perry, 31, isn't just married to two women—he was married to six women, five of whom live in Pasco County. The New Port Richey man has no children with any of his wives, sheriff's officials say.

Pasco sheriff's deputies charged him Sunday with bigamy, as well as forgery of marriage and divorce documents.

"I wanted to kill him," Theresa said. "I was hurt, I felt deceived...I felt betrayed and humiliated that he would ever think of doing a thing like that."

Perry is accused of marrying five women between November 1982 and November 1991, all the while remaining married to his first wife, Kathryn Elizabeth Ferrier. He married her in June 1981. Five of the marriages occurred in Pasco County.

For the most part, Perry was not living with more than one wife at any given time, authorities said. In fact, he told deputies, he thought some of the women had divorced him.

Perry apparently tried to divorce only one of his wives. In November 1991, he sought a divorce from his fifth wife, the former Kathy Jean Kirkland. That was granted November 18, 1991. One day later, Perry married Theresa, then 23 and a good friend of Kathy Jean's.

In fact, Theresa paid for the divorce. But the divorce was not valid because Perry had never been legally married to Kathy Jean Kirkland, sheriff's Sgt. Oonagh Guenkel said.

"It's like I told Kathy," Theresa Perry said. "I paid $600 something (for the divorce), and I didn't have to because you're not married to him."

James Perry's exceptional marriage history began June 24, 1981. Then 19, he married Ferrier, of New Port Richey, who had just turned 18.

Less than 18 months later, on November 12, 1992, Perry married 30-year old Judith Ann Lighthill.

Perry then went nearly two years without marrying another woman. But on November 2, 1984, he married 17 year-old Keli Raegenea Summers of Dade City.

Nearly three years passed during which Perry had three wives. He moved to South Carolina and lived there about two years, marrying Kimberly Coleman, 23, on October 21, 1987.

Coleman said she and Perry continued to have marital relations through early 1989, although Perry had married a fifth time, to Kirkland, 36, of Bayonnet Point, on December 14, 1988.

When questioned by deputies about his marital history, Perry had difficulty recalling his third wife,

Guenkel said.

"But once her name was mentioned to him, he remembered her," Guenkel said.

Theresa Perry separated from James Perry several months ago and has obtained a **domestic violence injunction against him.** She alleged that he has physically abused her, and Pasco sheriff's spokesman Jon Powers said several of the other wives made similar allegations.

Perry remained in the Central Pasco Detention Center on Monday, his bail set at $14,000. The forgery charges mostly stem from falsifying marriage licenses by stating that he was not married.

"Unfortunately, there is no central registry for cross-referencing records of marriages," Guenkel said. "It is not the duty of the clerks to research someone's marriage background. When you sign a marriage license, you are making a sworn statement."

Theresa Perry said she just hopes this never happens to anyone else.

"I just want everyone to know that before you walk down that aisle, before you say, 'I do', go check those computers," she said. **"I hate to say it. It sounds awful. You should trust the person you're going to marry, but you never know."**

(Reprinted by permission, *St. Petersburg Times*)

NOTES

State Records

The state licenses many professions, trades, and crafts. Write to the Secretary of State and submit your subject's name to be searched for any licensure by the state. The following are some occupations that may require licensing.

Aircraft Mechanics
Airports
Alarm Contractor
Alarm Installers
Auctioneers
Auto Inspectors
Auto Wreckers
Bankers
Barbers
Bill Collectors
Builders/Carpenters
Building Contractors
Building Wreckers
Carpet Cleaners
Certified Public Accountants
Embalmers
Investigators
Notary Public

Pawnbrokers
Pest Controllers
Pet Groomers
Pharmacists
Pilots
Real Estate Agents
   and Brokers
Scrap Dealers
Security Dealers
Security Guards
Stockbrokers
Surveyors
Talent Agents
Teachers
Therapists
Veterinarians
X-Ray Technicians

If your subject is licensed by the state for any of the above occupations or any others not listed, then you will be able to receive, at least, the following information from the licensing board; work and home **address**, length of time the subject has been licensed, the schools attended to be certified, if applicable, date of birth, any complaints lodged against the subject, and name of any **spouse**.

Of course, the most important information will be the addresses you are given, but you may want to take special note of any complaints filed. A court or hearing date may be scheduled in the near future and the exact date and location will be listed. Wait to see if your "friend" tells you about this hearing he has to attend.

COLLEGES AND UNIVERSITIES

There are over 3,500 colleges and universities in the United States. If you are aware of the institution of higher learning that your subject attended, then inquiring about "directory information" may yield more facts. The term "directory information" is used to describe the information that the school will release to the public about the student. Remember to look at yearbooks on the high school and college level to make sure the picture is the same as your subject's. **The assuming and switching of identity is widespread and one of the easiest avenues used for deception are education records and degrees.**

The following is a quote from Florida State University regarding the school's "directory information" policy:

"Prior consent of the student is **not required** for disclosure of portions of the educational record defined by the institution as DIRECTORY INFORMATION, which can be released via official media of the University:

Name, date, and place of birth
Local address
Permanent address
Telephone listing
Classification
Major field of study
Participation in official university activities and sports
Weight and height of members of athletic teams
Dates of attendance at the university
Degrees, honors, and awards received
The most recently attended educational institution

Stanford University's "directory information" policy is quoted as follows: "The University regards the following items of information as 'directory information,' i.e., information **available to any person** upon specific request:

Student name
Sex
Class status
Major
Local address and/or Stanford Post Office Box number
Local phone number
Permanent or legal address
Summer address
Summer phone number
Residence assignment and room or apartment number
Stanford student identification number
Specific quarters or semesters of registration at Stanford
Stanford degree(s) awarded and date(s), degree major(s)
University degree honors
Institution attended immediately prior to Stanford

Even though the permanent address listed may be years old, you may want to check the owner of record with the tax collector to see if the family of your subject is still the owner. Also, do not overlook the summer residence that is listed. The address will, in many instances, prove to be a vacation home that the subject's family still owns. Your subject's neighbors or friends may be a source of background information.

The date of birth and place of birth is of obvious value. You now have an exact date of birth that can be utilized to access the driving record of the subject. Even though years have passed, you may want to try calling the telephone numbers listed. In many instances, these numbers will still be good numbers that will enable you to contact the family.

LOTTERY WINNINGS

Even though you have no reason to believe that your "friend" has ever won the lottery, you may want to check. All winners who had single tickets worth over $600 must give their name, address, and Social Security Number to collect. Write to the state lottery commission in the state or states in which your subject has spent time. Ask if he was ever a winner, and they will search their records for you because it is public information. Also, you may want to search for **lottery winnings in your subject's wife or ex-wife's name.** Your "friend" may cry poverty but have community property wealth he may not have told you about. If your "friend" has any children, you will want to check under their names, because the money could have been converted into trust funds for the children, even though your subject may have full control of the fund with discretionary spending authority.

HUNTING AND FISHING LICENSES

Even if your subject tries to hide home addresses on other public records, the subject may have been issued a license for hunting or fishing, if this is his sport. The reason the subject would want to have a current license is to avoid being arrested by a game warden or other law enforcement official when enjoying his sport. Write to the state and submit a request asking that a search be conducted on your subject so that you may ascertain if he has a hunting or fishing license. If you are successful with your inquiry, you will receive the subject's current address and the current status of the license. States constantly change the laws insofar as access to these records. Several states have recently become completely computerized in the hunting and fishing license division, so their records are actually more accessible than before. There are a few states that do not have a statewide listing. These particular states will inform you to search on the city or county records level.

HUNTING AND FISHING LICENSES

ALABAMA

http://www.state.al.us/
Hunting and Fishing Licenses
Department of Conservation
State of Alabama
State Administrative Building
Montgomery, Alabama 36130

ALASKA

http://www.state.ak.us/
Hunting and Fishing Licenses
State of Alaska
P.O. Box 6188 Annex
Anchorage, Alaska 99502

ARIZONA

http://www.gf.state.az.us
Hunting and Fishing Licenses
Game and Fish Department
State of Arizona
2221 West Greenway Road
Phoenix, Arizona 85023

ARKANSAS

http://www.agfc.state.ar.us
Hunting and Fishing Licenses
State of Arkansas
2 Natural Resources Drive
Little Rock, Arkansas 72205

CALIFORNIA

http://www.dfg.ca.gov
Hunting and Fishing Licenses
State of California
P.O. Box 11319
Sacramento, California 95853

COLORADO

http://www.dnr.state.co.us/edo/-
wildlife.html
Hunting and Fishing Licenses
Division of Parks and Outdoor Recreation
State of Colorado
13787 South Highway 85
Littleton, Colorado 80125

CONNECTICUT

http://www.state.ct.us/
Hunting and Fishing Licenses
State of Connecticut
165 Capitol Avenue
Hartford, Connecticut 06106

DELAWARE

http://www.dnrec.state.de.us/fandw.htm
Hunting and Fishing Licenses
Division of Fish and Wildlife
State of Delaware
P.O. Box 1401
Dover, Delaware 19903

DISTRICT OF COLUMBIA

http://www.washingtondc.gov/
Hunting and Fishing Licenses
District of Columbia
550 Water Street, S.W.
Washington, DC 20024

FLORIDA

http://www.state.fl.us/gsd/
Hunting and Fishing Licenses
Department of Natural Resources
State of Florida
3900 Commonwealth Boulevard
Tallahassee, Florida 32399

GEORGIA

http://www.state.ga.us/
Hunting and Fishing Licenses
Department of Natural Resources
State of Georgia
270 Washington Street, S.W.
Atlanta, Georgia 30034

HAWAII

http://www.state.hi.us/
Hunting and Fishing Licenses
State of Hawaii
79 South Nimitz Highway
Honolulu, Hawaii 96813

IDAHO

http://www.state.id.us/
Hunting and Fishing Licenses
State of Idaho
2177 Warm Springs Avenue
Boise, Idaho 83720

ILLINOIS

http://dnr.state.il.us/
Hunting and Fishing Licenses
Conservation Department
State of Illinois
524 South Second Street
Springfield, Illinois 62701

INDIANA

http://www.state.in.us/dnr/fishwild/index.htm
Hunting and Fishing Licenses
Department of Natural Resources
State of Indiana
402 West Washington St.
Indianapolis, Indiana 46204

IOWA

http://www.state.ia.us/
Hunting and Fishing Licenses
State Conservation Commission
State of Iowa
Wallace Building
Des Moines, Iowa 50319

KANSAS

http://www.kdwp.state.ks.us/
Hunting and Fishing Licenses
Kansas Department of Wildlife
R.R. No. 2, Box 54A
Pratt, Kansas 67124

KENTUCKY

http://www.kfwis.state.ky.us
Hunting and Fishing Licenses
Department of Natural Resources
1 Game Farm Road
Frankfort, Kentucky 40601

LOUISIANA

http://www.state.la.us/
Hunting and Fishing Licenses
Department of Wildlife and Fisheries
State of Louisiana
P.O. Box 14796
Baton Rouge, Louisiana 70898

MAINE

http://www.state.me.us/ifw/homepage.htm
Hunting and Fishing Licenses
Department of Fisheries and Wildlife
State of Maine
284 State Street
Augusta, Maine 04333

MARYLAND

http://www.state.md.us/
Hunting and Fishing Licenses
Department of Natural Resources
State of Maryland
P.O. Box 1869
Annapolis, Maryland 21404–1869

MASSACHUSETTS

http://www.state.ma.us/
Hunting and Fishing Licenses
Commonwealth of Massachusetts
100 Nashua Street
Boston, Massachusetts 02114

MICHIGAN

http://www.state.mi.us/
Hunting and Fishing Licenses
State of Michigan
7064 Crowner Drive
Lansing, Michigan 48918

MINNESOTA

http://www.state.mn.us/
Hunting and Fishing Licenses
Department of Natural Resources
State of Minnesota
500 Lafayette Road
Saint Paul, Minnesota 55146

MISSISSIPPI

http://www.state.ms.us/its/msportal.nsf?Open
Hunting and Fishing Licenses
Department of Wildlife Conservation
P.O. Box 451
Jackson, Mississippi 39205

MISSOURI

http://www.state.mo.us/
Hunting and Fishing Licenses
Department of Conservation
State of Missouri
2901 West Truman Boulevard
Jefferson City, Missouri 65102

MONTANA

http://www.fwp.state.mt.us
Hunting and Fishing Licenses
State of Montana
1420 East Sixth Avenue
Helena, Montana 59620

NEBRASKA

http://www.ngpc.state.ne.us/fish/fish-ing.html
Hunting and Fishing Licenses
State Game and Parks Commission
State of Nebraska
2200 North 33rd Street
Lincoln, Nebraska 68503

NEVADA

http://colorado.state.nv.us/cnr/nvwildlife
Hunting and Fishing Licenses
Department of Wildlife
State of Nevada
P.O. Box 10678
Reno, Nevada 89520

NEW HAMPSHIRE

http://www.wildlife.state.nh.us
Hunting and Fishing Licenses
State of New Hampshire
10 Hazen Drive
Concord, New Hampshire 03305

NEW JERSEY

http://www.state.nj.us/
Hunting and Fishing Licenses
State of New Jersey
P.O. Box 7068
West Trenton, New Jersey 08625

NEW MEXICO

http://www.state.nm.us/
Hunting and Fishing Licenses
Natural Resources Department
State of New Mexico
P.O. Box 1147
Santa Fe, New Mexico 87504

NEW YORK

http://www.dec.state.ny.us/
Hunting and Fishing Licenses
State of New York
Empire State Plaza
Albany, New York 12238

NORTH CAROLINA

http://www.state.nc.us/
Hunting and Fishing Licenses
Wildlife Resources Commission
State of North Carolina
512 North Salisbury Street
Raleigh, North Carolina 27604

NORTH DAKOTA

http://www.state.nd.us/
Hunting and Fishing Licenses
State Game and Fish Department
State of North Dakota
2121 Lovett Avenue
Bismarck, North Dakota 58505

OHIO

http://www.dnr.state.oh.us/odnr/wildlife/index.html
Hunting and Fishing Licenses
Department of Natural Resources
State of Ohio
Fountain Square
Columbus, Ohio 43224

OKLAHOMA

http://www.state.ok.us/
Hunting and Fishing Licenses
State of Oklahoma
2501 North Lincoln
Oklahoma City, Oklahoma 73194

OREGON

http://www.dfw.state.or.us
Hunting and Fishing Licenses
State of Oregon
3000 Market Street, N.E.
Salem, Oregon 97310

PENNSYLVANIA

http://www.state.pa.us/
Hunting and Fishing Licenses
Commonwealth of Pennsylvania
3532 Walnut Street
Harrisburg, Pennsylvania 17105

PUERTO RICO

http://fortaleza.govpr.org/
Hunting and Fishing Licenses
Commonwealth of Puerto Rico
GPO Box 2829
San Juan, Puerto Rico 00936

RHODE ISLAND

http://www.state.ri.us/dem/regs.htm#FandW
Hunting and Fishing Licenses
State of Rhode Island
22 Hayes Street
Providence, Rhode Island 02903

SOUTH CAROLINA

http://www.state.sc.us/
Hunting and Fishing Licenses
State of South Carolina
P.O. Box 11710
Columbia, South Carolina 29211

SOUTH DAKOTA

http://www.state.sd.us/state/executive/gfp/
index.htm
Hunting and Fishing Licenses
State of South Dakota
412 West Missouri Street
Pierre, South Dakota 57501

TENNESSEE

http://www.state.tn.us/
Hunting and Fishing Licenses
Tennessee Wildlife Resources Agnecy
Ellington Agriculture Center
Nashville, Tennessee 37204

TEXAS

http://www.state.tx.us/
Hunting and Fishing Licenses
State of Texas
4200 Smith School Road
Austin, Texas 78744

UTAH

http://www.state.ut.us/
Hunting and Fishing Licenses
State of Utah
1095 Motor Avenue
Salt Lake City, Utah 84116

VERMONT

http://www.anr.state.vt.us/fw/fwhome/-
index.htm
Hunting and Fishing Licenses
State of Vermont
103 Main Street
Waterbury, Vermont 05676

VIRGINIA

http://www.state.va.us/
Hunting and Fishing Licenses
Commission of Game and Inland Fisheries
State of Virginia
P.O. Box 11104
Richmond, Virginia 23230

VIRGIN ISLANDS

http://www.virginisles.com/
Hunting and Fishing Licenses
Department of Natural Resources
State of Virgin Islands
Nisky Center, Suite 231
St. Thomas, U.S. Virgin Islands 00803

WASHINGTON

http://www.wa.gov/wdfw
Hunting and Fishing Licenses
Department of Natural Resources
State of Washington
P.O. Box 43135
Olympia, Washington 98504

WEST VIRGINIA

http://www.state.wv.us/
Hunting and Fishing Licenses
Department of Natural Resources
State of West Virginia
1800 Washington Street, East
Charleston, West Virginia 25305

WISCONSIN

http://www.state.wi.us/
Hunting and Fishing Licenses
Department of Natural Resources
State of Wisconsin
P.O. Box 7921
Madison, Wisconsin 53707

WYOMING

http://gf.state.wy.us
Hunting and Fishing Licenses
Game and Fish Department
State of Wyoming
5400 Bishop Boulevard
Cheyenne, Wyoming 82002

STATE OF WASHINGTON
DEPARTMENT OF FISHERIES
Post Office Box 43135, Olympia, Washington 98504-3135 • (206) 902-2200 SCAN 902-2200 TDD 902-2207

March 3, 1993

Dear Mr. Culligan:

Attached is a copy of the Request for Public Records you submitted to the Washington Department of Fisheries.

A thorough search of our records has been done, and no information was found.

If you have any questions, you may contact me at (206) 902-2470.

Sincerely,

Nancy Stewart, License Specialist
Commercial License Division

Most states do not charge for inquiries regarding hunting and fishing licenses. This response indicates a thorough search was conducted free of charge.

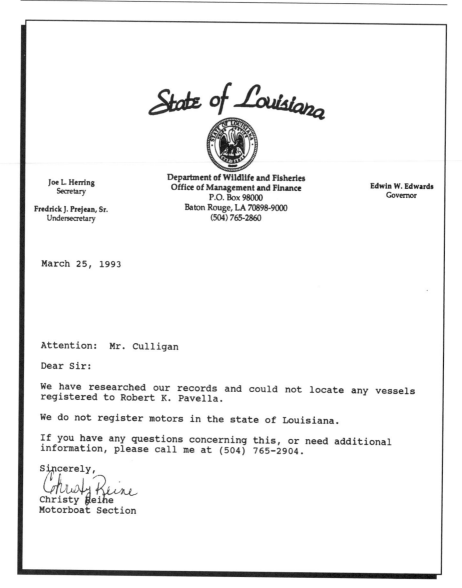

State of Louisiana

Joe L. Herring
Secretary

Fredrick J. Prejean, Sr.
Undersecretary

Department of Wildlife and Fisheries
Office of Management and Finance
P.O. Box 98000
Baton Rouge, LA 70898-9000
(504) 765-2860

Edwin W. Edwards
Governor

March 25, 1993

Attention: Mr. Culligan

Dear Sir:

We have researched our records and could not locate any vessels registered to Robert K. Pavella.

We do not register motors in the state of Louisiana.

If you have any questions concerning this, or need additional information, please call me at (504) 765-2904.

Sincerely,

Christy Reihe
Motorboat Section

If you receive a response that states that your subject does not have any boat or vessel ownership, then you may want to check any ownership under his company name. He may have chosen to hide his ownership because he is aware that this would become a marital asset when you marry. Use Chapter 11 to find out if he has any corporations under his name. Even though you are unaware that he may own a business, you will still want to check with corporations. **Many individuals don't have any business entity at all but use the corporation to hide assets.**

Nothing has been highlighted in this article. The content says it all and these instances may have been prevented with a check on the background of the boyfriends.

Sun-Sentinel

The Trouble with Boyfriends

"Paramours" are taking a deadly toll on children in Florida, with child abuse cases often pointing to boyfriends.

By Jill Young Miller
Staff Writer

Amy Lynn Mitich lived two months, then she was killed. Her crying did her in, her mother told police.

On March 2, she led police to Amy's body. It had been stuffed in a cardboard suitcase and tossed in a lake near Deerfield Beach.

Amy's mother—who had lied at first and reported the baby kidnaped—told police her boyfriend, Richard Hamlin, had tried to stop the baby's cries with an afghan. Amy suffocated. The mother, Laurel Mitich and Hamlin are charged with murder.

Nine-pound Amy's death put her in a gruesome category: children who, authorities say, have suffered or died at the hands of their mothers' boyfriends.

"It's an increasing problem," says Catherine Deans, a spokeswoman for Florida's Department of Health and Rehabilitative Services.

Boyfriends or girlfriends are responsible for one out of five child abuse deaths in Florida, according to figures from HRS.

In the 4-1/2 years from January 1986 through June 1990, they killed 38 children in Florida.

In just the next 12 months, they killed 29 more.

"The boyfriend comes in, and the child is really nothing to him except a nuisance or an aggravation or, in the case of sexual abuse, a temptation," says Doug Fulton, the lead prosecutor in the Palm Beach County murder of a 2-year old girl, Shunta Caraway. "Many times you get a mother who's working or who is out at the time, and the child is left with the boyfriend—and away we go."

Shunta died in 1990, her small body covered with more than 100 welts and bruises. The child had been beaten for dropping food, splashing bathwater, strewing crayons. Authorities called her death one of the worst cases of child abuse in the county's history.

"She cried out in pain, asking me to make him stop," the child's mother, Tiffany Caraway, testified. "I tried to, but I couldn't."

For her part in her child's death, Caraway is serving a seven-year prison sentence. Her boyfriend, John Bynes, was sentenced to life in prison with no chance of parole for 25 years.

"It's a heartbreaking thing," HRS spokeswoman Deans says. "In a lot of families, you may have one paramour who's there for a while and then another paramour who's there for a while, and the bond between that person and child may not be there."

Consider the fate of 3-year-old Thomas Kidwell. He lived in an apartment west of Fort Lauderdale until he died, beaten, last year. According to police, the mother's boyfriend blamed the death on her, then he changed his story and said he beat the child because the boy had soiled his pants. The boyfriend, Victor James Vance, is in jail, charged with murder and sexual battery.

Scott Bragg, 2-1/2, also died a brutal death. "God, I never thought I'd be shopping for my boy's casket," Scott's stunned mother, Jennifer Lumpkin, told a reporter in 1991. But one night in May, Lumpkin left their Coral Springs apartment to work delivering newspapers. Later, her boyfriend woke up and stepped on Scott, who was sleeping on the floor.

"I stood straight up on his stomach," 200-pound Christopher Rigsbee told police. "Then I noticed he had (feces) in his pants, and I stepped on his stomach again with a little harder force."

He stomped the boy to death. Rigsbee was sentenced to 32 years in prison.

Florida calls the boyfriend/girlfriend category of abusers "paramour" and doesn't divide it into males and females. But, overall, more than twice as many children in Florida are killed by men than by women.

Experts are quick to point out that children's parents abuse and murder them more than anyone else does. But if what's happening in Florida is an indication, parents' lovers are taking an increasingly deadly toll on children.

"Whether it's typical or not typical, it's appalling," says Andrea J. Sedlak, who led a national study of child abuse in 1986. At that time, Westat Inc., a private research firm in Maryland, concluded that parents' boyfriends or girlfriends were responsible for only 2.5 percent of child abuse in cases where perpetrators' identities were known. Current national figures on the problem are not available.

No one comprehends why some men brutalize or kill their girlfriends' children, but child advocates offer some ideas.

"If the boyfriend demands attention and the focus of the mom, then who is the greatest competitor for that attention? It is a crying child," says Jack Levine, Executive Director of the Florida Center for Children & Youth, and advocacy organization in Tallahassee. "In that competition, **the child weights 10 pounds or 20, and the boyfriend is 10 times that. The power to eliminate the competition is enormous.**"

Especially when that power also is turned against the mother.

"You're dealing many times with families that are troubled anyway," Deans says. "If, for instance, a mother is being abused by a paramour, she may not really be aware or think that she is in a position to do much if she thinks the children are (being abused). Her concern may be her life."

Tiffany Caraway, for instance, knew her boyfriend was abusing Shunta but didn't stand up to him, prosecutor Fulton says. "She knew it, but she was more or less a prisoner in her own house, in her own situation."

Joy Byers, Spokeswoman for the Chicago-based National Committee for Prevention of Child Abuse, worries about the situations parents get their children into.

"Sometimes parents—whether it be due to loneliness, or emotional need, or financial need or whatever—may establish relationships with people they don't really know very well," Byers says.

Maybe those people aren't used to children, she says. Maybe they're jealous of the time and attention the parent gives the child.

Maybe they don't want to be reminded of the girlfriend's past.

Maybe they're dangerous.

Says Byers, **"A parent who trusts a new person with the care of their child or children without knowing very much about that person is really taking a risk."** Unfortunately, many mothers take that risk because they can't afford or find good child care, says child advocate Levine. "Single parents are simply desperate for supervision of their kids."

More than 20,000 Florida children are on waiting lists for child care, he says.

"When kids are left alone without the basics of safety and security, then the very next chapter begins: child abused, child molested, child killed."

(Reprinted by permission, the *Sun Sentinel*)

NOTES

Federal Records

MILITARY RECORDS

Under the Freedom of Information Act, you are permitted access to the following information about military personnel:

Full name
Rank
Gross salary
Past duty assignments
Awards and decorations
Attendance at military schools

Write to the appropriate address listed in this chapter so you can ascertain whether your subject was in the military. What awards and decorations did he really get? Where had he been stationed? *Does he have any other families* **at these ports of call? Check out any financial obligations he may have had at locations of duty assignments.** If your subject has a close relative in the Armed Forces, then you will want to order their records. This relative can turn out to be an excellent source and may give you information about your subject, if you feel this is the route to go in doing this background investigation.

MILITARY LOCATOR SERVICES

The military will supply you with the current unit number and installation to which a person on active duty is assigned. If the person is retired, a letter will be forwarded to them.

ARMY

Active Duty
Army Locator
Fort Benjamin, Indiana 46249

Retired
Army Personnel Center
Attention: DARP—PAS
9700 Page Boulevard
Saint Louis, Missouri 63132

AIR FORCE

Active Duty
Air Force Locator Service
Air Force Military Personnel Center
Randolph Air Force Base,
Texas 78150

Retired
Retired Personnel Command
Air Force Military Personnel Center
Randolph Air Force Base,
Texas 78150

NAVY

Active Duty
Naval Personnel Command
Locator Service
NMC–21
Washington, DC 20307

Retired
Retired Personnel Command
Locator Service
4400 Dauphin Street
New Orleans, Louisiana 70149

MARINE CORPS

Active Duty
Marine Corps Locator Service
MMRD–10
Commandant of the Marine Corps
Washington, DC 20380

Retired
Marine Corps Retired
Locator Service
MMRD–06
Commandant of the Marine Corps
Washington, DC 20380

COAST GUARD

Active Duty	*Retired*
United States Coast Guard	United States Coast Guard
Locator Service	Retired Locator Service
Commandant–G-PIM	G–PS–5
2100 Second Street, Southwest	2100 Second Street, SW
Washington, DC 20593	Washington, DC 20593

The following addresses are to be used when you need to get someone's military records. Of course, provide as much identifying information about your subject as possible.

ARMY: Chief, Information Access Section
HQ USAISC (ASQNS-OP-F)
Hoffman I, Room 1146
2461 Eisenhower Avenue
Alexandria, Virginia 22331-0301

AIR FORCE: Secretary of the Air Force
Freedom of Information Manager
SAF/AADS (FOIA)
Pentagon, Room 4A1088C
Washington, DC 20330-1000

NAVY: Director, OPNAV Services and Security Division
OP-09B30
Pentagon, Room 5E521
Washington, DC 20350-2000

MARINE CORPS: Freedom of Information and Privacy Act
Office (Code MI-3)
Headquarters, U.S. Marine Corps, Room 4327
Washington, DC 20380-0001

COAST GUARD: Freedom of Information Act
Commandant of the Coast Guard
2100 Second Street, Southwest
Washington, DC 20593-0201

PATERNITY AND CHILD SUPPORT LOCATOR SERVICE

http://www.acf.dhhs.gov/

If you want to contact your subject because of a paternity or child support matter, then you may use the following address. This center will locate your subject and then guide you on what procedures to follow.

Armed Services Community and Family Support
Attention: TAPC–PDO–IP
200 Stovall Street
Alexandria, Virginia 22331

UNITED STATES CIVIL SERVICE

http://www.opm.gov

If your subject is a current or retired civil servant, then you will want to write to the Office of Personnel Management. They will give you the work site address of the current employer.

United States Office of Personnel Management
1900 East E Street
Washington, DC 20415

RAILROAD RETIREMENT BOARD

http://www.rrb.gov

The Railroad Retirement Board administers the retirement and survivor benefit programs provided to the nation's railroad workers and their families. If your subject was a railroad worker and you believe that they may be collecting benefits.

Railroad Retirement Board
844 Rush Street
Chicago, Illinois 60611

UNITED STATES PUBLIC HEALTH PERSONNEL

http://www.os.dhhs.gov/phs/corps/welcom1.html

You may write to the following address if your subject has ever been employed by the United States Public Health Service. If your subject is currently employed, you will be supplied with their grade and salary information, employment address, and date that employment started.

United States Public Health Service
Department of Health and Human Services
PHS/05G/DCP
5600 Fishers Lane
Parklawn Building, Room 4–35
Rockville, Maryland 20857

NUCLEAR REGULATORY COMMISSION (NRC)

http://www.nrc.gov

NRC regulates commercial nuclear power reactors; nonpower research reactors; fuel-cycle facilities; medical, academic, and industrial uses of nuclear materials; and the transport, storage, and disposal of nuclear materials and waste. **NRC also maintains applications and licenses of persons and companies that export nuclear material and equipment from the United States.**

SECURITIES AND EXCHANGE COMMISSION (SEC)

http://www.sec.gov

Your "friend" may own stock in companies that you know nothing about. The SEC is a good source of information insofar as stock ownership. These records include the following:

Financial statements
Identification of officers and directors

Identification of owners of more than 10 percent of a
corporation's stock

A description of the registrant's properties and
businesses

A description of the significant provisions of the
security to be offered for sale and its relationship
to the registrant's other capital securities

Identification of events of interest to investors

Identification of accountants and attorneys

A history of the business

**SEC maintains files on individuals and firms that have been
reported to it as having violated federal or state securities laws.** The information contained in these files pertains to official actions taken against such
persons and firms, including denials, refusals, suspensions, and revocations
of registrations; injunctions, fraud orders, stop orders, cease-and-desist orders;
and arrests, indictments, convictions, sentences, and other official actions.

The Securities and Exchange Commission Summary lists the changes
in beneficial ownership by officers, directors, and principal stockholders of
securities listed and registered on a national securities exchange or those relating to public utility companies and certain closed-end investment companies.

Copies of the documents maintained by SEC are available at its regional
or branch offices in the following cities: Atlanta, Georgia; Miami, Florida;
Boston, Massachusetts; Chicago, Illinois; Cleveland, Ohio; Detroit, Michi-
gan; St. Louis, Missouri; Denver, Colorado; Salt Lake City, Utah; Fort Worth,
Texas; Los Angeles, California; San Francisco, California; New York, New
York; Seattle, Washington; Washington, DC; and Philadelphia, Pennsylvania.

Corporate filings include the following:

**Annual Report of Publicly Traded Company (Form
10-K)—excerpts or complete report via DIALOG or
Lexis databases, both of which are discussed in
Chapter 4**

**Quarterly Report of Publicly Traded Company
(Form 10–Q)—same as Form 10–K**

**Registration of Security (Form 8–A)—prospectus,
data relative to the issuer**

Registration of Security by the Successor to (Form 8–B)—name of issuer, relationship to primary registrant/issuer

FEDERAL AVIATION ADMINISTRATION

http://www.faa.gov/

If your subject is a pilot or owns an aircraft, you may write to the Federal Aviation Administration. A search will be conducted by name. The subject's address, date of birth, pilot rating, and even the date of the last medical exam will be furnished to you if the subject has a pilot's license.

You may wish to order a list of any aircraft your subject may own. The request for a search can be conducted by your subject's name or by the name of the company he owns. If there is a listing of an aircraft, you will be given the address that the aircraft is registered to, the year and make of the aircraft, the name of pilots that will utilize the aircraft, and the name of an insurance carrier.

Once you have the registration number for an aircraft, the name of all the previous owners may be retrieved. These former owners may have a personal knowledge of the habits and personal details of the life of your subject. Order a copy of the bill of sale of the aircraft that your subject owns. This document will contain much information, including witnesses to the signing of the bill of sale and their addresses, the name of the financial institution that may have a lien on the aircraft, and the names and addresses of any other owners. The aforementioned sources may be able to direct you to the location of your subject if your subject cannot be located at the address listed on the registration.

Federal Aviation Administration
P.O. Box 25504
Oklahoma City, Oklahoma 73125

INTERSTATE COMMERCE COMMISSION

http://www.dot.gov

If your subject is in any form of the transportation business that crosses state lines, there will be records with important information on file. The Interstate Commerce Commission regulates moving companies, trucking firms, and many other entities that use the nation's interstate highway system.

Interstate Commerce Commission
12th Street and Constitution Avenue
Washington, DC 20423

UNITED STATES COURT OF MILITARY APPEALS

http://jaglink.jag.af.mil

The United States Court of Military Appeals was created by Congress in 1950 and is composed of three civilian judges. Even though this court operates as part of the Department of Defense for administrative purposes, it is independent of any influence from the military. The court's function is to be an impartial final appeals board for members of the military who have been convicted of crimes.

You will want to order a photocopy of your subject's complete court file if they have ever availed themselves of this avenue of redress. The date of birth, Social Security Number, grade and rank information, addresses, and the details of the court case will be part of the file.

United States Court of Military Appeals
450 E Street NW
Washington, DC 20442

UNITED STATES COURT OF VETERANS APPEALS

http://www.armfor.uscourts.gov/

Your subject may be a veteran of the Armed Forces that had made an appeal to the United States Court of Veterans Appeals. Cases are filed, in some cases, decades after the veteran had been separated from the service.

Much information such as Social Security Number, date of birth, and home address will be in this public record. Spouse and dependent information will be included if applicable.

United States Court of Veterans Appeals
625 Indiana Avenue
Washington, DC 20004

THE UNITED STATES CLAIMS COURT

http://www.fedcir.gov

The United States Claims Court may have been used by your subject to make a claim against the federal government. If you had heard that at one time your subject had filed suit, then you can write and order a photocopy of the court file. You will be able to learn such information as the Social Security Number, date of birth, home and business address, and the spouse information of the subject. The amount of any award of damages will be listed.

United States Claims Court
717 Madison Place, Northwest
Washington, DC 20005

UNITED STATES TAX COURT

http://ustaxcourt.gov

Congress created the United States Tax Court to provide a forum where a taxpayer may dispute a deficiency in taxes claimed by the Internal Revenue Service. The court allows only cases where the amount disputed is $10,000 or less.

Write to the tax court for a photocopy of the court file if you believe your subject may have had a case heard in this arena. The file will contain much information that will be of a personal nature, such as Social Security Number, home and business address, name of spouse, and nature of the tax dispute.

United States Tax Court
400 Second Street, Northwest
Washington, DC 20217

GENERAL SERVICES ADMINISTRATION

http://gsa.gov

The General Services Administration's function is to evaluate and award contracts to firms so that they may supply products or services to branches of the federal government. If your subject is a business person and you have reason to believe that he may have conducted business with the federal government, then you will want to request photocopies of the files containing the contracts that have been or presently are in force.

The contracts will have the business, and, in many instances, home address, Social Security Number, personal references, business and bank references, former addresses, and other important information regarding the subject that will assist you in your search for the subject.

General Services Administration
CAIR/Room 3016
18th & F Street, Northwest
Washington, DC 20405

UNITED STATES GOVERNMENT DEPOSITORY LIBRARIES

http://www.access.gpo.gov/su_docs/dpos/adpos003.html

Libraries that are considered complete and well-rounded are selected by the Superintendent of Documents to participate in the Depository Library Program. These libraries will receive all federal government publications free of charge if they pledge to make available free access to their facilities for all library patrons.

The libraries selected to be United States Government Depository Libraries must maintain a high standard of responsiveness, inventory, and access. This is a quote from the Congressional edict that will clearly demonstrate that the government is serious about the accountability of the Depository Libraries:

"The Superintendent of Documents shall make firsthand
investigation of conditions for which need is indicated and
include the results of investigations in his annual report. When

*he ascertains that the number of books in a depository library is below ten thousand, other than Government publications, or it has ceased to be maintained so as to be **accessible to the public,** or that the Government publications which have been furnished the library have not been properly maintained, he shall delete the library from the list of depository libraries if the library fails to correct the unsatisfactory conditions within six months."*

I used these particular libraries because they provide a level of service and availability of different publications that I require for research. These libraries, for instance, have on hand crisscross directories. These directories can be accessed two ways:

1. The listings are by telephone number. Look for a telephone number in the numerical listing and, if the number is a published number, it will show the name and address of the person with that telephone number.

2. The listings are by address. You may look up a street address, and you will be shown the name of the occupant and the telephone number corresponding to the address. All of the information on the neighbors will, of course, also be in the sequence.

The library will have the books for the locale you are in, and, in many instances, the books for the surrounding cities will be available. The libraries also keep the previous issues of the criss-cross directories for several years. The importance of these publications is obvious. You may have retrieved a telephone number in your search but no address. Now you have the means to find the address. Or you may have an address, but no telephone number.

If the information operator is not of any assistance because your subject does not have the telephone number listed under his name, use the crisscross directory. Retrieval of the telephone number at the subject's address is possible because the telephone listing is by address, not name. From these books, you now have the names, addresses, and telephone numbers of all the neighbors of your subject.

The library will have a publication called *Directory of United States Public and Private Companies.* You will want to review this reference if you believe your subject to be an owner of a business. The list of more than 107,000 business (of which 90 percent are privately held) includes the names of the principals in the business, address, regular and fax telephone numbers, financial information, and corporate structure information. Search for the company name you feel the subject may be using. Many persons will move to another state and use basically the same company name that they had used previously.

You may want to refer to the publication that is called the *Congressional Directory*. Not only does this book list the names, addresses, and telephone numbers of members of Congress, but it contains the names, addresses, and telephone numbers of every Freedom of Information officer in every agency of the federal government. **You are permitted to ask if your subject is an employee of any department of government by just directing your inquiry to the appropriate Freedom of Information officer.**

If your subject was or is a member of any union, trade organization, hobby group, or club, then you will be able to access the address and telephone number of the desired organization. Ask for the Gale Research edition of organizations, and you will have more than 47,000 entries to assist you in locating the correct information. The international edition lists more than 10,300 entries. Write to the above-noted sources and ask if your subject is a member, and, if so, what local chapter or unit he or she belongs to. This will give you a defined geographical location to start or continue your search in. This is an excellent technique to use, because just about everyone will belong to some type of organization. Even if your subject does not want to be found, they probably will still maintain a membership in a local group of the organization that they belonged to when they were in the mainstream.

DIRECTORY OF CORPORATE AFFILIATIONS— WHO OWNS WHOM?

This three-volume annual directory provides information on almost 150,000 public and private parent, subsidiary, and associate companies in the United States and overseas. Entries are arranged first by the parent's location, and then hierarchically by the company's organization. Criteria for inclusion is revenue in excess of $10 million or a work force in excess of 300 for U.S. companies, and revenue in excess of $50 million for non-U.S. firms. A two-volume master index provides access by company name, brand name, location, **personnel**, and standard industrial classification code.

DUN & BRADSTREET'S
MILLION DOLLAR DIRECTORY

This three-volume Dun & Bradstreet directory contains information on over 20,000 public and 140,000 private utilities, transportation companies, banks, trust companies, mutual and stock insurance companies, wholesalers, and retailers. The type of information available includes annual sales, **corporate officers, locations, phone numbers**, type of business, and number of employees. To be included in the directory, a company must be a headquarters or a single location and have 250 or more employees, $25 million or more in sales, or a net worth of $500,000 or more. Company names are arranged alphabetically. A two-volume index is arranged by location and standard industrial classification code.

FOREIGN REPRESENTATIVES
IN THE U.S. YELLOW BOOK

Does your "friend" say they work for a foreign entity? This directory has sections on foreign corporations, foreign-based financial institutions, foreign governments (embassies and consulates), intergovernmental organizations, non-U.S. media, and **personnel** who represent foreign corporations and government in the United States. **It includes officials' titles, addresses, and telephone and fax numbers.**

MOODY'S INTERNATIONAL MANUAL

Does your "friend" say they own a foreign firm? This manual contains background and financial information on over 3,000 foreign firms. It is arranged by country, and gives economic and political information and statistics for each geographical area. It provides statistical information regarding foreign stock exchanges, consumer price indexes, money market rates, imports, and exports.

MOODY'S INVESTORS SERVICES

Does your "friend" say they own an American company? Moody's broad business sector manuals cover companies whose stock is traded in the New

York and American stock exchanges, regional American stock exchanges, and in over-the-counter transactions. Each entry contains history and background; data on acquisitions, mergers, and subsidiaries; business and product descriptions; **names and titles of officers and directors;** number of stockholders and employees; location of plants and properties; the headquarters' phone number and address; and financial statements. Separate annual volumes with weekly supplements cover industries, transportation, utilities, and banking. Another series supplies detailed data on corporate and government bond sales and ratings.

STANDARD & POOR'S CORPORATION RECORDS

Does your "friend" say they are a director or an officer of a company? Originally provided to Standard & Poor subscribers, this directory is now available on CD-ROM. The records cover over 12,000 publically traded companies and 34,000 subsidiaries, affiliates, and privately held firms. Coverage consists of a company's brief history, financial statements, capital structure, lines of business, subsidiaries, and **officers and directors.** Information on 70,000 executives is also available.

AMERICAN MEDICAL DIRECTORY

Does your "friend" say they are a doctor? The directory has **listings of doctors—by state and city, year of birth, medical school and year of graduation, year of license, residence and office addresses, specialties, and membership in associated medical organizations. A name index of all doctors is provided.**

In addition to the directories focusing on individuals that are listed in this section, several other directories cited in this chapter, under other sections, contain information about individuals. These other directories are the Associations Yellow Book; Directory of Corporate Affiliations—Who Owns Whom; Dun & Bradstreet's Million Dollar Directory; Law Firms Yellow Book; Martindale-Hubbell Law Directory; Moody's Bank and Finance Manual; National Directory of Law Enforcement Administrators, Prosecutors, Correctional Institutions, and Related Agencies; National Trade and Professional Associations in the United States; Standard & Poor's Corporation Records; Standard & Poor's Register of Corporations, Directors and Executives; and Thomson Bank Directory.

CONGRESSIONAL DIRECTORY

Does your "friend" say they work for the federal government? This directory is prepared by the Joint Committee on Printing and is the official directory of the Congress. It presents short bibliographies of each member of the Senate and the House—listed by states and districts, respectively. It includes such additional data as his or her committee memberships, terms of service, administrative assistant and/or secretary, and room and telephone numbers. The Congressional Directory also lists officials of the courts; the military establishments; and other federal departments and agencies, including the District of Columbia government, governors of states and territories, foreign diplomats; and members of the press, radio, and television galleries. The directory is available both in paper format and online. The database is updated irregularly as changes are provided by the Joint Committee on Printing.

CORPORATE YELLOW BOOK

Does your "friend" say they are the director of a large corporation? This is a directory of the people who manage, direct, and shape the largest public and privately held companies in the United States. It enables subscribers to access corporate leaders, including board members who are taking increased responsibility for corporate decision making. The directory features (1) over 1,000 leading corporations and over 7,500 subsidiaries and divisions; (2) **names and titles of over 45,000 executives, including more than 10,000 corporate board members** and their outside affiliations; (3) over **18,700 direct-dial telephone numbers of executives;** (4) business descriptions and annual revenues; (5) addresses, telephone and fax numbers, and Internet addresses of corporate headquarters and domestic and foreign subsidiaries and divisions; and (6) Washington DC, government affairs offices, with addresses and telephone and fax numbers.

DEFENSE ORGANIZATION SERVICE

Does your "friend" say they have a top level job at the Defense Department? From Carroll Publishing Company, this service provides coverage exclusively for the Department of Defense (DOD). Detailed charts describe the organization and list the **staff of the Office of the Secretary, the Joint Chiefs of Staff,** the unified commands, and the individual services. Indexes reference locations, acronyms, key words, personal names, and program elements. This source is updated monthly.

FEDERAL REGIONAL YELLOW BOOK

Does your "friend" say they are an administrator at a federal department or agency? This yellow book describes federal regional offices located outside Washington, DC It contains over 3,000 regional directors and over 29,000 administrative staff of federal departments and agencies. It also has information on **administrators and professional staff** at federal laboratories, research centers, military installations, and service academies.

FEDERAL STAFF DIRECTORY

Does your "friend" say they are employed by an international organization? Another Congressional Quarterly tool, this item is similar to the Federal Yellow Book. One of its strong points is its "Quasi-Official, International and Non-Government Organizations" section that describes the mission and lists the **staff of almost 50 such organizations**. In addition, it contains over **2,600 biographies of key executives and senior staff** as well as entries for U.S. ambassadors to other countries and other countries' ambassadors to the United States. It is indexed by key word/subject and individual/personal name. It is updated semiannually.

FEDERAL YELLOW BOOK

Does your "friend" say they work for the White House executive branch? This quarterly publication provides detailed listings of **the names, locations, and telephone numbers of more than 40,000 staff members in the White House, the executive departments, and the independent agencies.** Like its Congressional counterpart, it has subject, organization, and staff indexes. Over 4,000 fax numbers and e-mail addresses are also included.

GOVERNMENT AFFAIRS YELLOW BOOK

Does your "friend" say they are a lobbyist? This yellow book lists over 18,000 government affairs professionals who lobby at both the state and federal levels. It details the issues the lobbyists contest, as well as the coalitions they form to advance their legislative agenda. Five indexes are included—on organization, subject, current legislative issues, geographical location, and individual name. Biographical data is included on each professional.

JUDICIAL YELLOW BOOK

Does your "friend" say they work for a federal court? This directory provides detailed biographical information for **state and federal judges and gives information on each judge's staff, including law clerks.** It features more than 2,000 judges in the federal court system, and more than 1,200 state judges of the highest appellate courts.

MUNICIPAL YELLOW BOOK

Does your "friend" say they are a government official of a city or county? This directory provides information on over **30,000 elected and appointed officials in U.S. cities, counties, and authorities, including name, address, and telephone and fax numbers.** It contains sections on cities and counties, which feature complex hierarchies of municipal officials. This directory also has listings for local departments, agencies, subdivisions, and branches.

STATE YELLOW BOOK

Does your "friend" say they are a state employee? This directory provides information on who's who in the executive and legislative branches of the 50 state governments, as well as American Samoa, Guam, Puerto Rico, and the Virgin Islands. It has both a subject and **personnel index and includes information on government officials,** departments, agencies, and legislative committees. Informational profiles of all states and territories are also provided.

WHO'S WHO SERIES

Does your "friend" say they are an important person who has many awards and degrees? This biennial series of international, U.S., regional, and professional biographical sources contains information submitted by the individual at the request of the publisher. *Who's Who in America* contains entries for over **100,000 nationally prominent individuals,** and the regional and professional volumes cover many thousands more people who are renowned in a locality or an occupation. Each entry includes information about an **individual's family, schooling, profession, writings, and awards and about offices held** by the individual. Indexing is by location, profession, who retired, and who died. Non-U.S.-wide titles, while following the same format as U.S. entries, do not have indexes.

ASSOCIATIONS YELLOW BOOK

Does your "friend" say they are an executive of an association? This is a directory of major trade and professional associations. Semiannual editions of the Associations Yellow Book provide current information on executive turnovers, changes in staff and governing boards, mergers, and name changes. It features (1) **over 45,000 officers, executives, and staff;** with titles, affiliations, education, and telephone and fax numbers, at more than 1,175 associations with budgets over $1 million; (2) addresses and e-mail addresses and telephone and fax numbers of headquarters and branches, and Internet addresses for headquarters; (3) boards of directors, with outside affiliations; (4) committees and chairmen, Washington representatives, political action committees, and foundations; (5) publications, including editors; and (6) annual budget, tax status, number of employees, and number of members.

NATIONAL TRADE AND PROFESSIONAL ASSOCIATIONS
(In the United States)

Does your "friend" say they are a member of a trade association? This annual directory lists about 7,500 active U.S. national trade and professional associations, labor unions, scientific societies, and technical organizations. Alphabetically arranged entries contain the name, location, telephone, and fax numbers, **executives' names,** history, recurring publication titles, budget amount, membership count, and annual meeting times. The directory has subject, geographical, budget, executive, acronym, and management firm indexes.

THOMSON BANK DIRECTORY
(Replaces the Rand McNally Bankers Directory)

Does your "friend" say they are an officer or a director of a bank? This semiannual directory in four volumes is a guide to all U.S. and non-U.S. banks. Entries include: the name, address, and telephone number of the bank; type of charter; funds processor; automated clearinghouse; holding company; asset rank; financial figures; balance sheets; **officers and directors;** branches; subsidiaries; and foreign offices.

LAW FIRM AND LAW ENFORCEMENT DIRECTORIES
Law Firms Yellow Book

Does your "friend" say they are a corporate attorney? This directory has information on 715 of the largest corporate law firms in the United States. It focuses on the **4,500 administrators and 10,000 attorneys** in these firms, and it is indexed by specialties, law schools, management/administrative personnel, geography, and personnel. It is updated semiannually.

MARTINDALE-HUBBELL LAW DIRECTORY

Does your "friend" say they are a member of a corporate law department? This 19-volume annual directory contains over 900,000 entries consisting of profiles of law firms, corporate law departments, state bar associations, and law schools; biographies of lawyers in private and corporate practice; and descriptions of legal service, supplier, and consultant firms in the United States and Canada. **Indexing is by individual,** firm, specialty, and geographic area. The 4-volume International Law Directory, which is part of the 19-volume work, has similar entries and indexes for non-U.S. and non-Canadian firms and individuals. It includes law digests for 140 countries and is available electronically on CD-ROM and LEXIS.

NATIONAL DIRECTORY OF LAW ENFORCEMENT ADMINISTRATORS, PROSECUTORS, CORRECTIONAL INSTITUTIONS, AND RELATED AGENCIES

Does your "friend" say they are an important member of the law enforcement community? This annual source lists the following information: **names, addresses, telephone numbers, and fax numbers of city chiefs of police, county sheriffs, district attorneys, state highway patrols, and federal law enforcement agencies.**

LLOYD'S DIRECTORIES ABOUT THE SHIPPING INDUSTRY
(List of Ship Owners)

Does your "friend" say they own a ship? This list includes over **40,000 owners, managers, and managing agents** for vessels listed in the Register of Ships. It is published annually in August and includes postal addresses; telephone, telex, and telefax numbers; fleet lists; and a geographical index. Subscribers receive eight cumulative supplements with the list.

REGISTER OF OFFSHORE UNITS, SUBMERSIBLES, AND UNDERWATER SYSTEMS

Does your "friend" say that they are involved in the offshore drilling business and that is why they need to be away for long periods of time? This register is published annually in October. It contains sections listing mobile drilling rigs, submersibles, underwater systems, work units (ships, barges, and platforms) used for a variety of offshore work, **owners**, and addresses of offshore support ships with their fleet lists.

VOYAGE RECORD

Does your "friend" say they need to travel for months at a time on a commercial vessel but there is no way you can tell where they are? This record details the recent voyage history of 22,000 vessels in commercial service by reporting movements collected continually by Lloyd's agents worldwide. It is a companion to the Shipping Index, which lists the historical movements of vessels.

INDEX MEDICUS

This monthly classified index of the world's biomedical literature (including research, clinical practice, administration, policy issues, and health-care services) is produced by the National Library of Medicine. It covers publications in all principal languages, and includes periodical articles and other analytical material; as well as books, pamphlets, and theses. The January issue includes lists of the periodicals indexed and medical subject headings used. Quarterly and annual cumulations are provided, and electronic access via commercial databases and CD-ROM is also available.

NEWS MEDIA YELLOW BOOK

Over 31,000 reporters, writers, editors, and producers at more than 2,900 national news media organizations are listed in this yellow book. It features 12 media categories—on newspapers, news services, and bureaus; television, radio, and cable stations and networks; publishers; independent journalists; and consumer, trade, and association magazines. This directory is fully updated on a quarterly basis.

PUBLIC AFFAIRS INFORMATION SERVICE

This subject index to the articles, books, documents, microfiche, pamphlets, and reports in the public affairs field is published monthly and cumulated annually. Each year, it includes selective indexing to more than 1,600 periodicals and 8,000 books from around the world. It contains factual and statistical information about political science, government, legislation, economics, and sociology. It is also available electronically via CD-ROMs and commercial databases.

READER'S GUIDE TO PERIODICAL LITERATURE

This guide indexes articles by subject and author in over 225 popular magazines. It is published semimonthly and cumulates annually. Each entry includes the article's author, title, and pages, as well as the periodical's title, volume, and date. The presence of graphic material is also noted. This tool is also available electronically on a commercial database and on CD-ROM.

THE NEW YORK TIMES INDEX

This source, published semimonthly and cumulated annually, includes an exact reference to the date, section, page, and column of *The New York Times* edition in which articles will be found. It contains cross-references to names and related topics, and has a brief synopsis of articles. Electronic access to the index is available in many forms from many sources; searchable, full-text files in the NEXIS and Dow Jones databases; a searchable, full-text CD-ROM called *The New York Times* ONDISC; and a searchable, full-text Internet site known as THE NEW YORK TIMES ON THE WEB.

ABSTRACT AND TITLE COMPANIES

Abstract and title companies generally develop an overview of the property, examine the title for liens and other conditions, and prepare a commitment to insure. Information contained in supporting records may include **transfer of property, locations, mortgage amounts, and releases of mortgages.**

SMALL BUSINESS ADMINISTRATION (SBA)

SBA guarantees loans made by commercial lenders to eligible small businesses; makes loans to businesses and individuals following federally declared disasters; and licenses investment companies to provide venture capital to eligible small businesses. SBA also (1) connects small firms owned by socially and economically disadvantaged Americans with contracts set aside by other federal agencies, and (2) seeks to increase federal contract opportunities for small businesses in general. SBA-guaranteed loans are made by private-sector lenders, with SBA promising to reimburse a specified percentage of any amount lost by the lender. By law, the amount of SBA's guarantee under its most popular and least restricted lending program is limited to $750,000, and the loan maturity to 25 years.

SBA may be the best source of financial and other information about the small businesses **(and their principals)** to which it provides assistance;

many of them are exempt from public disclosure laws because of their smallness. Records on businesses and individuals that have received SBA assistance are maintained by the division that administers the program involved. The local SBA district office maintains most records. Contact the local office of SBA's Office of Inspector General, Investigations Division, for assistance in obtaining records and other information.

JAILS AND PRISONS

One of the best, free-of-charge, and most overlooked research techniques are jails and prisons. When you absolutely cannot find someone, that person may be incarcerated. The following will assist you in checking whether or not your subject is in custody, and you may also use the contact numbers to start a background check on someone.

The Freedom of Information Act (5 USC 552) and the Privacy Act of 1974 (5 USC 552a) authorize the release of certain information about federal inmates to any member of the general public requesting it. This includes information such as name, age, and register number; as well as sentencing and confinement data (offense, date sentenced, institution of confinement, etc.). With a few exceptions, only inmates convicted of violating federal laws (laws of the United States) are sent to federal prisons. Individuals awaiting trial for violating federal laws are also held in federal prisons. The Federal Bureau of Prisons also houses a few state inmates. However, most inmates convicted of violating state or local laws are sent to state prisons or city or county jails.

How to Get Inmate Information: Write to the Freedom of Information Act (FOIA) office, 320 First St., NW, Washington, DC 20534. FOIA requests are processed within several weeks, and there is usually no charge for inmate location requests. However, please be aware that if you request additional information, you may be charged for research time.

Federal Inmates: For federal inmates released before 1982, please write to the Office of Communications and Archives, Federal Bureau of Prisons, 320 First St., NW, Washington, DC 20534. Attn: Historic Inmate Locator Request. Please include as much identifying information as possible, such as, name (including middle name or middle initial if known), aliases, date of birth, race, crime, approximate dates in prison, name of prison, etc. The more information you provide, the more quickly the request can be processed.

State Inmates: Most states have their own locator systems. Contact the Department of Corrections in your state for further information.

STATE PRISON WEBSITES

**Alabama Department
of Corrections**
(334) 240-9500
http://agencies.state.al.us/doc

Alaska Department of Corrections
(907) 269-7400
http://www.correct.state.ak.us/

Arizona Department of Corrections
(602) 542-5536
http://www.state.az.us/

**Arkansas Department
of Corrections**
(501) 247-6200
http://www.state.ar.us/doc

California Department of Corrections
(916) 445-7688
http://www.cdc.state.ca.us/

California Youth Authority
(916) 262-1480
http://www.cya.ca.gov/index.html

Colorado Department of Corrections
(719) 579-9580
http://www.doc.state.co.us/

**Connecticut Department
of Corrections**
(860) 566-4457
http://www.state.ct.us/doc/

Delaware Department of Corrections
(302) 739-5601
http://www.state.de.us/correct/

**District of Columbia
Department of Corrections**
(202) 673-7316
http://www.washingtondc.gov/agen-
cies/detail.asp?id=25

Florida Department of Corrections
(850) 488-5021
http://www.dc.state.fl.us/
Florida Department of Juvenile Justice
http://www.djj.state.fl.us/

Georgia Department of Corrections
(404) 656-4593
http://www.dcor.state.ga.us/

Georgia Department of Juvenile Justice
http://www.djj.state.ga.us/

Hawaii Department of Public Safety
(808) 587-1288
http://www.hawaii.gov/icsd/psd/psd.html

Idaho Department of Corrections
(208) 334-2318
http://www.corr.state.id.us/

Illinois Department of Corrections
(217) 522-2666
http://www.idoc.state.il.us/

Indiana Department of Corrections
(317) 232-5715
http://www.corrections.com/ICA
http://www.state.in.us/indcorrection/

Iowa Department of Corrections
(515) 281-4811
http://www.state.ia.us/corrections/doc/-
index.html

Kansas Department of Corrections
(913) 296-3310
http://www.ink.org/public/kdoc

**Kansas Regional
Juvenile Detention Center**
http://www.gardencity.net/fico/juvenile/

Kentucky Department of Corrections
(502) 564-4726
http://www.jus.state.ky.us/

**Louisiana Department of Public
Safety and Correctional Services**
(504) 342-6741
http://www.cole.state.la.us/

Maine Department of Corrections
(207) 287-4360
http://janus.state.me.us/corrections

**Maryland Department of Public
Safety and Correctional Services**
(410) 764-4003
http://www.dpscs.state.md.us/doc/

**Massachusetts Executive Office
of Public Safety**
(617) 727-7775
http://www.magnet.state.ma.us/doc/

Michigan Department of Corrections
(517) 373-0720
http://www.state.mi.us/mdoc

Minnesota Department of Corrections
(612) 642-0200
http://www.corr.state.mn.us/

Mississippi Department
of Corrections
(601) 359-5621
http://www.mdoc.state.ms.us/

Missouri Department of Corrections
(314) 751-2389
http://www.corrections.state.mo.us/

Montana Department of Corrections
(406) 444-3930
http://www.state.mt.us/cor/

**Nebraska Department
of Correctional Services**
(402) 471-2654
http://www.corrections.state.ne.us/

Nevada Department of Prisons
(702) 887-3285
http://www.state.nv.us/inprog.htm

**New Hampshire Department
of Corrections**
(603) 271-5600
http://www.state.nh.us/doc/

**New Jersey Department
of Corrections**
(609) 292-9860
http://www.state.nj.us/corrections

**New Mexico Department
of Corrections**
(505) 827-8709
http://www.state.nm.us/corrections/

**New York Department
of Correctional Services**
(518) 457-8126
http://www.docs.state.ny.us/

**North Carolina Department
of Corrections**
(919) 733-4926
http://www.doc.state.nc.us/

**North Dakota Department of
Corrections and Rehabilitation**
(701) 328-6390
http://www.state.nd.us/docr/Directory.htm

**Ohio Department of
Rehabilitation and Corrections**
(614) 752-1164
http://www.drc.ohio.gov/

**Ohio Department
of Youth Services**
http://www.state.oh.us/dys

**Oklahoma Department
of Corrections**
(405) 425-2500
http://www.doc.state.ok.us/

Oregon Department of Corrections
(503) 945-0920
http://www.doc.state.or.us/

**Pennsylvania Department
of Corrections**
(717) 975-4860
http://www.cor.state.pa.us/

**Rhode Island Department
of Corrections**
(401) 464-2611
http://www.doc.state.ri.us/

**South Carolina Department
of Corrections**
(803) 896-8555
http://www.state.sc.us/scdc/

**South Dakota Department
of Corrections**
(605) 773-3478
http://www.state.sd.us/corrections/adult.htm

**Tennessee Department
of Corrections**
(615) 741-2071
http://www.state.tn.us/correction

Texas Department of Criminal Justice
(409) 294-6231
http://www.tdcj.state.tx.us

Texas Youth Commission
http://www.tyc.state.tx.us/

Utah Department of Corrections
(801) 265-5500
http://www.cr.ex.state.ut.us/

**Vermont Department
of Corrections**
(802) 241-2442
http://www.doc.state.vt.us/

Virginia Department of Corrections
(804) 674-3000
http://www.cns.state.va.us/doc/

**Washington Department
of Corrections**
(360) 753-1573
http://www.wa.gov/doc/

**West Virginia Department
of Military Affairs and Public Safety**
(304) 558-2037
http://www.state.wv.us/wvdoc/htm

**Wisconsin Department
of Corrections**
(608) 266-4548
http://badger.state.wi.us/agencies/doc/

**Wyoming Department
of Corrections**
(307) 777-7405
http://doc.state.wy.us/corrections.html

I am reprinting the following government Websites (agency, organization, and bureau), because you may have an interest (perhaps on a personal note), in the statistics of crime in this country. The Office for Victims of Crime may also be of interest to you if you or someone you know was a victim of **your subject**. Some of the other links below include Websites of the Most Wanted because **your subject** may be listed.

America's Most Wanted
http://www.amw.com/

America's Most Wanted Criminals
http://cpcug.org/user/jlacombe/wanted.html

American Probation and Parole Association
http://www.appa-net.org/

Bureau of Justice Statistics
http://www.ojp.usdoj.gov/bjs

Corrections Connections—American Correctional Assn. and American Jail Assn.
http://www.corrections.com/index.html

Corrections Today—American Correctional Association's Magazine
http://www.corrections.com/aca/cortoday/index.html

Crime and Victims Statistics—US Bureau of Justice Statistics
http://www.ojp.usdoj.gov/bjs/

Crime Statistics by State
http://www.disastercenter.com/crime/

Crime Statistics Tutorial
http://crime.org/

FBI's 10 Most Wanted
http://www.fbi.gov/mostwanted.htm

FBI (Federal Bureau of Investigation)
http://www.fbi.gov/

Federal Judicial Center
http://www.fjc.gov/

Midwest Gang Investigators Association
http://www.mgia.org/

National Alliance of Gang Investigations
http://www.nagia.org/

National Archive of Criminal Justice Data
http://www.icpsr.umich.edu/nacjd

National Criminal Justice
http://www.sso.org/ncja

National Crime Statistics Link Guide
http://www.crime.org

National Institute of Corrections Information Center
http://www.nicic.org/

National Major Gang Task Force
http://www.nmgtf.org/

Office for Victims of Crime
http://www.ojp.usdoj.gov/ovc

Source Book of Criminal Justice Statistics (BJS)
http://www.albany.edu/sourcebook

US Alcohol, Tobacco and Firearms Most Wanted
http://www.atf.treas.gov/wanted/index.htm

US Bureau of Justice Statistics on Capital Punishment
http://www.ojp.usdoj.gov/bjs/cp.htm

US Department of Justice
http://www.usdoj.gov/

Victims National Criminal Justice Reference Service
http://www.ncjrs.org/

World's Most Wanted
http://mostwanted.com
http://www.mostwanted.org

The Abandoned Property Technique

Your subject may have had a period in his life he has chosen not to tell you about. **Perhaps he ran out on his wife, his children, his employer, his girlfriend or even the law.** He may have left some of his possessions.

In most instances, the state takes possession of the following if a person has disappeared for at least seven years:

Bank accounts
State Income tax refunds
Payroll checks
Overpayment of insurance premiums
Credit balance on credit cards
Utility refunds
Dividend checks
Annuity checks
Telephone deposit refunds
Safe deposit boxes

Each state maintains an alphabetical listing of all persons who have had property or monies held in escrow by the state. Write to any state in which your subject may have resided or in which he may have conducted any business.

If you find property held in your subject's name, simply write to the state asking for the full file. You will see where he lived, what valuables he left, if relatives had made a claim, etc. If your subject had to leave so suddenly that he did not take all his possessions, it would be wise to ask him about it and demand a precise and plausible answer as to **why.**

If you do not get an answer you can live with, then your subject may want to make a claim to get what is due him. After all, aren't the monies, properties or valuables to be yours if you do get married to this subject?

UNCLAIMED PROPERTY DEPARTMENTS

ALABAMA

http://www.treasury.state.al.us/website/-ucpd/ucpd_frameset.html
Alabama Revenue Department
Unclaimed Property Section
P.O. Box 327350-E
Montgomery, Alabama 36132

ALASKA

http://www.revenue.state.ak.us/tax/
Alaska Department of Revenue
Unclaimed Property Section
Box 8A
Juneau, Alaska 99811

ARIZONA

http://www.revenue.state.az.us/unclprop.htm
Arizona Department of Revenue
Unclaimed Property Processing Unit
1600 West Monroe, Sixth Floor
Phoenix, Arizona 85007

ARKANSAS

http://www.state.ar.us/auditor/unclprop/
Auditor of State
Unclaimed Property Department
230 State Capitol
Little Rock, Arkansas 72201

CALIFORNIA

http://scoweb.sco.ca.gov/scoucp/inquiry/index.htm
Office of the State Controller
Division of Unclaimed Property
P.O. Box 942850-N
Sacramento, California 94250

COLORADO

http://www.treasurer.state.co.us/payback.html
Colorado State Treasury
Great Colorado Payback
1560 Broadway, Ste. 1225
Denver, Colorado 80202

CONNECTICUT

http://www.state.ct.us/ott/ucp.html
Office of the State Treasurer
Unclaimed Property Division
20 Trinity Street
Hartford, Connecticut 06160

DELAWARE

http://www.state.de.us/revenue/
Delaware State Escheator
P.O. Box 89311-J
Wilmington, Delaware 19899

DISTRICT OF COLUMBIA
http://www.washingtondc.gov/
Department of Finance and Revenue
Unclaimed Property Division
300 Indiana Avenue N.W.
Washington, DC 20002

FLORIDA
http://up.dbf.state.fl.us/
Office of the Comptroller
Division of Finance
Abandoned Property Section
The Capitol
Tallahassee, Florida 32399

GEORGIA
http://www.state.ga.us/dor/ptd/ucp/
Georgia Department of Revenue
Property Tax Division
Unclaimed Property Section
405 Trinity—Washington Building
Atlanta, Georgia 30334

HAWAII
http://www.josephculligan.com/-
hawaii.html
Finance Division
Department of Budget and Finance
P.O. Box 150-O
Honolulu, Hawaii 96810

IDAHO
http://www2.state.id.us/tax/unclaimed_i
daho.htm
Unclaimed Property Section
State Tax Commission
P.O. Box 36-Y
Boise, Idaho 83722

ILLINOIS
http://www.cashdash.net/
State of Illinois
Department of Financial Institutions
Unclaimed Property Division
421 East Capitol Avenue
Springfield, Illinois 62706

INDIANA
http://www.state.in.us/serv/ag_ucp
Unclaimed Property Division
Office of the Attorney General
219 State House
Indianapolis, Indiana 46204

IOWA
http://www.treasurer.state.ia.us/
Unclaimed Property Division
State Treasurer's Office
Hoover State Office Building
Des Moines, Iowa 50319

KANSAS
http://www.treasurer.state.ks.us/upsearch
.htm
Division of Unclaimed Property
Office of State Treasurer
900 Jackson, Suite 201
Topeka, Kansas 66612

KENTUCKY
http://www.state.ky.us
Miscellaneous Excise Tax Section
Revenue Cabinet
The Capitol
Frankfort, Kentucky 40620

LOUISIANA
http://www.rev.state.la.us/Unclaimed.-
htm
Unclaimed Property Division
P.O. Box 91010-E
Baton Rouge, Louisiana 70821

MAINE
http://www.state.me.us/treasurer/prop-
erty.htm
Abandoned Property Division
Treasury Department
Station Number 39
Augusta, Maine 04333

MARYLAND

http://www.comp.state.md.us/unclaim.asp
Comptroller of the Treasurer
Unclaimed Property Division
301 West Preston Street
Baltimore, Maryland 21201

MASSACHUSETTS

http://www.magnet.state.ma.us/treas-
ury/abp.htm
Office of the Treasurer
Unclaimed Property Division
50 Franklin Street, Second Floor
Boston, Massachusetts 02110

MICHIGAN

http://www.mlive.com/news/miou.html
Escheats Division
Michigan Department of the Treasury
Lansing, Michigan 48922

MINNESOTA

http://www.commerce.state.mn.us/-
mainup.htm
Unclaimed Property Office
500 Metro Square Building
Saint Paul, Minnesota 55101

MISSISSIPPI

http://www.treasury.state.ms.us./claim.htm
State Treasury Department
Attention: Unclaimed Property
P.O. Box 138-D
Jackson, Mississippi 39205

MISSOURI

http://www.sto.state.mo.us/ucp/data-
base/search.htm
Unclaimed Property Department
P.O. Box 1272-R
Jefferson City, Missouri 65102

MONTANA

http://www.unclaimed.org/mainframe.asp
Department of Revenue
Abandoned Property Section
Mitchell Building
Helena, Montana 59620

NEBRASKA

http://www.state.ne.us
Office of the State Treasurer
Unclaimed Property Section
P.O. Box 94788
Capitol Building
Lincoln, Nebraska 68509

NEVADA

http://www.upd.state.nv.us/
Department of Commerce
Unclaimed Property Division
State Mail Room
Las Vegas, Nevada 89158

NEW HAMPSHIRE

http://www.state.nh.us/treasury/search.-
html
Abandoned Property Department
State House Annex
Room 121
Concord, New Hampshire 03301

NEW JERSEY

http://www.state.nj.us/treasury/taxa-
tion/unclaimsrch.htm
Department of the Treasury
Office of Financial Management
1 West State Street
Trenton, New Jersey 08625

NEW MEXICO

http://www.josephculligan.com/new-
mexico.html
Unclaimed Property Unit
Taxation and Revenue Department
P.O. Box 630-V
Santa Fe, New Mexico 87509

NEW YORK

http://www.osc.state.ny.us/cgi-
bin/db2www/ouffrm.d2w/input
New York State Comptroller
Office of Unclaimed Funds
P.O. Box 7003
Albany, New York 12225

NORTH CAROLINA

http://www.treasurer.state.nc.us/escheats/
fresc000.htm
Treasurer
Escheat and Unclaimed Property
325 North Salisbury Street
Raleigh, North Carolina 27611

NORTH DAKOTA

http://www.land.state.nd.us/
Unclaimed Property Division
State Land Department
Sixth Floor, State Capitol
Bismarck, North Dakota 58505

OHIO

http://www.josephculligan.com/ohio.html
Ohio Department of Commerce
Division of Unclaimed Funds
77 South High Street
Columbus, Ohio 43266

OKLAHOMA

http://www.kocotv.com/5oys/fortune.html
Oklahoma Tax Commission
Business Tax Division
Unclaimed Property Section
2501 Lincoln Boulevard
Oklahoma City, Oklahoma 73194

OREGON

http://rogue.sscgis.state.or.us/dsl/search.-
cfm
Division of State Lands
Unclaimed Property Division
1600 State Street
Salem, Oregon 97310

PENNSYLVANIA

http://www.treasury.state.pa.us/Unclaimed-
PropertyInquiry.html
Department of Revenue
Abandoned and Unclaimed Property
Bureau of Administrative Services
2850 Turnpike Industrial Park
Middletown, Pennsylvania 17057

PUERTO RICO

Secretary of the Treasury
Unclaimed Property Division
San Juan, Puerto Rico 00940

RHODE ISLAND

http://www.state.ri.us/treas/moneylst.htm
Office of General Treasurer
Unclaimed Property Division
P.O. Box 1435-S
Providence, Rhode Island 02901

SOUTH CAROLINA

http://www.state.sc.us/treas/uprop/search
.html
South Carolina Tax Division
P.O. Box 125-I
Columbia, South Carolina 29214

SOUTH DAKOTA

http://www.state.sd.us/state/executive/-
treasurer/prop.htm
Unclaimed Property Administrator
500 East Capitol
Pierre, South Dakota 57501

TENNESSEE

http://www.state.tn.us
Unclaimed Property Division
Andrew Jackson Building
11th Floor
Nashville, Tennessee 37219

TEXAS

http://www.window.state.tx.us/comp-
trol/unclprop/upsearch.html
Office of the State Treasurer
P.O. Box 12608-N
Capitol Station
Austin, Texas 78711

UTAH

http://www.treasurer.state.ut.us/
Utah State Treasurer
Unclaimed Property Division
219 State Capitol
Salt Lake City, Utah 84114

VERMONT

http://www.tre.state.vt.us/
Abandoned Property Division
Office of State Treasurer
133 State Street
Montpelier, Vermont 05602

VIRGINIA

http://www.trs.state.va.us/
Division of Unclaimed Property
P.O. Box 3-R-G
Richmond, Virginia 23207

WASHINGTON

http://dor.wa.gov/index.asp?//unclaim/-index.htm
Unclaimed Property Section
Department of Revenue
P.O. Box 448-T
Olympia, Washington 98507

WEST VIRGINIA

http://www.wvtreasury.com/search_un-claimed_property_databa.htm
Office of the Treasurer of State
Division of Unclaimed Property
The State Capitol, Room E-147
Charleston, West Virginia 25305

WISCONSIN

http://prd1.state.wi.us/servlet/trdUn-claimProperty
Office of State Treasurer
Unclaimed Property Division
P.O. Box 2114-H
Madison, Wisconsin 53701

WYOMING

http://www.state.wy.us/~sot/text_unc_-prop.html
Office of the State Treasurer
Unclaimed Property Division
State Capitol Building
Cheyenne, Wyoming 82002

Bankruptcy Records

In 2000, the number of individuals filing for bankruptcy was 1,243,923. If you have reason to believe that your subject has ever filed for bankruptcy, or will file for bankruptcy, these records are an excellent source to retrieve background information. They are public information. Even if your subject's petition for bankruptcy was rejected by the bankruptcy court because of the new, tougher bankruptcy law, the subject's petitions and all the important information contained within will be open for public inspection.

The petition file will contain the subject's Social Security Number, date of birth, current and former addresses, **names of any children,** bank accounts, stock ownership, employment history (including a list of the salaries and fringe benefits earned for the past several years), and a list of all property including vehicles and other **important financial and personal information.** Compare this information to what your subject has told you to be true. If your subject had a spouse, her Social Security Number, date of birth and other vital information will be included in the file. You will now have all the necessary personal data on her if you decide to find her and make contact to query her about your subject.

The Vehicle Identification Number (VIN) of each vehicle listed as an asset in the bankruptcy proceeding will be listed. You may access the current address of each vehicle by writing to the appropriate motor vehicle department (see Chapter 1) so you can determine if he has vehicles registered to an address of which you are not aware. Property that the subject can retain because it qualifies as being exempt from the bankruptcy will be listed. Look for the address to which any tax payments are sent.

Chapter 7 is commonly known as "liquidation" bankruptcy, and any person or business may file. Chapter 11 is a reorganization of debt. Chapter 13 is an adjustment of debts for a wage earner. This option is available to individuals with a regular income and who have fixed, unsecured debts less than $100,000 and secured debts of less than $350,000.

BANKRUPTCY COURTS

ALABAMA

United States Bankruptcy Court
500 South 22nd Street
Birmingham, Alabama 35233
http://www.alnd.uscourts.gov

United States Bankruptcy Court
P.O. Box 1248-I
Montgomery, Alabama 36192
http://www.alnd.uscourts.gov

United States Bankruptcy Court
P.O. Box 2865-S
Mobile, Alabama 36652
http://www.als.uscourts.gov

ALASKA

United States Bankruptcy Court
222 West 7th Avenue
Anchorage, Alaska 99513
http://www.akd.uscourts.gov

ARIZONA

United States Bankruptcy Court
230 North 1st Avenue
Phoenix, Arizona 85025
http://www.azb.uscourts.gov

United States Bankruptcy Court
110 South Church
Tucson, Arizona 85702
http://www.azb.uscourts.gov

ARKANSAS

United States Bankruptcy Court
P.O.Box 2381-A
Little Rock, Arkansas 72203
http://www.arwd.uscourts.gov

CALIFORNIA

United States Bankruptcy Court
1130 O Street
Fresno, California 93721
http://www.caed.uscourts.gov

United States Bankruptcy Court
325 West F Street
San Diego, California 92101-6998
http://www.casb.uscourts.gov

United States Bankruptcy Court
235 Pine Street, 19th Floor
San Francisco, California 94104
http://www.canb.uscourts.gov

United States Bankruptcy Court
1130 12th Street, Suite C
Modesto, California 95354
http://www.caeb.uscourts.gov

COLORADO

United States Bankruptcy Court
721 19th Street
Denver, Colorado 80202-2508
http://www.co.uscourts.gov

CONNECTICUT

United States Bankruptcy Court
450 Main Street
Hartford, Connecticut 06103
http://www.ctb.uscourts.gov

DELAWARE

United States Bankruptcy Court
824 Market Street, 5th Floor
Wilmington, Delaware 19801
http://www.deb.uscourts.gov

DISTRICT OF COLUMBIA

United States Bankruptcy Court
333 Constitution Avenue, Northwest
Washington, DC 20001
http://www.dcd.uscourts.gov

FLORIDA

United States Bankruptcy Court
4921 Memorial Highway, #200
Tampa, Florida 33634
http://www.flmd.uscourts.gov

United States Bankruptcy Court
311 W. Monroe Street, #206
Jacksonville, Florida 32202
http://www.flmb.uscourts.gov

United States Bankruptcy Court
227 North Bronough Street
Tallahassee, Florida 32301
www.flnd.uscourts.gov

United States Bankruptcy Court
51 Southwest 1st Avenue, Room 1517
Miami, Florida 33130
http://www.flmd.uscourts.gov

United States Bankruptcy Court
299 East Broward Boulevard
Fort Lauderdale, Florida 33301
http://www.flmp.uscourts.gov

GEORGIA

United States Bankruptcy Court
P.O. Box 1957-W
433 Cherry Street
Macon, Georgia 31202
http://www.gamb.uscourts.gov

United States Bankruptcy Court
75 Spring Street
Atlanta, Georgia 30303
http://www.ganb.uscourts.gov

United States Bankruptcy Court
P.O. Box 8347-E
Savannah, Georgia 31412
www.ganb.uscourts.gov

HAWAII

United States Bankruptcy Court
P.O. Box 50121-S
1132 Bishop Street, Suite 250-L
Honolulu, Hawaii 96813
http://www.hib.uscourts.gov

IDAHO

United States Bankruptcy Court
P.O. Box 2600-O
550 W. Fort St. MSC 042
Boise, Idaho 83724
http://www.id.uscourts.gov

ILLINOIS

United States Bankruptcy Court
P.O. Box 2438-M
Springfield, Illinois 62705
http://www.ilcb.uscourts.gov

United States Bankruptcy Court
219 South Dearborn Street
Chicago, Illinois 60604
http://www.ilnb.uscourts.gov

United States Bankruptcy Court
P.O. Box 309
750 Missouri Avenue
East St. Louis, Illinois 62201
http://www.ilsb.uscourts.gov

INDIANA

United States Bankruptcy Court
204 South Main Street
South Bend, Indiana 46601
http://www.innd.uscourts.gov

United States Bankruptcy Court
610 Connecticut Street
Gary, Indiana 46402
http://www.innb.uscourts.gov

United States Bankruptcy Court
46 East Ohio Street
Indianapolis, Indiana 46204
http://www.insd.uscourts.gov

IOWA

United States Bankruptcy Court
425 Second St. SE
Cedar Rapids, Iowa 52407
http://www.ianb.uscourts.gov

KANSAS

United States Bankruptcy Court
401 North Market Street
Wichita, Kansas 67202
http://www.ksb.uscourts.gov

KENTUCKY

United States Bankruptcy Court
P.O. Box 1111-E
100 East Vine St. #200
Lexington, Kentucky 40507
http://www.kyeb.uscourts.gov

United States Bankruptcy Court
601 West Broadway
Louisville, Kentucky 40202
http://www.kywd.uscourts.gov

LOUISIANA

United States Bankruptcy Court
500 Camp Street
New Orleans, Louisiana 70130
http://www.laed.uscourts.gov

United States Bankruptcy Court
500 Fannin Street
Shreveport, Louisiana 71109
http://www.lawb.uscourts.gov

United States Bankruptcy Court
412 North 4th Street
Baton Rouge, Louisiana 70802
http://www.laed.uscourts.gov

MAINE

United States Bankruptcy Court
537 Congress St.
Portland, Maine 04101
http://www.meb.uscourts.gov

MARYLAND

United States Bankruptcy Court
101 West Lombard Street
Baltimore, Maryland 21201
http://www.mdd.uscourts.gov

MASSACHUSETTS

United States Bankruptcy Court
1101 Thomas O'Neill Federal Building
Boston, Massachusetts 02222-1074
http://www.mab.uscourts.gov

MICHIGAN

United States Bankruptcy Court
211 W. Fort Street
Detroit, Michigan 48226
http://www.mieb.uscourts.gov

United States Bankruptcy Court
110 Michigan Street. NW
Grand Rapids, Michigan 49503
http://www.miwd.uscourts.gov

MINNESOTA

United States Bankruptcy Court
316 North Robert Street
Saint Paul, Minnesota 55101
http://www.mnb.uscourts.gov

United States Bankruptcy Court
300 South 4th Street
Minneapolis, Minnesota 55415
http://www.mnb.uscourts.gov

MISSISSIPPI

United States Bankruptcy Court
301 W. Commerce St.
Aberdeen, Mississippi 39730
http://www.msnb.uscourts.gov

United States Bankruptcy Court
245 East Capitol Street, Suite 316
Jackson, Mississippi 39201
http://www.mssd.uscourts.gov

United States Bankruptcy Court
725 Washington Loop
Biloxi, Mississippi 39530
http://www.msnd.uscourts.gov

MISSOURI

United States Bankruptcy Court
211 N. Broadway
St. Louis, Missouri 63102-2734
http://www.moed.uscourts.gov

United States Bankruptcy Court
400 E. 9th St., Room 1800
Kansas City, Missouri 64106
http://www.moept.uscourts.gov

MONTANA

United States Bankruptcy Court
400 N. Main St.
Butte, Montana 59701
http://www.mtb.uscourts.gov

NEBRASKA

United States Bankruptcy Court
215 N. 17th St., Room 8400
Omaha, Nebraska 68102
http://www.ned.uscourts.gov

United States Bankruptcy Court
460 Federal Building
100 Centennial Mall
Lincoln, Nebraska 68508
http://ned.uscourts.gov

NEVADA

United States Bankruptcy Court
300 Las Vegas Boulevard, Room 3210
Las Vegas, Nevada 89101
http://www.nvb.uscourts.gov

United States Bankruptcy Court
300 Booth Street, Room 1109
Reno, Nevada 89509
http://nvb.uscourts.gov

NEW HAMPSHIRE

United States Bankruptcy Court
55 Pleasant Street, Room 110
Concord, New Hampshire 03301-3941
http://www.nhd.uscourts.gov

NEW JERSEY

United States Bankruptcy Court
401 Market Street, 2nd Floor
Camden, New Jersey 08101
http://www.njb.uscourts.gov

United States Bankruptcy Court
402 E. State Street
Trenton, New Jersey 08608
http://www.njb.uscourts.gov

United States Bankruptcy Court
50 Walnut Street
Newark, New Jersey 07102
http://www.njb.uscourts.gov

NEW MEXICO

United States Bankruptcy Court
421 Gold Avenue SW, Room 314
Albuquerque, New Mexico 87103
http://www.nmcourt.fed.us/bkdocs

NEW YORK

United States Bankruptcy Court
225 Cadman Plaza East
Brooklyn, New York 11201
http://www.nyed.uscourts.gov

United States Bankruptcy Court
1 Bowling Green
New York, New York 10004
http://www.nysb.uscourts.gov

United States Bankruptcy Court
445 Broadway, Room 222
Albany, New York 12207-2924
www.nynd.uscourts.gov

United States Bankruptcy Court
300 Pearl St., Suite 250
Buffalo, New York 14202-2501
www.nywb.uscourts.gov

United States Bankruptcy Court
100 State Street
Rochester, New York 14614
http://www.nywb.uscourts.gov

NORTH CAROLINA

United States Bankruptcy Court
1760 Parkwood Blvd
Wilson, North Carolina 27894-2807
http://www.nceb.uscourts.gov

United States Bankruptcy Court
300 Fayetteville Street Mall
P.O. Box 144-B
Raleigh, North Carolina 27602-1441
http://www.ncmb.uscourts.gov

United States Bankruptcy Court
P.O. Box 26100-O
101 S. Edgeworth St.
Greensboro, North Carolina 27401
http://www.ncmb.uscourts.gov

United States Bankruptcy Court
100 Otis Street
Asheville, North Carolina 28801
http://www.ncwd.uscourts.gov

NORTH DAKOTA

http://www.ndb.uscourts.gov
United States Bankruptcy Court
P.O. Box 1110-O
655 First Avenue N
Fargo, North Dakota 58107

OHIO

United States Bankruptcy Court
1716 Spielbusch Avenue
Toledo, Ohio 43624
http://www.ohnb.uscourts.gov

United States Bankruptcy Court
127 Public Square
Cleveland, Ohio 44114-1309
http://www.ohnb.uscourts.gov

United States Bankruptcy Court
2 South Main Street
Akron, Ohio 44308
http://www.ohnb.uscourts.gov

United States Bankruptcy Court
125 Market Street
Youngstown, Ohio 44501
http://www.ohnb.uscourts.gov

United States Bankruptcy Court
201 Cleveland Avenue SW
Canton, Ohio 44702
http://www.ohnb.uscourts.gov

OKLAHOMA

United States Bankruptcy Court
224 S. Boulder Avenue
Tulsa, Oklahoma 74103
http://www.oknb.uscourts.gov

United States Bankruptcy Court
111 W. 4th Street, Room 229
Okmulgee, Oklahoma 74447
http://www.okeb.uscourts.gov

United States Bankruptcy Court
201 Dean McGee Avenue
Oklahoma City, Oklahoma 73102
http://oknb.uscourts.gov

OREGON

United States Bankruptcy Court
P.O. Box 1335-U
Eugene, Oregon 97440
http://www.ord.uscourts.gov/

United States Bankruptcy Court
1001 Southwest Fifth Avenue
Portland, Oregon 97204
http://www.ord.uscourts.gov

PENNSYLVANIA

United States Bankruptcy Court
600 Grant Street
Pittsburgh, Pennsylvania 15219
http://www.pawb.uscourts.gov

United States Bankruptcy Court
197 South Main Street
Wilkes Barre, Pennsylvania 18701
http://www.pamd.uscourts.gov

United States Bankruptcy Court
601 Market Street, Room 2609
Philadelphia, Pennsylvania 19106-1797
http://www.paed.uscourts.gov

RHODE ISLAND

United States Bankruptcy Court
380 Westminster Mall
Providence, Rhode Island 02903
http://www.rib.uscourts.gov

SOUTH CAROLINA

United States Bankruptcy Court
P.O. Box 1448-S
1100 Laurel Street
Columbia, South Carolina 29202
http://www.scb.uscourts.gov

SOUTH DAKOTA

United States Bankruptcy Court
400 S. Phillips Avenue, Room 117
Sioux Falls, South Dakota 57117
http://www.sdb.uscourts.gov

TENNESSEE

United States Bankruptcy Court
800 Market Street, Suite 330
Knoxville, Tennessee 37902
http://www.tneb.uscourts.gov

United States Bankruptcy Court
701 Broadway, P.O. Box 24890-J
Nashville, Tennessee 37202
http://www.tnmb.uscourts.gov

TEXAS

United States Bankruptcy Court
200 East Ferguson Street
Tyler, Texas 75702
http://www.txeb.uscourts.gov

United States Bankruptcy Court
1100 Commerce Street, Room 12A24
Dallas, Texas 75242-1496
http://www.txnb.uscourts.gov

United States Bankruptcy Court
501 West 10th Street
Fort Worth, Texas 76102-3643
http://www.txnb.uscourts.gov

United States Bankruptcy Court
1205 Texas Avenue
Lubbock, Texas 79401-4002
http://www.txnb.uscourts.gov

United States Bankruptcy Court
P.O. Box 15960-O
Amarillo, Texas 79105-0960
http://www.txeb.uscourts.com

United States Bankruptcy Court
515 Rusk Avenue
Houston, Texas 77002
http://www.txnd.uscourts.gov

United States Bankruptcy Court
P.O. Box 1439-E
San Antonio, Texas 78295
http://www.txeb.uscourts.com

UTAH

United States Bankruptcy Court
350 South Main Street
Salt Lake City, Utah 84101
http://www.state.ut.us/government.htm

VERMONT

United States Bankruptcy Court
P.O. Box 6648-P
Rutland, Vermont 05702
http://www.state.vt.us/

VIRGINIA

United States Bankruptcy Court
200 South Washington Street
Alexandria, Virginia 22314
http://www.vaeb.uscourts.gov

United States Bankruptcy Court
1100 E. Main St., Suite 310
Richmond, Virginia 23219-3515
http://www.vaeb.uscourts.gov

United States Bankruptcy Court
600 Granby Street, 4th Floor
Norfolk, Virginia 23510
http://www.vaeb.uscourts.gov

United States Bankruptcy Court
101 25th Street, Room 106
Newport News, Virginia 23607
http://vaeb.uscourts.com

United States Bankruptcy Court
210 Church Avenue SW, Room 200
Roanoke, Virginia 24011
http://www.vawb.uscourts.gov

WASHINGTON

United States Bankruptcy Court
904 W. Riverside, Suite 304
P.O. Box 2164-I
Spokane, Washington 99201
http://www.waeb.uscourts.gov

United States Bankruptcy Court
1200 Sixth Avenue, Room 315
Seattle, Washington 98101
http://www.wawb.uscourts.gov

WEST VIRGINIA

United States Bankruptcy Court
324 Main Street,
Clarkesburg, West Virginia 26302
http://www.wvnb.uscourts.gov

United States Bankruptcy Court
12th and Chapline Streets
Wheeling, West Virginia 26003
http://www.wvnb.uscourts.gov

WISCONSIN

United States Bankruptcy Court
517 East Wisconsin Avenue
Milwaukee, Wisconsin 53202
http://www.wieb.uscourts.gov

United States Bankruptcy Court
P.O. Box 548
Madison, Wisconsin 53701
http://www.wieb.uscourts.gov

WYOMING

United States Bankruptcy Court
2120 Capitol Avenue
Cheyenne, Wyoming 82001
http://www.wyb.uscourts.gov

John L. Cawler
Name
59 Huser Lane Apt. 23
Street
Nanuet, New York   10954
City, State, Zip
914-675-7723
Telephone

☐ Attorney for Debtor(s)   (If applicable) Attorney's

☒ Debtor In Pro SE   State Bar I.D. No _____

RECORDED

MAR 20 1993

CLERK OF CIRCUIT

UNITED STATES BANKRUPTCY COURT
Northeast   **DISTRICT OF** New York

In re _____
*[Set forth here all names including married, maiden, and trade
names used by debtor within last 6 years.]*

John L. Cawler   Debtor
Cawler Liquor Store
Cawler Food and Gas Station
Barbara Cawler
Barbara Cawler's Secretarial Service
Social Security No(s). 078-90-0064   and all
Employer's Tax Identification Nos.*[If any]*_____

Case No. 93-827361-9

Chapter Chapter 13

NOTICE OF AVAILABLE CHAPTERS BY THE CLERK OF THE COURT

1. Section 342(b) of 11 U.S. Code ("The Bankruptcy Code") states:
   "Prior to the commencement of a case under this title by an individual whose debts are primarily consumer debts, the clerk shall give written notice to such individual that indicates each chapter of this title under which such individual may proceed."

2. If your debts are primarily consumer ones (as opposed to business debts) and they do not exceed $100,000.00 unsecured or $350,000.00 secured (11 U.S.C. § 109(e)), you are eligible to file under Chapter 13 and to use future income to pay all or a portion of your existing debts.

3. You are also eligible to file under Chapter 11 ($500.00 filing fees) for debt reorganization.

4. You are not eligible to file under Chapter 9.

5. You are eligible to file under Chapter 7 ("straight bankruptcy"), whereby debts are eliminated and your non-exempt assets are liquidated by the trustee for the benefit of your creditors.

6. You may be eligible to file under Chapter 12.

7. All general filing eligibility is subject to 11 U.S.C. §§ 109, 727(a)(8) and (9), and 707(b). Consult your attorney.

Robert T. Vernon, Jr.
Clerk of the Court

I HAVE READ THE ABOVE "NOTICE OF AVAILABLE CHAPTERS".

Signature of Debtor

Signature of Joint Debtor

You will be able to find your subject in the bankruptcy files by name only. When you find the first application to the bankruptcy court, you will note that you now have the case number. Pull the entire file using this number. The subject's Social Security Number is listed along with any other important information, including the address, home telephone number, spouse's name, etc. Pay attention to the type of bankruptcy your subject claimed. Earlier in this chapter, I explained what types of bankruptcies an individual can claim. If the subject claimed Chapter 11, then he may have only reorganized his debt, **and he may still be making payments to creditors years later.**

NOTES

Workers'
Compensation Records

When the background profile on your subject does not reveal a driver's license, vehicle or boat registration, a license for one of the hundreds of professions that require licensing by the state, or any of the other facets of a normal paper trail, then turn to the Workers' Compensation Bureau.

Persons who receive benefits from the Workers' Compensation Bureau are those who have suffered injuries during the performance of their jobs. Your subject may be a **complete phony and may be collecting monies from worker's compensation.** Many workers' compensation claim cases require that the person not engage in any employment and may restrict sports activities, traveling outside the home or routine functions, such as driving an automobile. This would account for the odd behavior of your subject if he does not do any of the aforementioned activities.

Many states will provide a complete file which, of course, may yield information including addresses, previous employers, **spouses**, dependents, etc. It is important to remember that states may change their policies on releasing compensation information. Many states, including California, Florida, and New Jersey, consider Workers' Compensation files public records, whereas certain states will not release information. Write and inquire about the current policy using the following list.

WORKERS COMPENSATION

ALABAMA

http://www.dir.state.al.us/wc.htm
Workman's Compensation Division
Industrial Relation Building
649 Monroe St.
Montgomery, Alabama 36131
(334) 242-2868 or (800) 528-5166

ALASKA

http://www.labor.state.ak.us/wc/wcbrochr.htm
Workers' Compensation Division
P.O. Box 25512
Juneau, Alaska 99802
(907) 465-2790

ARIZONA

http://www.statefund.com/toc.htm
State Compensation Fund
3031 North Second Street, Suite 110
Phoenix, Arizona 85012
(602) 631-2900
Fax: (602) 631-2955

ARKANSAS

http://www.awcc.state.ar.us/ruleind.html
Workers' Compensation Commission
4th and Spring Streets
Little Rock, Arkansas 72203-0950
(501) 682-3930 or (800) 622-4472

CALIFORNIA

http://www.dir.ca.gov/
Commission on Health, Safety, and
Workers' Compensation
455 Golden Gate Avenue, 10th Floor
San Francisco, California 94102
(415) 703-4220

COLORADO

http://workerscomp.cdle.state.co.us
Division of Workers' Compensation
1515 Arapahoe
Denver, Colorado 80202-2117
(303) 575-8700 or (888) 390-7936

CONNECTICUT

http://wcc.state.ct.us
Workers' Compensation Commission
21 Oak Street
Hartford, Connecticut 06106
(860) 493-1500
Fax: (860) 247-1361

DELAWARE

http://www.state.de.us/
Industrial Accident Board
820 North French Street
Wilmington, Delaware 19801

DISTRICT OF COLUMBIA

http://www.washingtondc.gov/
Office of Workers' Compensation
P.O. Box 56098
Washington, DC 20011

FLORIDA

http://www.fdles.state.fl.us/wc/
Division of Workers' Compensation
2810 Sharer Road, Suite 27
Tallahassee, Florida 32312-2107
(850) 922-0426
Fax: (850) 414-1238

GEORGIA

http://www.ganet.org/sbwc
Board of Workers' Compensation
270 Peachtree Street NW
Atlanta, Georgia 30303-1299
(404) 656-2048

HAWAII

http://www.uhwo.hawaii.edu/clear/HRS
386-1.html
Disability Compensation Division
96-043 Ala Ike
Pearl City, Hawaii 96782-3366
(808) 454-4774
Fax: (808) 454-4776

IDAHO

http://www.state.id.us/
Idaho Industrial Commission
317 Main Street
Boise, Idaho 83720

ILLINOIS

http://www.state.il.us/agency/iic
Illinois Industrial Commission
100 West Randolph St. #8-200
Chicago, Illinois 60601
(312) 814-6611

INDIANA

http://www.state.in.us/wkcomp
Workers' Compensation
Industrial Board
402 W. Washington Street, Rm. W-196
Indianapolis, Indiana 46204
(317) 232-3809

IOWA

http://www.state.ia.us/
Industrial Commissioner's Office
1000 East Grand Street
Des Moines, Iowa 50319

KANSAS

http://www.hr.state.ks.us/wc/html/wc.htm
Workers' Compensation
Department of Human Resources
800 SW Jackson, Room 600
Topeka, Kansas 66612-1227
(785) 296-3441

KENTUCKY

http://www.state.ky.us/agencies/
Kentucky Labor Cabinet
1047 U.S. 127S, Suite 4
Frankfort, Kentucky 40601
(502) 573-3505

LOUISIANA

http://www.state.la.us/
Office of Workers' Compensation
224 Florida Blvd, Suite 100
Baton Rouge, Louisiana 70801
(225) 219-4378 or (800) 209-7175
Fax: (225) 219-4377

MAINE

http://www.state.me.us/
Workers' Compensation Commission
24 Stone Street
Augusta, Maine 04330
(207) 287-2308 or (800) 400-6854

MARYLAND

http://www.charm.net/~wcc
Workers' Compensation Commission
6 North Liberty Street
Baltimore, Maryland 21201-3785
(410) 767-0900 or (800) 492-0479
Fax: (410) 333-8122

MASSACHUSETTS

http://www.magnet.state.ma.us/wcac
Workers' Compensation Advisory Council
600 Washington Street
Boston, Massachusetts 02111
(617) 727-4900 x 378
Fax: (617) 727-7122

MICHIGAN

http://www.cis.state.mi.us/wkrcomp/
Workers' Compensation Appellate Commission
1375 S. Washington
Lansing, Michigan 48909-7968
(517) 334-9719
Fax: (517) 334-9750

MINNESOTA

http://www.doli.state.mn.us/workcomp.html
Minnesota Department
of Labor and Industry
443 Layafette Road N.
St. Paul, Minnesota 55155
(651) 297-4377 or (800) 342-5354

MISSISSIPPI

http://www.mwcc.state.ms.us
Workers' Compensation Commission
1428 Lakeland Drive
Jackson, Mississippi 39216
(601) 987-4294 or (800) 840-3550

MISSOURI

http://www.dolir.state.mo.us/wc
Division of Workers' Compensation
P.O. Box 58
Jefferson City, Missouri 65102-0058
(573) 751-4231
Fax: (573) 751-2012

MONTANA

http://www.state.mt.us/
Division of Workers' Compensation
5 South Last Chance Gulch
Helena, Montana 59604

NEBRASKA

http://www.state.ne.us/
Workers' Compensation Court
P.O. Box 98908
Lincoln, Nebraska 65809

NEVADA

http://www.state.nv.us/
Department of Industrial Relations
1390 South Curry Street
Carson City, Nevada 98710

NEW HAMPSHIRE

http://www.state.nh.us/
Workers' Compensation Board
19 Pillsbury Street
Concord, New Hampshire 03301

NEW JERSEY

http://www.state.nj.us/
Division of Workers' Compensation
State Office Building, Room 381
Trenton, New Jersey 08625

NEW MEXICO

http://www.state.nm.us/
Workers' Compensation Division
P.O. Box 27198
Albuquerque, New Mexico 87125

NEW YORK

http://www.ci.nyc.ny.us/
State Insurance Fund
199 Church Street
New York, New York 10007

NORTH CAROLINA

http://www.state.nc.us/
Industrial Commission
430 North Salisbury Street
Raleigh, North Carolina 27611

NORTH DAKOTA

http://www.state.nd.us/
Workers' Compensation Bureau
4007 North State Street
Bismarck, North Dakota 58501

OHIO

http://www.state.oh.us/
Bureau of Workers' Compensation
246 North High Street
Columbus, Ohio 43215

OKLAHOMA

http://www.state.ok.us/
Oklahoma Workers' Compensation Court
1915 North Stiles
Oklahoma City, Oklahoma 73105

OREGON

http://www.state.or.us/
Department of Insurance and Finance
Labor and Industries Building
Salem, Oregon 97310

PENNSYLVANIA

http://www.state.pa.us/
Bureau of Workers' Compensation
1171 South Cameron Street
Harrisburg, Pennsylvania 17104

PUERTO RICO

http://fortaleza.govpr.org/
State Insurance Fund
GPO Box 5038
San Juan, Puerto Rico 00936

RHODE ISLAND

http://www.state.ri.us/
Department of Workers' Compensation
610 Manton Avenue
Providence, Rhode Island 02909

SOUTH CAROLINA

http://www.state.sc.us/
Industrial Commission
1615 Marian Street
Columbia, South Carolina 29202

SOUTH DAKOTA

http://www.state.sd.us/
Department of Labor
700 Governors Drive
Pierre, South Dakota 57501

TENNESSEE

http://www.state.tn.us/
Workers' Compensation Division
501 Union Building
Nashville, Tennessee 37219

TEXAS

http://www.state.tx.us/
Industrial Accident Board
200 East Riverside Drive
Austin, Texas 78704

UTAH

http://www.state.tx.us/
Workers' Compensation Fund
P.O. Box 510250
Salt Lake City, Utah 84151

VERMONT

http://www.state.vt.us/
Department of Labor and Industry
120 State Street
Montpelier, Vermont 05602

VIRGINIA

http://www.state.va.us/
Industrial Commission
P.O. Box 1794
Richmond, Virginia 23220

WASHINGTON

http://access.wa.gov/
Department of Labor and Industries
General Administration Building
Olympia, Washington 98504

WEST VIRGINIA

http://www.state.wv.us/
Workers' Compensation Appeal Board
601 Morris Street
Charleston, West Virginia 25301

WISCONSIN

http://www.state.wi.us/
Workers' Compensation Bureau
P.O. Box 7901
Madison, Wisconsin 53707

WYOMING

http://www.state.wy.us
Workers' Compensation Division
122 West 25th Street
Cheyenne, Wyoming 82002

STATE OF INDIANA   EVAN BAYH - GOVERNOR

WORKER'S COMPENSATION BOARD   402 West Washington Street, Room W196
Rogelio Dominguez - Chairman   Indianapolis, Indiana 46204
                                        Telephone: (317) 232-3808

March 23, 1993

          RE: Robert K. Pavella - S. S. #242-23-8376
               Date of Birth: June 17, 1935

Dear Mr. Culligan:

This will acknowledge receipt of your request of February 16 1993,
concerning the above named individual.

Be advised that a diligent search of our files fails to reveal any worker's
compensation records filed by or on behalf of Mr. Panus while employed in
our State. However, this Board is not liable for any oversight or any
reliance thereof. If you feel further investigation is necessary, you
should do so.

Sincerely yours,

WORKER'S COMPENSATION BOARD OF INDIANA

DOUGLAS MEAGHER
Executive Secretary

You will note that the letter states "while employed in our state." Beware
that Workers' Compensation cases are routinely transferred to other states
under reciprocal agreements because many times an individual has to move,
"to a warmer climate because of health reasons." The receiving state will
have jurisdiction over the claimant and will monitor the case. That is why
this letter had the caveat "not liable for any oversight," since these cases
are not on file with the regular cases. If your inquiry yields a response stating your subject did have a claim, then evaluate the paperwork that is sent
to you. See what addresses, telephone numbers, and spouses' names are
listed, but most important of all, see when the benefits stopped. If he is still
collecting and you are aware he is currently employed, **there may be an
arrest for fraud in this man's future.**

STATE OF ALASKA

DEPARTMENT OF LABOR

DIVISION OF WORKERS' COMPENSATION

WALTER J. HICKEL, GOVERNOR

1111 WEST 8TH, ROOM 305
P.O. BOX 25512
JUNEAU, ALASKA 99802-5512
PHONE: (907) 465-2790
FAX: (907) 465-2797

March 11, 1993

RE: Claims information request on Robert K. Pavella

There are no claims on record for this individual. If you have any
questions, please contact me at 465-6046.

Sincerely,

Susan N. Oldacres
Secretary

Most states will give you a prompt response as illustrated above. You will
have telephone numbers to query the Workers' Compensation Department
if you have any further questions. When you get a response of "no claims
on record" and you feel that this person did have a claim, then you will
want to make another inquiry. Ask if the search was made manually or by
computer. Most of the states have been on computer for the past several
years but did not input all the older files in the computer. If the response
tells you it was done by a computer, ask that a manual search be conducted
through the old files.

BRERETON C. JONES
GOVERNOR

WORKERS' COMPENSATION BOARD
JUDGE ARMAND ANGELUCCI, CHAIRMAN
LARRY M. GREATHOUSE, MEMBER
WALTER W. TURNER, MEMBER

COMMISSIONER
L. T. GRANT

ADMINISTRATIVE LAW JUDGES
RICHARD H. CAMPBELL, JR.
W. BRUCE COWDEN, JR.
THOMAS A. DOCKTER
LLOYD R. EDENS
EDWARD L. FOSSETT
JAMES L. KERR
DENIS S. KLINE
DWIGHT T. LOVAN
RONALD W. MAY
THOMAS A. NANNEY
WILLARD B. PAXTON
ROGER D. RIGGS
GEORGE S. SCHUHMANN
IRENE C. STEEN
DONNA H. TERRY

DEPARTMENT OF WORKERS' CLAIMS
Perimeter Park West, Building C
1270 Louisville Road
Frankfort, Kentucky 40601
Telephone (502) 564-5550

Dear Sir or Madam:

The Department of Workers' Claims has received your request
for a work history or claim check on the attached
individual(s).

Using the information contained within your original
letter, such as the employee name and his/her social
security number, I checked back to 1978 and have been
unable to locate any **lost time injuries**, claims or
agreements.

If you have any questions concerning this matter, please
do not hesitate to contact me.

Sincerely,

Deborah S. Wingate
Open Records Specialist

This agency does not discriminate on the basis of race, color, national
origin, sex, religion, age or disability in employment or provision of services.

Printed on recycled paper

The above response indicates that this Department of Workers Compensation searched back to 1978. In this case, you will note that this specialist not only searched for any claims but also for "agreements." **Many times an employee will elect to cut a deal for a one-time sum of money instead of receiving a monthly payment.** Usually these agreements will show up in a normal trace but I suggest you ask specifically for a search for any "agreements," like I did in this case. "Agreements" paperwork will give you much information about your subject that was heretofore unknown to you.

Workers' Compensation Division
21 Labor & Industries Building, Salem, OR 97310   FAX: (503) 378-6828

Oregon

DEPARTMENT OF
INSURANCE AND
FINANCE

February 25, 1993

RE: Claimant: Robert K. Pavella
     SSN: 242/23/8376

     DOB: 6/17/35

This is in response to your letter requesting information on the
above-captioned claimant.

Based on the information provided, the claimant identified in your letter has
not been found in our data system. Claims are submitted to the Department
only when they are disabling or a denial has been issued.

R. Sherwood

Rebecca A. Sherwood
Information Unit
Operations Section

This letter states that the claims are only sent to this office when a claim is disabling or the state has denied the claim. An active claim that has not been adjudicated will not show up, so you may want to write another inquiry in several months. When you get a response that indicates your subject has made no workers' compensation claim, you will want to write another letter using other variations of your subject's name. In the above case, the second requests would include the names Pavelli, Pavello, Pavell and Bob, Bobby, Roberto, etc.

NOTES

Corporations
and UCC Filings

A person is listed in state corporate records if he is an officer, director, or registered agent. Write to the corporation division of your state government. Most states will be able to provide a list of all persons with a particular name, the names of the corporations with which they are associated, and the addresses of the corporations. Many times the **home addresses** will be listed for officers and directors in smaller corporations.

The corporate division will also conduct a search that will generate a list of all persons with a particular name who have a Uniform Commercial Code transaction. The UCC, in most states, is a transaction that is intended to create a security interest in personal property or fixtures, including goods, documents, instruments, general intangibles, chattel paper, and a contract that creates a security interest in a chattel trust, trust deed, equipment trust, conditional sale, trust receipt, and lease or consignment intended as security.

If your subject has, for example, ever lent money or equipment to someone who has opened a business or has borrowed money or equipment, then he would be listed in UCC transactions. When you isolate your subject on the UCC list, you will want to order a complete photocopy of the transaction. This will show the business and/or **home** address of the subject, the names of any witnesses, the name of the business, and the name of the other party to the transaction.

Your subject may not want you to know the full **extent of his wealth.**

He may hide monies, properties, vehicles, etc., in the name of a corporation. We all have known someone who has said he has his automobiles, condominiums, and houses under the "company" name. Now you will be able to find the "company."

When you get the name of the corporation(s) in which your subject is involved, you will want to check for automobiles, boats, planes, property, etc., under the corporation name.

Since most organizations, teams, churches, associations, and clubs require incorporation, your subject may be listed as having an involvement in a corporation. You may find out social activities that may have interested your subject in his life before you, which, of course, will give you new places and people to explore so that your background and investigation will be comprehensive.

SECRETARIES OF STATE

ALABAMA

http://www.sos.state.al.us
Office of the Secretary of State
Corporations Division
State of Alabama
P.O. Box 5616-R
Montgomery, Alabama 36103

ALASKA

http://www.state.ak.us/
Division of Corporations
State of Alaska
P.O. Box 110807-O
Juneau, Alaska 99811

AMERICAN SAMOA

Corporations
Territory of American Samoa
Moata Fona
Pago Pago, American Samoa 96799

ARIZONA

http://www.state.az.us/
Arizona Corporation Commission
Secretary of State
State of Arizona
1200 West Washington
Phoenix, Arizona 85005

ARKANSAS

http://www.state.ar.us/
Office of the Secretary of State
Corporation Department
State of Arkansas
State Capital
Little Rock, Arkansas 72201

CALIFORNIA

http://www.state.ca.us/
Office of the Secretary of State
Corporation Division
State of California
1230 J Street
Sacramento, California 95814

COLORADO

http://www.state.co.us/gov_dir/sos
Department of State
Corporation Section
1560 Broadway, Suite 200
Denver, Colorado 80202

CONNECTICUT

http://www.sots.state.ct.us/
Office of the Secretary of State
Corporations
30 Trinity Street
Hartford, Connecticut 06106

DELAWARE

http://www.state.de.us/
Secretary of State
Division of Corporations
State of Delaware
P.O. Box 793-B
Dover, Delaware 19903

DISTRICT OF COLUMBIA

Recorder of Deeds
Recorder of Deeds Building
6th and D Street, N.W.
Washington, DC 20001

FLORIDA

http://www.dos.state.fl.us/
Office of the Secretary of State
Division of Corporations
State of Florida
P.O. Box 6327-I
Tallahassee, Florida 32301

GEORGIA

http://www.sos.state.ga.us/
Office of the Secretary of State
Corporations
State of Georgia
#2 Martin Luther King Jr. Drive S.E.
Atlanta, Georgia 30034

GUAM

Corporations
Government of Guam
P.O. Box 2796-N
Agana, Guam 96910

HAWAII

http://www.state.hi.us/
Department of Regulatory Agencies
Corporations
State of Hawaii
1010 Richards Street
Honolulu, Hawaii 96813

IDAHO

http://www.idsos.state.id.us/
Office of the Secretary of State
Corporations
State of Idaho
Statehouse, Room 203
Boise, Idaho 83720

ILLINOIS

http://www.sos.state.il.us/
Office of the Secretary
Corporation Department
State of Illinois
Centennial Building, Room 328
Springfield, Illinois 62756

INDIANA

http://www.state.in.us/sos
Office of the Secretary of State
Corporation Division
State of Indiana
Statehouse, Room 155
Indianapolis, Indiana 46204

IOWA

http://www.sos.state.ia.us
Office of the Secretary of State
Corporation Division
East 14th & Walnut Streets
Des Moines, Iowa 50319

KANSAS

http://www.kssos.org
Office of the Secretary of State
Corporation Services
Statehouse, Room 200
Topeka, Kansas 66612

KENTUCKY

http://www.sos.state.ky.us
Office of the Secretary of State
Corporation Department
State of Kentucky
P.O. 718-B
Frankfort, Kentucky 40602

LOUISIANA

http://www.sec.state.la.us
Department of State
Corporation Division
State of Louisiana
P.O. Box 94125-A
Baton Rouge, Louisiana 70804

MAINE

http://www.state.me.us/sos/sos.htm
Secretary of State
Bureau of Corporations
State of Maine
Statehouse, Station 101
Augusta, Maine 04333

MARSHALL ISLANDS

Corporations
P.O. Box 100-R
Republic of the Marshall Islands
Mojuro, Marshall Islands 96960

MARYLAND

http://www.sos.state.md.us
Department of Assessments & Taxations
Corporations
State of Maryland
301 West Preston Street
Baltimore, Maryland 21201

MASSACHUSETTS

http://www.magnet.state.ma.us/sec
Secretary of the Commonwealth
Corporations Division
One Ashburton Place, Room 1713
Boston, Massachusetts, 02133

MICHIGAN

http://www.sos.state.mi.us
Department of Commerce
Corporation Division
State of Michigan
6546 Mercantile Drive
Lansing, Michigan 48909

MICRONESIA

Corporations
Department of Resources
& Development
FSM National Government
Kolonia, Ponape, E.C.I. 96941

MINNESOTA

http://www.sos.state.mn.us
Office of the Secretary of State
Corporation Division
State of Minnesota
State Office Building, Room 180
St. Paul, Minnesota 55155

MISSISSIPPI

http://www.sos.state.ms.us
Office of the Secretary of State
Corporations
State of Mississippi
P.O. Box 136
Jackson, Mississippi 39205

MISSOURI

http://mosl.sos.state.mo.us
Office of the Secretary of State
Corporations
State of Missouri
P.O. Box 1159
Jefferson City, Missouri 65101

MONTANA

http://www.state.mt.us/
Office of the Secretary of State
Corporations Bureau
State Capitol, Room 202
Helena, Montana 59620

NEBRASKA

http://www.state.ne.us/
Office of the Secretary of State
Corporation Department
State of Nebraska
301 Centennial Mall South
Lincoln, Nebraska 68509

NEVADA

http://sos.state.nv.us
Office of the Secretary of State
Corporation Department
State of Nevada
Capitol Complex
Carson City, Nevada 89710

NEW HAMPSHIRE

http://www.state.nh.us/
Office of the Secretary of State
Corporate Division
State of New Hampshire
Statehouse Annex, Room 204
Concord, New Hampshire 03301

NEW JERSEY

http://www.state.nj.us/state
Office of the Secretary of State
Corporations
State of New Jersey
Statehouse, CN 308
Trenton, New Jersey 08625

NEW MEXICO

http://web.state.nm.us/
Secretary of State
State Corporation Commission
State of New Mexico
State Office Building, Room 420
Santa Fe, New Mexico 87503

NEW YORK

http://www.state.ny.us/
Department of State
Division of Corporations
State of New York
162 Washington Avenue
Albany, New York 12231

NORTH CAROLINA

http://www.state.nc.us/
Office of the Secretary of State
Corporation Division
300 North Salisbury Street
Raleigh, North Carolina 27611

NORTH DAKOTA

http://www.state.nd.us/
Office of the Secretary of State
Division of Corporations
State of North Dakota
601 East Boulevard Avenue
Bismarck, North Dakota 58501

OHIO

http://www.state.oh.us/
Office of the Secretary of State
Corporations Department
State of Ohio
50 East Broad Street
Columbus, Ohio 43215

OKLAHOMA

http://www.state.ok.us/
Office of the Secretary of State
Corporation Department
State of Oklahoma
State Capitol Building, Room 101
Oklahoma City, Oklahoma 73105

OREGON

http://www.state.or.us/
Department of Commerce
Corporation Division
State of Oregon
158 12th Street, N.E.
Salem, Oregon 97310

PENNSYLVANIA

http://www.state.pa.us/
Office of the Secretary of State
Corporations Bureau
State of Pennsylvania
North Office Building, Room 308
Harrisburg, Pennsylvania 17120

PUERTO RICO

Corporation Division
Commonwealth of Puerto Rico
Fortaleza Street #50
San Juan, Puerto Rico 00904

RHODE ISLAND

http://www.state.ri.us/
Secretary of State
Corporation Division
State of Rhode Island
270 Westminister Mall
Providence, Rhode Island 02903

SOUTH CAROLINA

http://www.state.sc.us/
Office of the Secretary of State
Corporation Department
State of South Carolina
P.O. Box 11350
Columbia, South Carolina 29211

SOUTH DAKOTA

http://www.state.sd.us/
Office of the Secretary of State
Corporation Department
State of South Dakota
500 East Capitol
Pierre, South Dakota 57501

TENNESSEE

http://www.state.tn.us/
Office of the Secretary of State
Corporation Section
State of Tennessee
James K. Polk, Building, Room 500
Nashville, Tennessee 37219

TEXAS

http://www.sos.state.tx.us
Office of the Secretary of State
Corporations Section
State of Texas
P.O. Box 13193-K
Austin, Texas 78711

UTAH

http://www.state.ut.us/
Secretary of State
Corporations
State of Utah
160 East Third Street
Salt Lake City, Utah 84145

VERMONT

http://www.state.vt.us/
Office of the Secretary of State
Corporations
109 State Street, Pavilion Building
Montpelier, Vermont 05602

VIRGIN ISLANDS

Corporations
Territory of Virgin Islands
Charlette Amalie, St. Thomas
Virgin Islands 00801

VIRGINIA

http://www.soc.state.va.us
Secretary of State
State Corporation Commission
P.O. Box 1197
Richmond, Virginia 23209

WASHINGTON

http://access.wa.gov/
Office of the Secretary of State
Corporations
211 12th Street
Olympia, Washington 98504

WEST VIRGINIA

http://www.state.wv.us/
Office of the Secretary of State
Corporations
State Capitol Building
Charleston, West Virginia 25305

WISCONSIN

http://www.state.wi.us/
Office of the Secretary of State
Division of corporations
P.O. Box 7648-E
Madison, Wisconsin 53707

WYOMING

http://soswy.state.wy.us
Office of the Secretary of State
Corporation
110 Capitol Building
Cheyenne, Wyoming 82002

CANADIAN AGENCIES

ALBERTA

Department of Corporate Affairs
Corporate Registry
10365 97th Street
Edmonton, Alberta T5J 3W7

BRITISH COLUMBIA

Ministry of Corporate Affairs
940 Blanchard Street
Victoria, British Columbia V8W 3E6

MANITOBA

Department of Corporate Affairs
Corporations
10th Floor, Woodsworth Building
405 Broadway Avenue
Winnipeg, Manitoba R3C 3L6

NEW BRUNSWICK

Corporations
348 King Street, Lynch Bldg, 2nd Floor
P.O. Box 6000
Fredericton, New Brunswick E3B 5H1

NEWFOUNDLAND & LABRADOR

Department of Justice
Corporations
P.O. 4750
St. John's, Newfoundland A1C 5T7

NORTHWEST TERRITORIES

Department of Justice
and Public Services
Corporations
Yellowknife, Northwest Territories
X1A 2L9

NOVA SCOTIA

Department of the Attorney General
Corporations
1660 Hollis Street
Halifax, Nova Scotia B3J 2Y4

PRINCE EDWARD ISLAND

Department of Justice
Corporations
73 Rochford Street
Charlottetown,
Prince Edward Island C1A 7N8

ONTARIO

Department of Corporate Affairs
Corporations
555 Yonge Street
Toronto, Ontario M7A 2H6

QUEBEC

Bureau de L'Inspecteur General des
Institutions Financieres
800 Place d'Youville
Quebec, P.Q. G1R 4Y5

SASKATCHEWAN

Department Commercial Affairs
Corporations Branch
1871 Smith Street
Regina, Saskatchewan S4P 3V7

YUKON

Department of Corporate Affairs
Corporate Affairs
P.O. Box 2703-R
Whitehorse, Yukon Y1A 2C6

State of Arkansas
Office of Secretary of State
Little Rock

LIEN SEARCH CERTIFICATE

Uniform Commercial Code

Re: ROBERT K. PAVELLA

STATE OF ARKANSAS
COUNTY OF PULASKI

      I, Bill McCuen, Secretary of State of the State of Arkansas and as such keeper of the records, do hereby certify that the records of this office

(xx)   fail to show any form of financing against the above named.

( )   shows the following information on financing for the above named.

SECURED PARTY NAME & ADDRESS	ASSIGNED TO NAME & ADDRESS	FILE NO.	DATE & HOUR OF FILING

IN TESTIMONY WHEREOF, I have hereunto set my hand and Official Seal on this _____ 19th _____ day of ___ March ___ ,19 93 _____

W.J. "Bill" McCuen
Secretary of State

By _Margaret Mader_

I ran the name Robert K. Pavella for a Uniform Commercial Code. If this individual had been on file for any UCC transaction, then I would have been able to find out what banks had loaned him money, what collateral he had put up, what person, if any, had co-signed the lien agreement. Pay particular note to the length of time the loan is for. Your subject may have also signed to be personally responsible for a loan and this, as you are aware, **would become your obligation after you marry him.** Remember to check each state in which he has resided for corporations and UCC transactions.

STATE OF ALABAMA

OFFICE OF THE SECRETARY OF STATE

BUSINESS DIVISION

BILLY JOE CAMP
SECRETARY OF STATE

February 25, 1993

P.O. BOX 5616
MONTGOMERY, AL 36103

Re: Robert K. Pavella

Dear Sir/Madam:

An examination of the foreign and domestic corporate records on file in this office discloses no record of a corporation(s) by the above name.

With kindest regards, I am

Sincerely,

Billy Joe Camp
Secretary of State

BJC:rj

CORPORATIONS	LANDS & TRADEMARKS	UNIFORM COMMERCIAL CODE
(205) 242-5324	(205) 242-5325	(205) 242-5231

This will be the typical response from most states. You will note that there was no mention of any charge for this search on Robert K. Pavella. When there is information on file about your subject, you will want to order the Articles of Incorporation, which will show the original officers, and the annual report, which shows current officers. Your subject may still be in business with his ex-wife, which is something you should know about. When you receive the paperwork on the corporations of your subject, you will want to look closely for any amendments. Amendments are added after incorporation to change by-laws, but many times amendments will give power of attorney or **full ownership to another person who is not mentioned in any other corporate papers.**

SECRETARY
of STATE

Ralph Munro

3-23-93

CORPORATIONS DIVISION
2nd Floor Republic Building
505 E Union Avenue
P O Box 40234
Olympia WA 98504-0234
Information (206) 753-7115
Receptionist (206) 753-7120

CF

RE: ROBERT K. PAVELLA

Thank you for contacting the Corporations Division. In response to your
information request, we report the following:

_____   Annual Report(s) enclosed at $1.00 each. **PLEASE REMIT $**_____.

__X__   As of this date, we have no record of an active or inactive corporation(s)
that was dissolved since 1971, under the name(s) provided.

__X__   As of this date, we have no record of a current limited partnership(s),
or one that has merged into another entity, changed its name, or dissolved
since 1971, under the name provided.

_____   A corporation, under the name provided, was incorporated on _____
however, has not yet filed a list of officers

_____   The check submitted to this office with the enclosed statement has been
endorsed for deposit.   However, since we are unable to return the
requested information we are returning your check.

_____   Since the refund process is so costly, your check is being returned.
Please resubmit your request together with the fee of $ _____. Your
check has been endorsed for deposit, however, it has not been cashed by
the state.

_____   Other:

ENCLOSE A COPY OF THIS MEMO WITH YOUR PAYMENT
IN ORDER TO RECEIVE PROPER CREDIT

****
FOR OFFICE USE ONLY

PHOTO COPIES	AMT. REC'D:	BY:	DATE REC'D:

This state did a search back to 1971 which is a total of 22 years, free of charge.
Note that even when there is a charge, it is minimal, as in the case of an
annual report for $1.00. Note that your subject could have merged with
another company, changed his company name or dissolved his corporation
and it would have shown up during the search. Many corporation departments even extend credit when ordering records as is illustrated in the above
letter. Notice that a corporation can be incorporated but not list officers immediately. If this is the case with your inquiry, then you will want to send a
request for a list of officers in several months so that you can see **who your
"friend's" business associates are.**

National Cemetery System

Your subject may be sharp and has hidden his past well, but if he was in the service, you may want to use the National Cemetery System. This System was created by President Lincoln in 1862, and 12 cemeteries were established. In 1933, an Executive Order authorized the transfer of national cemeteries from the War Department (now Department of the Army) to the National Park Service, Department of the Interior. In June 1973, the national cemeteries were transferred from the Department of the Army to the Veterans Administration. Within the Veterans Administration, the National Cemetery System is the responsibility of the Department of Memorial Affairs.

Use the National Cemetery System to find dependents of the subject. If your subject was in the Armed Forces, the reserves or a member of the public health service, your subject may have dependents who are buried in one of the National Cemeteries. Here are the guidelines for the burial of a dependent:

A. The eligible **spouse** of an active duty member or veteran

B. The minor children of an eligible active duty member or veteran. For purpose of burial in a national cemetery, a minor child is a person who is unmarried and,

    1. Who is under the age of 21 years;

    2. Who, after attaining the age of 21 years and until completion of

education or training (but not after attaining the age of 23 years), is pursuing a course of instruction at an educational institution.

C. Unmarried adult children of an eligible active duty member or veteran if they become permanently incapable of self-support because of a physical or mental disability incurred before attaining the age of 21 years.

If your subject has a family member buried, write and ask for the records of interment. This will yield information about your subject, including date of birth, Social Security Number and addresses. Is this information the same as he told you? If you unexpectedly learn about a deceased spouse, then there may be children of which you were not informed. Remember, children can make a claim against the **estate** after you marry your subject and he dies. Or you may find that your subject has children buried of which you aren't aware and that may mean there is an ex-wife or current wife that may be able to make **claims against an estate** you and the subject may accumulate.

NATIONAL CEMETEREY SYSTEM

ALABAMA

Fort Mitchell National Cemetery
P.O. Box 2517
Phoenix City, Alabama 36867

Mobile National Cemetery
1202 Virginia Street
Mobile, Alabama 36604

ALASKA

Fort Richardson National Cemetery
P.O. Box 5-498
Fort Richardson, Alaska 99505

Sitka National Cemetery
P.O. Box 1065
Sitka, Alaska 99835

ARIZONA

Prescott National Cemetery
500 Highway 89N
Prescott, Arizona 86301

National Memorial Cemetery
23029 North Cave Creek Road
Phoenix, Arizona 85024

ARKANSAS

Fayetteville National Cemetery
700 Government Avenue
Fayetteville, Arkansas 72701

Fort Smith National Cemetery
522 Garland Avenue and South 6th Street
Fort Smith, Arkansas 72901

Little Rock National Cemetery
2523 Confederate Boulevard
Little Rock, Arkansas 72206

CALIFORNIA

Fort Rosecrans National Cemetery
P.O. Box 6237
San Diego, California 92106

Golden Gate National Cemetery
1300 Sneath Lane
San Bruno, California 94066

Los Angeles National Cemetery
950 South Sepulveda Boulevard
Los Angeles, California 90049

Riverside National Cemetery
22495 Van Buren Boulevard
Riverside, California 92508
San Francisco National Cemetery
P.O. Box 29012
San Francisco, California 94129

COLORADO
Fort Logan National Cemetery
3698 South Sheridan Boulevard
Denver, Colorado 80235

Fort Lyon National Cemetery
Virginia Medical Center
Fort Lyon, Colorado 81038

FLORIDA
Barrancas National Cemetery
Naval Air Station
Pensacola, Florida 32508

Bay Pines National Cemetery
P.O. Box 477
Bay Pines, Florida 33504

Florida National Cemetery
P.O. Box 337
Bushnell, Florida 33513

St. Augustine National Cemetery
104 Marine Street
St. Augustine, Florida 32084

GEORGIA
Marietta National Cemetery
500 Washington Avenue
Marietta, Georgia 30060

HAWAII
**National Memorial Cemetery
of the Pacific**
2177 Puowaina Drive
Honolulu, Hawaii 96813

ILLINOIS
Alton National Cemetery
600 Pearl Street
Alton, Illinois 62003

Camp Butler National Cemetery
R.R. #1
Springfield, Illinois 62707
Danville National Cemetery
1900 East Main Street
Danville, Illinois 61832

Mound City National Cemetery
Junction—Highway 37 & 51
Mound City, Illinois 62963

Quincy National Cemetery
36th and Maine Street
Quincy, Illinois 62301

Rock Island National Cemetery
Rock Island Arsenal
Rock Island, Illinois 61299

INDIANA
Crown Hill National Cemetery
700 West 38th Street
Indianapolis, Indiana 46208

Marion National Cemetery
VA Medical Center
Marion, Indiana 46952

New Albany National Cemetery
1943 Ekin Avenue
New Albany, Indiana 47150

IOWA
Keokuk National Cemetery
1701 J Street
Keokuk, Iowa 52632

KANSAS
Fort Leavenworth
National Cemetery
Fort Leavenworth, Kansas 66027

Fort Scott National Cemetery
P.O. Box 917
Fort Scott, Kansas 66701

Leavenworth National Cemeteries
P.O. Box 1649
Leavenworth, Kansas 66048

KENTUCKY

Camp Nelson National Cemetery
6980 Danville Road
Nicholasville, Kentucky 40356

Cave Hill National Cemetery
701 Baxter Avenue
Louisville, Kentucky 40204

Danville National Cemetery
377 North First Street
Danville, Kentucky 40442

Lebanon National Cemetery
R.R. #1, Box 616
Lebanon, Kentucky 40033

Lexington National Cemetery
833 West Main Street
Lexington, Kentucky 40508

Mill Springs National Cemetery
Rural Route #2, P.O. Box 172
Nancy, Kentucky 42544

Zachary Taylor National Cemetery
4701 Brownsboro Road
Louisville, Kentucky 40207

LOUISIANA

Alexandria National Cemetery
209 Shamrock Avenue
Pineville, Louisiana 71360

Baton Rouge National Cemetery
220 North 19th Street
Baton Rouge, Louisiana 70806

Port Hudson National Cemetery
Route No. 1, Box 185
Zachary, Louisiana 70791

MAINE

Togus National Cemetery
VA Medical and
Regional Office Center
Togus, Maine 04330

MARYLAND

Annapolis National Cemetery
800 West Street
Annapolis, Maryland 21401

Baltimore National Cemetery
5501 Frederick Avenue
Baltimore, Maryland 21228

Loudon Park National Cemetery
3445 Frederick Avenue
Baltimore, Maryland 21229

MASSACHUSETTS

Massachusetts National Cemetery
P.O. Box 100
Bourne, Massachusetts 02532

MICHIGAN

Fort Custer National Cemetery
15501 Dickman Road
Augusta, Michigan 49012

MINNESOTA

Fort Snelling National Cemetery
7601 34th Avenue, South
Minneapolis, Minnesota 55450

MISSISSIPPI

Biloxi National Cemetery
P.O. Box 4968
Biloxi, Mississippi 39535

Corinth National Cemetery
1551 Horton Street
Corinth, Mississippi 38834

Natchez National Cemetery
61 Cemetery Road
Natchez, Mississippi 39102

MISSOURI

**Jefferson Barracks
National Cemetery**
101 Memorial Drive
St. Louis, Missouri 63125

Jefferson City National Cemetery
1024 East McCarty Street
Jefferson City, Missouri 65101

Springfield National Cemetery
1702 East Seminole Street
Springfield, Missouri 65804

NEBRASKA

Fort McPherson National Cemetery
HCO 1, Box 67
Maxwell, Nebraska 69151

NEW JERSEY

Beverly National Cemetery
RD #1, Bridge Boro Road
Beverly, New Jersey 08010

Finn's Point National Cemetery
R.F.D. No. 3, Fort Mott Road,
Box 542
Salem, New Jersey 08079

NEW MEXICO

Fort Bayard National Cemetery
P.O. Box 189
Bayard, New Mexico 88036

Santa Fe National Cemetery
P.O. Box 88
Santa Fe, New Mexico 87501

NEW YORK

Bath National Cemetery
VA Medical Center
Bath, New York 14810

Calverton National Cemetery
210 Princeton Boulevard
Calverton, New York 11933

Cypress Hills National Cemetery
625 Jamaica Avenue
Brooklyn, New York 11208

Long Island National Cemetery
P.O. Box 250
Farmingdale, New York 11735

Woodlawn National Cemetery
1825 Davis Street
Elmira, New York 14901

NORTH CAROLINA

New Bern National Cemetery
1711 National Avenue
New Bern, North Carolina 28560

Raleigh National Cemetery
501 Rock Quarry Road
Raleigh, North Carolina 27610

Salisbury National Cemetery
202 Government Road
Salisbury, North Carolina 28144

Wilmington National Cemetery
2011 Market Street
Wilmington, North Carolina 28403

OHIO

Dayton National Cemetery
VA Medical Center
4100 West Third Street
Dayton, Ohio 45428

OKLAHOMA

Fort Gibson National Cemetery
R.R. #2, P.O. Box 47
Fort Gibson, Oklahoma 74434

OREGON

Eagle Point National Cemetery
2763 Riley Road
Eagle Point, Oregon 97524

Roseburg National Cemetery
VA Medical Center
Roseburg, Oregon 97470

Williamette National Cemetery
11800 S.E. Mt. Scott Blvd
Portland, Oregon 97266

PENNSYLVANIA

Indiantown Gap National Cemetery
P.O. Box 187
Annville, Pennsylvania 17003

Philadelphia National Cemetery
Haines Street and Limekiln Pike
Philadelphia, Pennsylvania 19138

PUERTO RICO

Puerto Rico National Cemetery
P.O. Box 1298
Bayamon, Puerto Rico 00621

SOUTH CAROLINA

Beaufort National Cemetery
1601 Boundary Street
Beaufort, South Carolina 29902

Florence National Cemetery
803 East National Cemetery Road
Florence, South Carolina 29501

SOUTH DAKOTA

Black Hills National Cemetery
P.O. Box 640
Sturgis, South Dakota 57785

Fort Meade National Cemetery
VA Medical Center
Fort Meade, South Dakota 57785

Hot Springs National Cemetery
VA Medical Center
Hot Springs, South Dakota 57747

TENNESSEE

Chattanooga National Cemetery
1200 Bailey Avenue
Chattanooga, Tennessee 37404

Knoxville National Cemetery
939 Tyson Street, N.W.
Knoxville, Tennessee 37917

Memphis National Cemetery
3568 Townes Avenue
Memphis, Tennessee 38122

Mountain Home National Cemetery
P.O. Box 8
Mountain Home, Tennessee 37684

Nashville National Cemetery
1420 Gallatin Road, South
Madison, Tennessee 37115

TEXAS

Fort Bliss National Cemetery
P.O. Box 6342
Fort Bliss, Texas 79906

Fort Sam Houston National Cemetery
1520 Harry Wurzbach Road
San Antonio, Texas 78209

Houston National Cemetery
10410 Veterans Memorial Drive
Houston, Texas 77038

Kerrville National Cemetery
VA Medical Center
3600 Memorial Boulevard
Kerrville, Texas 78028

San Antonio National Cemetery
517 Paso Hondo Street
San Antonio, Texas 78202

VIRGINIA

Alexandria National Cemetery
1450 Wilkes Street
Alexandria, Virginia 22314

Balls Bluff National Cemetery
P.O. Box 200
Leesburg, Virginia 22075

City Point National Cemetery
10th Avenue and Davis Street
Hopewell, Virginia 23860

Cold Harbor National Cemetery
Route 156 North
Mechanicsville, Virginia 23111

Culpeper National Cemetery
305 U.S. Avenue
Culpeper, Virginia 22701

Danville National Cemetery
721 Lee Street
Danville, Virginia 24541

Fort Harrison National Cemetery
8620 Varina Road
Richmond, Virginia 23231

Glendale National Cemetery
9301 Willis Church Road
Richmond, Virginia 23231

Hampton National Cemetery
Cemetery Road at Marshall Avenue
Hampton, Virginia 23669

Hampton National Cemetery
VA Medical Center
Hampton, Virginia 23669

Quantico National Cemetery
P.O. Box 10
Triangle, Virginia 22172
Richmond National Cemetery
1701 Williamsburg Road
Richmond, Virginia 23231

Seven Pines National Cemetery
400 East Williamsburg Road
Sandson, Virginia 23150

Staunton National Cemetery
901 Richmond Avenue
Staunton, Virginia 24401

Winchester National Cemetery
401 National Avenue
Winchester, Virginia 22601

WEST VIRGINIA
Grafton National Cemetery
431 Walnut Street
Grafton, West Virginia 26354

West Virginia National Cemetery
Route 2, Box 127
Pruntytown, West Virginia 26354

WISCONSIN
Wood National Cemetery
P.O. Box 500
VA Medical Center
Milwaukee, Wisconsin 53295

NOTES

The Internet

In the late 1960s, during the "cold war," nuclear war was foremost in our minds because of the military power of Russia. There was not an open and meaningful dialogue between the two superpowers. I, like many of my readers, remember when we had bomb shelters built in our homes. The threat of nuclear war was very real, even to the point of having "air raid" drills at school where we would go into the halls, put our hands behind our heads, and lean against the wall. China had developed nuclear weapons but at that point did not have the capability to deliver bombs to their designated targets worldwide. The United States was the superpower that decided to seriously explore an alternative method of communication should a nuclear holocaust impair or destroy surface or satellite communication.

An America that suffered the calamity of massive destruction would need a network of communications linked from city to city, county to county, state to state. The solution proposed by many was to make the current system of communication that was being used destruction-proof, by burying cable and lines, by making more use of satellites, and by building smaller phases and parts of the current communication network. The solution was not the preceding, because the destructive capacity of nuclear war makes no system of communication impregnable to the impact of nuclear blast and the subsequent fallout.

Another question that had been asked and could not be answered was that if a network of communication could be created, then who would be in control? From what place would the command operate from? If there were essential parts of the system destroyed, including the demise of the person in command, then how would there be a leader to be custodian of the communication network?

The Department of Defense had an agency called the Defense Advanced Research Projects Agency (DARPA), and the researchers developed many proposals. One idea that kept coming to the surface was a system of communications that would have no central command or authority. The intention was not to usurp the authority of the President of the United States, but rather to ensure continuity.

Another proposal was that no matter what network was to be in place as a "doomsday" backup, it was to be operable in the worst of all possible scenarios—that being total destruction of ground links in communication. An important part of the network would be that all parts of the new communications system would work both independently of each other and dependent with each other—sort of a centralized, yet decentralized, system.

And much to their credit, the founders of this new network thought of an important consideration and sought to resolve it at the outset. If one part of this system was destroyed, the other parts would pick up and deliver the instructions. That is why today when we send e-mail to someone, the message is sent along a different route each time. You can call it the path of least resistance. Whatever avenue is open at the second you send your e-mail is the way it travels. If the system would be able to work independently, then if someone sent a message over this system, it would go to many computers and the message could be retrieved by any computer going to any other computer because the message would be everywhere. If destruction has arrived, then instructions to rebuild would need to be sent over the new network. Instructions for the health and welfare of the public would be delivered by this system. Instructions from the Defense Department would be sent so a military infrastructure could be maintained. Timely news reports could be sent to allow the mass populace to know what was happening. So as you can see, information in the form of instructions was of paramount importance. The vehicle would be messages. You can see now where we are going with this—e-mail.

In 1968, UCLA, at the request and funding of the United States Department of Defense, started a small network of four computers to see if a decentralized, yet connected, communication network could work. Four computers transferred data on dedicated high-speed transmission lines. In 1971, UCLA and its sister institutions of higher learning expanded the network to eight computers, and the next year the system was expanded even more, to 37 computers online.

The mid 1970s saw a continued rapid expansion of the communication network that was started by UCLA. A decentralized system where anyone could go online, yet be connected to other computers in the network, offered possibilities heretofore not thought of by anyone.

In 1983, the Defense Department took away its funding from UCLA. The military made its own network, for security reasons, and named it MIL-NET, which of course, stands for *military network*. The same year, the Department of Defense invited the National Science Foundation to assist in the administration and coordination of the many computers that were coming online.

The many computers that were coming online daily created a need for further identification of the computers. Six basic categories were created, and they were: gov, mil, edu, com, org, and net. The network that UCLA started became known as the Internet.

I will explain the basics of the Internet because it is important that we are reminded of how incredible this recent communications tool is. What is more amazing is that there is not one central owner or controlling authority of the Internet! It is a coalition of millions of computers that speak the same computer language with the common goal of exchanging information and commerce.

The Internet is a computer network that has one master terminal that acts, sort of, like a Grand Central Station. Messages from all computers asking to be routed to a specific location come into it, and then the messages are dispatched to their proper location.

When you send a request to go to a site from your computer, you usually see a name, such as IBM.COM. (This is explained more, later in this chapter.) That address is really a string of numbers underneath. Those numbers are then sent to the master computer, the numbers are read, and it then gets funneled to IBM.COM.

This is accomplished because the Internet has its own language called Hypertext Transfer Protocol, or HTTP. The Web uses hypertext as its way of exchanging information. Hypertext is a string of words and numbers that links computers and documents to each other—hence, the name links that you are so familiar with.

Hypertext is created by making a language that is called Hypertext Markup Language, or HTML. Within the lines of information of HTML, tags or small lines of data are placed. These little bits of additional information are actually the instructions to the computer to produce on your monitor features such as font size, graphics, colors, sounds, and other multimedia effects. A single hypertext string sometimes has many, many links to other information and documents.

We even have different names for some types of hypertext. Java is a popular type of tag used extensively. When you go to a Website and you see a banner with a moving or jumping image, or you see a banner scrolling information, then that is Java. Java got its name because a group of young, industrious people got together to try to make a fancier hypertext. They wanted a hypertext that was not just text or still pictures. It was an arduous task, but they were successful and created a very different type of hypertext. They did not know what to call their creation, and all around their work area they saw strewn about paper cups that had contained coffee. They though that Java would be an appropriate and different name. Remember, odd names are more the norm instead of the exception on the Internet. All one has to do is look to Amazon or Yahoo to see creative and odd names.

FTP, which is the abbreviation for File Transfer Protocol, is the actual method by which files are transferred between computers. FTP allows the smooth and uninterrupted transference of text, books, articles, software, games, graphics, images, sounds, multimedia, video images, still photographs, spreadsheets, and much more.

Electronic mail, or e-mail, is the means by which computer users contact each other in an instant—worldwide and free of charge. E-mail brings forth what the Internet does best, which is allowing people to communicate. That was the basis of the Web. Do not ever put anything in e-mail communication that you do not want a third party to see. E-mail does not afford you the confidence, security, and sanctity that using a credit card on a secure server gives you. Your Internet Service Provider (ISP) has access to all your e-mail. That is just one example of who can see your e-mail. Sending attachments on e-mail allows you to send pictures, even in color, to your designated recipient. The process of sending accompaniments in e-mail is referred to as sending MIME attachments. MIME stands for Multimedia Internet Mail Extension.

Groups and forums are, basically, a worldwide electronic bulletin board where millions of computer users exchange information on every possible subject. One of the joys of the Internet and e-mail is the ability of everyone to participate in forums and groups that are of interest to them. Whether it is a favorite hobby, sport, educational interest, or something personal, there are people who want to communicate with you. There are no locks on the doors, and chat groups are open 24 hours a day.

The major difference between groups and forums and e-mail is the fact that group and forum messages are stored on central computers and are not a one-on-one e-mail communication. It is a group e- mail endeavor. You can even use a search engine using keywords, phrases, or someone's name to see if it has been mentioned in a group or forum session, because search engines sweep and catalog the contents of groups and forums. A great feature of groups and forums is that you can reply to one person, or you can reply to all members, by just a keystroke.

Still another fine feature in groups and forums is instant messaging. That means participants around the world can "talk" to each other by typing in real time and having their thoughts and ideas visible to many other people immediately. This allows for the exchanging of ideas from people worldwide instantly, which was heretofore not available in any medium.

The Internet, or Web, is made of files most commonly called pages, or home pages. Home pages can be visited by typing in the URL. URL stands for Uniform Resource Locator. The URL is the specific Internet address of the home page that is stored on an Internet Service Provider's computer that is connected to the Internet. Every file on the Internet has a unique URL. URLs are translated into numeric addresses using the Internet Domain Name System (DNS). Since numeric strings are difficult to remember, alphanumeric addresses are used.

For example, this is a URL for my home page:

http://www.josephculligan.com

Here is what the Uniform Resource Locator consists of:

The Protocol is: **http**
Host computer name: **www**
Domain name: **josephculligan**
Top level domain: **com**

The top-level domains (TLDs) that are common:

com	commercial enterprise
edu	educational institution
gov	U.S. government
mil	U.S. military
net	network access provider
org	nonprofit organizations

You need a software program called a Web browser to access the Internet Web. There are two types of browsers. The first is graphical: Sound, text, images, graphics, audio, and video are received through a graphical software program such as Netscape Navigator and Internet Explorer. Navigation is done by pointing and clicking a mouse on highlighted words and graphics. The second web browser is text: Lynx is a browser that allows you to visit the Internet in text form only. Navigating is done by highlighting emphasized words on the monitor with the arrow up-and-down keys. Then you key the forward arrow (or Enter) key to follow the link.

Web browsers come with several plug-ins that will allow you to use multimedia functions. There are many multimedia programs and real-time communication programs available today. You can even listen to radio stations anywhere in the world. I have provided links to thousands of radio stations on my Website.

You can even watch video with the sound that is not staccato and jumpy as it was a few short years ago. The video and sound is just about as smooth as you will see on your television at home. You can access sites of the news networks and watch the same video that was shown on the nightly television news. One advantage of watching the video on your monitor is that your computer can download the video. You do not need a video tape, and if the story is of sufficient interest, you can send the video via the Internet to your friends or business associates. The biggest obstacle until recently has been the slow download times when trying to save videos. Technology has now expanded multimedia capability by creating streaming data. Streaming data allows audio or video files to be played as they are downloading into your computer. You may also download or just watch real-time events such as press conferences, speeches, news events, concerts, and much more.

❧ ❧ ❧

SMILEYS

The following symbols are what is known on the Internet as *smileys*. If a smiley does not look correct, then you may want to tilt your head to the left to view them properly. :) Please remember that most smileys come in two forms—with a nose and without.

0:) or 0:-) = Angel

:ll or :-ll = Angry

:@ or :-@ = Angry or screaming

>:-(= Angry, annoyed

I-l = Asleep

;)= or ;-)= = Big grin

:1 or :-1 = Bland face

:o or :-o = Bored

:c or :-c = Bummed out

:'(o or :'-(= Crying/sad

:> or :-> = Devilish grin

:6 or :-6 = Eating something sour

}) or }-) = Evil

:] or :-] = Friendly

:(or :-(= Frowning

:/ or :-/ = Frustrated

8) or 8-) = Glasses

:D or :-D = Grinning

{ } = Hug

:*) or :-*) = Kiss

:x or :-x = Kissing

:))) or :-))) = Laughing or double chin

:,) or :,-) = Laughing tears

:$ or :-$ = Mouth wired shut

:X or :-X = Mute

:l or :-l = Not talking

:Y or :-Y = Quiet aside

:[or :-[= Real downer

:< or :-< = Sad

:> or :-> = Sarcastic

B) or B-) = Shades

=:0 or =:-) = Shocked

:Z or :-Z = Sleeping

:) or :-) = Smiling

:O or :-O = Surprised

:() or :-() = Talking

:P or :-P = Tongue out

:and or :-and = Tongue-tied

l) or l-) = Trekkie

:^(= Unhappy, looking away

;) or ;-) = Winking

:} or :-} = Wry Smile

ACCESSING GOVERNMENT FORMS

I have mentioned for years how important it is to check applications of a subject so you can find information that is not available elsewhere. Let us take a look at what an application for a firearm permit filed through the Department of Alcohol, Tobacco, and Firearms (ATF) will yield. The applicant must give their full name, former and current addresses for ten years, former and current employment, Social Security Number, date of birth, the names of three references, name of next of kin, home and business telephone numbers (whether they are unlisted or not), and much more. I have included the following links so that you can go online and see what different applications are out there.

If your subject had been employed in the radio or television business, then you may want to pull up a blank form to see what information the subject was required to give. If you find a need for the data, then you can order a copy of the application that they submitted when they were a disk jockey or radio announcer. There are literally thousands of jobs that require applications that are subject to public inspections. In my chapter on state records, you will recall the many occupations I listed that require licensing, and all the applications for those jobs are open for review by the public.

The importance of applications and forms that people fill out is underestimated. In the aforementioned description of what is on the ATF application for a firearm permit, you can see that the information forms the basis of a background check. So, if you ever need to do a very complete background on a prospective mate, or possible business associates, or even someone you are going to lend money to, then it is worth the time and effort to figure out what type of licenses they have and ask the government for copies of the applications. Of course, forms and applications are excellent sources of information for finding someone because even though they may have filled out an application years ago, you can get information such as the names of relatives, the Social Security Number, the date of birth, and much more.

I am including many government Websites in the following pages, but also some for your personal use that will provide you with legal forms and applications at no charge. If you own land, rent out an apartment, or have filed a lawsuit against someone, the following sites will provide you with the proper paperwork, and much of it will be free of charge.

GOVERNMENT APPLICATIONS, DOCUMENTS, AND LEGAL FORMS—ONLINE

All About Forms
http://www.allaboutforms.com

I am glad that this site is listed first because they give so much. Here is a quote from their Website. It says it all: *Free Legal Forms! Why pay for generic legal forms when you can get them for free? At All About Forms, we want to help you with your legal needs. We offer this service for free for thanking you for making our site successful.*

Bureau of Alcohol, Tobacco, and Firearms Forms
http://www.atf.treas.gov/

Your subject may have had to apply for a certain type of firearm permit through this agency. If so, then the application is public record. This application yields much information and is an excellent source for getting background information on someone, such as schooling, previous addresses, relatives, employment, and criminal record—no matter how minor and much more. If you are doing a background check on someone, then see if they have an application on file with the ATF.

Copyright Forms
http://www.loc.gov/copyright

If your subject had ever received a copyright, then the application is on file and is public information. But what most people do not realize is that if your subject had applied for a copyright and did not receive it, then the information is still on file and subject to public scrutiny. The copyright applications ask many questions that your subject may never let anyone else know. You can be also assured that the address the subject gave on the various forms and applications to the copyright office are correct and true. There isn't anyone who risks losing a copyright by giving incorrect information.

Corporate and Securities Forms
http://www.jefren.com/DOWNLOAD.HTML

Documents include Employees Stock Deferral Plan and Directors Stock Deferral Plan, Equity Based Long Term Incentive Plan, Indemnification Agreement, Liquidating Trust Agreement, Non-Employee Directors Deferred Compensation Plan, Restricted Stock Award Plan, Stock Appreciation Rights Plan, Standby Equity Agreement, Stock Option Plan, Stock Option Plan for Non-Employee Directors, Subordinated Debenture, Voting Trust Agreement and Voting Trust, and Warrant documents.

Federal Communications Commission Forms
http://www.fcc.gov/forms/

If your subject was ever a radio disc jockey or a broadcaster of any type, then their application and subsequent renewal are public record and available from the FCC. This site will give you the latest address to write to for information.

FEMA Forms
http://www.fema.gov/library/lib04.htm

Flood hazard, hurricane, and many other natural disasters are what FEMA responds to. Your subject may have filled out an application for aid from this government entity. There are many parts of the country that consistently have weather-related problems, so if your subject is in one of those areas, then see if they applied for assistance in the form of a loan or grant. This is an excellent way to find people who lived an anonymous life in a trailer, but then were caught up in a weather-related storm.

General Business Forms
http://www.lectlaw.com/formb.htm

Applications and forms include bulk sale, stock purchase, contracts, corporate, joint venture, partnership, employment, consulting, indemnity, promissory notes, and other paperwork business uses.

General Forms and Model Documents
http://www.courttv.com/legalhelp/business/forms/

Documents include arbitration, copyright, distributorships, e-mail policy, employee handbook, sexual harassment policies, corporate minutes, software development, and confidentiality agreements.

General Legal Documents
http://www.tiac.net/users/nmayhews/legal.htm

Documents and forms include promissory notes, notice of default, demand for payment, notice of delinquent account, installment agreement, credit application, security agreement, subordination agreements, leases, termination of tenancy, assignments, bills of sale, contracts, bulk sale, employment, corporate minutes, and other business documents.

Immigration and Naturalization Forms
http://www.ins.usdoj.gov/graphics/

Some of the applications and forms that people fill out are restricted. The status of availability, as with all public records, changes constantly. As you see elsewhere in the section, I list many different applications and forms. This is to give you some idea of what type of form your subject may have filled out if they would have had an occasion to do so. You can view the complete form online. Some applications and forms may be of more interest to you than others because of the situation that your subject may have been in when they had filled out the particular form giving information. In general, the following includes immigration, naturalization, employment, and asylum forms:

G-28	Notice of Entry of Appearance as Attorney or Representative
G-639	Freedom of Information/Privacy Act Request

G-731	Inquiry about Status of 1-551 Alien Registration Card
G-942	Application Survey (for INS Employment)
I-9	Employment Eligibility Verification
I-90	Application to Replace Permanent Resident Card $110
I-129F	Petition for Alien Fiancé(e)
I-129S	Nonimmigrant Petition Based on Blanket L Petition
I-129W	Petition for Non-immigrant Worker Filing Fee Exemption
I-130	Petition for Alien Relative
I-131	Application for Travel Document
I-193	Application for Waiver of Passport

Health and Human Services Forms
http://directory.psc.gov/

If your subject has ever done business with the Department of Health and Human Services, then there will be much information for you. The department conducts other business with 32 other federal agencies, independent establishments, and government corporations.

Law Practice Forms
http://www.lectlaw.com/forma.htm

Documents include checklists, demand letters, fee agreements, litigation practice forms, affidavit, declarations, applications, answers, complaints, and many more litigation-type documents.

Legaldocs
http://www.legaldocs.com/~usalaw/misc-s.htm

Applications, documents, and forms, including last will and testament, living wills, durable powers of attorney, promissory note, request for credit report, request to correct credit report, child-care authorization, automobile insurance claim, homeowner's insurance claim, and hunting lease.

Office of Personnel Management
Federal Employees Retirement Program
http://www.opm.gov/retire/

This is such an important site because if your subject ever worked for the federal government (as 11,400,000 living people have done, as over 27 million deceased people have done, and as 5,300,000 current employees are doing), then they would be listed in one of the links on the OPM site. There are so many applications your subject may have filled out or programs that your subject may have used and that, of course, creates a paper trail. This site is also excellent for personal reasons also because if you or any of your family members have worked for the federal government or are now employed, then you will want to take a look at the links I have included below for your review. You will be convinced that you should also visit their Website.

Passport Application Forms
http://travel.state.gov/get_forms.html

In the previous chapter on federal records, I go into detail on the use of passport records, which you may want to review. The United States Department of State has created a comprehensive site that will facilitate any research you may need to do.

Hackers

There are so many stories in the news where the actions of hackers are made to sound like they are full of adventure and daring. The federal government has now been finding, and very aggressively prosecuting, hackers who break into government computers and sell the information. I am including the law so you can see how serious the government is about protecting the sanctity of computer files. **Do things legally on the Internet because there are enough resources out there so that there is no need to do otherwise.**

§1030. Fraud and related activity in connection with computers

(a) Whoever—
(1) having knowingly accessed a computer without authorization or exceeding authorized access, and by means of such conduct having obtained information that has been determined by the United States Government pursuant to an Executive order or statute to require protection against unauthorized disclosure for reasons of national defense or foreign relations, or any restricted data, as defined in paragraph y. of section 11 of the Atomic Energy Act of 1954, with reason to believe that such information so

obtained could be used to the injury of the United States, or to the advantage of any foreign nation willfully communicates, delivers, transmits, or causes to be communicated, delivered, or communicated, delivered, or transmitted the same to any person not entitled to receive it, or willfully retains the same and fails to deliver it to the officer or employee of the United States entitled to receive it;

(2) intentionally accesses a computer without authorization or exceeds authorized access, and thereby obtains

(A) information contained in a financial record of a financial institution, or of a card issuer as defined in section 1602 (n) of title 15, or contained in a file of a consumer reporting agency on a consumer, as such terms are defined in the Fair Credit Reporting Act (15 U.S.C. 1681 et seq.);

(B) information from any department or agency of the United States; or

(C) information from any protected computer if the conduct involved an interstate or foreign communication;

(3) intentionally, without authorization to access any nonpublic computer of a department or agency of the United States, accesses such a computer of that department or agency that is exclusively for the use of the Government of the United States or, in the case of a computer not exclusively for such use is used by or for the Government of the United States and such conduct affects that use by or for the Government of the United States;

(4) knowingly and with intent to defraud, accesses a protected computer without authorization, or exceeds authorized access, and by means of such conduct furthers the intended fraud and obtains anything of value, unless the object of the fraud and the thing obtained consists only of the use of the computer and the value of such use is not more than $5,000 in any one-year period;

(5)

(A) knowingly causes the transmission of a program, information, code, or command, and as a result of such conduct, intentionally causes damage without authorization, to a protected computer;

(B) intentionally accesses a protected computer without authorization, and as a result of such conduct, recklessly causes damage; or

(C) intentionally accesses a protected computer without authorization, and as a result of such conduct, causes damage;

(6) knowingly and with intent to defraud traffics (as defined in section 1029) in any password or similar information through which a computer may be accessed without authorization, if

(A) such trafficking affects interstate or foreign commerce; or

(B) such computer is used by or for the government of the United States;

(7) with intent to extort from any person, firm, association, educational institution, financial institution, government entity, or other legal entity, any money or other thing of value, transmits in interstate or foreign commerce any communication containing any threat to cause damage to a protected computer;

shall be punished as provided in subsection (c) of this section.

(b) Whoever attempts to commit an offense under subsection (a) of this section shall be punished as provided in subsection (c) of this section.

(c) The punishment for an offense under subsection (a) or (b) of this section is,

(1)

(A) a fine under this title or imprisonment for not more than ten years, or both, in the case of an offense under subsection (a) (1) of this section, which does not occur after a conviction for another offense under this section, or an attempt to commit an offense punishable under this subparagraph; and

(B) a fine under this title or imprisonment for not more than twenty years, or both, in the case of an offense under subsection (a) (1) of this section which occurs after a conviction for another offense under this section, or an attempt to commit an offense punishable under this subparagraph; and

(2)

(A) a fine under this title or imprisonment for not more than one year, or both, in the case of an offense under subsection (a) (2), (a) (3), (a) (5) or (a) (6) of this section which does not occur after a conviction for another offense under this section, or an attempt to commit an offense punishable under this subparagraph; and

(B) a fine under this title or imprisonment for not more than 5 years, or both, in the case of an offense under subsection (a) (2) if

(i) the offense was committed for purpose of commercial advantage or private financial gain.

(ii) the offense was committed in furtherance of any criminal or tortious act in violation of the Constitution or laws of the United States or of any State; or

(iii) the value of the information obtained exceeds $5,000.00;

(C) a fine under this title or imprisonment for not more than ten years, or both, in the case of an offense under subsection (a) (2), (a) (3) or (a) (6) of this section which occurs after a conviction for another offense under this section, or an attempt to commit an offense punishable under this subparagraph; and

(3)

(A) a fine under this title or imprisonment for not more than five years, or both, in the case of an offense under subsection (a) (4), (a) (5) (A), (a) (5) (B), or (a) (7) of this section which does not occur after a conviction for another offense under this section, or an attempt to commit an offense punishable under this subparagraph; and

(B) a fine under this title or imprisonment for not more than ten years, or both, in the case of an offense under subsection (a) (4), (a) (5) (A), (a) (5) (B), (a) (5) (C), or (a) (7) of this section which occurs after a conviction for another offense under this section, or an attempt to commit an offense punishable under this subparagraph; and

(d) The United States Secret Service shall, in addition to any other agency having such authority, have the authority to investigate offenses under subsections (a) (2) (A), (a) (2) (B), (a) (3), (a) (4), (a) (5), and (a) (6) of this section. Such authority of the United States Secret Service shall be exercised in accordance with an agreement which shall be entered into by the Secretary of the Treasury and the Attorney General.

(e) As used in this section:

(1) the term "computer" means an electronic, magnetic, optical, electrochemical, or other high speed data processing device performing logical, arithmetic, or storage functions, and includes any data storage facility or communications facility directly related to or operating in conjunction with such device, but such term does not include an automated typewriter or typesetter, a portable hand held calculator, or other similar device;

(2) the term "protected computer" means a computer:

(A) exclusively for the use of a financial institution or the United States Government or, in the case of a computer not exclusively for such use, used by or for a financial institution or the United States government and the conduct constituting the offense affects that use by or for the financial institution or the government; or

(B) which is used in interstate or foreign commerce of communications;

(3) the term "State" includes the District of Columbia, the Commonwealth of Puerto Rico, and any other commonwealth, possession or territory of the United States;

(4) the term "financial institution" means:

(A) an institution with deposits insured by the Federal Deposit Insurance Corporation;

(B) the Federal Reserve or a member of the Federal Reserve including any Federal Reserve Bank;

(C) a credit union with accounts insured by the National Credit Union Administration;

(D) a member of the Federal home loan bank system and any home loan bank;

(E) any institution of the Farm Credit System under the Farm Credit Act of 1971;

(F) a broker-dealer registered with the Securities and Exchange Commission pursuant to section 15 of the Securities Exchange Act of 1934;

(G) the Securities Investor Protection Corporation;

(H) a branch or agency of a foreign bank (as such terms are defined in paragraphs (1) and (3) of section 1(b) of the International Banking Act of 1978); and

(I) an organization operating under section 25 or section 25(a) of the Federal Reserve Act

(5) the term "financial record" means information derived from any record held by a financial institution pertaining to a customer's relationship with the financial institution;

(6) the term "exceeds authorized access" means to access a computer with authorization and to use such access to obtain or alter information in the computer that the accessor is not entitled so to obtain or alter;

(7) the term "department of the United States" means the legislative or judicial branch of the Government, or one of the executive departments enumerated in section 101 of title 5; and

(8) the term 'damage' means any impairment to the integrity or availability of data, a program, a system, or information, that—

(A) causes loss aggregating at least $5,000 in value during any one-year period to one or more individuals;

(B) modifies or impairs, or potentially modifies or impairs, the medical examination, diagnosis, treatment, or care of one or more individuals;

(C) causes physical injury to any person; or

(D) threatens public health or safety; and

(9) the term 'government entity' includes the Government of the United States, any State or political subdivision of the United States, any foreign country, and any state, province, municipality, or other political subdivision of a foreign country.

(f) This section does not prohibit any lawfully authorized investigative, protective, or intelligence activity of a law enforcement agency of the United States, a State, or a political subdivision of a State, or of an intelligence agency of the United States.

(g) Any person who suffers damage or loss by reason of a violation of the section may maintain a civil action against the violator to obtain compensatory damages and injunctive relief or other equitable relief. Damages for violations involving damage as defined in subsection (e) (8) (A) are limited to economic damages. No action may be brought under this subsection unless such action is begun within 2 years of the date of the act complained of or the date of the discovery of the damage.

(h) The Attorney General and the Secretary of the Treasury shall report to the Congress annually, during the first 3 years following the date of the enactment of this subsection, concerning investigations and prosecutions under section 1030 (a) (5) of title 18, United States Code.

❧ ❧ ❧

APPENDIX

County Mailing Addresses

The following addresses are county mailing addresses in the United States that you will need. Chapter 5 showed the myriad of public records from divorce files to property records to voter's registration that can be accessed from the county hall of records.

Also, you will want to use these addresses to write away and make inquiries as to what arrest record information is on file for your subject. Use the title of "Chief Administrator Judge" on the top of the county mailing addresses. You may also want to use these addresses to make inquiries as to what arrest record information is on file for your subject. Put the name "Chief Administrative Judge" on top of the county mailing address.

ALABAMA

http://www.archives.state.al.us/referenc/vital.html

Autauga County
4th and Court Streets
Prattville, Alabama 36067

Baldwin County
County Courthouse
P.O. Box 459-J
Bay Minnette, Alabama 36507

Barbour County
County Courthouse
P.O. Box 758-O
Eufaula, Alabama 36027-0758

Bibb County
Courthouse Square
Centerville, Alabama 35042

Blount County
County Courthouse
P.O. Box 549
Oneonta, Alabama 35121

Bullock County
County Courthouse
P.O. Box 71-E
Union Springs, Alabama 36089

Butler County
County Courthouse
P.O. Box 756-Y
Greenville, Alabama 36037

Calhoun County
County Courthouse
1702 Noble St. Suite 102
Anniston, Alabama 36201

Chambers County
County Courthouse
Lafayette, Alabama 36862

Cherokee County
Courthouse on Main St.
Centre, Alabama 35960

Chilton County
County Courthouse
P.O. Box 270-E
Clanton, Alabama 35045

Choctaw County
County Courthouse
117 South Mulberry St.
Butler, Alabama 36904

Clarke County
County Courthouse
117 Court St.
Grove Hill, Alabama 36451

Clay County
County Courthouse
P.O. Box 1120
Ashland, Alabama 36251

Cleburne County
406 Vickery St.
Heflin, Alabama 36264

Coffee County
County Courthouse
P.O. Box 1256
Enterprise, Alabama 36331

Colbert County
County Courthouse
201 N. Main St.
Tuscumbia, Alabama 35647

Conecuh County
County Courthouse
P.O. Box 149
Evergreen, Alabama 36410

Coosa County
County Courthouse
P.O. Box 218
Rockford, Alabama 35136

Covington County
County Courthouse
P.O. Box 789
Andalusia, Alabama 36240

Crenshaw County
County Courthouse
P.O. Box 328
Luverne, Alabama 36049

Cullman County
County Courthouse
P.O. Box 237
Cullman, Alabama 35055

Dale County
County Courthouse
P.O. Box 580
Ozark, Alabama 36361

Dallas County
County Courthouse
P.O. Box 997
Selma, Alabama 36702

Dekalb County
County Courthouse
301 S. Grand Ave.
Fort Payne, Alabama 35967

Elmore County
County Courthouse
P.O. Box 280
Wetumpka, Alabama 36092

Escambia County
County Courthouse
P.O. Box 557
Brewton, Alabama 36427

Etowah County
County Courthouse
800 Forrest Ave.
Gadsden, Alabama 35902

Fayette County
County Courthouse
P.O. Box 509
Fayette, Alabama 35555

Franklin County
County Courthouse
410 N. Jackson St.
Russellville, Alabama
35653

Geneva County
County Courthouse
P.O. Box 430
Geneva, Alabama 36340

Greene County
County Courthouse
P.O. Box 790
Eutaw, Alabama 35462

Hale County
1001 Main St.
Greensboro, Alabama
36744

Henry County
County Courthouse
101 West Court Square St.
Abbeville, Alabama 36310

Houston County
County Courthouse
P.O. Box 6406
Dothan, Alabama 36302

Jackson County
County Courthouse
P.O. Box 128
Scottsboro, Alabama 35768

Jefferson County
County Courthouse
716 N. 21st St.
Birmingham, Alabama
35263

Lamar County
County Courthouse
P.O. Box 338
Vernon, Alabama 35592

Lauderdale County
County Courthouse
P.O. Box 1059
Florence, Alabama 35631

Lawrence County
County Courthouse
14330 Court St.
Moulton, Alabama 35650

Lee County
County Courthouse
215 South 9th St.
Opelika, Alabama
36803-2266

Limestone County
County Courthouse
310 West Washington St.
Athens, Alabama 35611

Lowndes County
County Courthouse
P.O. Box 5
Hayneville, Alabama 36040

Macon County
County Courthouse
210 N. Elm St.
Tuskegee, Alabama 36083

Madison County
100 Courthouse Square SE
Huntsville, Alabama 35801

Marengo County
101 East Coats Ave.
Linden, Alabama 36748

Marion County
County Courthouse
P.O. Box 1687
Hamilton, Alabama 35570

Marshall County
County Courthouse
425 Gunter Ave.
Guntersville, Alabama
35976

Mobile County
County Courthouse
109 Government St.
Mobile, Alabama 36602

Monroe County
County Courthouse
South Mount Plaza Ave.
Monroeville, Alabama
36461

Montgomery County
County Courthouse
P.O. Box 223
Montgomery, Alabama
36140

Morgan County
County Courthouse
302 Lee St. NE
Decatur, Alabama 35601

Perry County
County Courthouse
P.O. Box 478
Marion, Alabama 36756

Pickens County
County Courthouse
P.O. Box 370
Carrollton, Alabama 35447

Pike County
County Courthouse
120 West Church St.
Troy, Alabama 36081

Randolph County
County Courthouse
P.O. Box 249
Wedowee, Alabama 36278

Russell County
County Courthouse
P.O. Box 700
Phoenix City, Alabama
36868

Shelby County
County Courthouse
P.O. Box 825
Columbiana, Alabama
35051

St Clair County
County Courthouse
P.O. Box 220
Ashville, Alabama 35953

Sumter County
County Courthouse
Franklin St.
Livingston, Alabama 35470

Talladega County
County Courthouse
P.O. Box 755
Talladega, Alabama 35160

Tallapoosa County
County Courthouse
125 N. Broadnax St.
Dadeville, Alabama 36853

Tuscaloosa County
County Courthouse
714 Greensboro Ave.
Tuscaloosa, Alabama
35401

Walker County
County Courthouse
P.O. Box 502
Jasper, Alabama 35502

Washington County
County Courthouse
P.O. Box 549
Chatom, Alabama 36518

Wilcox County
County Courthouse
P.O. Box 668
Camden, Alabama 36726

Winston County
County Courthouse
P.O. Box 27
Double Springs, Alabama
35553

ALASKA

http://www.hss.state.ak.us/dph/bvs/bvs_home.htm

Aleutians East Borough
P.O. Box 349
Sandpoint, Alaska 99661

Anchorage Borough
P.O. Box 196650
Anchorage, Alaska 99519

Bristol Bay Borough
P.O. Box 189
Naknek, Alaska 99633

Denali Borough
P.O. Box 480
Healy, Alaska 99743

Fairbanks North Star Borough
809 Pioneer Rd.
Fairbanks, Alaska 99701

Haines Borough
P.O. Box 1209
Haines, Alaska 99827

Juneau Borough
155 S. Seward St.
Juneau, Alaska 99801

Kenai Peninsula Borough
144 N. Binkley St.
Soldolna, Alaska 99669

Ketchikan Borough
344 Front St.
Ketchikan, Alaska 99901

Kodiak Borough
710 Mill Bay Rd.
Kodiak, Alaska 99615

Matanuska-Susitna Borough
350 E. Dahlia Ave.
Palmer, Alaska 99645

North Slope Borough
P.O. Box 69
Barrow, Alaska 99723

Northwest Arctic Borough
P.O. Box 1110
Kotzebue, Alaska 99752

Silka Borough
100 Lincoln St.
Sitka, Alaska 99835

Yakutat Borough
P.O. Box 160
Yakutat, Alaska 99689

ARIZONA

http://www.state.az.us/

Apache County
P.O. Box 365
St. Johns, Arizona 85936

Cochise County
P.O. Box CK
Bisbee, Arizona 85603

Coconino County
100 E. Birch Ave.
Flagstaff, Arizona 86001

Gila County
1400 E. Ash St.
Globe, Arizona 85501

Graham County
800 W. Main St.
Safford, Arizona 85546

Greenlee County
Webster St.
Clifton, Arizona 85533

La Paz County
1713 S. Kola Ave.
Parker, Arizona 85344

Maricopa County
201 W. Jefferson St.
Phoenix, Arizona 85003

Mohave County
401 E. Spring St.
Kingman, Arizona 86401

Navajo County
P.O. Box 668
Holbrook, Arizona 86025

Pima County
150 West Congress St.
Tucson, Arizona 85701

Pinal County
P.O. Box 827
Florence, Arizona 85232

Santa Cruz County
P.O. Box 1265
Nogales, Arizona 85628

Yavapai County
Clerk of Superior Court
Prescott, Arizona 86301

Yuma County
198 S. Main St.
Yuma, Arizona 85364

ARKANSAS

http://www.state.ar.us

Arkansas County Clerk
P.O. Box 719
Stuttgart, Arkansas
72160-0719

Ashley County Clerk
215 E. Jefferson Ave.
Hamburg, Arkansas 71646

Baxter County Clerk
County Courthouse
Mountain Home, Arkansas
72653-4065

Benton County Clerk
P.O. Box 699
Bentonville, Arkansas
72712-0699

Boone County Clerk
100 N. Main, Suite 201
Harrison, Arkansas 72601

Bradley County Clerk
County Courthouse
Warren, Arkansas 71671

Calhoun County Clerk
P.O. Box 626
Hampton, Arkansas
71744-0626

Carroll County Clerk
210 West Church St.
Berryville, Arkansas
72616-4233

Chicot County Clerk
County Courthouse
Lake Village, Arkansas
71653

Clark County Clerk
County Courthouse Square
Arkadelphia, Arkansas
71923

Clay County Clerk
P.O. Box 306
Piggott, Arkansas 72454

Cleburne County Clerk
301 W. Main St.
Heber Springs, Arkansas
72543

Cleveland County Clerk
Main and Magnolia Streets
Rison, Arkansas 71665

Columbia County Clerk
1 Court Square
Magnolia, Arkansas 71753

Conway County Clerk
117 S. Moose St.,
Rm. 203
Morrilton, Arkansas
72110-3427

Craighead County Clerk
511 Union St.
Jonesboro, Arkansas
72401-2849

Crawford County Clerk
3rd and Main Streets
Van Buren, Arkansas
72946-5765

Crittenden County Clerk
County Courthouse
Marion, Arkansas 72364

Cross County Clerk
705 E. Union St.
Wynne, Arkansas
72396-3039

Dallas County Clerk
206 3rd St. W.
Fordyce, Arkansas 71742

Desha County Clerk
P.O. Box 188
Arkansas City, Arkansas
71630-0188

Drew County Clerk
210 S. Main St.
Monticello, Arkansas
71655

Faulkner County Clerk
801 Locust St
Conway, Arkansas 72032

Franklin County Clerk
Courthouse
Ozark, Arkansas 72949

Fulton County Clerk
P.O. Box 278
Salem, Arkansas
72576-0278

Garland County Clerk
501 Ouachita Ave.
Hot Springs, Arkansas
71901-5154

Grant County Clerk
Main and Center Streets
Sheridan, Arkansas 72150

Greene County Clerk
320 W. Court, Rm. 102
Paragould, Arkansas 72450

Hempstead County Clerk
P.O. Box 1420
Hope, Arkansas 71801

**Hot Springs County
Clerk**
3rd and Locust St.
Malvern, Arkansas 72104

Howard County Clerk
421 N. Main St.
Nashville, Arkansas
71852-2008

**Independence
County Clerk**
192 E. Main St.
Batesville, Arkansas
72501-3135

Izard County Clerk
P.O. Box 95
Melbourne, Arkansas
72556

Jackson County Clerk
P.O. Box 641
Newport, Arkansas
72112-0641

Jefferson County Clerk
P.O. Box 6317
Pine Bluff, Arkansas
71611-6317

Johnson County Clerk
P.O. Box 57
Clarksville, Arkansas
72830

Lafayette County Clerk
#2 Courthouse Square
Lewisville, Arkansas 71845

Lawrence County Clerk
315 W. Main St., Rm. 1
Walnut Ridge, Arkansas
72476-0553

Lee County Clerk
15 E. Chestnut St.
Marianna, Arkansas
72360-2302

Lincoln County Clerk
Drew and Wiley Streets
Star City, Arkansas 71667

Little River County Clerk
351 N. 2nd St.
Ashdown, Arkansas 71822

Logan County Clerk
Broadway St.
Booneville, Arkansas
72927

Lonoke County Clerk
P.O. Box 431
Lonoke, Arkansas 72086

Madison County Clerk
P.O. Box 37
Huntsville, Arkansas
72740-0037

Marion County Clerk
Courthouse Square
Yellville, Arkansas 72687

Miller County Clerk
400 Laurel St.
Texarkana, Arkansas 75502

Mississippi County Clerk
Walnut and 2nd Streets
Blytheville, Arkansas
72315

Monroe County Clerk
123 Madison St.
Clarendon, Arkansas
72029-2742

**Montgomery County
Clerk**
P.O. Box 717
Mount Ida, Arkansas 71957

Nevada County Clerk
County Courthouse
Prescott, Arkansas 71857

Newton County Clerk
P.O. Box 410
Jasper, Arkansas 72641

Ouachita County Clerk
145 Jefferson St.
Camden, Arkansas 71701

Perry County Clerk
P.O. Box 358
Perryville, Arkansas
72126-0358

Phillips County Clerk
626 Cherry St.
Helena, Arkansas 72342

Pike County Clerk
Washington St.
Murfreesboro, Arkansas
71958

Poinsett County Clerk
Courthouse Square
Harrisburg, Arkansas
72432

Polk County Clerk
507 Church Ave.
Mena, Arkansas 71953

Pope County Clerk
100 W. Main St.
Russellville, Arkansas
72801

Prairie County Clerk
P.O. Box 278
Des Arc, Arkansas 72040-
0278

Pulaski County Clerk
405 W. Markham St.
Little Rock, Arkansas
72201-1407

Randolph County Clerk
201 Marr St
Pocahontas, Arkansas
72455-3322

Saline County Clerk
200 N. Main St.
Benton, Arkansas 72015

Scott County Clerk
P.O. Box 1578
Waldron, Arkansas
72958-1578

Searcy County Clerk
P.O. Box 297
Marshall, Arkansas 72650

Sebastian County Clerk
6th and Rogers
Fort Smith, Arkansas
72901

Sevier County Clerk
115 N. 3rd St.
De Queen, Arkansas 71832

Sharp County Clerk
County Courthouse
Ash Flat, Arkansas 72513

St. Francis County Clerk
313 S. Izard St.
Forrest City, Arkansas
72335-3856

Stone County Clerk
P.O. Box 120
Mountain View, Arkansas
72560

Union County Clerk
101 N. Washington Ave.
El Dorado, Arkansas 71730

Van Buren County Clerk
Rt.6, Box 254-9
Clinton, Arkansas 72031

**Washington
County Clerk**
280 N. College St.,
Suite 300
Fayetteville, Arkansas
72701-5309

White County Clerk
300 N. Spruce St.
Searcy, Arkansas
72143-7720

Woodruff County Clerk
500 N. 3rd St.
Augusta, Arkansas
72006-2056

Yell County Clerk
P.O. Box 219
Danville, Arkansas 72833

CALIFORNIA
http://www.state.ca.us/

Alameda County
1106 Madison St., 1st Fl
Oakland, California 94607

Alpine County
99 Water St.
Markleeville, California
96120

Amador County
500 Argonaut Lane
Jackson, California 95642

Butte County
25 County Center Dr.
Oroville, California
95965-3316

Calaveras County
Government Center
San Andreas, California
95249

Colusa County
546 Jay St.
Colusa, California
95932-2491

Contra Costa County
730 Las Juntas
Martinez, California
94553-1233

Del Norte County
450 H St.
Crescent City, California
95531-4021

El Dorado County
360 Fair Lane
Placerville, California
95667

Fresno County
220 Tulare St., Rm. 303
Frenso, California 93721

Glenn County
526 W. Sycamore St.
Willows, California 95988

Humboldt County
714 4th St.
Eureka, California 95501

Imperial County
940 Main St., Rm. #206
El Centro, California 92243

Inyo County
168 N. Edwards St.
Independence, California
93526

Kern County
1655 Chester Ave.
Bakersfield, California
93301

Kings County
1400 W. Lacey Blvd.
Hanford, California
93230-5905

Lake County
255 N. Forbes St.
Lakeport, California
95453-4731

Lassen County
220 S. Lassen St., Suite 5
Susanville, California
96130

Los Angeles County
Los Angeles Registrar-
Recorder/County Clerk
P.O. Box 53120
Los Angeles, California
90053-0120

Madera County
209 W. Yosemite Ave.
Madera, California
93637-3534

Marin County
3501 Civic Center Dr.,
Rm. 234
San Rafael, California
94903

Mariposa County
P.O. Box 35
Mariposa, California 95338

Mendocino County
501 Low Gap Rd., Rm. 1020
Ukiah, California 95482

Merced County
2222 M St.
Merced, California
95340-3729

Modoc County
200 Court St.
Alturas, California
96101-4026

Mono County
P.O. Box 537
Bridgeport, California
93517-0537

Monterey County
240 Church St., Rm. 305
Salinas, California 93902

Napa County
900 Coombs St., Rm. 116
Napa, California 94559

Nevada County
950 Maidu Ave.
Nevada City, California
95959-2504

Orange County
12 Civic Center Plaza,
Rm. 106
Santa Ana, California
92701

Placer County
2954 Richardson Dr.
Auburn, California 95603

Plumas County
520 Main St. Rm. 102
Quincy, California
95971-9366

Riverside County
2724 Gateway Dr.
Riverside, California 92502

Sacramento County
600 8th St., Rm. 108
Sacramento, California
95814

San Benito County
440 5th St., Rm. 206
Hollister, California
95023-3843

San Bernardino County
222 W. Hospitality Lane.
San Bernardino, California
92415

San Diego County
1600 Pacific Highway,
Rm. 260
San Diego, California
92112-4147

San Francisco County
Birth and Death Records:
San Francisco Dept of
Public Health
101 Grove St. Rm. 105
San Francisco, California
94102

Marriage Records:
San Francisco
County Recorder
875 Stevenson St., Rm. 100
San Francisco, California
94103

San Joaquin County
24 S. Hunter #304
Stockton, California 95201

San Luis Obispo County
1144 Monterey St., Suite A
San Luis Obispo,
California 93408

San Mateo County
401 Marshall St., 6th Fl.
Redwood City, California
94063-1636

Santa Barbara County
1100 Anacapa St.
Santa Barbara, California
93101-2000

Santa Clara County
Birth, Death,
Marriage Records:
Santa Clara
County Recorder
70 West Hedding St.
San Jose, California 95112

Divorce Records:
Santa Clara County
Superior Court
191 N. 1st St.
San Jose, California
53113-1001

Santa Cruz County
701 Ocean St., Rm. 230
Santa Cruz, California
95060

Shasta County
1500 Court St.
Redding, California
96001-1662

Sierra County
P.O. Box D
Downieville, California
95936-0398

Siskiyou County
P.O. Box 338
Yreka, California
96097-9910

Solano County
701 Texas St.
Fairfield, California 94533

Sonoma County
585 Fiscal Dr.
Santa Rosa, California
95403

Stanislaus County
P.O. Box 1098
Modesto, California
95353–1098

Sutter County
433 2nd St.
Yuba City, California
95991-5524

Tehama County
P.O. Box 250
Red Bluff, California
96080-0250

Trinity County
P.O. Box 1258
Weaverville, California
96093-1258

Tulare County
Tulare County Civic
Center, Rm. 203
Visalia, California 93291

Tuolumne County
2 S. Green St.
Sonora, California
95370-4617

Ventura County
800 S. Victoria Ave.
Ventura, California
93009-1260

Yolo County
625 Court St., Rm. 105
Woodland, California
95695

Yuba County
935 14th St.
Marysville, California
95901

COLORADO
http://www.state.co.us/

Adams County
450 S. 4th Ave.
Brighton, Colorado 80601

Alamosa County
P.O. Box 178
Alamosa, Colorado 81101

Arapahoe County
5334 Prince St.
Littleton, Colorado
80120-1136

Archuleta County
P.O. Box 148
Pagosa Springs, Colorado
81147-0148

Baca County
741 Main St.
Springfield, Colorado
81073-0116

Bent County
P.O. Box 350
Las Animas, Colorado
81054-0350

Boulder County
3450 Broadway
Boulder, Colorado 80304

Chaffee County
P.O. Box 699
Salida, Colorado
81201-0699

Cheyenne County
P.O. Box 67
Cheyenne Wells, Colorado
80810-0067

Clear Creek County
P.O. Box 2000
Georgetown, Colorado
80444-2000

Conejos County
P.O. Box 157
Conejos, Colorado
81129-0157

Costilla County
P.O. Box 100
San Luis, Colorado 81152

Crowley County
6th and Main St.
Ordway, Colorado 81063

Custer County
205 S. 6th St.
Westcliffe, Colorado 81252

Delta County
501 Palmer St.
Delta, Colorado
81416-1725

Denver County
Clerk and
Recorder's Office
1437 Bannock St., Rm. 281
Denver, Colorado 80202

Dolores County
4th and Main St.
Dove Creek, Colorado
81324-0164

Douglas County
301 Wilcox St.
Castle Rock, Colorado
80104-2440

Eagle County
P.O. Box 537
Eagle, Colorado
81631-0850

El Paso County
Vital Statistics Section
301 S. Union Blvd.
Colorado Springs,
Colorado 80910
(719) 520-7475

Elbert County
751 Ute Ave.
Kiowa, Colorado
80117-9315

Fremont County
615 Macon Ave.
Cannon City, Colorado
81212

Garfield County
109 8th St.
Glenwood Springs,
Colorado 81601-3362

Gilpin County
P.O. Box 366
Central City, Colorado
80427-0366

Grand County
308 Byers Ave.
Hot Sulphur Springs,
Colorado 80451

Gunnison County
200 E. Virginia Ave.
Gunnison, Colorado
81230-2248

Hinsdale County
P.O. Box 403
Lake City, Colorado 81235

Huerfano County
400 Main St., Rm. 201
Walsenburg, Colorado
81089-2034

Jackson County
P.O. Box 337
Walden, Colorado
80480-0337

Jefferson County
260 S. Kipling St.
Lakewood, Colorado 80226

Kiowa County
1305 Golf St.
Eads, Colorado
81036-0037

Kit Carson County
P.O. Box 248
Burlington, Colorado
80807-0248

La Plata County
1060 E. 2nd Ave.
Durango, Colorado
81301-5157

Lake County
P.O. Box 964
Leadville, Colorado 80461

Larimer County
1525 Blue Spruce Dr.
Fort Collins, Colorado
80524-2004

Las Animas County
1st and Maple St.
Trinidad, Colorado 81082

Lincoln County
718 3rd Ave.
Hugo, Colorado 80821

Logan County
315 Main St.
Sterling, Colorado 80751

Mesa County
515 Patterson Rd.
Grand Junction, Colorado
81506

Mineral County
P.O. Box 70
Creede, Colorado
81130-0070

Moffat County
221 W. Victory Way
Craig, Colorado
81625-2732

Montezuma County
109 W. Main St.
Cortez, Colorado
81321-3154

Montrose County
P.O. Box 1289
Montrose, Colorado
81402-1289

Morgan County
231 Ensign St.
Fort Morgan, Colorado
80701-0596

Otero County
P.O. Box 511
LaJunta, Colorado
81050-0511

Ouray County
541 4th St.
Ouray, Colorado
81427-0615

Park County
501 Main St.
Fairplay, Colorado
80440-0220

Phillips County
221 S. Interocean Ave.
Holyoke, Colorado
80734-1534

Pitkin County
530 E. Main St.
Aspen, Colorado 81611

Prowers County
301 S. Main St.
Lamar, Colorado
81052-1046

Pueblo County
211 W. 10th St.
Pueblo, Colorado
81003-2905

Rio Blanco County
P.O. Box 1150
Meeker, Colorado 81641

Rio Grande County
P.O. Box 160
Del Norte, Colorado
81132-0160

Routt County
P.O. Box 773598
Steamboat Springs,
Colorado 80477

Saguache County
P.O. Box 356
Saguache, Colorado
81149-0356

San Juan County
P.O. Box 466
Silverton, Colorado 81433

San Miguel County
305 W. Colorado
Telluride, Colorado 81435

Sedgwick County
P.O. Box 3
Julesburg, Colorado
80737-0003

Summitt County
208 E. Lincoln St.
Breckenridge, Colorado
80424

Teller County
P.O. Box 959
Cripple Creek, Colorado
80813-0959

Washington County
150 Ash Ave.
Akron, Colorado
80720-1510

Weld County
915 10th St.
Greeley, Colorado
80631-3811

Yuma County
Third and Ash
Wray, Colorado 80758

CONNECTICUT
http://www.state.ct.us/

Fairfield County Clerk
1061 Main St.
Bridgeport, Connecticut
06601-4222

Hartford County Clerk
95 Washington St.
Hartford, Connecticut
06106-4406

Litchfield County Clerk
20 West St.
Litchfield, Connecticut
06759

Middlesex County Clerk
1 Court St.
Middletown, Connecticut
06457-3442

New Haven County Clerk
235 Church St.
New Haven, Connecticut
06510-0998

**New London
County Clerk**
181 State St.
New London, Connecticut
06320

Tolland County Clerk
69 Brooklyn St.
Vernon Rockville,
Connecticut 06066-3643

Windham County Clerk
Courthouse
Putnam, Connecticut 06260

DELAWARE
http://www.state.de.us/

Kent County Clerk
414 Federal St.
Dover, Delaware
19901-3615

New Castle County Clerk
800 N. French St.
Wilmington, Delaware
19801-3590

Sussex County Clerk
P.O. Box 743
Georgetown, Delaware
19947

FLORIDA
http://www.state.fl.us/

Alachua County Clerk
21 E. University Ave.
Gainesville, Florida
32602-3028

Baker County Clerk
55 N. 3rd St.
MacClenny, Florida
32063-2101

Bay County Clerk
300 E. 4th St.
Panama City, Florida
32402-2269

Bradford County Clerk
P.O. Box B
Starke, Florida 32091-1286

Brevard County Clerk
700 S. Park Ave.
Titusville, Florida 32781

Broward County Clerk
2421 S.W. 6th Ave.
Ft. Lauderdale, Florida
33315

Calhoun County Clerk
425 E. Central Ave.
Blountstown, Florida
32424-2242

Charlotte County Clerk
514 E. Grace St.
Punta Gorda, Florida 33950

Citrus County Clerk
110 N. Apopka Ave.
Inverness, Florida 33450

Clay County Clerk
P.O. Box 698
Green Cove Springs,
Florida 32043-0698
(904) 284-6300

Collier County Clerk
3301 Tamiami Trail
Naples, Florida
33962-4902

Columbia County Clerk
35 N. Herndaz St.
Lake City, Florida 32055

Dade County Clerk
1350 NW 14th St.
Miami, Florida 33125

De Soto County Clerk
P.O. Box 591
Arcadia, Florida 34265

Dixie County Clerk
P.O. Box 1206
Cross City, Florida 32628

Duval County Clerk
515 W. 6th St.
Jacksonville, Florida
32206-4397

Escambia County Clerk
223 S. Palafox Pl.
Pensacola, Florida
32501-5845

Flagler County Clerk
200 E. Moody Blvd
Bunnell, Florida
32110-0787

Franklin County Clerk
33 Market St., Suite 203
Apalachicola, Florida
32320

Gadsden County Clerk
10 E. Jefferson St.
Quincy, Florida
32351-0231

Gilchrist County
112 S. Main St.
Trenton, Florida
32693-0037

Glades County Clerk
P.O. Box 10
Moore Haven, Florida
33471-0010

Gulf County Clerk
1000 5th St.
Port St. Joe, Florida
32456-1648

Hamilton County Clerk
P.O. Box 789
Jasper, Florida 32052

Hardee County Clerk
412 W. Orange St.
Wauchula, Florida
33873-2831

Hendry County Clerk
P.O. Box 1760
La Belle, Florida
33935-1760

Hernando County Clerk
20 N. Main St.
Brooksville, Florida 34601

Highlands County Clerk
430 S. Commerce Ave.
Attn: Recording Dept.
Sebring, Florida
33870-3701

**Hillsborough
County Clerk**
1105 E. Kennedy Blvd,
Rm. 276
Tampa, Florida 33602

Holmes County Clerk
201 N. Oklahoma St.
Bonifay, Florida
32425-2243

**Indian River
County Clerk**
1840 25th St.
Vero Beach, Florida
32960-3365

Jackson County Clerk
P.O. Box 510
Marianna, Florida
32446-0510

Jefferson County Clerk
P.O. Box 547
Monticello, Florida 32344

Lafayette County Clerk
P.O. Box 88
Mayo, Florida 32066-0088

Lake County Clerk
315 W. Main St.
Tavares, Florida
32778-3813

Lee County Clerk
2115 2nd St.
Fort Myers, Florida
33902-2469

Leon County Clerk
301 S. Monroe St.
Tallahassee, Florida 32301

Levy County Clerk
P.O. Box 610
Bronson, Florida
32621-0610

Liberty County Clerk
P.O. Box 399
Bristol, Florida 32321-0399

Madison County Clerk
P.O. Box 237
Madison, Florida
32340-0237

Manatee County Clerk
410 East 6th Ave.
Bradenton, Florida
34208-1928

Marion County Clerk
Department of Vital
Records
1801 S. E. 32nd Ave.
Ocala, Florida 34471

Martin County Clerk
Health Department
620 S. Dixie Highway
Stuart, Florida 34994

Monroe County Clerk
500 Whitehead St.
Key West, Florida
33040-6547

Nassau County Clerk
P.O. Box 456
Fernandina Beach, Florida
32034-0456

**Okaloosa County Public
Health Unit**
221 Hospital Dr. NE
Ft. Walton Beach, Florida
32548

**Okeechobee
County Clerk**
304 NW 2nd St.
Okeechobee, Florida 34972

Orange County Clerk
832 W. Central Blvd.,
Rm. 200
Orlando, Florida 32805

Osceola County Clerk
12 S. Vernon Ave.
Kissimmee, Florida
32741-5188

Palm Beach County Clerk
Vital Statistics Department
705 N. Olive Ave.
West Palm Beach, Florida
33402

Pasco County Clerk
38053 E. Live Oak Ave.
Dade City, Florida 33525

**Pinellas County Health
Department**
Vital Statistics
300 31st St. N., Suite 100
St. Petersburg, Florida
33713

Polk County Clerk
255 N. Broadway Ave.
Bartow, Florida 33830

Putnam County Clerk
P.O. Box 758
Palatka, Florida
32078-0758

Santa Rosa County Clerk
801 Caroline St. SE
Milton, Florida 32570-4978

Sarasota County Clerk
2000 Main St.
Sarasota, Florida 34237

Seminole County Clerk
300 N. Park Ave.
Sanford, Florida
32771-1244

St. Johns County P.H.U.
180 Marine St.
St. Augustine, Florida
32084

St. Lucie County Clerk
221 South Indian River Dr.
Ft. Pierce, Florida 34950

Sumter County Clerk
209 N. Florida St.
Bushnell, Florida
33513-9308

Suwannee County Clerk
200 South Ohio Ave.
Live Oak, Florida 32060

Taylor County Clerk
P.O. Box 620
Perry, Florida 32347-0620

Union County Clerk
55 W. Main St.
Lake Butler, Florida
32054-1637

Volusia County Clerk
120 W. Indiana Ave.
De Land, Florida
32720-4210

Wakulla County Clerk
P.O. Box 337
Crawfordville, Florida
32327-0337

Walton County Clerk
P.O. Box 1260
De Funiak Springs, Florida
32434-1260

**Washington
County Clerk**
203 W. Cypress Ave.
Chipley, Florida
32428-1821

GEORGIA

http://www.state.ga.us/

Appling County Clerk
100 N. Oak St.
Baxley, Georgia 31513

Atkinson County Clerk
P.O. Box 855
Pearson, Georgia 31642

Bacon County Clerk
502 W. 12th St.
Alma, Georgia 31510

Baker County Clerk
P.O. Box 548
Newton, Georgia 31770

Baldwin County Clerk
201 W. Hancock St.
Milledgeville, Georgia
31061

Banks County Clerk
P.O. Box 130
Homer, Georgia 30547

Barrow County Clerk
310 S. Broad St., Suite 321
Winder, Georgia 30680

Bartow County Clerk
135 W. Cherokee Ave.,
Suite 251
Cartersville, Georgia 30120

Ben Hill County Clerk
401 E. Central Ave.
Fitzgerald, Georgia 31750

Berrien County Clerk
105 E. Washington Ave.
Nashville, Georgia
31639-0446

Bibb County Clerk
Attn: Vital Records
171 Emery Hwy
Macon, Georgia 31217

Bleckley County Clerk
306 2nd St. SE
Cochran, Georgia
31014-1622

Brantley County Clerk
P.O. Box 398
Nahunta, Georgia 31553

Brooks County Clerk
P.O. Box 665
Quitman, Georgia
31643-0665

Bryan County Clerk
401 S. College St.
Pembroke, Georgia 31321

Bullock County Clerk
1 W. Altman St.
Statesboro, Georgia 30458

Burke County Clerk
6th and Liberty St.
Waynesboro, Georgia
30830-0062

Butts County Clerk
P.O. Box 320
Jackson, Georgia 30233

Calhoun County Clerk
Courthouse Square
Morgan, Georgia 31766

Camden County Clerk
P.O. Box 99
Woodbine, Georgia 31569

Candler County Clerk
705 N. Lewis St.
Metter, Georgia 30439

Carroll County Clerk
311 Newnan St.
Carrollton, Georgia
30117-1620

Catoosa County Clerk
Health Dept-Vital Records
182 Tiger Trail
Ringgold, Georgia
30736-1712

Charlton County Clerk
100 3rd St.
Folkston, Georgia
31537-3706

Chatham County Clerk
P.O. Box 31416
Savannah, Georgia 31406

**Chattahoochee
County Clerk**
P.O. Box 299
Cusseta, Georgia 31805

Chattooga County Clerk
P.O. Box 211
Summerville, Georgia
30747

Cherokee County Clerk
90 North St.
Canton, Georgia
30114-2725

Clarke County Clerk
325 E. Washington St.
Athens, Georgia
30601-2776

Clay County Clerk
P.O. Box 550
Ft. Gaines, Georgia
31751-0550

Clayton County Clerk
112 Smith St.
Jonesboro, Georgia 30236

Clinch County Clerk
100 Court Square
Homerville, Georgia
31634-1415

Cobb County Clerk
1650 County
Services Pkwy.
Marietta, Georgia 30008

Coffee County Clerk
County Courthouse
Douglas, Georgia 31533

Colquitt County Clerk
P.O. Box 886
Moultrie, Georgia 31776

Columbia County Clerk
P.O. Box 58
Appling, Georgia 30802

Cook County Clerk
212 N. Hutchinson Ave.
Adel, Georgia 31620

Coweta County Clerk
P.O. Box 945
Newnan, Georgia
30264-0945

Crawford County Clerk
P.O. Box 420
Knoxville, Georgia
31050-0420

Crisp County Clerk
210 7th St. South
Cordele, Georgia 31015

Dade County Clerk
P.O. Box 417
Trenton, Georgia
30752-0417

Dawson County Clerk
P.O. Box 192
Dawsonville, Georgia
30534

Decatur County Clerk
P.O. Box 234
Bainbridge, Georgia 31717

Dekalb County Clerk
445 Winn Way-Box 987
Decatur, Georgia 30031

Dodge County Clerk
P.O. Box 818
Eastman, Georgia
31023-0818

Dooly County Clerk
P.O. Box 322
Vienna, Georgia
31092-0322

Dougherty County Clerk
225 Pine Ave.
Albany, Georgia
31701-2561

Douglas County Clerk
6754 Broad St.
Douglasville, Georgia
30134-1711

Early County Clerk
105 Courthouse Square
Blakely, Georgia
31723-0525

Echols County Clerk
P.O. Box 118
Statenville, Georgia 31648

Effingham County Clerk
901 N. Pine St.
Springfield, Georgia
31329-0307

Elbert County Clerk
Elbert County Courthouse
14 N. Oliver St.
Elberton, Georgia 30635

Emanuel County Clerk
101 S. Main St.
Swainsboro, Georgia 30401

Evans County Clerk
3 Freeman St.
Claxton, Georgia 30417

Fannin County Clerk
P.O. Box 245
Blue Ridge, Georgia 30513

Fayette County Clerk
145 Johnson Ave.
Fayetteville, Georgia 30214

Floyd County Clerk
315 W. 10th St.
Rome, Georgia 30161-2678

Forsyth County Clerk
P.O. Box 128
Cumming, Georgia
30130-0128

Franklin County Clerk
Courthouse Square
Carnesville, Georgia 30521

Fulton County Clerk
99 Butler St. SE, 2nd Fl.
Atlanta, Georgia 30303

Gilmer County Clerk
1 Westside Square
Ellijay, Georgia
30540-1071

Glascock County Clerk
P.O. Box 231
Gibson, Georgia 30810

Glynn County Clerk
701 G St.
Brunswick, Georgia 31520

Gordon County Clerk
100 S. Wall St. Annex 1
Calhoun, Georgia 30701

Grady County Clerk
250 N. Broad St.
Cairo, Georgia 31728-4101

Greene County Clerk
113-C N. Main St.
Greensboro, Georgia 30642

Gwinnett County Clerk
75 Langley Dr.
Lawrenceville, Georgia
30245

Habersham County Clerk
P.O. Box 227
Clarkesville, Georgia
30523-0227

Hall County Clerk
116 Spring St. East
Gainesville, Georgia 30501

Hancock County Clerk
Courthouse Square–
Drawer G
Sparta, Georgia 31087

Haralson County Clerk
P.O. Box 488
Buchanan, Georgia
30113-0488

Harris County Clerk
P.O. Box 528
Hamilton, Georgia 31811

Hart County Clerk
P.O. Box 128
Hartwell, Georgia 30643

Heard County Clerk
North River St.
Franklin, Georgia 30217

Henry County Clerk
345 Phillips Dr.
McDonough, Georgia
30253-3425

Houston County Clerk
200 Carl Vinson Pkwy.
Warner Robbins, Georgia
31088-5808

Irwin County Clerk
710 N. Irwin Ave.
Ocilla, Georgia
31774-0287

Jackson County Clerk
P.O. Box 68
Jefferson, Georgia 30549

Jasper County Clerk
County Courthouse
Monticello, Georgia 31064

Jeff Davis County Clerk
Jeff Davis St.
Hazlehurst, Georgia 31539

Jefferson County Clerk
P.O. Box 658
Louisville, Georgia
30434-0658

Jenkins County Clerk
P.O. Box 797
Millen, Georgia
30442-0797

Johnson County Clerk
P.O. Box 269
Wrightsville, Georgia
31096-0269

Jones County Clerk
P.O. Box 1359
Gray, Georgia 31032

Lamar County Clerk
327 Thomaston St.
Barnesville, Georgia
30204-1612

Lanier County Clerk
100 W. Main St.
Lakeland, Georgia
31635-1116

Laurens County Clerk
2121 Bellevue Rd.
Dublin, Georgia 31021

Lee County Clerk
P.O. Box 56
Leesburg, Georgia
31763-0056

Liberty County Clerk
Courthouse Square
Hinesville, Georgia 31313

Lincoln County Clerk
P.O. Box 340
Lincolnton, Georgia
30817-0340

Long County Clerk
P.O. Box 426
Ludowici, Georgia 31316

Lowndes County Clerk
P.O. Box 1349
Valdosta, Georgia
31603-1349

Lumpkin County Clerk
99 Courthouse Hill, Suite A
Dahlonega, Georgia 30533

Macon County Clerk
P.O. Box 216
Oglethorpe, Georgia 30168

Madison County Clerk
P.O. Box 147
Danielsville, Georgia
30633-0147

Marion County Clerk
Courthouse Square
Buena Vista, Georgia
31803-0481

McDuffie County Clerk
P.O. Box 28
Thomson, Georgia 30824

McIntosh County Clerk
P.O. Box 453
Darien, Georgia 31305

Meriwether County Clerk
P.O. Box 608
Greenville, Georgia 30222

Miller County Clerk
155 S. 1st St.
Colquitt, Georgia
31737-1284

Mitchell County Clerk
12 Broad St.
Camilla, Georgia 31730

Monroe County Clerk
P.O. Box 817
Forsyth, Georgia
31029-0187

**Montgomery
County Clerk**
P.O. Box 295
Mt. Vernon, Georgia
30445-0295

Morgan County Clerk
141 E. Jefferson St.
Madison, Georgia
30650-1361

Murray County Clerk
3rd Ave.
Chatsworth, Georgia
30705-0023

Muscogee County Clerk
1000 10th St.
Columbus, Georgia
31901-2617

Newton County Clerk
1113 Usher St.
Covington, Georgia
30209-3155

Oconee County Clerk
15 Water St.
Watkinsville, Georgia
30677-0145

Oglethorpe County Clerk
P.O. Box 70
Lexington, Georgia 30648

Paulding County Clerk
116 Main St.
Dallas, Georgia
30132-1441

Peach County Clerk
205 W. Church St.
Ft. Valley, Georgia
31030-0468

Pickens County Clerk
211-1 N. Main St.
Jasper, Georgia
30143-9501

Pierce County Clerk
P.O. Box 646
Blackshear, Georgia 31516

Pike County Clerk
P.O. Box 377
Zebulon, Georgia
30295-0377

Polk County Clerk
100 Prior St. #101
Cedartown, Georgia 30125

Pulaski County Clerk
P.O. Box 29
Hawkinsville, Georgia
31036-0029

Putnam County Clerk
108 S. Madison Ave.
Eatonton, Georgia 31024

Quitman County Clerk
P.O. Box 7
Georgetown, Georgia
31754

Rabun County Clerk
P.O. Box 925
Clayton, Georgia 30525

Randolph County Clerk
Court St.
Cuthbert, Georgia 31740

Richmond County Clerk
530 Greene St.
Augusta, Georgia 30911

Rockdale County Clerk
922 Court St. NE
Conyers, Georgia 30012

Schley County Clerk
P.O. Box 352
Ellaville, Georgia
31806-0352

Screven County Clerk
216 Mims Rd.
Sylvania, Georgia 30467

Seminole County Clerk
P.O. Box 458 County
Courthouse
Donalsonville, Georgia
31745-0458

Spalding County Clerk
132 E. Solomon St.
Griffin, Georgia
30223-3312

Stephens County Clerk
P.O. Box 386
Toccoa, Georgia
30577-0386

Stewart County Clerk
P.O. Box 157
Lumpkin, Georgia
31815-0157

Sumter County Clerk
P.O. Box 246
Americus, Georgia 31709

Talbot County Clerk
P.O. Box 155
Courthouse Square
Talbotton, Georgia
31827-0155

Taliaferro County Clerk
P.O. Box 114
Courthouse Square
Crawfordville, Georgia
30631

Tattnall County Clerk
Main and Brazell Streets
Reidsville, Georgia 30453

Taylor County Clerk
P.O. Box 148
Butler, Georgia 31006

Telfair County Clerk
Courthouse Square
McRae, Georgia 31055

Terrell County Clerk
955 Forrester Dr. SE
Dawson, Georgia
31742-0525

Thomas County Clerk
P.O. Box 1582
Thomasville, Georgia
31799

Tift County Clerk
P.O. Box 826
Tifton, Georgia
31793-0826

Toombs County Clerk
Courthouse Square and
Hwy 280
Lyons, Georgia 30436

Towns County Clerk
P.O. Box 178
Hiawassee, Georgia 30546

Treutlen County Clerk
P.O. Box 88
Soperton, Georgia
30457-0088

Troup County Clerk
900 Dallas St.
LaGrange, Georgia 30241

Twiggs County
101 Magnolia St.
Jeffersonville, Georgia
31044-0202

Union County Clerk
Rural Route 8, Box 8005
Blairsville, Georgia
30512-9808

Upson County Clerk
P.O. Box 889
Thomaston, Georgia 30286

Walker County Clerk
P.O. Box 445
Lafayette, Georgia
30728-0445

Walton County Clerk
Court St. Annex 1
Monroe, Georgia 30655

Ware County Clerk
800 Church St.
Waycross, Georgia
31502-1069

Warren County Clerk
100 Main St.
Warrenton, Georgia 30828-0046

Washington County Clerk
P.O. Box 271
Sandersville, Georgia
31082-0271

Wayne County Clerk
174 N. Brunswick St.
Jesup, Georgia 31545

Webster County Clerk
P.O. Box 29
Preston, Georgia
31824-0029

Wheeler County Clerk
P.O. Box 477
Alamo, Georgia 30411

White County Clerk
1657 S. Main St.
Cleveland, Georgia 30528

Whitfield County Clerk
300 W. Crawford St.
Dalton, Georgia 30722

Wilcox County Clerk
Courthouse Square
Abbeville, Georgia 31001

Wilkes County Clerk
23 E. Court St.
Washington, Georgia
30673-1516

Wilkinson County Clerk
100 Main St.
Irwinton, Georgia 31042

Worth County Clerk
201 N. Main
Sylvester, Georgia
31791-2100

HAWAII

http://www.state.hi.us/

Hawaii County Clerk
25 Aupuni St.
Hilo, Hawaii 96720-4252

Honolulu County Clerk
City Hall
Honolulu, Hawaii
96813-3014

Kauai County Clerk
4396 Rice St.
Lihue, Hawaii 96766-1337

Maui County
200 S. High St.
Wailuku, Hawaii
96793-2155

IDAHO

http://www.state.id.us/

Ada County Clerk
650 Main St.
Boise, Idaho 83702-5960

Adams County Clerk
P.O. Box 48
Council, Idaho 83612-0048

Bannock County Clerk
624 E. Center St., Rm. 211
Pocatello, Idaho
83201-6274

Bear Lake County Clerk
7 E. Center St.
Paris, Idaho 83261

Benewah County Clerk
318 Highland.
St. Maries, Idaho 83861

Bingham County Clerk
501 N. Maple St.
Blackfoot, Idaho 83221

Blaine County Clerk
206 1st Ave., South,
Suite 200
Hailey, Idaho 83333

Boise County Clerk
P.O. Box 157
Idaho City, Idaho
83631-0157

Bonner County Clerk
215 S. 1st Ave.
Sandpoint, Idaho
83664-1305

Bonneville County Clerk
605 N. Capital Ave.
Idaho Falls, Idaho
83402-3582

Boundary County Clerk
315 Kootnal St.
Bonners Ferry, Idaho
83805-0419

Butte County Clerk
P.O. Box 737
Arco, Idaho 83213-0737

Camas County Clerk
P.O. Box 430
Fairfield, Idaho
83327-0430

Canyon County Clerk
1115 Albany St.
Caldwell, Idaho
83605-3542

Caribou County Clerk
159 S. Main St.
Soda Springs, Idaho
83276-1427

Cassia County Clerk
County Courthouse
Burley, Idaho 83318-1862

Clark County Clerk
P.O. Box 205
Dubois, Idaho 83423-0205

Clearwater County Clerk
P.O. Box 586
Orofino, Idaho 83544-0586

Custer County Clerk
P.O. Box 597
Challis, Idaho 83226

Elmore County Clerk
150 S. 4th East
Mountain Home, Idaho
83647

Franklin County Clerk
39 W. Oneida St.
Preston, Idaho 83263-1234

Fremont County Clerk
151 W. 1st North
St. Anthony, Idaho 83445

Gem County Clerk
415 E. Main St.
Emmett, Idaho 83617-3049

Gooding County Clerk
P.O. Box 417
Gooding, Idaho
83330-0417

Idaho County Clerk
320 W. Main St.
Grangeville, Idaho
83530-1948

Jefferson County Clerk
120 N. Clark St.
Rigby, Idaho 83442-1462

Jerome County Clerk
300 N. Lincoln Ave.
Jerome, Idaho 83338

Kootenai County Clerk
501 N. Government Way
Coeur d'Alene, Idaho
83814-2915

Latah County Clerk
522 S. Adams St.
Moscow, Idaho 83843

Lemhi County Clerk
206 Courthouse Dr.
Salmon, Idaho 83467-3943

Lewis County Clerk
510 Oak St.
Nez Perce, Idaho 83543

Lincoln County Clerk
111 W. B St.
Shoshone, Idaho
83352-0800

Madison County Clerk
P.O. Box 389
Rexburg, Idaho
83440-0389

Minidoka County Clerk
715 G St.
Rupert, Idaho 83350-0474

Nez Perce County Clerk
P.O. Box 896
Lewiston, Idaho
83501-0896

Oneida County Clerk
10 Court St.
Malad City, Idaho 83252

Owyhee County Clerk
P.O. Box 128
Murphy, Idaho 83650

Payette County Clerk
1130 Third Ave. N.
Payette, Idaho 83661-2473

Power County Clerk
543 Bannock Ave.
American Falls, Idaho
83211-1200

Shoshone County Clerk
P.O. Box 1049
Wallace, Idaho 83873-1049

Teton County Clerk
89 N. Main
Driggs, Idaho 83422

Twin Falls County Clerk
P.O. Box 126
Twin Falls, Idaho 83303

Valley County Clerk
P.O. Box 737
Cascade, Idaho 83611-0737

**Washington
County Clerk**
P.O. Box 670
Weisor, Idaho 83672-0670

ILLINOIS
http://www.state.il.us/

Adams County Clerk
521 Vermont St.
Quincy, Illinois 62301

Alexander County Clerk
2000 Washington Ave.
Cairo, Illinois 62914

Bond County Clerk
P.O. Box 407
Greenville, Illinois 62246

Boone County Clerk
601 N. Main St.
Belvidere, Illinois 61008

Brown County Clerk
21 W. Court St.
Mt. Sterling, Illinois 62353

Bureau County Clerk
County Courthouse
Princeton, Illinois 61356

Calhoun County Clerk
P.O. Box 187
Hardin, Illinois 62047-0187

Carroll County Clerk
P.O. Box 152
Mt. Carroll, Illinois
61053-0152

Cass County Clerk
100 E. Springfield St.
Virginia, Illinois 62691

Champaign County Clerk
1776 E. Washington St.
Urbana, Illinois 61801

Christian County Clerk
600 N. Main St.
Taylorville, Illinois
62568-0190

Clark County Clerk
501 Archer Ave.
Marshall, Illinois 62441

Clay County Clerk
P.O. Box 160
Louisville, Illinois
62858-0160

Clinton County Clerk
850 Fairfax
Carlyle, Illinois 62231

Coles County Clerk
651 Jackson Ave., Rm. 122
Charleston, Illinois 61920

Cook County Clerk
118 N. Clark St.
Chicago, Illinois 60602

Crawford County Clerk
P.O. Box 602
Robinson, Illinois
62454-0602

**Cumberland
County Clerk**
Courthouse Square
Toledo, Illinois 62468-0146

Dekalb County Clerk
110 E. Sycamore St.
Sycamore, Illinois
60178-1448

DeWitt County Clerk
201 W. Washington St.
Clinton, Illinois 61727

Douglas County Clerk
401 S. Center St.
Tuscola, Illinois
61953-0067

DuPage County Clerk
421 N. Farm Rd.
Wheaton, Illinois
60187-3978

Edgar County Clerk
115 W. Court St., Rm. J
Paris, Illinois 61944

Edwards County Clerk
50 E. Main St.
Albion, Illinois 62806

Effingham County Clerk
P.O. Box 628
Effingham, Illinois
62401-0628

Fayette County Clerk
221 S. 7th St.
Vandalia, Illinois 62471

Ford County Clerk
200 W. State St. Rm. 101
Paxton, Illinois 60957

Franklin County Clerk
202 W. Main St.
Benton, Illinois 62918

Fulton County Clerk
100 N. Main St.
Lewistown, Illinois
61542-1409

Gallatin County Clerk
P.O. Box 550
Shawneetown, Illinois
62984

Greene County Clerk
519 N. Main St.
Carrollton, Illinois 62016

Grundy County Clerk
111 E. Washington St.
Morris, Illinois 60450

Hamilton County Clerk
Courthouse
McLeansboro, Illinois
62859

Hancock County Clerk
Court House
Carthage, Illinois 62321

Hardin County Clerk
Main St.
Elizabethtown, Illinois
62931

Henderson County Clerk
P.O. Box 308
Oquawka, Illinois 61469

Henry County Clerk
100 S. Main St.
Cambridge, Illinois 61238

Iroquois County Clerk
550 S. 10th St.
Watseka, Illinois
60970-1810

Jackson County Clerk
1001 Walnut St.
Murphysbobo, Illinois
62966-2194

Jasper County Clerk
100 W. Jordan St.
Newton, Illinois
62448-1973

Jefferson County Clerk
100 S. 10th St.
Mt. Vernon, Illinois 62864

Jersey County Clerk
210 W. Pearl St.
Jerseyville, Illinois
62052-1675

Jo Daviess County Clerk
330 N. Bench St.
Galena, Illinois 61036

Johnson County Clerk
400 Court Square
Vienna, Illinois 62995

Kane County Clerk
719 S. Batavia Ave.,
Bldg B
Geneva, Illinois
60134-2722

Kankakee County Clerk
189 E. Court St.
Kankakee, Illinois 60901

Kendall County Clerk
110 W. Fox St.
Yorkville, Illinois 60560

Knox County Clerk
200 S. Cherry St.
Galesburg, Illinois
61401-4912

Lake County Clerk
18 N. County St., Rm. 101
Waukegan, Illinois
60085-4364

Lasalle County Clerk
707 E. Etna Rd County
Gov. Ctr.
Ottawa, Illinois
61350-1033

Lawrence County Clerk
County Courthouse
Lawrenceville, Illinois
62439

Lee County Clerk
P.O. Box 329
Dixon, Illinois 61021

Livingston County Clerk
112 W. Madison St.
Pontiac, Illinois 61764

Logan County Clerk
601 Broadway St.
Lincoln, Illinois 62656

Macon County Clerk
141 S. Main
Decatur, Illinois 62523

Macoupin County Clerk
County Courthouse
Carlinville, Illinois 62626

Madison County Clerk
155 N. Main St.
Edwardsville, Illinois
62025

Marion County Clerk
P.O. Box 637
Salem, Illinois 62881-0637

Marshall County Clerk
122 N. Prairie St.
Lacon, Illinois 61540-1216

Mason County Clerk
County Courthouse
100 N. Broadway
Havana, Illinois
62644-0090

Massac County Clerk
P.O. Box 429
Metropolis, Illinois
62960-0429

**McDonough
County Clerk**
County Courthouse
Macomb, Illinois 61455

McHenry County Clerk
2200 N. Seminary Ave.
Woodstock, Illinois 60098

McLean County Clerk
Court House, Rm. 102
Bloomington, Illinois
61702

Menard County Clerk
P.O. Box 456
Petersburg, Illinois 62675

Mercer County Clerk
100 SE 3rd St.
Aledo, Illinois 61231

Monroe County Clerk
Courthouse 100 S. Main St.
Waterloo, Illinois 62298

**Montgomery
County Clerk**
1 Courthouse Square
Hillsboro, Illinois 62049

Morgan County Clerk
300 W. State St.
Jacksonville, Illinois
62650-2061

Moultrie County Clerk
Courthouse
Sullivan, Illinois 61951

Ogle County Clerk
P.O. Box 357
Oregon, Illinois
61061-0357

Peoria County Clerk
324 Main St.
Peoria, Illinois 61602

Perry County Clerk
P.O. Box 438
Pinckneyville, Illinois
62274

Piatt County Clerk
101 W. Washington St.
Monticello, Illinois 61856

Pike County Clerk
Route 36
Pittsfield, Illinois 62363

Pope County Clerk
Courthouse
Golconda, Illinois 62938

Pulaski County Clerk
P.O. Box 218
Mound City, Illinois
62963-0218

Putnam County Clerk
Courthouse
Hennepin, Illinois 61327

Randolph County Clerk
Courthouse
Chester, Illinois 62233

Richland County Clerk
103 W. Main St.
Olney, Illinois 62450

**Rock Island
County Clerk**
1504 3rd Ave.
Rock Island, Illinois 61201

Saline County Clerk
Courthouse
Harrisburg, Illinois 62946

Sangamon County Clerk
200 S. 9th St., Rm. 101
Springfield, Illinois 62701

Schuyler County Clerk
Courthouse
Rushville, Illinois 62681

Scott County Clerk
Courthouse
Winchester, Illinois 62694

Shelby County Clerk
324 E. Main St.
Shelbyville, Illinois 62565

St. Clair County Clerk
10 Public Square
Belleville, Illinois
62220-1623

Stark County Clerk
130 W. Main St.
Toulon, Illinois 61483

Stephenson County Clerk
15 N. Galena Ave.
Freeport, Illinois
61032-4348

Tazewell County Clerk
4th and Court St.
Pekin, Illinois 61554

Union County Clerk
311 W. Market St.
Jonesboro, Illinois 62952

Vermilion County Clerk
6 N. Vermilion St.
Danville, Illinois
61832-5842

Wabash County Clerk
4th and Market St.
Mt. Carmel, Illinois 62863

Warren County Clerk
Courthouse
Monmouth, Illinois 61462

**Washington
County Clerk**
Courthouse
Nashville, Illinois 62263

Wayne County Clerk
300 E. Main St.
Fairfield, Illinois
62837-0187

White County Clerk
Courthouse
Carmi, Illinois 62821

Whiteside County Clerk
200 E. Knox St.
Morrison, Illinois 61270

Will County Clerk
302 N. Chicago St.
Joliet, Illinois 60432

Williamson County Clerk
200 W. Jefferson St.
Marion, Illinois
62959-3061

Winnebago County Clerk
404 Elm St., Rm. 103
Rockford, Illinois 61101

Woodford County Clerk
P.O. Box 38
Eureka, Illinois 61530

INDIANA
http://www.state.in.us/

Adams County Clerk
Adams County Service
Complex
313 W. Jefferson St,
Rm. 314
Decatur, Indiana 46733

Allen County Clerk
One E..Main St.
Ft. Wayne, Indiana
46802-1804

**Bartholomew
County Clerk**
440 Third St., Suite 303
Columbus, Indiana
47201-6798

Benton County Clerk
700 E. 5th St., Suite 15
Fowler, Indiana
47944-1556

Blackford County Clerk
100 N. Jefferson
Hartford City, Indiana
47348

Boone County Clerk
416 W. Camp St.
Lebanon, Indiana
46052-2161

Brown County Clerk
P.O. Box 281
Nashville, Indiana 47448

Carroll County Clerk
Courthouse, 101 W. Main
Delphi, Indiana 46923

Cass County Clerk
200 Court Park, Gov. Bldg
Logansport, Indiana 46947

Clark County Clerk
1216 Akers Ave.
Jeffersonville, Indiana
47130

Clay County Clerk
Courthouse, 609 E.
National Ave.
Brazil, Indiana 47834

Clinton County Clerk
211 N. Jackson St.
Frankfort, Indiana 46041

Crawford County Clerk
306 Oak Hill Circle
English, Indiana 47118

Daviess County Clerk
Courthouse, 200 E. Walnut
Washington, Indiana 47501

Dearborn County Clerk
215-B W. High St.
Lawrenceburg, Indiana
47025

Decatur County Clerk
801 N. Lincoln
Greensburg, Indiana 47240

Dekalb County Clerk
215 E. 9th, Suite 201
Auburn, Indiana 46706

Delaware County Clerk
100 W. Main St.
Muncie, Indiana 47305

Dubois County Clerk
602 Main St.
Jasper, Indiana 47546

Elkhart County Clerk
608 Oakland Ave.
Elkhart, Indiana 46516

Fayette County Clerk
111 W. 4th St.
Connersville, Indiana
47331

Floyd County Clerk
1917 Bono Rd.
New Albany, Indiana
47150

Fountain County Clerk
210 S. Perry St.
Attica, Indiana 47918

Franklin County Clerk
459 Main St.
Brookville, Indiana 47012

Fulton County Clerk
1009 W. 3rd St.
Rochester, Indiana
46975-1546

Gibson County Clerk
Courthouse Annex
800 S. Prince St.
Princeton, Indiana 47670

Grant County Clerk
401 S. Adams St.
Marion, Indiana 46953

Greene County Clerk
Courthouse
Bloomfield, Indiana 47424

Hamilton County Clerk
One Hamilton County Sq.,
Suite 30
Noblesville, Indiana 46060

Hancock County Clerk
9 E. Main St., Rm. 105
Greenfield, Indiana 46140

Harrison County Clerk
245 Atwood St.,
North Wing.
Corydon, Indiana
47112-1333

Hendricks County Clerk
County Gov. Center
355 S. Washington St.
Danville, Indiana 46122

Henry County Clerk
208 S. 12th St.
New Castle, Indiana 47362

Howard County Clerk
120 Fast Mulberry,
Rm. 206
Kokomo, Indiana 46901

Huntington County Clerk
Courthouse, Rm. 205
Huntington, Indiana 46750

Jackson County Clerk
207 N. Pine St.
Seymour, Indiana 47220

Jasper County Clerk
105 W. Kellner Blvd.
Rensselaer, Indiana
47978-2888

Jay County Clerk
120 N. Court St.
Portland, Indiana 47371

Jefferson County Clerk
715 Green Rd.
Madison, Indiana 47250

Jennings County Clerk
P.O. Box 323
Vernon, Indiana 47282

Johnson County Clerk
86 W. Court St.
Franklin, Indiana 46131

Knox County Clerk
624 Broadway St.
Vincennes, Indiana
47591-5338

Kosciusko County Clerk
100 W. Center St.
Warsaw, Indiana
46580-2846

La Grange County Clerk
114 W. Michigan St.
LaGrange, Indiana 46761

La Porte County Clerk
809 State St.
La Porte, Indiana 46350

Lake County Clerk
2293 N. Main St.
Crown Point, Indiana
46307

Lawrence County Clerk
2419 Mitchell Rd.
Bedford, Indiana 47421

Madison County Clerk
206 E. 9th St.
Anderson, Indiana
46016-1538

Marion County Clerk
3838 N. Rural St.
Indianapolis, Indiana
46205

Marshall County Clerk
112 W. Jefferson St.,
Rm. 103
Plymouth, Indiana 46563

Martin County Clerk
P.O. Box 716
Shoals, Indiana 47581

Miami County Clerk
Courthouse, Rm. 110
Peru, Indiana 46970-2231

Monroe County Clerk
119 W. 7th St.
Bloomington, Indiana
47402-0547

**Montgomery
County Clerk**
307 Binford St. - Basement
Crawfordsville, Indiana
47933

Morgan County Clerk
180 S. Main St., Suite 252
Martinsville, Indiana 46151

Newton County Clerk
210 E. State St.
Morocco, Indiana 47963

Noble County Clerk
2090 N. State Rd. 9,
Suite C
Albion, Indiana
46701-1049

Ohio County Clerk
515 Second St.
Rising Sun, Indiana 47040

Orange County Clerk
205 E. Main St.
Paoli, Indiana 47454

Owen County Clerk
Courthouse, First Fl.
Spencer, Indiana 47460

Parke County Clerk
116 W. High St., Rm. 10
Rockville, Indiana 47872

Perry County Clerk
Courthouse Annex
Cannelton, Indiana
47520-1251

Pike County Clerk
801 Main St.
Petersburg, Indiana 47567

Porter County Clerk
155 Indiana Ave., Suite 104
Valparaiso, Indiana 46383

Posey County Clerk
126 E. 3rd St.
Mt.Vernon, Indiana 47620

Pulaski County Clerk
125 S. Riverside Dr.,
Suite 205
Winamac, Indiana 46996

Putnam County Clerk
Courthouse, 4th Fl.
Greencastle, Indiana 46135

Randolph County Clerk
211 S. Main St.
Winchester, Indiana 47394

Ripley County Clerk
107 N. Washington St.
Versailles, Indiana
47042-0177

Rush County Clerk
Courthouse, Rm. 5
Rushville, Indiana 46173

Scott County Clerk
1471 N. Gardner St.
Scottsburg, Indiana 47170

Shelby County Clerk
53 W. Polk St.
Shelbyville, Indiana 46176

Spencer County Clerk
Courthouse, 3rd Fl., Rm. 1
Rockport, Indiana
47635-0012

St. Joseph County Clerk
227 W. Jefferson Blvd.
South Bend, Indiana 46601

Starke County Clerk
Courthouse, 1st Fl.
Main St.
Knox, Indiana 46534

Steuben County Clerk
55 S. Public Square
Angola, Indiana 46703

Sullivan County Clerk
102 N. Section St.
Sullivan, Indiana 47882

**Switzerland
County Clerk**
211 E. Main St.
Vevay, Indiana 47043

Tippecanoe County Clerk
20 N. 3rd St.
Lafayette, Indiana
47901-1211

Tipton County Clerk
1000 S. Main St.
Tipton, Indiana 46072

Union County Clerk
26 W. Union St.
Liberty, Indiana
47353-1350

**Vanderburgh
County Clerk**
One NW Martin Luther
King Blvd
Admin. Bldg., Rm. 127
Evansville, Indiana
47708-1888

Vermillion County Clerk
825 S. Main St.
Newport, Indiana 47966

Vigo County Clerk
201 Cherry St.
Terre Haute, Indiana
47807-2986

Wabash County Clerk
Memorial Hall
89 West Hill St.
Wabash, Indiana
46992-2015

Warren County Clerk
210 S. Perry St.
Attica, Indiana 47918

**Warrick
County Clerk**
215 S. First St.
Boonville, Indiana 47601

**Washington
County Clerk**
35 Public Square
Salem, Indiana 47167

Wayne County Clerk
Admin. Bldg.
401 E. Main St.
Richmond, Indiana
47375-1172

Wells County Clerk
223 W. Washington St.
Bluffton, Indiana 46714

White County Clerk
P.O. Box 838
Monticello, Indiana 47960

Whitley County Clerk
101 W. Market, Suite A
Columbia City, Indiana
46725-2402

IOWA
http://www.state.ia.us/

Adair County Clerk
P.O. Box L
Greenfield, Iowa
50849-1290

Adams County Clerk
Davis and 9th
Corning, Iowa 50841

Allamakee County Clerk
P.O. Box 248
Waukon, Iowa 52172-0248

Appanoose County Clerk
County Courthouse
Centerville, Iowa 52544

Audubon County Clerk
County Courthouse
Audubon, Iowa 50025

Benton County Clerk
100 E. 4th St.
Vinton, Iowa 52349

**Black Hawk
County Clerk**
316 E. 5th St.
Waterloo, Iowa
50703-4712

Boone County Clerk
County Courthouse
Boone, Iowa 50036

Bremer County Clerk
415 E. Bremer Ave.
Waverly, Iowa 50677

Buchanan County Clerk
210 5th Ave. Nebraska
Independence, Iowa 50644

**Buena Vista
County Clerk**
P.O. Box 1186
Storm Lake, Iowa
50588-1186

Butler County Clerk
P.O. Box 325
Allison, Iowa 50602-0307

Calhoun County Clerk
P.O. Box 273
Rockwell City, Iowa 50579

Carroll County Clerk
P.O. Box 867
Carroll, Iowa 51401-0867

Cass County Clerk
7th St. Courthouse
Atlantic, Iowa 50022

Cedar County Clerk
400 Cedar St.
Tipton, Iowa 52772-1752

**Cerro Gordon County
Clerk**
220 N. Washington Ave.
Mason City, Iowa
50401-3254

Cherokee County Clerk
P.O. Box F
Cherokee, Iowa 51012

Chickasaw County Clerk
Prospect St.
New Hampton, Iowa 50659

Clarke County Clerk
117½ S. Main St.
Osceola, Iowa 50213-1299

Clay County Clerk
215 W. 4th St.
Spencer, Iowa 51301-0604

Clayton County Clerk
111 High St.
Elkader, Iowa 52043

Clinton County Clerk
P.O. Box 157
Clinton, Iowa 52732-0157

Crawford County Clerk
P.O. Box 546
Denison, Iowa 51442-0546

Dallas County Clerk
801 Court St.
Adel, Iowa 50003-1447

Davis County Clerk
Courthouse Square
Bloomfield, Iowa
52537-1600

Decatur County Clerk
207 N. Main St.
Leon, Iowa 50144-1647

Delaware County Clerk
P.O. Box 527
Manchester, Iowa
52057-0527

Des Moines County Clerk
513 N. Main St.
Burlington, Iowa
52601-5221

Dickinson County Clerk
18th and Hill County
Courthouse
Spirit Lake, Iowa 51360

Dubuque County Clerk
720 Central Ave.
Dubuque, Iowa
52001-7079

Emmet County Clerk
609 1st Ave. N.
Estherville, Iowa 51334

Fayette County Clerk
Vine St.
West Union, Iowa 52175

Floyd County Clerk
101 S. Main St.
Charles City, Iowa
50616-2756

Franklin County Clerk
12 First Ave. NW
Hampton, Iowa
50441-0026

Fremont County Clerk
Courthouse Square
Sidney, Iowa 51652-0549

Greene County Clerk
County Courthouse
Jefferson, Iowa
50129-2294

Grundy County Clerk
700 G Ave.
Grundy Center, Iowa
50638-1440

Guthrie County Clerk
200 N. 5th St.
Guthrie Center, Iowa
50115-1331

Hamilton County Clerk
County Courthouse
Webster City, Iowa
50595-3158

Hancock County Clerk
855 State St.
Garner, Iowa 50438

Hardin County Clerk
Edgington Ave.
Eldora, Iowa 50627-1741

Harrison County Clerk
113 N. 2nd Ave.
Logan, Iowa 51546-1331

Henry County Clerk
100 E. Washington St.
Mt. Pleasant, Iowa
52641-1931

Howard County Clerk
218 N. Elm St.
Cresco, Iowa 52136-1522

Humboldt County Clerk
County Courthouse
Dakota City, Iowa
50529-9999

Ida County Clerk
401 Moorehead St.
Ida Grove, Iowa
51445-1429

Iowa County Clerk
Court Ave.
Marengo, Iowa 52301

Jackson County Clerk
201 W. Platt St.
Maquoketa, Iowa
52060-2243

Jasper County Clerk
100 1st St.
Newton, Iowa 50208-0666

Jefferson County Clerk
P.O. Box 984
Fairfield, Iowa 52556-0984

Johnson County Clerk
913 S. Dubuque St.
Iowa City, Iowa
52244-1350

Jones County Clerk
High St.
Anamosa, Iowa 52205

Keokuk County Clerk
Courthouse Square
Sigourney, Iowa
52591-1499

Kossuth County Clerk
114 W. State St.
Algona, Iowa 50511-2613

Lee County Clerk
P.O. Box 1443
Ft. Madison, Iowa
52627-1443

Linn County Clerk
50 3rd Ave. Bridge
Cedar Rapids, Iowa
52401-1704

Louisa County Clerk
117 S. Main St.
Wapello, Iowa 52653-1547

Lucas County Clerk
County Courthouse
Chariton, Iowa 50049

Lyon County Clerk
206 S. 2nd Ave.
Rock Rapids, Iowa
51246-1597

Madison County Clerk
P.O. Box 152
Winterset, Iowa
50273-0152

Mahaska County Clerk
P.O. Box 30
Oskaloosa, Iowa
52577-0030

Marion County Clerk
P.O. Box 497
Knoxville, Iowa
50138-0497

Marshall County Clerk
17 E. Main St.
Marshalltown, Iowa
50158-4906

Mills County Clerk
418 Sharp St.
Glenwood, Iowa
51534-1756

Mitchell County Clerk
County Courthouse
Osage, Iowa 50461

Monona County Clerk
610 Iowa Ave.
Onawa, Iowa 51040

Monroe County Clerk
County Courthouse
Albia, Iowa 52531

**Montgomery
County Clerk**
105 Coolbaugh St.
Red Oak, Iowa 51566

Muscatine County Clerk
P.O. Box 327
Muscatine, Iowa
52761-0327

O'Brien County Clerk
155 S. Hayes
Primghar, Iowa 51245

Osceola County Clerk
614 5th Ave.
Sibley, Iowa 51249-1704

Page County Clerk
112 E. Main St.
Clarinda, Iowa 51632-2197

Palo Alto County Clerk
11th and Broadway
Emmetsburg, Iowa 50536

Plymouth County Clerk
3rd Ave. and 2nd St. SE
Le Mars, Iowa 51031

Pocahontas County Clerk
Court Square County
Courthouse
Pocahontas, Iowa 50574

Polk County Clerk
500 Mulberry St., Rm. 304
Des Moines, Iowa
50309-4238

**Pottawattamie
County Clerk**
227 S. 6th St.
Council Bluffs, Iowa 51501

Poweshiek County Clerk
302 E. Main St.
Montezuma, Iowa 50171

Ringgold County Clerk
County Courthouse
Mt. Ayr, Iowa 50854

Sac County Clerk
P.O. Box 368
Sac City, Iowa 50583-0368

Scott County Clerk
416 W. 4th St.
Davenport, Iowa 52801

Shelby County Clerk
P.O. Box 431
Harlan, Iowa 51537-0431

Sioux County Clerk
210 Central Ave. SW
Orange City, Iowa
51041-1751

Story County Clerk
900 6th St.
Nevada, Iowa 50201-2004

Tama County Clerk
County Courthouse
Toledo, Iowa 52342-0306

Taylor County Clerk
County Courthouse
Bedford, Iowa 50833

Union County Clerk
300 N. Pine St.
Creston, Iowa 50801-2430

Van Buren County Clerk
P.O. Box 475
Keosauqua, Iowa
52565-0475

Wapello County Clerk
4th and Court St.
Ottumwa, Iowa
52501-2599

Warren County Clerk
P.O. Box 379
Indianola, Iowa
50125-0379

**Washington
County Clerk**
P.O. Box 391
Washington, Iowa 52353

Wayne County Clerk
P.O. Box 424
Corydon, Iowa 50060-0424

Webster County Clerk
703 Central Ave.
Ft. Dodge, Iowa 50501

Winnebago County Clerk
126 S. Clark St.
Forest City, Iowa
50436-1793

Winneshiek County Clerk
201 W. Main St.
Decorah, Iowa 52101

Woodbury County Clerk
101 Court St.
Sioux City, Iowa
51101-1909

Worth County Clerk
1000 Central Ave.
Northwood, Iowa
50459-1523

Wright County Clerk
P.O. Box 306
Clarion, Iowa 50525-0306

KANSAS
http://www.state.ks.us/

Allen County Clerk
1 North Washington St.
Iola, Kansas 66749-2841

Anderson County Clerk
100 E. 4th Ave.
Garnett, Kansas 66032

Atchison County Clerk
423 N. 5th St.
Atchison, Kansas 66002

Barber County Clerk
120 E. Washington Ave.
Medicine Lodge, Kansas
67104-1421

Barton County Clerk
P.O. Box 1089
Great Bend, Kansas 67530

Bourbon County Clerk
210 S. National Ave.
Fort Scott, Kansas 66701

Brown County Clerk
Courthouse Square
Hiawatha, Kansas 66434

Butler Country Clerk
200 W. Central Ave.
El Dorado, Kansas 67042

Chase County Clerk
P.O. Box 547
Cottonwood Falls, Kansas
66845

**Chautauqua County
Clerk**
215 N. Chautauqua St.
Sedan, Kansas 67361-1326

Cherokee County Clerk
300 E. Maple
Columbus, Kansas
66725-1806

Cheyenne County
P.O. Box 985
St. Francis, Kansas
67756-0985

Clark County Clerk
P.O. Box 886
Ashland, Kansas 67831

Clay County Clerk
P.O. Box 98
Clay Center, Kansas
67432-0098

Cloud County Clerk
811 Washington St.
Concordia, Kansas
66901-3415

Coffey County Clerk
6th and Neosho
Burlington, Kansas 66839

Comanche County Clerk
P.O. Box 397
Coldwater, Kansas
67029-0397

Cowley County Clerk
311 E. 9th Ave.
Winfield, Kansas 67156

Crawford County Clerk
County Courthouse
P.O. Box 249
Girard, Kansas 66743–249

Decatur County Clerk
120 E. Hall
Oberlin, Kansas 67749

Dickinson County Clerk
P.O. Box 248
Abilene, Kansas 67410

Doniphan County Clerk
Main St.
Troy, Kansas 66087

Douglas County Clerk
111 E. 11th St.
Lawrence, Kansas
66044-2912

Edwards County Clerk
312 Massachusetts Ave.
Kinsley, Kansas
67547-1059

Elk County Clerk
P.O. Box 606
Howard, Kansas 67349

Ellis County Clerk
1204 Fort St.
Hays, Kansas 67601-3831

Ellsworth County Clerk
P.O. Box 396
Ellsworth, Kansas
67439-0396

Finney County Clerk
P.O. Box M
Garden City, Kansas
67846-0450

Ford County Clerk
Central and Spruce St.
Dodge City, Kansas 67801

Franklin County Clerk
3rd and Main St.
Ottawa, Kansas 66067

Geary County Clerk
8th and Franklin
Junction City, Kansas
66441

Gove County Clerk
P.O. Box 128
Gove, Kansas 67736-0128

Graham County Clerk
410 N. Pomeroy St.
Hill City, Kansas
67642-1645

Grant County Clerk
108 S. Glenn St.
Ulysses, Kansas
67880-2551

Gray County Clerk
P.O. Box 487
Cimarron, Kansas 67835

Greeley County Clerk
P.O. Box 277
Tribune, Kansas
67879-0277

Greenwood County Clerk
311 N. Main St.
Eureka, Kansas
67045-0268

Hamilton County Clerk
N. Main St.
Syracuse, Kansas 67878

Harper County Clerk
County Courthouse
Anthony, Kansas 67003

Harvey County Clerk
P.O. Box 687
Newton, Kansas 67114

Haskell County Clerk
P.O. Box 518
Sublette, Kansas 67877

Hodgeman County Clerk
P.O. Box 247
Jetmore, Kansas 67854

Jackson County Clerk
Courthouse Square
Holton, Kansas 66436

Jefferson County Clerk
P.O. Box 321
Oskaloosa, Kansas
66066-0321

Jewell County Clerk
307 N. Commercial St.
Mankato, Kansas
66956-2025

Johnson County Clerk
111 South Cherry,
Suite 1200
Olathe, Kansas 66061

Kearny County Clerk
305 N. Main St.
Lakin, Kansas 67860

Kingman County Clerk
130 N. Spruce St.
Kingman, Kansas 67068

Kiowa County Clerk
211 E. Florida Ave.
Greensburg, Kansas
67054-2211

Labette County Clerk
P.O. Box 387
Oswego, Kansas 67356

Lane County Clerk
144 S. Lane
Dighton, Kansas
67839-0788

**Leavenworth
County Clerk**
601 S. Third St.,
Suite 3051
Leavenworth, Kansas
66048

Lincoln County Clerk
216 E. Lincoln Ave.
Lincoln, Kansas 67455

Linn County Clerk
P.O. Box B
Mound City, Kansas
66056-0601

Logan County Clerk
710 W. 2nd St.
Oakley, Kansas
67748-1251

Lyon County Clerk
402 Commercial St.
Emporia, Kansas
66801-4000

Marion County Clerk
Courthouse Square
P.O. Box 219
Marion, Kansas
66861-0219

Marshall County Clerk
1201 Broadway
Marysville, Kansas
66508-1844

McPherson County Clerk
Kansas and Maple St.
McPherson, Kansas
67460-0425

Meade County Clerk
200 N. Fowler St.
Meade, Kansas 67864-0278

Miami County Clerk
120 S. Pearl St.
Paola, Kansas 66071

Mitchell County Clerk
P.O. Box 190
Beloit, Kansas 67420

**Montgomery
County Clerk**
P.O. Box 446
Independence, Kansas
67301

Morris County Clerk
501 W. Main St.
Council Grove, Kansas
66846

Morton County Clerk
P.O. Box 1116
Elkhart, Kansas
67950-1116

Nemaha County Clerk
607 Nemaha St.
Seneca, Kansas 66538

Neosho County Clerk
P.O. Box 237
Erie, Kansas 66733

Ness County Clerk
202 W. Sycamore St.
Ness City, Kansas 67560

Norton County Clerk
Courthouse
Norton, Kansas 67654

Osage County Clerk
717 Topeka Ave.
Lyndon, Kansas 66451

Osborne County Clerk
W. Main St.
Osborne, Kansas 67473

Ottawa County Clerk
307 N. Concord St.
Minneapolis, Kansas 67467

Pawnee County Clerk
715 Broadway
Larned, Kansas
67550-3054

Phillips County Clerk
3rd and State St.
Phillipsburg, Kansas 67661

**Pottawatomie
County Clerk**
P.O. Box 187
Westmoreland, Kansas
66549

Pratt County Clerk
300 S. Ninnescah St.
Pratt, Kansas 67124

Rawlins County Clerk
607 Main St.
Atwood, Kansas
67730-1839

Reno County Clerk
206 W. 1st Ave.
Hutchinson, Kansas
67501-5245

Republic County Clerk
County Courthouse
Route 1
Belleville, Kansas
66935-9801

Rice County Clerk
101 W. Commercial St.
Lyons, Kansas 67554

Riley County Clerk
110 Courthouse Plaza
Manhattan, Kansas
66502-6018

Rooks County Clerk
115 N. Walnut St.
Stockton, Kansas
67669-1663

Rush County Clerk
715 Elm St.
LaCrosse, Kansas 67548

Russell County Clerk
P.O. Box 113
Russell, Kansas 67665

Saline County Clerk
300 W. Ash St.
Salina, Kansas 67401-2335

Scott County Clerk
303 Court St.
Scott City, Kansas
67871-1122

Sedgwick County Clerk
525 N. Main St.
Wichita, Kansas 67203

Seward County Clerk
415 N. Washington Ave.
Liberal, Kansas
67901-3462

Shawnee County Clerk
200 SE 7th St.
Topeka, Kansas
66603-3922

Sheridan County Clerk
P.O. Box 899
Hoxie, Kansas 67740-0899

Sherman County Clerk
813 Broadway
Goodland, Kansas 67735

Smith County Clerk
218 S. Grant St.
Smith Center, Kansas
66967-2708

Stafford County Clerk
209 N. Broadway St.
St. John, Kansas 67576

Stanton County Clerk
P.O. Box 190
Johnson, Kansas 67855

Stevens County Clerk
200 E. 6th St.
Hugoton, Kansas
67951-2652

Sumner County Clerk
500 N. Washington Ave.
Wellington, Kansas
67152-4064

Thomas County Clerk
300 N. Court St.
Colby, Kansas 67701-2439

Trego County Clerk
216 N. Main St.
Wakeeney, Kansas
67672-2102

Wabaunsee County Clerk
215 Kansas St.
Alma, Kansas 66401-9797

Wallace County Clerk
313 Main St.
Sharon Springs, Kansas
67758

Washington County Clerk
214 C St.
Washington, Kansas
66968-1928

Wichita County Clerk
P.O. Box 968
Leoti, Kansas 67861

Wilson County Clerk
615 Madison St.
Fredonia, Kansas 66736

Woodson County Clerk
105 W. Rutledge St.
Yates Center, Kansas 66783

Wyandotte County Clerk
710 N. 7th St.
Kansas City, Kansas
66101-3047

KENTUCKY

http://www.state.ky.us/

Adair County Clerk
425 Public Square
Columbia, Kentucky
42728-1451

Allen County Clerk
P.O. Box 336
Scottsville, Kentucky
42164-0036

Anderson County Clerk
151 S. Main St.
Lawrenceburg, Kentucky
40342-1175

Ballard County Clerk
P.O. Box 145
Wickliffe, Kentucky
42087-0145

Barren County Clerk
103 Courthouse Square
Glasgow, Kentucky
42141-2812

Bath County Clerk
Main St.
Owingsville, Kentucky
40360-0609

Bell County Clerk
P.O. Box 156
Pineville, Kentucky
40977-0156

Boone County Clerk
2950 E. Washington St.
Burlington, Kentucky
41005-0874

Bourbon County Clerk
P.O. Box 312
Paris, Kentucky
40361-0312

Boyd County Clerk
2800 Louisa St.
Catlettsburg, Kentucky
41129-1116

Boyle County Clerk
321 W. Main St., Rm. 123
Danville, Kentucky
40422-1848

Bracken County Clerk
Locus St.
Brooksville, Kentucky
41004-0147

Breathitt County Clerk
1127 Main St.
Jackson, Kentucky
41339-1194

**Breckenridge
County Clerk**
Courthouse Square
Hardinsburg, Kentucky
40143-0538

Bullitt County Clerk
149 N. Walnut St.
Shepherdsville, Kentucky
40165-0006

Butler County Clerk
Courthouse on Main St.
Morgantown, Kentucky
42261

Caldwell County Clerk
100 E. Market St., Rm. 3
Princeton, Kentucky
42445-1675

Calloway County Clerk
101 S. 5th St.
Murray, Kentucky
42071-2569

Campbell County Clerk
340 York St.
Newport, Kentucky 41071

Carlisle County Clerk
West Court St.
Bardwell, Kentucky 42023

Carroll County Clerk
County Courthouse
440 Main St.
Carrollton, Kentucky
41008-1064

Carter County Clerk
Courthouse, Rm. 232
Grayson, Kentucky 41143

Casey County Clerk
Courthouse Square
Liberty, Kentucky 42539

Christian County Clerk
511 S. Main St.
Hopkinsville, Kentucky
42240-2368

Clark County Clerk
34 S. Main St.
Winchester, Kentucky
40391

Clay County Clerk
316 Main St., Suite 143
Manchester, Kentucky
40962-0463

Clinton County Clerk
212 Washington
Albany, Kentucky 42602

Crittenden County Clerk
107 S. Main St.
Marion, Kentucky
42064-1507

**Cumberland
County Clerk**
P.O. Box 275
Burkesville, Kentucky
42717

Daviess County Clerk
212 St. Ann St., Rm. 105
Owensboro, Kentucky
42302-0389

Edmonson County Clerk
Main and Cross St.
Brownsville, Kentucky
42210

Elliott County Clerk
P.O. Box 225
Sandy Hook, Kentucky
41171-0710

Estill County Clerk
130 Main St.
Irvine, Kentucky 40336

Fayette County Clerk
162 W. Main St.
Lexington, Kentucky
40507

Fleming County Clerk
100 Court Square
Flemingsburg, Kentucky
41041

Floyd County Clerk
3rd Ave. Courthouse
Prestonsburg, Kentucky
41653

Franklin County Clerk
P.O. Box 338
Frankfort, Kentucky 40602

Fulton County Clerk
Moulton and Wellington St.
Hickman, Kentucky
42050-0126

Gallatin County Clerk
P.O. Box 616
Warsaw, Kentucky 41095

Garrard County Clerk
Public Square
Lancaster, Kentucky
40444-1057

Grant County Clerk
P.O. Box 469
Courthouse Basement
Williamstown, Kentucky
41097-0469

Graves County Clerk
902 W. Broadway
Mayfield, Kentucky
42066-2021

Grayson County Clerk
10 Public Square
Leitchfield, Kentucky
42754

Green County Clerk
203 W. Court St.
Greensburg, Kentucky
42743-1552

Greenup County Clerk
Courthouse, Rm. 204
Greenup, Kentucky 41144

Hancock County Clerk
County
Administration Bldg.
Hawesville, Kentucky
42348

Hardin County Clerk
14 Public Square
Elizabethtown, Kentucky
42701

Harlan County Clerk
205 Central St.
Harlan, Kentucky 40831

Harrison County Clerk
190 W. Pike St.
Cynthiana, Kentucky
40131

Hart County Clerk
Courthouse, Main St.
Munfordville, Kentucky
42765-0277

Henderson County
P.O. Box 374
Henderson, Kentucky
42420

Henry County Clerk
P.O. Box 615
New Castle, Kentucky
40050

Hickman County Clerk
110 E. Clay St.
Clinton, Kentucky 42031

Hopkins County Clerk
P.O. Box 737
Madisonville, Kentucky
42431

Jackson County Clerk
Courthouse, Rm. 108
McKee, Kentucky 40447

Jefferson County Clerk
527 W. Jefferson St.,
Rm 100
Louisville, Kentucky 40202

Jessamine County Clerk
101 Main St.
Nicholasville, Kentucky
40356

Johnson County Clerk
Courthouse on Court St.
Paintsville, Kentucky
41240

Kenton County
P.O. Box 1109
Covington, Kentucky
41012

Knott County Clerk
P.O. Box 446
Hindman, Kentucky 41822

Knox County Clerk
401 Court Square,
Suite 102
Barbourville, Kentucky
40906-0105

Larue County Clerk
County Courthouse
Hodgenville, Kentucky
42748

Laurel County Clerk
County Courthouse
London, Kentucky 40741

Lawrence County Clerk
122 S. Main Cross St.
Louisa, Kentucky 41230

Lee County Clerk
Courthouse, Rm. 11,
Main St.
Beattyville, Kentucky
41311

Leslie County Clerk
P.O. Box 916
Hyden, Kentucky 41749

Letcher County Clerk
P.O. Box 58
Whitesburg, Kentucky
41858

Lewis County Clerk
P.O. Box 129
Vanceburg, Kentucky
41179-0129

Lincoln County Clerk
102 E. Main St.
Stanford, Kentucky 40484

Livingston County Clerk
P.O. Box 400
Smithland, Kentucky
42081

Logan County Clerk
229 W. 3rd St.
Russellville, Kentucky
42276

Lyon County Clerk
P.O. Box 350
Eddyville, Kentucky
42038-0350

Madison County Clerk
101 W. Main St.
Richmond, Kentucky
40475

Magoffin County Clerk
P.O. Box 530
Salyersville, Kentucky
41465-0530

Marion County Clerk
120 W. Main St.
Lebanon, Kentucky 40033

Marshall County Clerk
1101 Main St.
Benton, Kentucky 42025

Martin County Clerk
P.O. Box 485
Inez, Kentucky 41224-0485

Mason County Clerk
P.O. Box 234
Maysville, Kentucky 41056

McCracken County Clerk
Washington and 7th St.
Paducha, Kentucky 42002

McCreary County Clerk
P.O. Box 699
Whitley City, Kentucky
42653

McLean County Clerk
210 Main St.
Calhoun, Kentucky 42327

Meade County Clerk
Fairway Dr.
Brandenburg, Kentucky
40108-0614

Menifee County Clerk
P.O. Box 123
Frenchburg, Kentucky
40322-0123

Mercer County Clerk
P.O. Box 426
Harrodsburg, Kentucky
40330

Metcalfe County Clerk
P.O. Box 850
Edmonton, Kentucky
42129

Monroe County Clerk
P.O. Box 188
Tompkinsville, Kentucky
42167

**Montgomery County
Clerk**
P.O. Box 414
Mt. Sterling, Kentucky
40353

Morgan County Clerk
505 Prestonsburg St.
West Liberty, Kentucky
41472

Muhlenberg
County Clerk
100 S. Main St.
Greenville, Kentucky
42345

Nelson County Clerk
311 E. Stephen Foster Ave.
Bardstown, Kentucky
40004-0312

Nicholas County Clerk
P.O. Box 227
Carlisle, Kentucky 40311

Ohio County Clerk
P.O. Box 85
Hartford, Kentucky 42347

Oldham County Clerk
100 W. Jefferson St.
La Grange, Kentucky
40031

Owen County Clerk
P.O. Box 338
Owenton, Kentucky 40359

Owsley County Clerk
154 Main St.
Booneville, Kentucky
41314

Pendleton County Clerk
P.O. Box 112
Falmouth, Kentucky 41040

Perry County Clerk
P.O. Box 150
Hazard, Kentucky
41701-0150

Pike County Clerk
320 Main St.
Pikeville, Kentucky 41501

Powell County Clerk
P.O. Box 548
Stanton, Kentucky 40380

Pulaski County Clerk
P.O. Box 724
Somerset, Kentucky
42501-0724

Robertson County Clerk
P.O. Box 75
Mt. Olivet, Kentucky
41064

Rockcastle County Clerk
Main St.
Mt. Vernon, Kentucky
40456-0365

Rowan County Clerk
672 E. Main St.
Morehead, Kentucky 40351

Russell County Clerk
P.O. Box 579
Jamestown, Kentucky
42629

Scott County Clerk
101 E. Main St.
Georgetown, Kentucky
40324

Shelby County Clerk
501 Main St.
Shelbyville, Kentucky
40066

Simpson County Clerk
103 W. Cedar
Franklin, Kentucky 42134

Spencer County Clerk
P.O. Box 544
Taylorsville, Kentucky
40071-0544

Taylor County Clerk
203 N. Court St., Suite 5
Campbellsville, Kentucky
42718

Todd County Clerk
P.O. Box 307
Elkton, Kentucky 42220

Trigg County Clerk
P.O. Box 1310
Cadiz, Kentucky 42211

Trimble County Clerk
P.O. Box 262
Bedford, Kentucky 40006

Union County Clerk
Main and Morgan Streets
Morganfield, Kentucky
42437

Warren County Clerk
429 E. 10th St.
Bowling Green, Kentucky
42101-2250

Washington
County Clerk
P.O. Box 446
Springfield, Kentucky
40069-0446

Wayne County Clerk
109 Main St.
Monticello, Kentucky
42633-0565

Webster County Clerk
25 Main St.
Dixon, Kentucky 42409

Whitley County Clerk
111 Main St.
Williamsburg, Kentucky
40769

Wolfe County Clerk
P.O. Box 400
Campton, Kentucky
41301-0400

Woodford County Clerk
County Courthouse
Main St.
Versailles, Kentucky 40383

LOUISIANA

http://www.state.la.us/

Acadia Parish Clerk
P.O. Box 1342
Crowley, Louisiana
70527-1342

Allen Parish Clerk
P.O. Box G
Oberlin, Louisiana
70655-2007

Ascension Parish Clerk
P.O. Box 192
Donaldsonville, Louisiana
70346

Assumption Parish Clerk
Martin Luther King Dr.
and Hwy 1
Napoleonville, Louisiana
70390

Avoyelles Parish Clerk
301 N. Main St.
Marksville, Louisiana
71351

Beauregard Parish Clerk
P.O. Box 310
De Ridder, Louisiana
70634-0310

Bienville Parish Clerk
300 Courthouse Square
Arcadia, Louisiana 71001

Bossier Parish Clerk
P.O. Box 369
Benton, Louisiana 71006

Caddo Parish Clerk
501 Texas St.
Shreveport, Louisiana
71101-5401

Calcasieu Parish Clerk
P.O. Box 1030
Lake Charles, Louisiana
70602-1030

Caldwell Parish Clerk
Courthouse
Columbia, Louisiana 71418

Cameron Parish Clerk
P.O. Box 549
Cameron, Louisiana
70631-0549

Catahoula Parish Clerk
P.O. Box 198
Harrisonburg, Louisiana
71340-0198

Claiborne Parish Clerk
Courthouse Square
Homer, Louisiana 71040

Concordia Parish Clerk
P.O. Box 790
Vidalia, Louisiana 71373

DeSoto Parish Clerk
P.O. Box 1206
Mansfield, Louisiana
71052

**East Baton Rouge
Parish Clerk**
222 St. Louis St.
Baton Rouge, Louisiana
70802-5817

East Carroll Parish Clerk
400 1st St.
Lake Providence, Louisiana
71254-2616

**East Feliciana
Parish Clerk**
P.O. Box 599
Clinton, Louisiana 70722

Evangeline Parish Clerk
Court St., 2nd Fl.
Ville Platte, Louisiana
70586

Franklin Parish Clerk
210 Main St.
Winnsboro, Louisiana
71295-2708

Grant Parish Clerk
Courthouse, Main St.
Colfax, Louisiana 71417

Iberia Parish Clerk
300 Iberia St.
New Iberia, Louisiana
70560

Iberville Parish Clerk
P.O. Box 423
Plaquemine, Louisiana
70765

Jackson Parish Clerk
500 E. Courthouse Ave.
Jonesboro, Louisiana
71251

Jefferson Parish Clerk
200 Derbigny St.
3rd Fl. Main Courthouse
Gretna, Louisiana
70054-0010

**Jefferson Davis
Parish Clerk**
P.O. Box 1409
Jennings, Louisiana 70546

Lafayette Parish Clerk
P.O. Box 4508
Lafayette, Louisiana
70502-4508

Lafourche Parish Clerk
209 Green St.
Thibodaux, Louisiana
70302

Lasalle Parish Clerk
P.O. Box 1372
Jena, Louisiana
71342-1372

Lincoln Parish Clerk
100 W. Texas Ave.
Ruston, Louisiana 71270

Livingston Parish Clerk
20180 Iowa St.
Livingston, Louisiana
70754

Madison Parish Clerk
100 N. City St.
Tallulah, Louisiana 71282

Morehouse Parish Clerk
125 E. Madison St.
Bastrop, Louisiana
71221-0509

**Natchitoches
Parish Clerk**
P.O. Box 799
Natchitoches, Louisiana
71458-0799

Orleans Parish Clerk
1300 Perdido St.
New Orleans, Louisiana
70112-2114

Ouachita Parish Clerk
300 St. John St.
Monroe, Louisiana
71201-7326

Plaquemines Parish Clerk
Courthouse
Pointe Ala Hache,
Louisiana 70082

**Pointe Coupee
Parish Clerk**
P.O. Box 86
New Roads, Louisiana
70760-0086

Rapides Parish Clerk
P.O. Box 952
Alexandria, Louisiana
71309-0952

Red River Parish Clerk
615 E. Carroll St.
Coushatta, Louisiana
71019-8731

Richland Parish Clerk
108 Courthouse Square
Rayville, Louisiana 71269

Sabine Parish Clerk
400 Court St.
Many, Louisiana 71449

St. Bernard Parish Clerk
8201 W. Judge Perez Dr.
Chalmette, Louisiana
70043-1611

St. Charles Parish Clerk
P.O. Box 302
Hahnville, Louisiana 70057

St. Helena Parish Clerk
Court Square
Greensburg, Louisiana
70441-0308

St. James Parish Clerk
P.O. Box 106
Convent, Louisiana 70723

**St. John The Baptist
Parish Clerk**
P.O. Box 38
Edgard, Louisiana 70049

St. Landry Parish Clerk
Court and Landry St.
Opelousas, Louisiana
70570

St. Martin Parish Clerk
County Courthouse
St. Martinville, Louisiana
70582-0009

St. Mary Parish Clerk
500 Main St.
Franklin, Louisiana 70538

**St. Tammany
Parish Clerk**
510 E. Boston
Covington, Louisiana
70433-2945

Tangipahoa Parish Clerk
P.O. Box 215
Amite, Louisiana 70422

Tensas Parish Clerk
Courthouse Square
St. Joseph, Louisiana
71366-0078

Terrebonne Parish Clerk
301 Goode St.
Houma, Louisiana
70360-1569

Union Parish Clerk
Main and Bayou St.
Farmerville, Louisiana
71241

Vermilion Parish Clerk
P.O. Box 790
Abbeville, Louisiana
70511-0790

Vernon Parish Clerk
201 S. 3rd St.
Leesville, Louisiana
71496-0040

Washington Parish Clerk
Washington and Main St.
Franklinton, Louisiana
70438-0607

Webster Parish Clerk
410 Main St.
Minden, Louisiana
71055-3325

West Baton Rouge
Parish Clerk
P.O. Box 107
Port Allen, Louisiana
70767

West Carroll
Parish Clerk
P.O. Box 630
Oak Grove, Louisiana
71263-0630

West Feliciana
Parish Clerk
Royal and Prosperity
St. Francisville, Louisiana
70775

Winn Parish Clerk
P.O. Box 951
Winnfield, Louisiana
71483-0951

MAINE

http://www.state.me.us/

Androscoggin
County Clerk
2 Turner St.
Auburn, Maine 04210-5953

Arooslook County Clerk
13 Hall St.
Fort Kent, Maine 04730

Cumberland
County Clerk
142 Federal St.
Portland, Maine 04101

Franklin County Clerk
38 Main St.
Farmington, Maine 04938

Hancock County Clerk
60 State St.
Ellsworth, Maine
04605-1926

Kennebec County Clerk
95 State St.
Augusta, Maine
04330-5611

Knox County Clerk
P.O. Box 885
Rockland, Maine
04841-0885

Lincoln County Clerk
High St. County
Courthouse
Wiscasset, Maine 04578

Oxford County Clerk
26 Western Ave.
South Paris, Maine
04281-1417

Penobscot County Clerk
97 Hammond St.
Bangor, Maine 04401

Piscataquis County Clerk
51 E. Main St.
Dover-Foxcroft, Maine
04426-1306

Sagadahoc County Clerk
752 High St.
Bath, Maine 04530-2436

Somerset County Clerk
County Courthouse
Skowhegan, Maine
04976-9801

Waldo County Clerk
73 Church St.
Belfast, Maine 04915-1705

Washington
County Clerk
P.O. Box 297
Machias, Maine
04654-0297

York County Clerk
Court St.
Alfred, Maine 04002

MARYLAND

http://www.state.md.us/

Allegany County Clerk
3 Pershing St.
Cumberland, Maryland
21502-3043

Anne Arundel
County Clerk
44 Calvert St.
Annapolis, Maryland
21401-1930

Baltimore County Clerk
401 Bosley Ave.
Towson, Maryland 21204

Baltimore City
County Clerk
6550 Reisterstown Plaza
Baltimore, Maryland
21202-3417

Calvert County Clerk
175 Main St.
Prince Frederick, Maryland
20678

Caroline County Clerk
P.O. Box 207
Denton, Maryland
21629-0207

Carroll County Clerk
225 N. Center St.
Westminster, Maryland
21157-5107

Cecil County Clerk
129 E. Main St., Rm. 108
Elkton, Maryland 21921

Charles County Clerk
P.O. Box B
La Plata, Maryland
20646-0167

Dorchester County Clerk
P.O. Box 26
Cambridge, Maryland
21613-0026

Frederick County Clerk
100 West Patrick St.
Frederick, Maryland 21701

Garrett County Clerk
203 S. Fourth St.
Oakland, Maryland
21550-1535

Harford County Clerk
20 West Courtland St.
Bel Air, Maryland
21014-3833

Howard County Clerk
3430 Courthouse Dr.
Ellicott City, Maryland
21043-4300

Kent County Clerk
Cross St.
Chestertown, Maryland
21620

**Montgomery
County Clerk**
101 Monroe St.
Rockville, Maryland
20850-2540

**Prince George's
County Clerk**
Administration Bldg.
Upper Marlboro, Maryland
20772-3050

**Queen Anne's
County Clerk**
107 N. Liberty St.
Centreville, Maryland
21617

Somerset County Clerk
P.O. Box 99
Princess Anne, Maryland
21853

St. Mary's County Clerk
P.O. Box 316 Peabody St.
Leonardtown, Maryland
20650

Talbot County Clerk
Courthouse
Easton, Maryland 21601

**Washington
County Clerk**
Summit Ave.
Hagerstown, Maryland
21740

Wicomico County Clerk
P.O. Box 198
Salisbury, Maryland 21801

Worcester County Clerk
Courthouse
Snow Hill, Maryland 21863

MASSACHUSETTS

http://www.state.ma.us/

Barnstable County Clerk
Rt. 6A
Barnstable, Massachusetts
02630

Berkshire County Clerk
44 Bank Row
Pittsfield, Massachusetts
01201-6202

Bristol County Clerk
11 Court St.
Taunton, Massachusetts
02780-3223

Dukes County Clerk
81 Main St.
Edgartown, Massachusetts
02539

Essex County Clerk
36 Federal St.
Salem, Massachusetts
01970

Franklin County Clerk
425 Main St.
Greenfield, Massachusetts
01301-3313

Hampden County Clerk
50 State St.
Springfield, Massachusetts
01103-2027

Hampshire County Clerk
33 King St.
Northampton,
Massachusetts 01060-3236

Middlesex County Clerk
208 Cambridge St.
Cambridge, Massachusetts
02141-1202

Nantucket County Clerk
16 Broad St.
Nantucket, Massachusetts
02554-3500

Norfolk County Clerk
649 High St.
Dedham, Massachusetts
02026-1831

Plymouth County Clerk
Russell St.
Plymouth, Massachusetts
02360

Suffolk County Clerk
1 Pemberton Square
Boston, Massachusetts
02108-1706

Worcester County Clerk
2 Main St.
Worcester, Massachusetts
01608-1116

MICHIGAN

http://www.state.mi.us/

Alcona County Clerk
106 Fifth St.
Harrisville, Michigan
48740-9789

Alger County Clerk
101 Court St.
Munising, Michigan
49862-1103

Allegan County Clerk
113 Chestnut St.
Allegan, Michigan
49010-1332

Alpena County Clerk
720 W. Chisholm St.
Alpena, Michigan
49707-2429

Antrim County Clerk
208 E. Cayuga St.
Bellaire, Michigan 49615

Arenac County Clerk
Courthouse
Standish, Michigan 48658

Baraga County Clerk
Courthouse
L'Anse, Michigan
49946-1085

Barry County Clerk
Courthouse
Hastings, Michigan 49058

Bay County Clerk
515 Center Ave.
Bay City, Michigan
48708-5941

Benzie County Clerk
Courthouse
Beulah, Michigan 49617

Berrien County Clerk
701 Main St.
Saint Joseph, Michigan
49085

Branch County Clerk
31 Division St.
Coldwater, Michigan 49036

Calhoun County Clerk
315 W. Green St.
Marshall, Michigan 49068

Cass County Clerk
120 N. Broadway
Cassopolis, Michigan
49031-1302

Charlevoix County Clerk
Courthouse
Charlevoix, Michigan
49720

Cheboygan County Clerk
P.O. Box 70
Cheboygan, Michigan
49721

Chippewa County Clerk
Courthouse
Sault Ste. Marie, Michigan
49783-2183

Clare County Clerk
P.O. Box 438
Harrison, Michigan
48625-0438

Clinton County Clerk
100 E. State St.
St. Johns, Michigan
48879-1571

Crawford County Clerk
200 W. Michigan Ave.
Grayling, Michigan
49738-1745

Delta County Clerk
310 Ludington St.
Escanaba, Michigan
49829-4057

Dickinson County Clerk
P.O. Box 609
Iron Mountain, Michigan
49801

Eaton County Clerk
1045 Independence Blvd
Charlotte, Michigan
48813-1033

Emmet County Clerk
200 Division St.
Petoskey, Michigan 49770

Genesee County Clerk
900 S. Saginaw St.
Flint, Michigan 48502

Gladwin County Clerk
401 W. Cedar
Gladwin, Michigan
48624-2023

Gogebic County Clerk
200 N. Moore St.
Bessemer, Michigan 49911

**Grand Traverse
County Clerk**
400 Boardman
Traverse City, Michigan
49684

Gratiot County Clerk
Courthouse
Ithaca, Michigan 48847

Hillsdale County Clerk
Courthouse
Hillsdale, Michigan 49242

Houghton County Clerk
401 E. Houghton Ave.
Houghton, Michigan
49931-2016

Huron County Clerk
250 E. Huron Ave.
Bad Axe, Michigan 48413

Ingham County Clerk
366 S. Jefferson St.
Mason, Michigan 48854

Ionia County Clerk
Courthouse
Ionia, Michigan 48846

Iosco County Clerk
P.O. Box 838
Tawas City, Michigan
48764-0838

Iron County Clerk
2 South 6th St.
Crystal Falls, Michigan
49920-1413

Isabella County Clerk
200 N. Main St.
Mt. Pleasant, Michigan
48858-2321

Jackson County Clerk
312 S. Jackson
Jackson, Michigan 49201

Kalamazoo County Clerk
201 W. Kalamazoo
Kalamazoo, Michigan
49007-3734

Kalkaska County Clerk
605 N. Birch
Kalkaska, Michigan
49646-9436

Kent County Clerk
300 Monroe, NW
Grand Rapids, Michigan
49503-2206

Keweenaw County Clerk
Courthouse
Eagle River, Michigan
49924

Lake County Clerk
P.O. Box B
Baldwin, Michigan
49304-0902

Lapeer County Clerk
Courthouse
Lapeer, Michigan 48446

Leelanau County Clerk
Courthouse
Leland, Michigan 49654

Lenawee County Clerk
425 N. Main St.
Adrian, Michigan 49221

Livingston County Clerk
200 E. Grand River
Howell, Michigan 48843

Luce County Clerk
East Court St.
Newberry, Michigan 49868

Mackinac County Clerk
100 Marley St.
St. Ignace, Michigan
49781-1457

Macomb County Clerk
40 N. Main
Mt. Clemens, Michigan
48043

Manistee County Clerk
415 Third St.
Manistee, Michigan
49660-1606

Marquette County Clerk
232 W. Baraga Ave.
Marquette, Michigan
49855-4710

Mason County Clerk
Courthouse
Ludington, Michigan
49431

Mecosta County Clerk
400 Elm St.
Big Rapids, Michigan
49307-1849

Menominee County Clerk
Courthouse
Menominee, Michigan
49858

Midland County Clerk
220 W. Ellsworth St.
Midland, Michigan 48640

Missaukee County Clerk
Courthouse
Lake City, Michigan 49651

Monroe County Clerk
106 E. First
Monroe, Michigan
48161-2143

Montcalm County Clerk
211 W. Main St.
Stanton, Michigan 48888

**Montmorency County
Clerk**
P.O. Box 415
Atlanta, Michigan 49709

Muskegon County Clerk
990 Terrace St.
Muskegon, Michigan
49442-3301

Newaygo County Clerk
1087 Newell St.
White Cloud, Michigan
49349

Oakland County Clerk
1200 N. Telegraph Rd.
Pontiac, Michigan
48053-1008

Oceana County Clerk
P.O. Box 153
Hart, Michigan 49420

Ogemaw County Clerk
Courthouse
West Branch, Michigan
48661

Ontonagon County Clerk
725 Greenland Rd.
Ontonagon, Michigan
49953-1423

Osceola County Clerk
301 W. Upton
Reed City, Michigan
49677-1149

Oscoda County Clerk
P.O. Box 399
Mio, Michigan 48647

Otsego County Clerk
225 W. Main St.
Gaylord, Michigan
49735-1348

Ottawa County Clerk
414 Washington St.
Grand Haven, Michigan
49417-1443

**Presque Isle
County Clerk**
151 E. Huron St.
Rogers City, Michigan
49779-1316

**Roscommon
County Clerk**
Courthouse
Roscommon, Michigan
48653

Saginaw County Clerk
111 S. Michigan
Saginaw, Michigan
48602-2019

Sanilac County Clerk
67 W. Sanilac Ave.
Sandusky, Michigan
48471-1060

Schoolcraft County Clerk
300 Walnut St.
Manistique, Michigan
49854-1414

Shiawassee County Clerk
Courthouse
Corunna, Michigan 48817

St. Clair County Clerk
201 McMorran Blvd.
Port Huron, Michigan
48060-4006

St. Joseph County Clerk
P.O. Box 189
Centreville, Michigan
49032-0189

Tuscola County Clerk
440 N. State St.
Caro, Michigan
48723-1555

Van Buren County Clerk
Courthouse
Paw Paw, Michigan
49079-1496

Washtenaw County Clerk
101 E. Huron St.
Ann Arbor, Michigan
48107-8645

Wayne County Clerk
728 City County Bldg.
Detroit, Michigan
48226-3413

Wexford County Clerk
Courthouse
Cadillac, Michigan 49601

MINNESOTA

http://www.state.mn.us/

Aitkin County Clerk
209 2nd St., NW
Aitkin, Minnesota 56431

Anoka County Clerk
325 E. Main St.
Anoka, Minnesota 55303

Becker County Clerk
915 Lake Ave.
Detroit Lakes, Minnesota
56502

Beltrami County Clerk
619 Beltrami Ave. NW
Bemidji, Minnesota 56601

Benton County Clerk
531 Dewey St.
Foley, Minnesota 56329

Big Stone County Clerk
20 SE 2nd St.
Ortonville, Minnesota
56278

Blue Earth County Clerk
P.O. Box 3524
Mankato, Minnesota
56001-4585

Brown County Clerk
P.O. Box 248
New Ulm, Minnesota
56073

Carlton County Clerk
301 Walnut
Carlton, Minnesota 55718

Carver County Clerk
600 E. 4th St.
Chaska, Minnesota 55318

Cass County Clerk
P.O. Box 3000
Walker, Minnesota 56484

Chippewa County Clerk
629 N. 11th St.
Montevideo, Minnesota
56265

Chisago County Clerk
313 N. Main St.
Center City, Minnesota
55012

Clay County Clerk
807 11th St. N.
Moorhead, Minnesota
56561

Clearwater County Clerk
213 Main Ave. N.
Bagley, Minnesota 56621

Cook County Clerk
P.O. Box 1150
Grand Marais, Minnesota
55604

**Cottonwood
County Clerk**
900 Third Ave.
Windom, Minnesota 56101

Crow Wing County Clerk
326 Laurel St.
Brainerd, Minnesota 56401

Dakota County Clerk
1590 W. Highway 55
Hastings, Minnesota 55033

Dodge County Clerk
22 E. Sixth St.
Mantorville, Minnesota
55955

Douglas County Clerk
305 Eighth Ave. W.
Alexandria, Minnesota
56308

Faribault County Clerk
P.O. Box 130
Blue Earth, Minnesota
56013

Fillmore County Clerk
101 Fillmore St.
Preston, Minnesota 55965

Freeborn County Clerk
411 S. Broadway
Albert Lea, Minnesota
56007

Goodhue County Clerk
509 W. Fifth St.
Red Wing, Minnesota
55066

Grant County Clerk
10 Second St. NE
Elbow Lake, Minnesota
56531

Hennepin County Clerk
300 S. Sixth St., 2nd Fl.
Minneapolis, Minnesota
55487-0999

Houston County Clerk
P.O. Box 29
Caledonia, Minnesota
55921

Hubbard County Clerk
Courthouse
Park Rapids, Minnesota
56470

Isanti County Clerk
555 18th Ave. SW
Cambridge, Minnesota
55008

Itasca County Clerk
123 Fourth St. NE
Grand Rapids, Minnesota
55744

Jackson County Clerk
P.O. Box 209
Jackson, Minnesota 56143

Kanabec County Clerk
18 N. Vine
Mora, Minnesota 55051

Kandiyohi County Clerk
400 SW Benson Ave. SW
Willmar, Minnesota 56201

Kittson County Clerk
410 S. Fifth St.
Hallock, Minnesota 56728

**Koochiching
County Clerk**
715 Fourth St.
International Falls,
Minnesota 56649

**Lac qui Parle
County Clerk**
P.O. Box 132
Madison, Minnesota 56256

Lake County Clerk
601 Third Ave.
Two Harbors, Minnesota
55616

**Lake of the Woods
County Clerk**
206 SE Eighth Ave.
Baudette, Minnesota 56623

Le Sueur County Clerk
88 S. Park Ave.
Le Center, Minnesota
56057

Lincoln County Clerk
319 N. Rebecca St.
Ivanhoe, Minnesota 56142

Lyon County Clerk
607 W. Main
Marshall, Minnesota 56258

Mahnomen County Clerk
County Courthouse
Mahnomen, Minnesota
56557

Marshall County Clerk
208 E. Colvin Ave.
Warren, Minnesota 56762

Martin County Clerk
201 Lake Ave.
Fairmont, Minnesota 56031

McLeod County Clerk
P.O. Box 127
Glencoe, Minnesota 55336

Meeker County Clerk
325 N. Sibley Ave.
Litchfield, Minnesota
55355

Mille Lacs County Clerk
635 2nd St. SE
Milaca, Minnesota 56353

Morrison County Clerk
213 First Ave. SE
Little Falls, Minnesota
56345

Mower County Clerk
201 First St. NE
Austin, Minnesota 55912

Murray County Clerk
2500 28th St.
Slayton, Minnesota 56172

Nicollet County Clerk
501 S. Minnesota Ave.
St. Peter, Minnesota 56082

Nobles County Clerk
P.O. Box 757
Worthington, Minnesota
56187

Norman County Clerk
16 E. Third Ave.
Ada, Minnesota 56510

Olmsted County Clerk
151 Fourth St. SE
Rochester, Minnesota
55904

Otter Tail County Clerk
P.O. Box 867
Fergus Falls, Minnesota
56538

Pennington County Clerk
P.O. Box 616
Thief River Falls,
Minnesota 56701

Pine County Clerk
315 Sixth St., Suite 3
Pine City, Minnesota 55063

Pipestone County Clerk
416 S. Hiawatha
Pipestone, Minnesota
56164

Polk County Clerk
P.O. Box 397
Crookston, Minnesota
56716-0397

Pope County Clerk
130 E. Minnesota Ave.
Glenwood, Minnesota
56334

Ramsey County Clerk
555 Cedar St.
St. Paul, Minnesota 55101

Red Lake County Clerk
124 N. Main St.
Red Lake Falls, Minnesota
56750

Redwood County Clerk
P.O. Box 130
Redwood Falls, Minnesota
56283

Renville County Clerk
500 E. DePue
Olivia, Minnesota 56277

Rice County Clerk
320 NW Third St., Suite 10
Faribault, Minnesota 55021

Rock County Clerk
204 E. Brown
Luverne, Minnesota 56156

Roseau County Clerk
606 Fifth Ave. SW, Rm. 20
Roseau, Minnesota 56751

Scott County Clerk
428 S. Holmes St.
Shakopee, Minnesota
55379

Sherburne County Clerk
13880 Highway 10
Elk River, Minnesota
55330

Sibley County Clerk
400 Court Ave.
Gaylord, Minnesota 55334

St. Louis County Clerk
100 N. Fifth Ave. W
Duluth, Minnesota 55801

Stearns County Clerk
705 Courthouse Square,
Rm. 125
St. Cloud, Minnesota
56303

Steele County Clerk
111 E. Main St.
Owatonna, Minnesota
55060

Stevens County Clerk
P.O. Box 530
Morris, Minnesota 56267

Swift County Clerk
301 14th St. N
Benson, Minnesota 56215

Todd County Clerk
215 First Ave. S
Long Prairie, Minnesota
56347

Traverse County Clerk
702 Second Ave. N
Wheaton, Minnesota
56296-0428

Wabasha County Clerk
625 Jefferson Ave.
Wabasha, Minnesota 55981

Wadena County Clerk
P.O. Box 415
Wadena, Minnesota 56482

Waseca County Clerk
307 N. State St.
Waseca, Minnesota 56093

**Washington
County Clerk**
1520 W. Frontage Rd.
Stillwater, Minnesota
55082

Watonwan County Clerk
P.O. Box 518
St. James, Minnesota
56081

Wilkin County Clerk
300 S. Fifth St.
Breckenridge, Minnesota
56520

Winona County Clerk
74 W. Third St.
Winona, Minnesota 55987

Wright County Clerk
10 NW Second St., Rm. 160
Buffalo, Minnesota
55313-1165

**Yellow Medicine
County Clerk**
415 Ninth Ave.
Granite Falls, Minnesota
56241

MISSISSIPPI

http://www.state.ms.us/
Adams County Clerk
115 S. Wall St.
Natchez, Mississippi 39120

Alcorn County Clerk
P.O. Box 112
Corinth, Mississippi 38834

Amite County Clerk
243 W. Main St.
Liberty, Mississippi 39645

Attala County Clerk
230 W. Washington St.
Kosciusko, Mississippi
39090

Benton County Clerk
P.O. Box 218
Ashland, Mississippi
38603-0218

Bolivar County Clerk
200 N. Court St.
Cleveland, Mississippi
38732

Calhoun County Clerk
P.O. Box 8
Pittsboro, Mississippi
38951-0008

Carroll County Clerk
Lexington St.
Carrollton, Mississippi
38917-0291

Chicasaw County Clerk
101 N. Jefferson
Houston, Mississippi 38851

Choctaw County Clerk
112 Quinn St.
Ackerman, Mississippi
39735-0250

Claiborne County Clerk
410 Main St.
Port Gibson, Mississippi
39150

Clark County Clerk
101 S. Archusa Ave.
Quitman, Mississippi
39355

Clay County Clerk
205 Court St.
West Point, Mississippi
39773-0815

Coahoma County Clerk
P.O. Box 98
Clarksdale, Mississippi
38614-0098

Copiah County Clerk
100 Caldwell Dr.
Hazlehurst, Mississippi
39083

Covington County Clerk
101 S. Elm Ave.
Collins, Mississippi 39428

DeSoto County Clerk
Courthouse
Hernando, Mississippi
38632

Forrest County Clerk
641 N. Main St.
Hattiesburg, Mississippi
39403-0951

Franklin County Clerk
Main St. Meadville,
Mississippi 39653

George County Clerk
320 Cox St.
Lucedale, Mississippi
39452

Greene County Clerk
Main St.
Leakesville, Mississippi
39451-0610

Grenada County Clerk
59 Green St.
Grenada, Mississippi
38901-1208

Hancock County Clerk
152 Main St.
Bay St. Louis, Mississippi
39520

Harrison County Clerk
Courthouse
Gulfport, Mississippi
39502

Hinds County Clerk
P.O. Box 686
Jackson, Mississippi
39205-0686

Holmes County Clerk
P.O. Box 239
Lexington, Mississippi
39095-0239

Humphreys County Clerk
102 Castleman St.
Belzoni, Mississippi
39038-0547

Issaquena County Clerk
129 Court St.
Mayersville, Mississippi
39113

Itawamba County Clerk
P.O. Box 776
Fulton, Mississippi 38843

Jackson County Clerk
P.O. Box 998
Pascagoula, Mississippi
39567

Jasper County Clerk
Court St.
Bay Springs, Mississippi
39422

Jefferson County Clerk
307 S. Main St.
Fayette, Mississippi 39069

**Jefferson Davis
County Clerk**
1025 Third St.
Prentiss, Mississippi
39474-1137

Jones County Clerk
415 N. 5th Ave.
Laurel, Mississippi
39441-3968

Kemper County Clerk
Bell St.
De Kalb, Mississippi 39328

Lafayette County Clerk
Town Square
Oxford, Mississippi 38655

Lamar County Clerk
203 Main St.
Purvis, Mississippi 39475

Lauderdale County Clerk
500 Constitution Ave.
Meridian, Mississippi
39302

Lawrence County Clerk
517 E. Broad St.
Monticello, Mississippi
39654-0040

Leake County Clerk
P.O. Box 72
Carthage, Mississippi
39051-0072

Lee County Clerk
200 W. Jefferson St.
Tupelo, Mississippi 38802

Leflore County Clerk
317 W. Market St.
Greenwood, Mississippi
38930

Lincoln County Clerk
300 S. 2nd St.
Brookhaven, Mississippi
39601

Lowndes County Clerk
521 Second Ave. N
Columbus, Mississippi
39701

Madison County Clerk
146 W. Center St.
Canton, Mississippi 39046

Marion County Clerk
250 Broad St. #2
Columbia, Mississippi
39429

Marshall County Clerk
128 E. Van Dorn Ave.
Holly Springs, Mississippi
38635

Monroe County Clerk
201 W. Commerce St.
Aberdeen, Mississippi
39730

**Montgomery
County Clerk**
614 Summit St.
Winona, Mississippi 38967

Neshoba County Clerk
401 Beacon St. #107
Philadelphia, Mississippi
39350-0067

Newton County Clerk
92 W. Broad St.
Decatur, Mississippi 39327

Noxubee County Clerk
505 S. Jefferson St.
Macon, Mississippi 39341

Oktibbeha County Clerk
101 W. Main St.
Starkville, Mississippi
39759

Panola County Clerk
215 S. Pocahontas St.
Batesville, Mississippi
38666

Pearl River County Clerk
200 S. Main St.
Poplarville, Mississippi
39470

Perry County Clerk
Main St.
New Augusta, Mississippi
39462-0198

Pike County Clerk
200 E. Bay St.
Magnolia, Mississippi
39652

Pontotoc County Clerk
11 E. Washington St.
Pontotoc, Mississippi
38863-0209

Prentiss County Clerk
100 N. Main St.
Booneville, Mississippi
38829

Quitman County Clerk
23 Chestnut St.
Marks, Mississippi 38646

Rankin County Clerk
301 E. Government St.
Brandon, Mississippi
39042

Scott County Clerk
100 E. Main St.
Forest, Mississippi 39074

Sharkey County Clerk
400 Locust St.
Rolling Fork, Mississippi
39159-0218

Simpson County Clerk
109 W. Pine Ave.
Mendenhall, Mississippi
39114

Smith County Clerk
123 Main St.
Raleigh, Mississippi 39153

Stone County Clerk
P.O. Drawer 7
Wiggins, Mississippi 39577

Sunflower County Clerk
200 Main St.
Indianola, Mississippi
38751-0988

**Tallahatchie
County Clerk**
1 Court Square
Charleston, Mississippi
38921-0330

Tate County Clerk
201 Ward St.
Senatobia, Mississippi
38668-2616

Tippah County Clerk
Main St.
Ripley, Mississippi 38663

Tishomingo County Clerk
1008 Battleground Dr.
Iuka, Mississippi 38852

Tunica County Clerk
1300 School St. #104
Tunica, Mississippi 38676

Union County Clerk
109 Main St. E
New Albany, Mississippi
38652-0847

Walthall County Clerk
P.O. Box 351
Tylertown, Mississippi
39667-0351

Warren County Clerk
1009 Cherry St.
Vicksburg, Mississippi
39180

**Washington
County Clerk**
900 Washington Ave.
Greenville, Mississippi
38702

Wayne County Clerk
609 Azalea Dr.
Waynesboro, Mississippi
39367

Webster County Clerk
Highway 9N
Walthall, Mississippi 39771

Wilkinson County Clerk
P.O. Box 516
Woodville, Mississippi
39669-0516

Winston County Clerk
115 S. Court Ave.
Louisville, Mississippi
39339-0188

Yalobusha County Clerk
132 Blackmur Dr.
Water Valley, Mississippi
38965

Yazoo County Clerk
211 E. Broadway St.
Yazoo City, Mississippi
39194

MISSOURI

http://www.state.mo.us/

Adair County Clerk
Courthouse
Kirksville, Missouri 63501

Andrew County Clerk
Courthouse
Savannah, Missouri 64485

Atchison County Clerk
40 Washington St.
Rock Port, Missouri 64482

Audrain County Clerk
Courthouse
Mexico, Missouri 65265

Barry County Clerk
Courthouse
Cassville, Missouri 65625

Barton County Clerk
Courthouse
Lamar, Missouri 64759

Bates County Clerk
Courthouse
Butler, Missouri 64730

Benton County Clerk
P.O. Box 1238
Warsaw, Missouri
65355-1238

Bollinger County Clerk
Courthouse
Marble Hill, Missouri
63764

Boone County Clerk
600 E. Broadway
Columbia, Missouri 65201

Buchanan County Clerk
Fifth and Jules
St. Joseph, Missouri 64501

Butler County Clerk
P.O. Box 332
Poplar Bluff, Missouri
63901-0332

Caldwell County Clerk
P.O. Box 67
Kingston, Missouri
64650-0067

Callaway County Clerk
Courthouse
Fulton, Missouri 65251

Camden County Clerk
1 Court Circle
Camdenton, Missouri
65020

**Cape Girardeau
County Clerk**
1 Barton Square
Jackson, Missouri 63755

Carroll County Clerk
Courthouse
Carrollton, Missouri 64633

Carter County Clerk
P.O. Box 517
Van Buren, Missouri
63965-0517

Cass County Clerk
Courthouse
Harrisonville, Missouri
64701

Cedar County Clerk
P.O. Box 158
Stockton, Missouri 65785

Chariton County Clerk
Courthouse
Keytesville, Missouri
65261

Christian County Clerk
Courthouse
Ozark, Missouri 65721

Clark County Clerk
Courthouse
Kahoka, Missouri 63445

Clay County Clerk
P.O. Box 99
Liberty, Missouri 64068

Clinton County Clerk
P.O. Box 245
Plattsburg, Missouri
64477-0245

Cole County Clerk
301 E. High
Jefferson City, Missouri
65101-3208

Cooper County Clerk
P.O. Box 123
Boonville, Missouri
65233-0123

Crawford County Clerk
Courthouse
Steelville, Missouri 65565

Dade County Clerk
Courthouse
Greenfield, Missouri 65661

Dallas County Clerk
P.O. Box 436
Buffalo, Missouri
65622-0436

Daviess County Clerk
Courthouse, 102 N. Main
Gallatin, Missouri 64640

DeKalb County Clerk
P.O. Box 248
Maysville, Missouri
64469-0248

Dent County Clerk
Courthouse
Salem, Missouri
65560-1298

Douglas County Clerk
Courthouse
Ava, Missouri 65608

Dunklin County Clerk
P.O. Box 188
Kennett, Missouri 63857

Franklin County Clerk
P.O. Box 311
Union, Missouri
63084-0311

Gasconade County Clerk
P.O. Box 295
Hermann, Missouri
65041-0295

Gentry County Clerk
Courthouse
Albany, Missouri 64402

Greene County Clerk
940 Boonville
Springfield, Missouri
65802

Grundy County Clerk
700 Main St.
Trenton, Missouri
64683-2063

Harrison County Clerk
Courthouse
Bethany, Missouri 64424

Henry County Clerk
Courthouse
Clinton, Missouri 64735

Hickory County Clerk
Courthouse
Hermitage, Missouri 65668

Holt County Clerk
Courthouse
Oregon, Missouri 64473

Howard County Clerk
Courthouse
Fayette, Missouri 65248

Howell County Clerk
Courthouse
West Plains, Missouri
65775

Iron County Clerk
P.O. Box 42
Ironton, Missouri
63650-0042

Jackson County Clerk
Kansas City, Missouri
64106

Jasper County Clerk
Courthouse
Carthage, Missouri 64836

Jefferson County Clerk
P.O. Box 100
Hillsboro, Missouri
63050-0100

Johnson County Clerk
Courthouse
Warrensburg, Missouri
64093

Knox County Clerk
Courthouse
Edina, Missouri 63537

Laclede County Clerk
Second and Adam Streets
Lebanon, Missouri 65536

Lafayette County Clerk
P.O. Box 357
Lexington, Missouri
64067-0357

Lawrence County Clerk
Courthouse
Mt. Vernon, Missouri
65712

Lewis County Clerk
Courthouse
Monticello, Missouri 63457

Lincoln County Clerk
201 Main St.
Troy, Missouri 63379-1127

Linn County Clerk
Courthouse
Linneus, Missouri 64653

Livingston County Clerk
P.O. Box 803
Chillicothe, Missouri
64601

Macon County Clerk
P.O. Box 382
Macon, Missouri 63552

Madison County Clerk
Court Square
Fredericktown, Missouri
63645

Maries County Clerk
Courthouse
Vienna, Missouri 65582

Marion County Clerk
Courthouse
Palmyra, Missouri 63461

McDonald County Clerk
P.O. Box 665
Pineville, Missouri 64856

Mercer County Clerk
Courthouse
Princeton, Missouri 64673

Miller County Clerk
P.O. Box 12
Tuscumbia, Missouri
65082-0012

Mississippi County Clerk
P.O. Box 304
Charleston, Missouri
63834-0304

Moniteau County Clerk
Courthouse
California, Missouri 65018

Monroe County Clerk
300 N. Main St.
Paris, Missouri 65275-1399

**Montgomery
County Clerk**
211 E. Third
Montgomery City, Missouri
63361-1956

Morgan County Clerk
104 N. Fisher
Versailles, Missouri
65084-1202

**New Madrid
County Clerk**
P.O. Box 68
New Madrid, Missouri
63869

Newton County Clerk
Courthouse
Neosho, Missouri 64850

Nodaway County Clerk
Courthouse
Maryville, Missouri 64468

Oregon County Clerk
Courthouse
Alton, Missouri 65606

Osage County Clerk
P.O. Box 826
Linn, Missouri 65051

Ozark County Clerk
Courthouse
Gainesville, Missouri
65655

Pemiscot County Clerk
Ward Ave.
Caruthersville, Missouri
63830

Perry County Clerk
Courthouse
Perryville, Missouri 63775

Pettis County Clerk
415 S. Ohio
Sedalia, Missouri
65301-4435

Phelps County Clerk
Third and Rolla St.
Rolla, Missouri 65401

Pike County Clerk
115 W. Main
Bowling Green, Missouri
63334

Platte County Clerk
Courthouse
Platte City, Missouri 64079

Polk County Clerk
Courthouse
Bolivar, Missouri 65613

Pulaski County Clerk
Courthouse
Waynesville, Missouri
65583

Putnam County Clerk
Courthouse
Unionville, Missouri 63565

Ralls County Clerk
Courthouse
New London, Missouri
63459-0444

Randolph County Clerk
S. Main St.
Huntsville, Missouri 65259

Ray County Clerk
Courthouse
Richmond, Missouri 64085

Reynolds County Clerk
Courthouse Square
Centerville, Missouri
63633

Ripley County Clerk
Courthouse
Doniphan, Missouri 63935

Saline County Clerk
Courthouse
Marshall, Missouri 65340

Schuyler County Clerk
P.O. Box 187
Lancaster, Missouri
63548-0187

Scotland County Clerk
Courthouse
Memphis, Missouri 63555

Scott County Clerk
Courthouse
Benton, Missouri 63736

Shannon County Clerk
P.O. Box 187
Eminence, Missouri
65466-0187

Shelby County Clerk
P.O. Box 186
Shelbyville, Missouri
63469-0186

St. Charles County Clerk
Third and Jefferson
St. Charles, Missouri
63301

St. Clair County Clerk
P.O. Box 334
Osceola, Missouri 64776

**St. Francois
County Clerk**
Courthouse
Farmington, Missouri
63640

St. Louis County Clerk
111 S. Meramec Ave.,
1st Fl.
Clayton, Missouri
63105-1711

St. Louis City Clerk
634 N. Grand Blvd.
St. Louis City, Missouri
63103-2803

Ste. Genevieve
County Clerk
55 S. Third
Ste. Genevieve, Missouri
63670

Stoddard County Clerk
Courthouse
Bloomfield, Missouri
63825

Stone County Clerk
Courthouse
Galena, Missouri 65656

Sullivan County Clerk
Courthouse
Milan, Missouri 63556

Taney County Clerk
Courthouse
Forsyth, Missouri 65653

Texas County Clerk
210 N. Grand
Houston, Missouri
65483-1224

Vernon County Clerk
Courthouse
Nevada, Missouri 64772

Warren County Clerk
116 W. Main
Warrenton, Missouri 63383

Washington County
Clerk
102 N. Missouri
Potosi, Missouri 63664

Wayne County Clerk
Courthouse
Greenville, Missouri 63944

Webster County Clerk
P.O. Box 529
Marshfield, Missouri 65706

Worth County Clerk
P.O. Box L
Grant City, Missouri
64456-0530

Wright County Clerk
P.O. Box 98
Hartville, Missouri
65667-0098

MONTANA
http://www.state.mt.us/

Beaverhead County Clerk
2 South Pacific St.
Cluster #3
Dillon, Montana 59725

Big Horn County Clerk
P.O. Drawer H
Hardin, Montana 59034

Blaine County
P.O. Box 278
Chinook, Montana 59523

Broadwater County Clerk
515 Broadway
Townsend, Montana 59644

Carbon County Clerk
P.O. Box 948
Red Lodge, Montana
59068

Carter County Clerk
P.O. Box 315
Ekalaka, Montana
59324-0315

Cascade County Clerk
415 2nd Ave. N., Rm. 203
Great Falls, Montana
59403

Chouteau County Clerk
1308 Franklin
Fort Benton, Montana
59442

Custer County Clerk
1010 Main St.
Miles City, Montana
59301-3419

Daniels County Clerk
P.O. Box 247
Scobey, Montana 59263

Dawson County Clerk
207 W. Bell St.
Glendive, Montana
59330-1616

Deer Lodge County Clerk
800 S. Main
Anaconda, Montana
59711-2999

Fallon County Clerk
10 W. Fallon Ave.
Baker, Montana 59313

Fergus County Clerk
712 W. Main
Lewistown, Montana
59457-2562

Flathead County Clerk
800 S. Main
Kalispell, Montana
59901-5435

Gallatin County Clerk
311 W. Main
Bozeman, Montana
59715-4576

Garfield County Clerk
P.O. Box 7
Jordan, Montana
59337-0007

Glacier County Clerk
512 Main St.
Cut Bank, Montana
59427-3016

**Golden Valley
County Clerk**
107 Kemp
Ryegate, Montana 59074

Granite County Clerk
P.O. Box J
Philipsburg, Montana
59858

Hill County Clerk
Courthouse
Havre, Montana
59501-3999

Jefferson County Clerk
P.O. Box H
Boulder, Montana 59632

**Judith Basic
County Clerk**
Courthouse
Stanford, Montana 59479

Lake County Clerk
106 Fourth Ave.
Polson, Montana
59860-2125

**Lewis and Clark
County Clerk**
316 N. Park
Helena, Montana
59601-5059

Liberty County Clerk
P.O. Box 549
Chester, Montana 59522

Lincoln County Clerk
512 California Ave.
Libby, Montana
59923-1942

Madison County Clerk
110 W. Wallace St.
Virginia City, Montana
59755

McCone County Clerk
P.O. Box 199
Circle, Montana 59215

Meagher County Clerk
P.O. Box 309
White Sulphur Springs,
Montana 59645

Mineral County Clerk
P.I. Box 550
Superior, Montana
59872-0550

Missoula County Clerk
Courthouse
Missoula, Montana
59802-4292

Musselshell County Clerk
P.O. Box 686
Roundup, Montana 59072

Park County Clerk
414 E. Callender
Livingston, Montana
59047-2746

Petroleum County Clerk
201 E. Main St.
Winnett, Montana 59087

Phillips County Clerk
314 Second Ave. W.
Malta, Montana 59538

Pondera County Clerk
20 Fourth Ave. SW
Conrad, Montana
59425-2340

**Powder River
County Clerk**
P.O. Box J
Broadus, Montana 59317

Powell County Clerk
409 Missouri
Deer Lodge, Montana
59722-1084

Prairie County Clerk
P.O. Box 125
Terry, Montana
59349-0125

Ravalli County Clerk
Courthouse
Hamilton, Montana 59840

Richland County Clerk
201 W. Main
Sidney, Montana
59270-4035

Roosevelt County Clerk
400 Second Ave. S.
Wolf Point, Montana
59201-1605

Rosebud County Clerk
P.O. Box 48
Forsyth, Montana 59327

Sanders County Clerk
Main St.
Thompson Falls, Montana
59873

Sheridan County Clerk
100 W. Laurel Ave.
Plentywood, Montana
59254-1619

Silver Bow County Clerk
155 W. Granite
Butte, Montana
59701-9256

Stillwater County Clerk
Courthouse
Columbus, Montana 59019

**Sweet Grass
County Clerk**
P.O. Box 460
Big Timber, Montana
59011

Teton County Clerk
P.O. Box 610
Choteau, Montana
59422-0610

Toole County Clerk
226 First St., S.
Shelby, Montana
59474-1920

Treasure County Clerk
P.O. Box 392
Hysham, Montana 59038

Valley County Clerk
501 Court Square, #2
Glasgow, Montana 59230

Wheatland County Clerk
P.O. Box 1903
Harlowton, Montana 59036

Wibaux County Clerk
200 S. Wibaux
Wibaux, Montana 59353

Yellowstone County Clerk
P.O. Box 35001
Billings, Montana
59107-5001

NEBRASKA

http://www.state.ne.us/

Adams County Clerk
500 W. Fifth, Rm. 109
Hastings, Nebraska 68901

Antelope County Clerk
Courthouse
Neligh, Nebraska 68756

Arthur County Clerk
P.O. Box 126
Arthur, Nebraska
69121-0126

Banner County Clerk
P.O. Box 67
Harrisburg, Nebraska
69345-0067

Blaine County Clerk
Courthouse
Brewster, Nebraska 68821

Boone County Clerk
222 S. Fourth St.
Albion, Nebraska
68620-1258

Box Butte County Clerk
510 Box Butte Ave.
Alliance, Nebraska 69301

Boyd County Clerk
Courthouse
Butte, Nebraska 68722

Brown County Clerk
Ainsworth, Nebraska
69210

Buffalo County Clerk
15th and Central Ave.
Kearney, Nebraska 68848

Burt County Clerk
111 N. Thirteenth St.
Tekamah, Nebraska
68061-1043

Butler County Clerk
Courthouse
David City, Nebraska
68632
(402) 367-3091

Cass County Clerk
Fourth and Main St.
Plattsmouth, Nebraska
68048

Cedar County Clerk
101 E. Centre
Hartington, Nebraska
68739

Chase County Clerk
P.O. Box 310
Imperial, Nebraska
69033-0310

Cherry County Clerk
P.O. Box 120
Valentine, Nebraska 69201

Cheyenne County Clerk
Courthouse
Sidney, Nebraska 69162

Clay County Clerk
111 W. Fairfield
Clay Center, Nebraska
68933

Colfax County Clerk
411 E. 11th St.
Schuyler, Nebraska 68661-
1940

Cuming County Clerk
Courthouse
West Point, Nebraska
68788

Custer County Clerk
431 S. Tenth Ave.
Broken Bow, Nebraska
68822-2001

Dakota County Clerk
Courthouse
Dakota City, Nebraska
68731

Dawes County Clerk
Courthouse
Chadron, Nebraska 69337

Dawson County Clerk
P.O. Box 370
Lexington, Nebraska
68850-0370

Deuel County Clerk
Courthouse
Chappell, Nebraska 69129

Dixon County Clerk
Courthouse
Ponca, Nebraska 68770

Dodge County Clerk
435 N. Park
Fremont, Nebraska 68025

Douglas County Clerk
1819 Farnam St., Rm. 402
Omaha, Nebraska 68183

Dundy County Clerk
Courthouse
Benkelman, Nebraska
69021

Fillmore County Clerk
Courthouse
Geneva, Nebraska 68361

Franklin County Clerk
405 15th Ave.
Franklin, Nebraska
68939-1309

Frontier County Clerk
P.O. Box 40
Stockville, Nebraska 69042

Furnas County Clerk
P.O. Box 387
Beaver City, Nebraska
68926-0387

Gage County Clerk
6th and Grant St.
Beatrice, Nebraska 68310

Garden County Clerk
Courthouse
Oshkosh, Nebraska 69154

Garfield County Clerk
P.O. Box 218
Burwell, Nebraska
68823-0218

Gosper County Clerk
P.O. Box 136
Elwood, Nebraska 68937

Grant County Clerk
P.O. Box 128
Hyannis, Nebraska 69350

Greeley County Clerk
P.O. Box 287
Greeley Center, Nebraska
68842-0287

Hall County Clerk
121 S. Pine
Grand Island, Nebraska
68801-6076

Hamilton County Clerk
Courthouse
Auroa, Nebraska 68818

Harlan County Clerk
Courthouse
Alma, Nebraska 68920

Hayes County Clerk
P.O. Box 67
Hayes Center, Nebraska
69032-0067

Hitchcock County Clerk
Courthouse
Trenton, Nebraska 69044

Holt County Clerk
Courthouse
O'Neill, Nebraska 68763

Hooker County Clerk
P.O. Box 184
Mullen, Nebraska
69152-0184

Howard County Clerk
P.O. Box 25
St. Paul, Nebraska
68873-0025

Jefferson County Clerk
411 Fourth St.
Fairbury, Nebraska
68352-2513

Johnson County Clerk
P.O. Box 416
Tecumseh, Nebraska
68450-0416

Kearney County Clerk
Courthouse
Minden, Nebraska 68959

Keith County Clerk
P.O. Box 149
Ogallala, Nebraska
69153-0149

Keya Paha County Clerk
P.O. Box 349
Springview, Nebraska
68778

Kimball County Clerk
114 E. Third St.
Kimball, Nebraska
69145-1401

Knox County Clerk
Courthouse
Center, Nebraska 68724

Lancaster County Clerk
555 Tenth St.
Lincoln, Nebraska
68508-2803

Lincoln County Clerk
Courthouse
North Platte, Nebraska
69101

Logan County Clerk
P.O. Box 8
Stapleton, Nebraska
69163-0008

Loup County Clerk
P.O. Box 187
Taylor, Nebraska
68879-0187

Madison County Clerk
P.O. Box 230
Madison, Nebraska 68748

McPherson County Clerk
P.O. Box 122
Tryon, Nebraska
69167-0122

Merrick County Clerk
P.O. Box 27
Central City, Nebraska
68826-0027

Morrill County Clerk
P.O. Box 610
Bridgeport, Nebraska
69336-0610

Nance County Clerk
Courthouse
Fullerton, Nebraska 68638

Nemaha County Clerk
1824 N. Street
Auburn, Nebraska
68305-2342

Nuckolls County Clerk
Courthouse
Nelson, Nebraska 68961

Otoe County Clerk
P.O. Box 249
Nebraska City, Nebraska
68410

Pawnee County Clerk
P.O. Box 431
Pawnee City, Nebraska
68420-0431

Perkins County Clerk
P.O. Box 156
Grant, Nebraska
69140-0156

Phelps County Clerk
P.O. Box 334
Holdrege, Nebraska
68949-0334

Pierce County Clerk
P.O. Box 218
Pierce, Nebraska
68767-0218

Platte County Clerk
2610 14th St.
Columbus, Nebraska
68601-4929

Polk County Clerk
Courthouse
Osceola, Nebraska 68651

Red Willow County Clerk
500 Norris Ave.
McCook, Nebraska
69001-2006

Richardson County Clerk
1701 Stone St.
Falls City, Nebraska 68355

Rock County Clerk
400 State St.
Bassett, Nebraska
68714-0367

Saline County Clerk
215 Court St.
Wilber, Nebraska
68465-0865

Sarpy County Clerk
1210 Golden Gate Dr.
Papillion, Nebraska
68046-2845

Saunders County Clerk
Chestnut St. Courthouse
Wahoo, Nebraska 68066

Scotts Bluff County Clerk
1825 Tenth St.
Gering, Nebraska
69341-2413

Seward County Clerk
P.O. Box 190
Seward, Nebraska 68434

Sheridan County Clerk
301 E. 2nd St.
Rushville, Nebraska
69360-0039

Sherman County Clerk
P.O. Box 456
Loup City, Nebraska
68853-0456

Sioux County Clerk
Courthouse, Main St.
Harrison, Nebraska 69346

Stanton County Clerk
804 Ivy St.
Stanton, Nebraska 68779

Thayer County Clerk
235 N. 4th St.
Hebron, Nebraska 68370

Thomas County Clerk
P.O. Box 226
Thedford, Nebraska 69166

Thurston County Clerk
106 S. 5th St.
Pender, Nebraska 68047

Valley County Clerk
125 S. 15th St.
Ord, Nebraska 68862-1409

**Washington County
Clerk**
1555 Colfax St.
Blair, Nebraska
68008-2022

Wayne County Clerk
510 N. Pearl St.
Wayne, Nebraska 68787

Webster County Clerk
621 N. Cedar St.
Red Cloud, Nebraska
68970

Wheeler County Clerk
County Courthouse
Bartlett, Nebraska 68622

York County Clerk
510 Lincoln Ave.
York, Nebraska 68467

NEVADA

http://www.state.nv.us/

**Carson City
County Clerk**
885 E. Musser St.
Carson City, Nevada 89701

Churchill County Clerk
190 W. First St.
Fallon, Nevada 89406-3309

Clark County Clerk
625 Shadow Lane
Las Vegas, Nevada 89101

Douglas County Clerk
P.O. Box 218
Minden, Nevada
89423-0218

Elko County Clerk
571 Idaho St.
Elko, Nevada 89801-3770

Esmeralda County Clerk
P.O. Box 547
Goldfield, Nevada
89103-0547

Eureka County Clerk
P.O. Box 677
Eureka, Nevada
89316-0677

Humbolt County Clerk
P.O. Box 352
Winnemucca, Nevada
89445-0352

Lander County Clerk
315 S. Humboldt
Battle Mountain, Nevada
89820-1655

Lincoln County Clerk
1 Main St.
Pioche, Nevada
89043-0090

Lyon County Clerk
31 S. Main St.
Yerington, Nevada
89447-0816

Mineral County Clerk
P.O. Box 1450
Hawthorne, Nevada
89415-1450

Nye County Clerk
P.O. Box 1031
Tonopah, Nevada 89049

Pershing County Clerk
P.O. Box 820
Lovelock, Nevada
89419-0820

Storey County Clerk
P.O. Box D
Virginia City, Nevada
89440-0139

Washoe County Clerk
P.O. Box 11130
Reno, Nevada 89520-0027

White Pine County Clerk
Campton Street
Ely, Nevada 89301

NEW HAMPSHIRE

http://www.state.nh.us/

Belknap County Clerk
P.O. Box 578
Laconia, New Hampshire
03247-0578

Carroll County Clerk
Administration Bldg.
Ossipee, New Hampshire
03864

Cheshire County Clerk
12 Court St.
Keene, New Hampshire
03431-3402

Coos County Clerk
Main Street
Lancaster, New Hampshire
03584

Grafton County Clerk
RR1, Box 65F
North Haverhill, New
Hampshire 03774-9708

**Hillsborough
County Clerk**
19 Temple St.
Nashua, New Hampshire
03060-3444

Merrimack County Clerk
163 N. Main St.
Concord, New Hampshire
03301-5068

**Rockingham
County Clerk**
Rt. 125
Brentwood, New
Hampshire 03830

Strafford County Clerk
P.O. Box 799
Dover, New Hampshire
03820-0799

Sullivan County Clerk
22 Main St.
Newport, New Hampshire
03773-0045

NEW JERSEY

http://www.state.nj.us/

Atlantic County Clerk
5901 Main St.
Mays Landing, New Jersey
08330

Bergen County Clerk
21 Main St.
Hackensack, New Jersey
07601-7017

Burlington County Clerk
49 Rancocas Rd.
Mount Holly, New Jersey
08060-1384

Camden County Clerk
5th and Mickle Blvd.
Camden, New Jersey
08103-4001

Cape May County Clerk
7 N. Main St.
Cape May, New Jersey
08210

**Cumberland
County Clerk**
Broad and Fayette Street
Bridgeton, New Jersey
08302

Essex County Clerk
920 Broad St., Rm. 111
Newark, New Jersey 07101

Gloucester County Clerk
1 N. Broad St.
Woodbury, New Jersey
08096-7376

Hudson County Clerk
595 Newark Ave.
Jersey City, New Jersey
07306-2394

Hunterdon County Clerk
71 Main St.
Flemington, New Jersey
08822

Mercer County Clerk
P.O. Box 8068
Trenton, New Jersey
08650-0068

Middlesex County Clerk
1 John F. Kennedy Square
New Brunswick, New
Jersey 08901

Monmouth County Clerk
Main St.
Freehold, New Jersey
07728-1255

Morris County Clerk
P.O. Box 900
Morristown, New Jersey
07960-0900

Ocean County Clerk
P.O. Box 2191
Toms River, New Jersey
08754

Passaic County Clerk
77 Hamilton St.
Paterson, New Jersey
07505-2018

Salem County Clerk
92 Market St.
Salem City, New Jersey
08079-1913

Somerset County Clerk
P.O. Box 3000
Somerville, New Jersey
08876-1262

Sussex County Clerk
4 Park Place
Newton, New Jersey 07860

Union County Clerk
2 Broad St.
Elizabeth, New Jersey
07201

Warren County Clerk
Rt. 519
Wayne Dumont Jr. Bldg.
Belvidere, New Jersey
07823

NEW MEXICO

http://www.state.nm.us/

Bernalillo County Clerk
One Civic Plaza NW
Albuquerque, New Mexico
87102

Catron County Clerk
P.O. Box 507
Reserve, New Mexico
87830

Chaves County Clerk
401 N. Main St.
Roswell, New Mexico
88201-4726

Cibola County Clerk
515 W. High St.
Grants, New Mexico
87020-2526

Colfax County Clerk
P.O. Box 1498
Raton, New Mexico
87740-1498

Curry County Clerk
700 N. Main St.
Clovis, New Mexico
88102-1168

DeBaca County Clerk
P.O. Box 347
Fort Sumner, New Mexico
88819

Dona Ana County Clerk
251 W. Amador Ave.
Las Cruces, New Mexico
88005

Eddy County Clerk
P.O. Box 1139
Carlsbad, New Mexico
88221-1139

Grant County Clerk
P.O. Box 898
Silver City, New Mexico
88062-0898

Guadalupe County Clerk
420 Parker Ave.
Santa Rosa, New Mexico
88435

Harding County Clerk
P.O. Box 1002
Mosquero, New Mexico
87733-1002

Hidalgo County Clerk
300 S. Shakespeare St.
Lordsburg, New Mexico
88045-1939

Lea County Clerk
P.O. Box 4C
Lovington, New Mexico
88260

Lincoln County Clerk
300 Central Ave.
Carrizozo, New Mexico
88301-0711

Los Alamos County Clerk
2300 Trinity Dr.
Los Alamos, New Mexico
87544-3051

Luna County Clerk
P.O. Box 1838
Deming, New Mexico
88031-1838

McKinley County Clerk
200 W. Hill Ave.
Gallup, New Mexico 87301

Mora County Clerk
P.O. Box 360
Mora, New Mexico 87732

Otero County Clerk
10th And New York Streets
Alamogordo, New Mexico
88310

Quay County Clerk
300 S. 3rd St.
Tucumcari, New Mexico
88401

Rio Arriba County Clerk
P.O. Box 158
Tierra Amarilla, New
Mexico 87575

Roosevelt County Clerk
Courthouse
Portales, New Mexico
88130

San Juan County Clerk
P.O. Box 550
Aztec, New Mexico 87410

San Miguel County Clerk
Courthouse
Las Vegas, New Mexico
87701

Sandoval County Clerk
P.O. Box 40
Bernalillo, New Mexico
87004

Santa Fe County Clerk
P.O. Box 1985
Santa Fe, New Mexico
87504

Sierra County Clerk
300 Date Street
Truth or Consequences,
New Mexico 87901-2362

Socorro County Clerk
131 Court St.
Socorro, New Mexico
87801

Taos County Clerk
P.O. Box 676
Taos, New Mexico 87571

Torrance County Clerk
9th and Allen
Estancia, New Mexico
87016

Union County Clerk
200 Court St.
Clayton, New Mexico
88415-0430

Valencia County Clerk
P.O. Box 1119
Los Lunas, New Mexico
87031

NEW YORK

http://www.state.ny.us/

Albany County Clerk
16 Eagle St.
Albany, New York
12207-1019

Allegany County Clerk
Courthouse
Belmont, New York 14813

Bronx County Clerk
1780 Grand Concourse
Bronx, New York 10457

Broome County Clerk
44 Hawley St.
Binghamton, New York
13901

Cattaraugus County Clerk
303 Court St.
Little Valley, New York
14755-1028

Cayuga County Clerk
160 Genesee St.
Auburn, New York
13021-3424

Chautauqua County Clerk
P.O. Box 292
Mayville, New York
14757-0292

Chemung County Clerk
210 Lake St.
Elmire, New York
14901-3109

Chenango County Clerk
5 Court St.
Norwich, New York 13815

Clinton County Clerk
137 Margaret St.
Plattsburgh, New York
12901-2933

Columbia County Clerk
Allen and Union St.
Courthouse
Hudson, New York 12534

Cortland County Clerk
60 Central Ave.
Cortland, New York
13045-2716

Delaware County Clerk
4 Court St.
Delhi, New York 13753

Dutchess County Clerk
222 Market St.
Poughkeepsie, New York
12601-3222

Erie County Clerk
92 Franklin St.
Buffalo, New York
14202-3904

Essex County Clerk
Court St.
Elizabethtown, New York
12932

Franklin County Clerk
63 W. Main St.
Malone, New York
12953-1817

Fulton County Clerk
County Bldg.
223 W. Main St.
Johnstown, New York
12905-2331

Genesee County Clerk
Main and Court St.
Batavia, New York 14020

Greene County Clerk
388 Main St.
Catskill, New York 12414

Hamilton County Clerk
Office Bldg.
Lake Pleasant, New York
12108

Herkimer County Clerk
P.O. Box 471
Herkimer, New York
13350-0471

Jefferson County Clerk
175 Arsenal St.
Watertown, New York
13601-2522

Kings County Clerk
360 Adams St.
Brooklyn, New York
11201-3712

Lewis County Clerk
7660 State St.
Lowville, New York
13367-1432

Livingston County Clerk
6 Court St.
Geneseo, New York 14454

Madison County Clerk
N. Court St.
Wampsville, New York
13163-0668

Monroe County Clerk
39 W. Main St.
Rochester, New York
14614

Montgomery County Clerk
Broadway
Fonda, New York 12068

Nassau County Clerk
1 West St.
Mineola, New York
11501-4812

New York City Vital Records
One Center Street,
Rm. 252
New York, New York
10007

New York County Clerk
60 Centre St.
New York, New York
10007-1402

Niagara County Clerk
Courthouse
Lockport, New York 14094

Oneida County Clerk
109 Mary St.
Utica, New York
13350-1921

Onondaga County Clerk
421 Montgomery St. #20
Syracuse, New York 13202

Ontario County Clerk
3907 County Rd. 46
Canandaigua, New York
14424

Orange County Clerk
255-275 Main St.
Goshen, New York
10924-1621

Orleans County Clerk
Courthouse Square
Albion, New York
14411-1449

Oswego County Clerk
West Oneida St.
Oswego, New York 13126

Otsego County Clerk
197 Main St.
Cooperstown, New York
13326-1129

Putnam County Clerk
40 Gleneida Ave.
Carmel, New York 10512

Queens County Clerk
88-11 Sutphin Blvd.
Jamaica, New York 11435

Rensselaer County Clerk
1600 7th Ave.
Troy, New York 12180

Richmond County Clerk
18 Richmond Terrace
Staten Island, New York
10301-1935

Rockland County Clerk
27 New Hempstead Rd.
New City, New York 10956

Saratoga County Clerk
40 McMasters St.
Ballston Spa, New York
12020-1908

Schenectady
County Clerk
City Hall, Rm. 107
Jay St.
Schenectady, New York
12305

Schoharie County Clerk
P.O. Box 549
Schoharie, New York
12157-0549

Schuyler County Clerk
105 Ninth St., Box 8
Watkins Glen, New York
14891

Seneca County Clerk
1 DiPronio Dr.
Waterloo, New York 13165

St. Lawrence
County Clerk
Courthouse
Canton, New York 13617

Steuben County Clerk
Courthouse at 3 Pulteney
Square
Bath, New York 14810

Suffolk County Clerk
County Center
Riverhead, New York
11901-3398

Sullivan County Clerk
100 Main St.
Monticello, New York
12701-1160

Tioga County Clerk
16 Court St.
Owego, New York 13827

Tompkins County Clerk
401 Harris B. Dates Dr.
Ithaca, New York 14850

Ulster County Clerk
244 Fair St.
Kingston, New York
12402-1800

Warren County Clerk
Route 9
Lake George, New York
12845

Washington
County Clerk
Upper Broadway
Fort Edward, New York
12828

Wayne County Clerk
9 Pearl St.
Lyons, New York
14489-0131

Westchester
County Clerk
110 Dr. Martin Luther
King Jr. Blvd
White Plains, New York
10601

Wyoming County Clerk
143 N. Main St.
Warsaw, New York
14569-1123

Yates County Clerk
110 Court St.,
County Bldg.
Penn Yan, New York 14527

NORTH CAROLINA
http://www.state.nc.us/

Alamance County Clerk
124 W. Elm St.
Graham, North Carolina
27253

Alexander County Clerk
201 First St. SW, Suite 1
Taylorsville,
North Carolina 28681

Alleghany County Clerk
P.O. Box 186
Sparta, North Carolina
28675

Anson County Clerk
P.O. Box 352
Wadesboro, North Carolina
28170

Ashe County Clerk
P.O. Box 367
Jefferson, North Carolina
28640

Avery County Clerk
P.O. Box 87
Newland, North Carolina
28657-0356

Beaufort County Clerk
P.O. Box 514
Washington,
North Carolina 27889

Bertie County Clerk
P.O. Box 340
Windsor, North Carolina
27983

Bladen County Clerk
P.O. Box 247
Elizabethtown,
North Carolina 28337

Brunswick County Clerk
P.O. Box 87
Bolivia, North Carolina
28422

Buncombe County Clerk
60 Court Plaza
Asheville, North Carolina
28801

Burke County Clerk
P.O. Box 936
Morganton, North Carolina
28655

Cabarrus County Clerk
P.O. Box 707
Concord, North Carolina
28026

Caldwell County Clerk
905 West Ave. NW
Lenoir, North Carolina
28645

Camden County Clerk
P.O. Box 190
Camden, North Carolina
27921

Carteret County Clerk
Courthouse Square
Admin. Bldg.
Beaufort, North Carolina
28516

Caswell County Clerk
P.O. Box 98
Yanceyville,
North Carolina 27379

Catawba County Clerk
P.O. Box 65
Newton, North Carolina
28658

Chatham County Clerk
P.O. Box 756
Pittsboro, North Carolina
27312

Cherokee County Clerk
Cherokee County
Courthouse
Murphy, North Carolina
28906

Chowan County Clerk
P.O. Box 487
Edenton, North Carolina
27932

Clay County Clerk
P.O. Box 118
Hayesville, North Carolina
28904-0118

Cleveland County Clerk
P.O. Box 1210
Shelby, North Carolina
28151-1210

Columbus County Clerk
P.O. Box 1086
Whiteville, North Carolina
28472

Craven County
406 Craven St.
New Bern, North Carolina
28560

**Cumberland
County Clerk**
P.O. Box 2039
Fayetteville,
North Carolina 28301-5749

Currituck County Clerk
P.O. Box 71
Currituck, North Carolina
27929-0039

Dare County Clerk
P.O. Box 70
Manteo, North Carolina
27954

Davidson County Clerk
P.O. Box 464
Lexington, North Carolina
27293

Davie County Clerk
123 S. Main St.
Mocksville, North Carolina
27028

Duplin County Clerk
P.O. Box 970
Kenansville,
North Carolina 28349

Durham County Clerk
414 E. Main St.
Durham, North Carolina
27701

Edgecombe County Clerk
P.O. Box 386
Tarboro, North Carolina
27886

Forsyth County Clerk
P.O. Box 20639
Winston-Salem,
North Carolina 27120

Franklin County Clerk
P.O. Box 545
Louisburg, North Carolina
27549

Gaston County Clerk
P.O. Box 1578
Gastonia, North Carolina
28053

Gates County Clerk
P.O. Box 345
Gatesville, North Carolina
27938

Graham County Clerk
P.O. Box 406
Robbinsville,
North Carolina 28771

Granville County Clerk
P.O. Box 427
Oxford, North Carolina
27565

Greene County Clerk
P.O. Box 68
Snow Hill, North Carolina
28580

Guilford County Clerk
P.O. Box 3427
Greensboro, North Carolina
27402

Halifax County Clerk
P.O. Box 67
Halifax, North Carolina
27839

Harnett County Clerk
729 S. Main St.
Lillington, North Carolina
27546

Haywood County Clerk
Haywood County
Courthouse
Waynesville,
North Carolina 28786

Henderson County Clerk
200 N. Grove St., Suite 129
Hendersonville,
North Carolina 28792

Hertford County Clerk
P.O. Box 36
Winton, North Carolina
27986

Hoke County Clerk
304 N. Main St.
Raeford, North Carolina
28376

Hyde County Clerk
P.O. Box 294
Swan Quarter,
North Carolina 27885-0337

Iredell County Clerk
P.O. Box 904
Statesville, North Carolina
28677-0788

Jackson County Clerk
401 Grindstaff Cove Rd
Sylva, North Carolina
28779

Johnston County Clerk
P.O. Box 118
Smithfield, North Carolina
27577

Jones County Clerk
P.O. Box 189
Trenton, North Carolina
28585

Lee County Clerk
P.O. Box 2040
Sanford, North Carolina
27311

Lenoir County Clerk
P.O. Box 3289
Kinston, North Carolina
28502

Lincoln County Clerk
Lincoln Co. Courthouse
Lincolnton, North Carolina
28092

Macon County Clerk
5 West Main St.
Franklin, North Carolina
28734

Madison County Clerk
P.O. Box 66
Marshall, North Carolina
28753

Martin County Clerk
P.O. Box 348
Williamston,
North Carolina 27892-0668

McDowell County Clerk
1 South Main St.
Marion, North Carolina
28752-1450

**Mecklenburg
County Clerk**
249 Billingsley Rd
Charlotte, North Carolina
28211

Mitchell County Clerk
P.O. Box 82
Bakersville, North Carolina
28705

**Montgomery
County Clerk**
P.O. Box 695
Troy, North Carolina 27371

Moore County Clerk
P.O. Box 1210
Carthage, North Carolina
28327

Nash County Clerk
P.O. Box 974
Nashville, North Carolina
27856

**New Hanover
County Clerk**
316 Princess St., Rm. 216
Wilmington,
North Carolina 28401

**Northampton County
Clerk**
P.O. Box 128
Jackson, North Carolina
27845

Onslow County Clerk
P.O. Box 159, Rm. 107
Jacksonville,
North Carolina 28540

Orange County Clerk
208 S. Cameron St.
Hillsborough,
North Carolina 27278

Pamlico County Clerk
P.O. Box 423
Bayboro, North Carolina
28515

Pasquotank County Clerk
P.O. Box 154
Elizabeth City, North
Carolina 27909

Pender County Clerk
P.O. Box 43
Burgaw, North Carolina
28425

**Perquimans
County Clerk**
P.O. Box 74
Hertford, North Carolina
27944

Person County Clerk
Courthouse Square
Roxboro, North Carolina
27573

Pitt County Clerk
P.O. Box 35
Greenville, North Carolina
27835

Polk County Clerk
P.O. Box 308
Columbus, North Carolina
28722

Randolph County Clerk
P.O. Box 4066
Asheboro, North Carolina
27203

Richmond County Clerk
114 E. Franklin St. #101
Rockingham,
North Carolina 28379

Robeson County Clerk
P.O. Box 22
Lumberton, North Carolina
28358

**Rockingham
County Clerk**
P.O. Box 56
Wentworth, North Carolina
27375

Rowan County Clerk
P.O. Box 2568
Salisbury, North Carolina
28145

Rutherford County Clerk
P.O. Box 551
Rutherfordton,
North Carolina 28139

Sampson County Clerk
P.O. Box 256
Clinton, North Carolina
28328

Scotland County Clerk
P.O. Box 769
Laurinburg, North Carolina
28352

Stanley County Clerk
P.O. Box 97
Albemarle, North Carolina
28002

Stokes County Clerk
P.O. Box 67
Danbury, North Carolina
27016

Surry County Clerk
P.O. Box 303
Dobson, North Carolina
27017

Swain County Clerk
P.O. Box 417
Bryson City,
North Carolina 28713

**Transylvania
County Clerk**
12 East Main St.
Brevard, North Carolina
28712

Tyrrell County Clerk
P.O. Box 449
Columbia, North Carolina
27925

Union County Clerk
P.O. Box 248
Monroe, North Carolina
28111

Vance County Clerk
122 Young St. Courthouse
Henderson, North Carolina
27536-2017

Wake County Clerk
10 Sunnybrook Rd
Raleigh, North Carolina
27620

Warren County Clerk
P.O. Box 506
Warrenton, North Carolina
27589-1929

**Washington
County Clerk**
P.O. Box 1007
Plymouth, North Carolina
27962-1007

Watauga County Clerk
842 W. King St., Suite 9
Boone, North Carolina
28607

Wayne County Clerk
P.O. Box 267
Goldsboro, North Carolina
27533

Wilkes County Clerk
Wilkes County Courthouse
Wilkesboro, North Carolina
28697

Wilson County Clerk
P.O. Box 1728
Wilson, North Carolina
27694

Yadkin County Clerk
P.O. Box 211
Yadkinville, North Carolina
27055

Yancey County Clerk
Courthouse, Rm. 4
Burnsville, North Carolina
28714

NORTH DAKOTA
http://www.state.nd.us/

Adams County Clerk
P.O. Box 469
Hettinger, North Dakota
58639

Barnes County Clerk
P.O. Box 774
Valley City, North Dakota
58072

Benson County Clerk
P.O. Box 213
Minnewaukan, North
Dakota 58351

Billings County Clerk
P.O. Box 138
Medora, North Dakota
58645

Bottineau County Clerk
314 W. 5th St.
Bottineau, North Dakota
58318

Bowman County Clerk
P.O. Box 379
Bowman, North Dakota
58623

Burke County Clerk
P.O. Box 219
Bowbells, North Dakota
58721

Burleigh County Clerk
P.O. Box 1055
Bismarck, North Dakota
58502

Cass County Clerk
P.O. Box 2806
Fargo, North Dakota 58108

Cavalier County Clerk
901 3rd St.
Langdon, North Dakota
58249

Dickey County Clerk
P.O. Box 336
Ellendale, North Dakota
58436

Divide County Clerk
P.O. Box 68
Crosby, North Dakota
58730-0049

Dunn County Clerk
P.O. Box 136
Manning, North Dakota
58642

Eddy County Clerk
524 Central Ave.
New Rockford, North
Dakota 58356-1698

Emmons County Clerk
P.O. Box 905
Linton, North Dakota
58552

Foster County Clerk
P.O. Box 257
Carrington, North Dakota
58421

Golden Valley County Clerk
P.O. Box 9
Beach, North Dakota 58621

Grand Forks County Clerk
P.O. Box 5939
Grand Forks, North Dakota 58201-1477

Grant County Clerk
P.O. Box 258
Carson, North Dakota 58529

Griggs County Clerk
P.O. Box 326
Cooperstown, North Dakota 58425-0326

Hettinger County Clerk
P.O. Box 668
Mott, North Dakota 58646

Kidder County Clerk
P.O. Box 66
Steele, North Dakota 58482-0110

La Moure County Clerk
P.O. Box 5
La Moure, North Dakota 58458

Logan County Clerk
P.O. Box 6
Napoleon, North Dakota 58561

McHenry County Clerk
P.O. Box 117
Towner, North Dakota 58788

McIntosh County Clerk
P.O. Box 179
Ashley, North Dakota 58413

McKenzie County Clerk
P.O. Box 524
Watford City, North Dakota 58854

McLean County Clerk
P.O. Box 1108
Washburn, North Dakota 58577

Mercer County Clerk
P.O. Box 39
Stanton, North Dakota 58571-0039

Morton County Clerk
210 Second Ave. NW
Mandan, North Dakota 58554-3124

Mountrail County Clerk
P.O. Box 69
Stanley, North Dakota 58784

Nelson County Clerk
P.O. Box 565
Lakota, North Dakota 58344

Oliver County Clerk
P.O. Box 125
Center, North Dakota 58530-0166

Pembina County Clerk
301 Dakota St. W, #6
Cavalier, North Dakota 58220-0160

Pierce County Clerk
240 SE Second St.
Rugby, North Dakota 58368-1830

Ramsey County Clerk
524 4th Ave., #4
Devils Lake, North Dakota 58301-2701

Ransom County Clerk
P.O. Box 626
Lisbon, North Dakota 58054

Renville County Clerk
P.O. Box 68
Mohall, North Dakota 58761-0068

Richland County Clerk
418 Second Ave. North
Wahpeton, North Dakota 58075

Rolette County Clerk
P.O. Box 460
Rolla, North Dakota 58367

Sargent County Clerk
P.O. Box 176
Forman, North Dakota 58032-0098

Sheridan County Clerk
P.O. Box 668
McClusky, North Dakota 58463-0636

Sioux County Clerk
P.O. Box L
Fort Yates, North Dakota 58538

Slope County Clerk
P.O. Box JJ
Amidon, North Dakota 58620-0449

Stark County Clerk
P.O. Box 130
Dickinson, North Dakota 58602-0130

Steele County Clerk
P.O. Box 296
Finley, North Dakota 58230

Stutsman County Clerk
511 Second Ave. SE
Jamestown, North Dakota
58401-4210

Towner County Clerk
P.O. Box 517
Cando, North Dakota
58324

Traill County Clerk
P.O. Box 805
Hillsboro, North Dakota
58045

Walsh County Clerk
600 Cooper Ave.
Grafton, North Dakota
58237-1542

Ward County Clerk
P.O. Box 5005
Minot, North Dakota 58701

Wells County Clerk
P.O. Box 596
Fessenden, North Dakota
58437-0596

Williams County Clerk
P.O. Box 2047
Williston, North Dakota
58802-1246

OHIO

http://www.state.oh.us/

Adams County Clerk
110 West Main
West Union, Ohio
45693-1347

Allen County Clerk
301 N. Main St.
Lima, Ohio 45801-4456

Ashland County Clerk
West 2nd St.
Ashland, Ohio 44805

Ashtabula County Clerk
25 W. Jefferson St.
Jefferson, Ohio
44047-1027

Athens County Clerk
Court and Washington St.
Athens, Ohio 45701-2888

Auglaize County Clerk
214 S. Wagner St.
Wapakoneta, Ohio 45895

Belmont County Clerk
101 Main St.
St. Clairsville, Ohio
43950-1224

Brown County Clerk
Danny L. Pride Courthouse
Georgetown, Ohio 45121

Butler County Clerk
130 High St.
Hamilton, Ohio 45011

Carroll County Clerk
119 Public Square
Carrollton, Ohio 44615

Champaign County Clerk
200 N. Main St.
Urbana, Ohio 43078

Clark County Clerk
529 E. Home Rd.
Springfield, Ohio 45502

Clermont County Clerk
76 South Riverside
Batavia, Ohio 45103-2602

Clinton County Clerk
46 S. South St.
Wilmington, Ohio
45177-2214

**Columbiana
County Clerk**
105 S. Market St.
Lisbon, Ohio 44432-1255

Coshocton County Clerk
349½ Main St.
Coshocton, Ohio
43812-1510

Crawford County Clerk
112 E. Mansfield St.
Bucyrus, Ohio 44820

Cuyahoga County Clerk
1200 Ontario St.
Cleveland, Ohio 44113

Darke County Clerk
4th and Broadway
Greenville, Ohio 45331

Defiance County Clerk
500 Court St.
Defiance, Ohio 43512-2157

Delaware County Clerk
91 N. Sandusky
Delaware, Ohio
43015-1703

Elyria City Clerk
202 Chestnut St.
Elyria, OH 44035

Erie County Clerk
323 Columbus Ave.
Sandusky, Ohio 44870

Fairfield County Clerk
224 E. Main St., Rm. 303
Lancaster, Ohio
43130-3842

Fayette County Clerk
110 East Court
Washington Court House,
Ohio 43160-1355

Franklin County Clerk
181 Washington Blvd.
Columbus, Ohio
43215-4095

Fulton County Clerk
210 S. Fulton
Wauseon, Ohio
43567-1355

Gallia County Clerk
18 Locust St.
Gallipolis, Ohio 45631

Geauga County Clerk
231 Main St.
Chardon, Ohio 44024

Greene County Clerk
45 N. Detroit St.
Xenia, Ohio 45385

Guernsey County Clerk
Wheeling Ave.
Cambridge, Ohio 43725

Hamilton County Clerk
230 East 9th St.
William Howard
Taft Center
Cincinnati, Ohio 45202

Hancock County Clerk
300 S. Main St.
Findlay, Ohio 45840-9039

Hardin County Clerk
Public Square
Kenton, Ohio 43326

Harrison County Clerk
100 W. Market St.
Cadiz, Ohio 43907

Henry County Clerk
660 N. Perry
Napoleon, Ohio
43545-1702

Highland County Clerk
P.O. Box 825
Hillsboro, Ohio
45133-0825

Hocking County Clerk
1 East Main St.
Logan, Ohio 43138-1207

Holmes County Clerk
East Jackson St.
Millersburg, Ohio 44654

Huron County Clerk
2 East Main St.
Norwalk, Ohio 44857

Jackson County Clerk
226 Main St.
Jackson, Ohio 45640

Jefferson County Clerk
301 Market St.
Steubenville, Ohio
43952-2133

Knox County Clerk
106 East High St.
Mount Vernon, Ohio
43050-3453

Lake County Clerk
33 Mill St.
Painesville, Ohio 44077

Lawrence County Clerk
5th and Park Ave.
Ironton, Ohio 45638

Licking County Clerk
20 South 2nd St.
Newark, Ohio 43055-9553

Logan County Clerk
Main and East Columbus
St., 2nd Fl.
Bellefontaine, Ohio
43311-0429

Lorain County Clerk
226 Middle Ave., Admin
Bldg. 4th Fl.
Elyria, Ohio 44035

Lucas County Clerk
635 N. Erie St.
Toledo, Ohio 43624

Madison County Clerk
1 North Main St., Rm. 205
London, Ohio 43140

Mahoning County Clerk
120 Market St.
Youngstown, Ohio
44503-1710

Marion County Clerk
114 N. Main St.
Marion, Ohio 43302-3030

Medina County Clerk
93 Public Square
Medina, Ohio 44256-2205

Meigs County Clerk
144 Butternut Ave.
Pomeroy, Ohio 45769

Mercer County Clerk
101 N. Main St.
Celina, Ohio 45822

Miami County Clerk
201 West Main St.
Troy, Ohio 45373-3239

Monroe County Clerk
101 N. Main St., Rm. 12
Woodsfield, Ohio 43793

**Montgomery
County Clerk**
451 West 3rd St.
Dayton, Ohio 45422

Morgan County Clerk
19 East Main St.
McConnelsville, Ohio
43756-1172

Morrow County Clerk
48 East High St.
Mount Gilead, Ohio 43338

**Muskingum
County Clerk**
401 Main St.
Zanesville, Ohio
43701-3567

Noble County Clerk
County Courthouse
Caldwell, Ohio 43724

Ottawa County Clerk
315 Madison St.
Port Clinton, Ohio
43452-1936

Paulding County Clerk
County Courthouse
Paulding, Ohio 45879

Perry County Clerk
P.O. Box 167
New Lexington, Ohio
43764

Pickaway County Clerk
207 S. Court St.
Circleville, Ohio 43113

Pike County Clerk
100 East Second
Waverly, Ohio 45690-1301

Portage County Clerk
203 West Main St.
Ravenna, Ohio 44266-2761

Preble County Clerk
100 Main St.
Eaton, Ohio 45320

Putnam County Clerk
245 East Main St.
Ottawa, Ohio 45875-1968

Richland County Clerk
50 Park Ave., East
Mansfield, Ohio
44902-1850

Ross County Clerk
425 Chestnut St., #2077
Chillicothe, Ohio
45601-2306

Sandusky County Clerk
100 North Park Ave.
Fremont, Ohio 43420-2454

Scioto County Clerk
602 7th St.
Portsmouth, Ohio
45662-3948

Seneca County Clerk
3140 S. State Route 100
Tiffin, Ohio 44883

Shelby County Clerk
129 East Court St.
Sidney, Ohio 45365

Stark County Clerk
115 Central Plaza North
Canton, Ohio 44702-1290

Summit County Clerk
209 South High St.
Akron, Ohio 44308

Trumbull County Clerk
418 South Main St.
Warren, Ohio 44481-1005

Tuscarawas County Clerk
Public Square
New Philadelphia, Ohio
44663

Union County Clerk
5th and Court St.
Marysville, Ohio 43040

Van Wert County Clerk
121 East Main St.,
2nd Fl.
Van Wert, Ohio 45891

Vinton County Clerk
Courthouse
McArthur, Ohio 45651

Warren County Clerk
320 East Silver St.
Lebanon, Ohio 45036-1816

**Washington
County Clerk**
205 Putnam St.
Marietta, Ohio 45750

Wayne County Clerk
P.O. Box 407
Wooster, Ohio 44691

Williams County Clerk
107 Butler St.
Bryan, Ohio 43506

Wood County Clerk
1 Courthouse Square
Bowling Green, Ohio
43402-2427

Wyandot County Clerk
County Courthouse
Upper Sandusky, Ohio
43351

OKLAHOMA

http://www.state.ok.us/

Adair County Clerk
P.O. Box 169
Stilwell, Oklahoma 74960

Alfalfa County Clerk
300 South Grand
Cherokee, Oklahoma
73728

Atoka County Clerk
201 East Court
Atoka, Oklahoma
74525-2045

Beaver County Clerk
111 West 2nd St.
Beaver, Oklahoma 73932

Beckham County Clerk
P.O. Box 67
Sayre, Oklahoma 73662

Blaine County Clerk
P.O. Box 138
Watonga, Oklahoma 73772

Bryan County Clerk
P.O. Box 1789
Durant, Oklahoma 74702

Caddo County Clerk
P.O. Box 10
Anadarko, Oklahoma
73005

Canadian County Clerk
Courthouse
El Reno, Oklahoma 73036

Carter County Clerk
First and B Street, SW
Ardmore, Oklahoma 73401

Cherokee County Clerk
213 West Delaware
Tahlequah, Oklahoma
74464-3639

Choctaw County Clerk
Choctaw County
Courthouse
Hugo, Oklahoma 74743

Cimarron County Clerk
P.O. Box 788
Boise City, Oklahoma
73933

Cleveland County Clerk
201 South Jones
Norman, Oklahoma 73069

Coal County Clerk
3 North Main St.
Coalgate, Oklahoma
74538-2832

Comanche County Clerk
Courthouse
Lawton, Oklahoma
73501-4326

Cotton County Clerk
301 North Broadway St.
Walters, Oklahoma
73572-1271

Craig County Clerk
301 W. Canadian
Vinita, Oklahoma 74301

Creek County Clerk
222 E. Dewey, Suite 200
Sapulpa, Oklahoma 74066

Custer County Clerk
P.O. Box 300
Arapaho, Oklahoma 73620

Delaware County Clerk
P.O. Box 309
Jay, Oklahoma 74346-0309

Dewey County Clerk
P.O. Box 368
Taloga, Oklahoma
73667-0368

Ellis County Clerk
100 South Washington
Arnett, Oklahoma
73832-0257

Garfield County Clerk
Rm. 101
Enid, Oklahoma 73701

Garvin County Clerk
Courthouse
Pauls Valley, Oklahoma
73075

Grady County Clerk
P.O. Box 1009
Chickasha, Oklahoma
73023-1009

Grant County Clerk
Courthouse
Medford, Oklahoma
73759-1243

Greer County Clerk
Courthouse
Mangum, Oklahoma 73554

Harmon County Clerk
Courthouse
Hollis, Oklahoma 73550

Harper County Clerk
P.O. Box 369
Buffalo, Oklahoma
73834-0369

Haskell County Clerk
202 East Main
Stigler, Oklahoma
74462-2439

Hughes County Clerk
P.O. Box 914
Holdenville, Oklahoma
74848-0914

Jackson County Clerk
Courthouse
Altus, Oklahoma 73521

Jefferson County Clerk
220 North Main St.
Waurika, Oklahoma
73573-2234

Johnston County Clerk
Courthouse
Tishomingo, Oklahoma
73460

Kay County Clerk
Courthouse
Newkirk, Oklahoma 74647

Kingfisher County Clerk
P.O. Box 118
Kingfisher, Oklahoma
73750

Kiowa County Clerk
Courthouse
Hobart, Oklahoma 73651

Latimer County Clerk
109 North Central
Wilburton, Oklahoma
74578-2440

LeFlore County Clerk
P.O. Box 218
Poteau, Oklahoma
74953-0607

Lincoln County Clerk
P.O. Box 126
Chandler, Oklahoma
74834-0126

Logan County Clerk
Courthouse
Guthrie, Oklahoma
73044-4939

Love County Clerk
405 West Main St.
Marietta, Oklahoma
73448-2848

Major County Clerk
East Broadway
Fairview, Oklahoma 73737

Marshall County Clerk
P.O. Box 58
Madill, Oklahoma 73446

Mayes County Clerk
Courthouse
Pryor, Oklahoma 74361

McClain County Clerk
P.O. Box 629
Purcell, Oklahoma 73080

McCurtain County Clerk
P.O.a Box 1078
Idabel, Oklahoma 74745

McIntosh County Clerk
P.O. Box 108
Eufaula, Oklahoma
74432-0108

Murray County Clerk
P.O. Box 240
Sulphur, Oklahoma
73086-0240

Muskogee County Clerk
P.O. Box 2307
Muskogee, Oklahoma
74402-2307

Nobel County Clerk
300 Courthouse Dr. #11
Perry, Oklahoma 73077

Nowata County Clerk
229 North Maple St.
Nowata, Oklahoma
74048-2654

Okfuskee County Clerk
P.O. Box 26
Okemah, Oklahoma
74859-0026

Oklahoma County Clerk
320 NW Robert S. Kerr
Oklahoma City, Oklahoma
73102-3441

Okmulgee County Clerk
P.O. Box 904
Okmulgee, Oklahoma
74447

Osage County Clerk
P.O. Box 87
Pawhuska, Oklahoma
74056-0087

Ottawa County Clerk
Courthouse
Miami, Oklahoma 74354

Pawnee County Clerk
Courthouse
Pawnee, Oklahoma
74058-2568

Payne County Clerk
Sixth and Husband
Stillwater, Oklahoma
74074

Pittsburg County Clerk
Courthouse
McAlester, Oklahoma
74501

Pontotoc County Clerk
P.O. Box 1425
Ada, Oklahoma 74820

Pottawatomie
County Clerk
325 N. Broadway
Shawnee, Oklahoma
74801-6919

Pushmataha
County Clerk
203 SW Third
Antlers, Oklahoma
74523-3899

Roger Mills County Clerk
P.O. Box 708
Cheyenne, Oklahoma
73628

Rogers County Clerk
219 South Missouri
Claremore, Oklahoma
74017-7832

Seminole County Clerk
Courthouse
Wewoka, Oklahoma 74884

Sequoyah County Clerk
120 East Chickasaw St.
Sallisaw, Oklahoma
74955-4655

Stephens County Clerk
Courthouse
Duncan, Oklahoma 73533

Texas County Clerk
P.O. Box 197
Guymon, Oklahoma
73942-0197

Tillman County Clerk
P.O. Box 992
Frederick, Oklahoma
73542

Tulsa County Clerk
500 South Denver
Tulsa, Oklahoma 74103-3826

Wagoner County Clerk
307 East Cherokee
Wagoner, Oklahoma
74467-4729

Washington County Clerk
420 South Johnstone
Bartlesville, Oklahoma
74003-6605

Washita County Clerk
P.O. Box 380
Cordell, Oklahoma 73632

Woods County Clerk
P.O. Box 386
Alva, Oklahoma 73717

Woodward County Clerk
1600 Main St.
Woodward, Oklahoma
73801-3046

OREGON

http://www.state.or.us/

Baker County Clerk
1995 Third St.
Baker, Oregon 97814-3363

Benton County Clerk
120 NW Fourth St.
Corvallis, Oregon
97330-4728

Clackamas County Clerk
906 Main St.
Oregon City, Oregon 97045

Clatsop County Clerk
749 Commercial
Astoria, Oregon 97103

Columbia County Clerk
Strand St.
St. Helens, Oregon 97051

Coos County Clerk
250 N. Baxter St.
Coquille, Oregon
97423-1899

Crook County Clerk
300 East Third St.
Prineville, Oregon
97754-1949

Curry County Clerk
P.O. Box 746
Gold Beach, Oregon
97444-0746

Deschutes County Clerk
1164 NW Bond
Bend, Oregon 97701-1905

Douglas County Clerk
1036 SE Douglas
Roseburg, Oregon
97470-3317

Gilliam County Clerk
221 S. Oregon St.
Condon, Oregon 97823

Grant County Clerk
200 South Canyon Blvd.
Canyon City, Oregon
97820

Harney County Clerk
450 North Buena Vista
Burns, Oregon 97720

Hood River County Clerk
309 State St.
Hood River, Oregon 97031

Jackson County Clerk
10 South Oakdale
Medford, Oregon
97501-2952

Jefferson County Clerk
66 South East D St.
Madras, Oregon
97741-1707

Josephine County Clerk
North West Sixth and C
Grants Pass, Oregon 97526

Klamath County Clerk
316 Main St.
Klamath Falls, Oregon
97601-6347

Lake County Clerk
513 Center St.
Lakeview, Oregon
97630-1539

Lane County Clerk
125 East Eighth Ave.
Eugene, Oregon
97401-2922

Lincoln County Clerk
225 West Olive St.
Newport, Oregon
97365-3811

Linn County Clerk
P.O. Box 100
Albany, Oregon
97321-0031

Malheur County Clerk
251 B Street West
Vale, Oregon 97918-0130

Marion County Clerk
Courthouse
Salem, Oregon 97301

Morrow County Clerk
P.O. Box 338
Heppner, Oregon
97836-0338

Multnomah County Clerk
426 SW Stark, 2nd Fl.
Portland, Oregon 97204

Polk County Clerk
850 Main Street
Dallas, Oregon 97338-3116

Sherman County Clerk
P.O. Box 365
Moro, Oregon 97039-0365

Tillamook County Clerk
201 Laurel Ave.
Tillamook, Oregon
97141-2394

Umatilla County Clerk
216 SE Fourth Ave.
Pendleton, Oregon
97801-2500

Union County Clerk
1100 L Ave.
La Grande, Oregon
97850-2121

Wallowa County Clerk
101 South River St.
Enterprise, Oregon
97828-0170

Wasco County Clerk
5th and Washington
The Dalles, Oregon 97058

**Washington
County Clerk**
155 North First Ave.
Hillsboro, Oregon
97124-3002

Wheeler County Clerk
P.O. Box 327
Fossil, Oregon 97830-0327

Yamhill County Clerk
5th and Evans
McMinnville, Oregon
97128

PENNSYLVANIA

http://www.state.pa.us/

Adams County Clerk
111 Baltimore St.
Gettysburg, Pennsylvania
17325-2312

Allegheny County Clerk
414 Grant St.
Pittsburgh, Pennsylvania
15219

Armstrong County Clerk
Market St.
Kittanning, Pennsylvania
16201

Beaver County Clerk
Courthouse
Beaver, Pennsylvania
15009

Bedford County Clerk
203 S. Juliana St.
Bedford, Pennsylvania
15522-1714

Berks County Clerk
633 Court St.
Reading, Pennsylvania
19601

Blair County Clerk
423 Allegheny St.
Hollidaysburg,
Pennsylvania 16648-2022

Bradford County Clerk
301 Main St.
Towanda, Pennsylvania
18848-1824

Bucks County Clerk
Main and Court St.
Doylestown, Pennsylvania
18901

Butler County Clerk
South Main St.
Butler, Pennsylvania 16001

Cambria County Clerk
200 South Center St.
P.O. Box 298
Ebensburg, Pennsylvania
15931

Cameron County Clerk
20 East 5th St.
Emporium, Pennsylvania
15834

Carbon County Clerk
P.O. Box 129 Courthouse
Jim Thorpe, Pennsylvania
18229

Centre County Clerk
Willowbank Bldg.
Bellefonte, Pennsylvania
16823

Chester County Clerk
601 Westtown Rd.,
Suite 080
West Chester, Pennsylvania
19380-0990

Clarion County Clerk
Main Street
Clarion, Pennsylvania
16214

Clearfield County Clerk
2 Market St.
Clearfield, Pennsylvania
16830-2404

Clinton County Clerk
County Courthouse
Lock Haven, Pennsylvania
17745

Columbia County Clerk
35 West Main St.
Bloomsburg, Pennsylvania
17815-1702

Crawford County Clerk
903 Diamond Park
Meadville, Pennsylvania
16335-2677

**Cumberland
County Clerk**
Hanover St.
Carlisle, Pennsylvania
17013

Dauphin County Clerk
Front and Market Street
Harrisburg, Pennsylvania
17101-2012

Delaware County Clerk
West Front St.
Media, Pennsylvania 19063

Elk County Clerk
P.O. Box 314
Ridgeway, Pennsylvania
15853

Erie County Clerk
140 West Sixth St.
Erie, Pennsylvania
16501-1011

Fayette County Clerk
61 East Main St.
Uniontown, Pennsylvania
15401-3514

Forest County Clerk
P.O. Box 423
Tionesta, Pennsylvania
16353

Franklin County Clerk
157 Lincoln Way, East
Chambersburg,
Pennsylvania 17201-2211

Fulton County Clerk
North Second St.
McConnellsburg,
Pennsylvania 17233

Greene County Clerk
93 East High St.
Waynesburg, Pennsylvania
15370

**Huntingdon
County Clerk**
223 Penn St.
Huntingdon, Pennsylvania
16652

Indiana County Clerk
825 Philadelphia
Indiana, Pennsylvania
15701-3934

Jefferson County Clerk
155 Jefferson Place
Brookville, Pennsylvania
15825-1236

Juniata County Clerk
P.O. Box 68
Miffintown, Pennsylvania
17059-0068

**Lackawanna
County Clerk**
Vital Statistics Office
100 Lackawanna Ave.
Scranton, Pennsylvania
18503

Lancaster County Clerk
50 North Duke St.
Lancaster, Pennsylvania
17603

Lawrence County Clerk
101 S. Mercer St.
New Castle, Pennsylvania
16101

Lebanon County Clerk
400 South Eighth St.
Lebanon, Pennsylvania
17042-6794

Lehigh County Clerk
455 Hamilton St.
Allentown, Pennsylvania
18105

Luzerne County Clerk
200 North River St.
Wilkes-Barre, Pennsylvania
18702-2685

Lycoming County Clerk
48 West Third St.
Williamsport, Pennsylvania
17701-6519

McKean County Clerk
P.O. Box 202
Smethport, Pennsylvania
16749

Mercer County Clerk
South Diamond St.
Mercer, Pennsylvania
16137

Mifflin County Clerk
20 North Wayne St.
Lewistown, Pennsylvania
17044-1770

Monroe County Clerk
Courthouse Square
Stroudsburg, Pennsylvania
18360

Montgomery County Clerk
P.O. Box 311
Norristown, Pennsylvania
19404

Montour County Clerk
29 Mill St.
Danville, Pennsylvania
17821-1945

Northampton County Clerk
7th and Washington St.
Easton, Pennsylvania
18042-7401

Northumberland County Clerk
2nd and Market St.
Sunbury, Pennsylvania
17801

Perry County Clerk
P.O. Box 37
New Bloomfield,
Pennsylvania 17068

Philadelphia County Clerk
3101 Market St. First Fl.
Philadelphia, Pennsylvania
19104

Pike County Clerk
506 Broad St.
Milford, Pennsylvania
18337-1511

Potter County Clerk
1 East Second St.
Coudersport, Pennsylvania
16915

Schuylkill County Clerk
N. 2nd St. and Laurel Blvd.
Pottsville, Pennsylvania
17901

Snyder County Clerk
11 West Market St.
Middleburg, Pennsylvania
17842

Somerset County Clerk
111 E. Union St.
Somerset, Pennsylvania
15501

Sullivan County Clerk
Main and Muncy
Laporte, Pennsylvania
18626

Susquehanna County Clerk
Courthouse
Montrose, Pennsylvania
18801

Tioga County Clerk
116-188 Main St.
Wellsboro, Pennsylvania
16901-1410

Union County Clerk
103 South 2nd St.
Lewisburg, Pennsylvania
17837-1903

Venango County Clerk
Liberty and 12th Street
Franklin, Pennsylvania
16323

Warren County Clerk
204 Fourth St.
Warren, Pennsylvania
16365-2318

Washington County Clerk
100 West Beau St.
Washington, Pennsylvania
15301-4402

Wayne County Clerk
925 Court St.
Honesdale, Pennsylvania
18431-9517

Westmoreland County Clerk
Westmoreland
County Court House
Main St.
Greensburg, Pennsylvania
15601-2405

Wyoming County Clerk
Courthouse Square
Tunkhannock,
Pennsylvania 18657-1216

York County Clerk
28 East Market St.
York, Pennsylvania
17401-1501

RHODE ISLAND

http://www.state.ri.us/

Bristol County Clerk
1 Dorrance Plaza
Bristol, Rhode Island
02809

Kent County Clerk
222 Quaker Lane
East Greenwich, Rhode
Island 02818

Newport County Clerk
Washington Square
Newport, Rhode Island
02840

Providence County Clerk
250 Benefit
Providence, Rhode Island
02903-2719

**Washington
County Clerk**
4800 Tower Hill Rd.
Wakefield, Rhode Island
02879

SOUTH CAROLINA

http://www.state.sc.us/

Abbeville County Clerk
P.O. Box 99
Abbeville, South Carolina
29620-0099

Aiken County Clerk
P.O. Box 583
Aiken, South Carolina
29802-0583

Allendale County Clerk
P.O. Box 126
Allendale, South Carolina
29810-0126

Anderson County Clerk
220 McGee Rd.
Anderson, South Carolina
29625

Bamberg County Clerk
P.O. Box 150
Bamberg, South Carolina
29003-0150

Barnwell County Clerk
P.O. Box 723
Barnwell, South Carolina
29812-0723

Beaufort County Clerk
Courthouse
Beaufort, South Carolina
29901

Berkeley County Clerk
223 North Live Oak Dr.
Moncks Corner,
South Carolina 29461-2331

Calhoun County Clerk
302 S. Railroad Ave.
St. Matthews,
South Carolina 29135-1452

Charleston County Clerk
4050 Bridgeview Dr.
North Charleston,
South Carolina 29405

Cherokee County Clerk
P.O. Box 866
Gaffney, South Carolina
26342

Chester County Clerk
P.O. Box 580
Chester, South Carolina
29706-0580

**Chesterfield
County Clerk**
P.O. Box 529
Chesterfield,
South Carolina 29709-0529

Clarendon County Clerk
P.O. Box E
Manning, South Carolina
29102-0136

Colleton County Clerk
P.O. Box 620
Walterboro, South Carolina
29488-0620

Darlington County Clerk
Courthouse
Darlington, South Carolina
29532-3213

Dillon County Clerk
P.O. Box 1220
Dillon, South Carolina
29536-1220

Dorchester County Clerk
101 Ridge St.
St. George, South Carolina
29477-2443

Edgefield County Clerk
215 Jeter St.
Edgefield, South Carolina
29824-1133

Fairfield County Clerk
P.O. Box 236
Winnsboro, South Carolina
29180-0236

Florence County Clerk
180 North Irby St.
Florence, South Carolina
29501-3456

**Georgetown
County Clerk**
715 Prince St.
Georgetown,
South Carolina 29440-3631

Greenville County Clerk
P.O. Box 2507
Greenville, South Carolina
29602

Greenwood County Clerk
528 Monument
Greenwood, South Carolina
29646-2643

Hampton County Clerk
P.O. Box 7
Hampton, South Carolina
29924-0007

Horry County Clerk
P.O. Box 288
Conway, South Carolina
29528-0288

Jasper County Clerk
P.O. Box 248
Ridgeland, South Carolina
29936-0248

Kershaw County Clerk
Courthouse
Camden, South Carolina
29020

Lancaster County Clerk
P.O. Box 1809
Lancaster, South Carolina
29720

Laurens County Clerk
P.O. Box 287
Laurens, South Carolina
29360-0287

Lee County Clerk
Courthouse Square
Bishopville, South Carolina
29010

Lexington County Clerk
Courthouse
Lexington, South Carolina
29072

Marion County Clerk
P.O. Box 295
Marion, South Carolina
29571-0295

Marlboro County Clerk
P.O. Box 996
Bennettsville,
South Carolina 29512-0996

**McCormick
County Clerk**
P.O. Box 86
McCormick,
South Carolina 28735

Newberry County Clerk
P.O. Box 278
Newberry, South Carolina
29108-0278

Oconee County Clerk
P.O. Box 158
Walhalla, South Carolina
29691-0158

**Orangeburg
County Clerk**
P.O. Box 100
Orangeburg,
South Carolina 29116-0100

Pickens County Clerk
P.O. Box 215
Pickens, South Carolina
29671-0215

Richland County Clerk
1701 Main St.
Columbia, South Carolina
29201-2833

Saluda County Clerk
Courthouse Square
Saluda, South Carolina
29138-1444

**Spartanburg
County Clerk**
180 Magnolia St.
Spartanburg,
South Carolina 29306

Sumter County Clerk
141 North Main St.
Sumter, South Carolina
29150-4965

Union County Clerk
P.O. Box G
Union, South Carolina
29379-0200

**Williamsburg
County Clerk**
203 North Brooks
Kingstree, South Carolina
29556

York County Clerk
P.O. Box 649
York, South Carolina
29745-0649

SOUTH DAKOTA
http://www.state.sd.us/

Aurora County Clerk
Courthouse
Plankinton, South Dakota
57368

Beadle County Clerk
Courthouse
Huron, South Dakota
57350

Bennett County Clerk
Main St.
Martin, South Dakota
57551

**Bon Homme
County Clerk**
Courthouse
Tyndall, South Dakota
57066

Brookings County Clerk
314 Sixth Ave.
Brookings, South Dakota
57006-2041

Brown County Clerk
111 South East First Ave.
Aberdeen, South Dakota
57401-4203

Brule County Clerk
300 South Courtland
Chamberlain, South Dakota
57325-1508

Buffalo County Clerk
Courthouse
Gann Valley, South Dakota
57341-0148

Butte County Clerk
Courthouse
Belle Fourche,
South Dakota 57717

Campbell County Clerk
P.O. Box 146
Mound City, South Dakota
57646

**Charles Mix
County Clerk**
Courthouse
Lake Andes, South Dakota
57356

Clark County Clerk
Courthouse
Clark, South Dakota 57225

Clay County Clerk
P.O. Box 403
Vermillion, South Dakota
57069-0403

Codington County Clerk
Courthouse
Watertown, South Dakota
57201

Corson County Clerk
200 First St. East
McIntosh, South Dakota
57641

Custer County Clerk
420 SW Mount Rushmore
Custer, South Dakota
57730-1934

Davison County Clerk
200 East 4th Ave.
Mitchell, South Dakota
57301-2631

Day County Clerk
710 West First St.
Webster, South Dakota
57274

Deuel County Clerk
P.O. Box 125
Clear Lake, South Dakota
57226

Dewey County Clerk
Courthouse
Timber Lake, South Dakota
57656

Douglas County Clerk
Courthouse
Armour, South Dakota
57313

Edmunds County Clerk
Courthouse
Ipswich, South Dakota
57451

Fall River County Clerk
906 North River St.
Hot Springs, South Dakota
57747-1387

Faulk County Clerk
Courthouse
Faulkton, South Dakota
57438

Grant County Clerk
210 East Fifth Ave.
Milbank, South Dakota
57252-2433

Gregory County Clerk
Courthouse
Burke, South Dakota 57523

Haakon County Clerk
Courthouse
Philip, South Dakota 57567

Hamlin County Clerk
Courthouse
Hayti, South Dakota 57241

Hand County Clerk
415 West First Ave.
Miller, South Dakota
57362-1346

Hanson County Clerk
Courthouse
Alexandria, South Dakota
57311

Harding County Clerk
Courthouse
Buffalo, South Dakota
57720

Hughes County Clerk
104 E. Capital
Pierre, South Dakota
57501-2563

Hutchinson County Clerk
Courthouse
Olivet, South Dakota
57052

Hyde County Clerk
P.O. Box 306
Highmore, South Dakota
57345-0306

Jackson County Clerk
Courthouse
Kadoka, South Dakota
57543

Jerauld County Clerk
Courthouse
Wessington Springs,
South Dakota 57382

Jones County Clerk
Courthouse
Murdo, South Dakota
57559

Kingsbury County Clerk
Courthouse
De Smet, South Dakota
57231

Lake County Clerk
P.O. Box 447
Madison, South Dakota
57042-0447

Lawrence County Clerk
644 Main St.
Deadwood, South Dakota
57732-1124

Lincoln County Clerk
100 East Fifth St.
Canton, South Dakota
57013-1732

Lyman County Clerk
Courthouse
Kennebec, South Dakota
57544

Marshall County Clerk
Courthouse
Britton, South Dakota
57430

McCook County Clerk
Courthouse
Salem, South Dakota
57058

McPherson County Clerk
P.O. Box L
Leola, South Dakota 57456

Meade County Clerk
1425 Sherman St.
Sturgis, South Dakota
57785-1452

Mellette County Clerk
P.O. Box C
White River, South Dakota
57579

Miner County Clerk
Courthouse
Howard, South Dakota
57349

Minnehaha County Clerk
415 N. Dakota Ave.
Sioux Falls, South Dakota
57102-0192

Moody County Clerk
P.O. Box 152
Flandreau, South Dakota
57028

Pennington County Clerk
P.O. Box 230
Rapid City, South Dakota
57709-0230

Perkins County Clerk
Courthouse
Bison, South Dakota 57620

Potter County Clerk
201 South Exene
Gettysburg, South Dakota
57442-1521

Roberts County Clerk
411 Second Ave. East
Sisseton, South Dakota
57262-1403

Sanborn County Clerk
Courthouse
Woonsocket, South Dakota
57385

Shannon County Clerk
906 North St.
Hot Springs, South Dakota
57747-1387

Spink County Clerk
210 East Seventh Ave.
Redfield, South Dakota
57469-1266

Stanley County Clerk
Courthouse
Fort Pierre, South Dakota
57532

Sully County Clerk
Courthouse
Onida, South Dakota 57564

Todd County Clerk
200 East Third St.
(c/o Tripp County)
Winner, South Dakota
57580-1806

Tripp County Clerk
200 East Third St.
Winner, South Dakota
57580-1806

Turner County Clerk
Main St.
Parker, South Dakota
57053

Union County Clerk
P.O. Box 757
Elk Point, South Dakota
57025-0757

Walworth County Clerk
P.O. Box 199
Selby, South Dakota
57472-0199

Yankton County Clerk
P.O. Box 155
Yankton, South Dakota
57078-0137

Ziebach County Clerk
Main St.
Dupree, South Dakota
57623

TENNESSEE

http://www.state.tn.us/

Anderson County Clerk
100 N. Main St.
Clinton, Tennessee 37716

Bedford County Clerk
104 Northside Square
Shelbyville, Tennessee
37160

Benton County Clerk
3 East Court Square, #101
Camden, Tennessee 38320

Bledsoe County Clerk
P.O. Box 149
Pikeville, Tennessee 37367

Blount County Clerk
345 Court St.
Maryville, Tennessee
37804

Bradley County Clerk
P.O. Box 46
Cleveland, Tennessee
37364-0046

Campbell County Clerk
195 Kentucky St.
Jacksboro, Tennessee
37757

Cannon County Clerk
Public Square
Woodbury, Tennessee
37190

Carroll County Clerk
P.O. Box 110
Huntingdon, Tennessee
38344-0110

Carter County Clerk
801 East Elk Ave.
Elizabethton, Tennessee
37643

Cheatham County Clerk
100 Public Square
Ashland City, Tennessee
37015-1711

Chester County Clerk
133 East Main St.
Henderson, Tennessee
38340

Claiborne County Clerk
1740 Main St., Suite 201
Tazewell, Tennessee 37879

Clay County Clerk
100 Courthouse Square
Celina, Tennessee 38551

Cocke County Clerk
111 Court Ave.
Newport, Tennessee 37821

Coffee County Clerk
300 Hillsboro Blvd
Manchester, Tennessee
37355

Crockett County Clerk
Courthouse
Alamo, Tennessee 38001

**Cumberland
County Clerk**
Main St.
Crossville, Tennessee
38555-9428

Davidson County Clerk
311 23rd Ave. North
Nashville, Tennessee 37203

Decatur County Clerk
P.O. Box 488
Decaturville, Tennessee
38329-0488

DeKalb County Clerk
County Courthouse,
Rm. 205
Smithville, Tennessee
37166

Dickson County Clerk
4 Court Square
Charlotte, Tennessee 37036

Dyer County Clerk
P.O. Box 1360
Dyersburg, Tennessee
38025-1360

Fayette County Clerk
P.O. Box 218
Somerville, Tennessee
38068-0218

Fentress County Clerk
Main St.
Jamestown, Tennessee
38556

Franklin County Clerk
1 South Jefferson St.
Winchester, Tennessee
37398

Gibson County Clerk
P.O. Box 228
Trenton, Tennessee 38382

Giles County Clerk
P.O. Box 678
Madison and First St.
Pulaski, Tennessee
38478-0678

Grainger County Clerk
Highway 11 West
Rutledge, Tennessee 37861

Greene County Clerk
Courthouse
Greeneville, Tennessee
37743

Grundy County Clerk
Hwy 56
Altamont, Tennessee 37301

Hamblen County Clerk
511 West Second N St.
Morristown, Tennessee
37814-3964

Hamilton County Clerk
625 Georgia Ave. #201
Chattanooga, Tennessee
37402

Hancock County Clerk
Main St.
Sneedville, Tennessee
37869

Hardeman County Clerk
100 N. Main
Bolivar, Tennessee
38008-2322

Hardin County Clerk
601 Main St.
Savannah, Tennessee 38372

Hawkins County Clerk
150 Washington St.
Rogersville, Tennessee
37857

Haywood County Clerk
100 N. Washington
Brownsville, Tennessee
38012-2557

Henderson County Clerk
17 Monroe St.
Lexington, Tennessee
38351

Henry County Clerk
100 W. Washington St.
Paris, Tennessee 38242

Hickman County Clerk
101 College St.
Centerville, Tennessee
37033

Houston County Clerk
100 Main St.
Erin, Tennessee 37061

Humphreys County Clerk
102 Thompson St. #2
Waverly, Tennessee 37185

Jackson County Clerk
101 E. Hull Ave.
Gainesboro, Tennessee
38562

Jefferson County Clerk
204 W. Main St.
Dandridge, Tennessee
37725

Johnson County Clerk
222 Main St.
Mountain City, Tennessee
37683-1612

Knox County Clerk
140 Dameron Ave.
Knoxville, Tennessee
37917-6413

Lake County Clerk
Church St.
Tiptonville, Tennessee
38079

Lauderdale County Clerk
Courthouse
Ripley, Tennessee 38063

Lawrence County Clerk
Courthouse
Lawrenceburg, Tennessee
38464

Lewis County Clerk
110 N. Park St.
Hohenwald, Tennessee
38462

Lincoln County Clerk
112 Main St. South
Fayetteville, Tennessee
37334

Loudon County Clerk
101 Mulberry St.
Loudon, Tennessee 37774

Macon County Clerk
104 Courthouse
Lafayette, Tennessee 37083

Madison County Clerk
Courthouse
Jackson, Tennessee 38301

Marion County Clerk
1 Courthouse Square
Jasper, Tennessee 37347

Marshall County Clerk
207 Marshall County
Courthouse
Lewisburg, Tennessee
37091

Maury County Clerk
Public Square
Columbia, Tennessee
38401

McMinn County Clerk
6 West Madison Ave.
Athens, Tennessee 37303

McNairy County Clerk
Courthouse
Selmer, Tennessee 38375

Meigs County Clerk
P.O. Box 218
Decatur, Tennessee
37322-0218

Monroe County Clerk
103 College St.
Madisonville, Tennessee
37354

**Montgomery County
Clerk**
Courthouse
Clarksville, Tennessee
37042

Moore County Clerk
P.O. Box 206
Lynchburg, Tennessee
37352

Morgan County Clerk
415 N. Kingston St.
Wartburg, Tennessee 37887

Obion County Clerk
Courthouse
Union City, Tennessee
37261

Overton County Clerk
317 East University St.
Livingston, Tennessee
38570

Perry County Clerk
P.O. Box 16
Linden, Tennessee
37096-0016

Pickett County Clerk
1 Courthouse Square
Byrdstown, Tennessee
38549

Polk County Clerk
Hwy 411
Benton, Tennessee 37307

Putnam County Clerk
29 Washington
Cookeville, Tennessee
38501

Rhea County Clerk
1475 Market St.
Dayton, Tennessee 37321

Roane County Clerk
200 W. Race St.
Kingston, Tennessee 37763

Robertson County Clerk
101 5th Ave. W
Springfield, Tennessee
37172

Rutherford County Clerk
26 N. Public Square
Murfreesboro, Tennessee
37130

Scott County Clerk
P.O. Box 69
Huntsville, Tennessee
37756

Sequatchie County Clerk
308 Cherry St.
Dunlap, Tennessee 37327

Sevier County Clerk
125 Court Ave. #202
Sevierville, Tennessee
37862

Shelby County Clerk
814 Jefferson Ave.
Memphis, Tennessee 38105

Smith County Clerk
211 Main St. North
Carthage, Tennessee 37030

Steward County Clerk
P.O. Box 67
Dover, Tennessee
37058-0067

Sullivan County Clerk
3411 Highway 126
Blountville, Tennessee
37617

Sumner County Clerk
155 East Main St.
Gallatin, Tennessee 37066

Tipton County Clerk
P.O. Box 528
Covington, Tennessee
38019-0528

Trousdale County Clerk
200 East Main St. #2
Hartsville, Tennessee
37074

Unicoi County Clerk
100 N. Main Ave.
Erwin, Tennessee
37650-0340

Union County Clerk
901 Main St.
Maynardville, Tennessee
37807-0395

Van Buren County Clerk
Courthouse Square
Spencer, Tennessee
38585-0126

Warren County Clerk
Courthouse
McMinnville, Tennessee
37110

**Washington
County Clerk**
Courthouse
Jonesboro, Tennessee
37659

Wayne County Clerk
P.O. Box 185
Waynesboro, Tennessee
38485

Weakley County Clerk
P.O. Box 587
Dresden, Tennessee 38225

White County Clerk
1 E. Bockman Way
Sparta, Tennessee 38583

Williamson County Clerk
1320 W. Main St.
Franklin, Tennessee 37064

Wilson County Clerk
228 E. Main St.
Lebanon, Tennessee 37087

TEXAS

http://www.state.tx.us/

Anderson County Clerk
500 N. Church St.
Palestine, Texas 75801

Andrews County Clerk
P.O. Box 727
Andrews, Texas 79714

Angelina County Clerk
P.O. Box 908
Lufkin, Texas 75902-0908

Aransas County Clerk
301 Live Oak
Rockport, Texas
78382-2744

Archer County Clerk
P.O. Box 458
Archer City, Texas 76351

Armstrong County Clerk
P.O. Box 309
Claude, Texas 79019-0309

Atascosa County Clerk
Circle Dr.
Jourdanton, Texas 78026

Austin County Clerk
1 East Main
Bellville, Texas
77418-1521

Bailey County Clerk
P.O. Box 735
Muleshoe, Texas
79347-0735

Bandera County Clerk
Courthouse
Bandera, Texas 78003

Bastrop County Clerk
803 Pine St.
Bastrop, Texas 78602-0577

Baylor County Clerk
Courthouse
Seymour, Texas 76380

Bee County Clerk
105 West Corpus Christi
Beeville, Texas 78102-5627

Bell County Clerk
Courthouse
Belton, Texas 76513

Bexar County Clerk
Courthouse
San Antonio, Texas
78285-5100

Blanco County Clerk
P.O. Box 65
Johnson City, Texas
78636-0065

Borden County Clerk
P.O. Box 124
Gail, Texas 79738

Bosque County Clerk
P.O. Box 617
Meridian, Texas
76665-0617

Bowie County Clerk
Courthouse
New Boston, Texas 75570

Brazoria County Clerk
P.O. Box D
Angleton, Texas
77515-1504

Brazos County Clerk
300 East 26th St. #314
Bryan, Texas 77803

Brewster County Clerk
P.O. Box 119
Alpine, Texas 79831

Briscoe County Clerk
P.O. Box 375
Silverton, Texas
79257-0375

Brooks County Clerk
Courthouse
Falfurrias, Texas 78355

Brown County Clerk
200 South Broadway
Brownwood, Texas
76801-3136

Burleson County Clerk
P.O. Box 57
Caldwell, Texas 77836

Burnet County Clerk
220 S. Pierce St.
Burnet, Texas 78611-3136

Caldwell County Clerk
Courthouse
Lockhart, Texas 78644

Calhoun County Clerk
211 South Ann
Port Lavaca, Texas
77979-4249

Callahan County Clerk
Courthouse
Baird, Texas 79504

Cameron County Clerk
964 East Harrison St.
Brownsville, Texas 78520

Camp County Clerk
126 Church St.
Pittsburg, Texas
75686-1346

Carson County Clerk
P.O. Box 487
Panhandle, Texas
79068-0487

Cass County Clerk
P.O. Box 468
Linden, Texas 75563-0468

Castro County Clerk
100 East Bedford
Dimmitt, Texas
79027-2643

Chambers County Clerk
P.O. Box 728
Anahuac, Texas
77514-0728

Cherokee County Clerk
Courthouse
Rusk, Texas 75785

Childress County Clerk
P.O. Box 4
Childress, Texas
79201-3755

Clay County Clerk
P.O. Box 548
Henrietta, Texas
76365-0548

Cochran County Clerk
Courthouse
Morton, Texas 79346

Coke County Clerk
P.O. Box 150
Robert Lee, Texas
76945-0150

Coleman County Clerk
P.O. Box 591
Coleman, Texas
76834-0591

Collin County Clerk
Courthouse
McKinney, Texas
75069-5655

**Collingsworth County
Clerk**
Courthouse
Wellington, Texas
79095-3037

Colorado County Clerk
P.O. Box 68
Columbus, Texas 78934

Comal County Clerk
100 Main Plaza, Suite 104
New Braunfels, Texas
78130

Comanche County Clerk
Courthouse
Comanche, Texas
76442-3264

Concho County Clerk
Courthouse
Paint Rock, Texas 76866

Cooke County Clerk
Courthouse
Gainesville, Texas 76240

Coryell County Clerk
Main St.
Gatesville, Texas 76528

Cottle County Clerk
P.O. Box 717
Paducah, Texas 79248

Crane County Clerk
P.O. Box 578
Crane, Texas 79731-0578

Crockett County Clerk
P.O. Box C
Ozona, Texas 76943-2502

Crosby County Clerk
Courthouse
Crosbyton, Texas
79322-2503

Culberson County Clerk
P.O. Box 158
Van Horn, Texas
79855-0158

Dallam County Clerk
P.O. Box 1352
Dalhart, Texas 79002-1352

Dallas County Clerk
509 Main St.
Dallas, Texas 75202-3507

Dawson County Clerk
P.O. Box 1268
Lamesa, Texas 79331-1268

De Witt County Clerk
307 N. Gonzales St.
Cuero, Texas 77954-2970

Deaf Smith County Clerk
Courthouse
Hereford, Texas
79045-5515

Delta County Clerk
200 West Dallas Ave.
Cooper, Texas 75432-1726

Denton County Clerk
P.O. Box 2187
Denton, Texas 76202-2187

Dickens County Clerk
Courthouse
Dickens, Texas 79229

Dimmit County Clerk
103 N. Fifth St.
Carrizo Springs, Texas
78834-3101

Donley County Clerk
Courthouse
Clarendon, Texas
79226-2020

Duval County Clerk
Courthouse
San Diego, Texas 78384

Eastland County Clerk
P.O. Box 110
Eastland, Texas
76448-0110

Ector County Clerk
Courthouse
Odessa, Texas 79763

Edwards County Clerk
P.O. Box 184
Rocksprings, Texas
78880-0184

El Paso County Clerk
500 East San Antonio
El Paso, Texas 79901-2421

Ellis County Clerk
Courthouse
Waxahachie, Texas
75165-3759

Erath County Clerk
Courthouse
Stephenville, Texas
76401-4219

Falls County Clerk
P.O. Box 458
Marlin, Texas 76661-0458

Fannin County Clerk
Courthouse
Bonham, Texas 75418

Fayette County Clerk
151 N. Washington St.
La Grange, Texas 78945

Fisher County Clerk
Courthouse
Roby, Texas 79543

Floyd County Clerk
P.O. Box 476
Floydada, Texas
79235-0476

Foard County Clerk
P.O. Box 539
Crowell, Texas 79227

Fort Bend County Clerk
301 Jackson
Richmond, Texas 77469

Franklin County Clerk
P.O. Box 68
Mount Vernon, Texas
75457-0068

Freestone County Clerk
P.O. Box 1017
Fairfield, Texas
75840-1017

Frio County Clerk
P.O. Box X
Pearsall, Texas 78061-1423

Gaines County Clerk
Courthouse
Seminole, Texas
79360-4341

Galveston County Clerk
P.O. Box 2450
Galveston, Texas 77553

Garza County Clerk
Courthouse
Post, Texas 79356-3242

Gillespie County Clerk
P.O. Box 551
Fredericksburg, Texas
78624-0551

Glasscock County Clerk
P.O. Box 190
Garden City, Texas
79739-0190

Goliad County Clerk
P.O. Box 5
Goliad, Texas 77963-0005

Gonzales County Clerk
Courthouse
Gonzales, Texas 78629

Gray County Clerk
200 N. Russell St.
Pampa, Texas 79065-6442

Grayson County Clerk
100 West Houston
Sherman, Texas 75090

Gregg County Clerk
P.O. Box 3049
Longview, Texas
75606-3049

Grimes County Clerk
P.O. Box 209
Anderson, Texas 77830

Guadalupe County Clerk
Courthouse
Seguin, Texas 78155-5727

Hale County Clerk
P.O. Box 710
Plainview, Texas
79073-0710

Hall County Clerk
Courthouse
Memphis, Texas
79245-3341

Hamilton County Clerk
Courthouse
Hamilton, Texas 76531

Hansford County Clerk
P.O. Box 367
Spearman, Texas
79081-0367

Hardeman County Clerk
Courthouse
Quanah, Texas 79252

Hardin County Clerk
P.O. Box 38
Kountze, Texas
77625-0038

Harris County Clerk
1001 Preston, 4th Fl.
Houston, Texas 77251

Harrison County Clerk
Courthouse
Marshall, Texas 75671

Hartley County Clerk
P.O. Box 22
Channing, Texas
79018-0022

Haskell County Clerk
P.O. Box 905
Haskell, Texas 79521

Hays County Clerk
Courthouse
San Marcos, Texas 78666

Hemphill County Clerk
P.O. Box 867
Canadian, Texas
79014-0867

Henderson County Clerk
Courthouse
Athens, Texas 75751

Hidalgo County Clerk
P.O. Box 58
Edinburg, Texas
78540-0058

Hill County Clerk
P.O. Box 398
Hillsboro, Texas
76645-0398

Hockley County Clerk
Courthouse
Levelland, Texas
79336-4529

Hood County Clerk
P.O. Box 339
Granbury, Texas
76048-0339

Hopkins County Clerk
P.O. Box 288
Sulphur Springs, Texas
75482-0288

Houston County Clerk
Courthouse
Crockett, Texas 75835

Howard County Clerk
P.O. Box 1468
Big Spring, Texas
79721-1468

Hudspeth County Clerk
Courthouse
Sierra Blanca, Texas 79851

Hunt County Clerk
P.O. Box 1316
Greenville, Texas
75401-1316

Hutchinson County Clerk
P.O. Box F
Stinnett, Texas 79083-0526

Irion County Clerk
Courthouse
Mertzon, Texas 76941

Jack County Clerk
100 Main St.
Jacksboro, Texas
76056-1746

Jackson County Clerk
115 West. Main St.
Edna, Texas 77957-2733

Jasper County Clerk
Courthouse
Jasper, Texas 75951

Jeff Davis County Clerk
P.O. Box 398
Fort Davis, Texas
79734-0398

Jefferson County Clerk
P.O. Box 1151
Beaumont, Texas 77704

Jim Hogg County Clerk
102 East Tilley
Hebbronville, Texas
78361-3554

Jim Wells County Clerk
Courthouse
Alice, Texas 78332-4845

Johnson County Clerk
Courthouse
Cleburne, Texas 76031

Jones County Clerk
P.O. Box 552
Anson, Texas 79501-0552

Karnes County Clerk
Courthouse
Karnes City, Texas
78118-2959

Kaufman County Clerk
Courthouse
Kaufman, Texas 75142

Kendall County Clerk
Courthouse
Boerne, Texas 78006

Kenedy County Clerk
P.O. Box 7
Sarita, TX 78385-0007

Kent County Clerk
P.O. Box 9
Jayton, Texas 79528-0009

Kerr County Clerk
700 Main Street
Kerrville, Texas 78028

Kimble County Clerk
501 Main St.
Junction, Texas
76849-4763

King County Clerk
Courthouse
Guthrie, Texas 79236

Kinney County Clerk
P.O. Box 9
Brackettville, Texas
78832-0009

Kleberg County Clerk
P.O. Box 1327
Kingsville, Texas
78364-1327

Knox County Clerk
County House
Benjamin, Texas 79505

La Salle County Clerk
P.O. Box 340
Cotulla, Texas 78014-0340

Lamar County Clerk
119 North Main
Paris, Texas 75460-4265

Lamb County Clerk
Courthouse
Littlefiled, Texas 79339

Lampasas County Clerk
P.O. Box 231
Lampasas, Texas
76550-0231

Lavaca County Clerk
Courthouse
Hallettsville, Texas 77964

Lee County Clerk
P.O. Box 419
Giddings, Texas
78942-0419

Leon County Clerk
P.O. Box 98
Centerville, Texas
75833-0098

Liberty County Clerk
1923 Sam Huston
Liberty, Texas 77575-4815

Limestone County Clerk
200 West State St.
Groesbeck, Texas
76642-1702

Lipscomb County Clerk
Courthouse
Lipscomb, Texas 79056

Live Oak County Clerk
P.O. Box 280
George West, Texas
78022-0280

Llano County Clerk
801 Ford, Rm. 101
Llano, Texas 78643

Loving County Clerk
Courthouse
Mentone, Texas 79754

Lubbock County Clerk
P.O. Box 10536
Lubbock, Texas 79408

Lynn County Clerk
Courthouse
Tahoka, Texas 79373

Madison County Clerk
101 West Main
Madisonville, Texas 77864

Marion County Clerk
P.O. Box F
Jefferson, Texas
75657-0420

Martin County Clerk
Courthouse
Stanton, Texas 79782

Mason County Clerk
P.O. Box 702
Mason, Texas 76856-0702

Matagorda County Clerk
1700 Seventh Street
Bay City, Texas
77414-5034

Maverick County Clerk
Courthouse
Eagle Pass, Texas 78853

McCulloch County Clerk
Courthouse
Brady, Texas 76825

McLennan County Clerk
225 W. Waco Dr.
Waco, Texas 76707

McMullen County Clerk
P.O. Box 235
Tilden, Texas 78072-0235

Medina County Clerk
Courthouse
Hondo, Texas 78861

Menard County Clerk
Courthouse
Menard, Texas 76659

Midland County Clerk
P.O. Box 211
Midland, Texas
79702-0211

Milam County Clerk
100 South Fannin
Cameron, Texas
76520-4216

Mills County Clerk
P.O. Box 646
Goldthwaite, Texas
76844-0646

Mitchell County Clerk
P.O. Box 1166
Colorado City, Texas
79512-1166

Montague County Clerk
P.O. Box 77
Montague, Texas
76251-0077

**Montgomery
County Clerk**
301 N. Main, Suite 128
Conroe, Texas 77301-2637

Moore County Clerk
P.O. Box 396
Dumas, Texas 79029-0396

Morris County Clerk
500 Broadnax St.
Daingerfield, Texas
75638-1304

Motley County Clerk
County Clerk
Matador, Texas 79224

**Nacogdoches
County Clerk**
101 West Main St.
Nacogdoches, Texas
75961-5119

Navarro County Clerk
300 West Third Ave.
Corsicana, Texas 75110

Newton County Clerk
P.O. Box 484
Newton, Texas 75966-0484

Nolan County Clerk
P.O. Box 98
Sweetwater, Texas 79556

Nueces County Clerk
901 Leopard
Corpus Christi, Texas
78401-3606

Ochiltree County Clerk
511 South Main St.
Perryton, Texas
79070-3154

Oldham County Clerk
P.O. Box 469
Vega, Texas 79092-0469

Orange County Clerk
801 Division St.
Orange, Texas 77630-6321

Palo Pinto County Clerk
Courthouse
Palo Pinto, Texas 76072

Panola County Clerk
Rm. 201
Carthage, Texas 75633

Parker County Clerk
1112 Santa Fe Dr.
Weatherford, Texas
76086-5827

Parmer County Clerk
P.O. Box 356
Farwell, Texas 79325-0356

Pecos County Clerk
103 West Callahan St.
Fort Stockton, Texas
79735-7101

Polk County Clerk
101 Church St. West
Livingston, Texas
77351-3201

Potter County Clerk
511 South Taylor
Amarillo, Texas
79101-2437

Presidio Country Clerk
P.O. Box 789
Marfa, Texas 79843-0789

Rains County Clerk
P.O. Box 187
Emory, Texas 75440-0187

Randall County Clerk
P.O. Box 660
Canyon, Texas 79015-0660

Reagan County Clerk
P.O. Box 100
Big Lake, Texas
76932-0100

Real County Clerk
P.O. Box 656
Leakey, Texas 78873-0656

Red River County Clerk
400 North Walnut St.
Clarksville, Texas 75426

Reeves County Clerk
P.O. Box 867
Pecos, Texas 79772-0867

Refugio County Clerk
P.O. Box 704
Refugio, Texas 78377-0704

Roberts County Clerk
P.O. Box 477
Miami, Texas 79059-0477

Robertson County Clerk
P.O. Box L
Franklin, Texas
77856-0300

Rockwall County Clerk
Courthouse
Rockwall, Texas 75087

Runnels County Clerk
P.O. Box 189
Ballinger, Texas
76821-0189

Rusk County Clerk
P.O. Box 758
Henderson, Texas
75653-0758

Sabine County Clerk
Courthouse
Hemphill, Texas 75948

**San Augustine
County Clerk**
106 Courthouse
San Augustine, Texas
75972

San Jacinto County Clerk
P.O. Box 669
Coldspring, Texas 77331

San Patricio
County Clerk
P.O. Box 578
Sinton, Texas 78387-0578

San Saba County Clerk
Courthouse
San Saba, Texas 76877

Schleicher County Clerk
Courthouse
Eldorado, Texas 76936

Scurry County Clerk
Courthouse
Snyder, Texas 79549

Shackelford
County Clerk
P.O. Box 247
Albany, Texas 76430-0247

Shelby County Clerk
P.O. Box 1987
Center, Texas 75935-1987

Sherman County Clerk
P.O. Box 270
Stratford, Texas
79084-0270

Smith County Clerk
100 N. Broadway
Tyler, Texas 75710-1018

Somervell County Clerk
P.O. Box 1098
Glen Rose, Texas
76043-1098

Starr County Clerk
Britton Ave.
Rio Grande City, Texas
78582

Stephens County Clerk
Courthouse
Breckenridge, Texas 76024

Sterling County Clerk
P.O. Box 55
Sterling City, Texas
76951-0055

Stonewall County Clerk
P.O. Box P
Aspermont, Texas
79502-0914

Sutton County Clerk
P.O. Box 481
Sonora, Texas 76950-0481

Swisher County Clerk
Courthouse
Tulia, Texas 79088-2245

Tarrant County Clerk
100 E. Weatherford St.
Fort Worth, Texas 76196

Taylor County Clerk
Courthouse
Abilene, Texas 79608

Terrell County Clerk
P.O. Box 410
Sanderson, Texas
79848-0410

Terry County Clerk
Courthouse
Brownfield, Texas
79316-4328

Throckmorton
County Clerk
P.O. Box 309
Throckmorton, Texas
76083-0309

Titus County Clerk
Courthouse
Mount Pleasant, Texas
75455

Tom Green County Clerk
112 West Beauregard
San Angelo, Texas
76903-5850

Travis County Clerk
1000 Guadalupe
Austin, Texas 78701-2336

Trinity County Clerk
P.O. Box 456
Groveton, Texas
75845-0456

Tyler County Clerk
100 Courthouse
Woodville, Texas
75979-5245

Upshur County Clerk
Courthouse
Gilmer, Texas 75644

Upton County Clerk
P.O. Box 465
Rankin, Texas 79778-0465

Uvalde County Clerk
P.O. Box 284
Uvalde, Texas 78802-0284

Val Verde County Clerk
P.O. Box 1267
Del Rio, Texas 78841-1267

Van Zandt County Clerk
P.O. Box 515
Canton, Texas 75103-0515

Victoria County Clerk
115 North Bridge
Victoria, Texas 77901-6513

Walker County Clerk
1100 University
Huntsville, Texas
77340-4631

Waller County Clerk
836 Austin St.
Hempstead, Texas
77445-4667

Ward County Clerk
Courthouse
Monahans, Texas 79756

**Washington
County Clerk**
P.O. Box K
Brenham, Texas
77833-0609

Webb County Clerk
204 McPherson Dr.
Laredo, Texas 78041-2712

Wharton County Clerk
P.O. Box 69
Wharton, Texas 77488

Wheeler County Clerk
P.O. Box 465
Wheeler, Texas
79096-0465

Wichita County Clerk
P.O. Box 1679
Wichita Falls, Texas
76307-1679

Wilbarger County Clerk
1700 Wilbarger Street
Vernon, Texas 76384-4742

Willacy County Clerk
Courthouse
Raymondville, Texas
78580-3533

Williamson County Clerk
P.O. Box 18
Georgetown, Texas
78627-0018

Wilson County Clerk
P.O. Box 27
Floresville, Texas
78114-0027

Winkler County Clerk
P.O. Box 1007
Kermit, Texas 79745-1007

Wise County Clerk
P.O. Box 359
Decatur, Texas 76234-0359

Wood County Clerk
P.O. Box 338
Quitman, Texas
75783-0338

Yoakum County Clerk
P.O. Box 309
Plains, Texas 79355-0309

Young County Clerk
P.O. Box 218
Graham, Texas 76046-0218

Zapata County Clerk
Courthouse
Zapata, Texas 78076

Zavala County Clerk
Courthouse
Crystal City, Texas
78839-3547

UTAH
http://www.state.ut.us/

Beaver County Clerk
105 East Center
Beaver, Utah 84713

Box Elder County Clerk
1 South Main St.
Brigham City, Utah
84302-2548

Cache County Clerk
655 East 1300 North
Logan, Utah 84341

Carbon County Clerk
120 E. Main St.
Price, Utah 84501

Daggett County Clerk
95 North 1st W.
Manila, Utah 84046

Davis County Clerk
28 East State St.
Farmington, Utah 84025

Duchesne County Clerk
P.O. Box 270
Duchesne, Utah 84021

Emery County Clerk
95 East Main St.
Castle Dale, Utah 84513

Garfield County Clerk
55 S. Main St.
Panguitch, Utah 84759

Grand County Clerk
125 East Center St.
Moab, Utah 84532

Iron County Clerk
68 South 100 East
Parowan, Utah 84761

Juab County Clerk
160 N. Main St.
Nephi, Utah 84648

Kane County Clerk
76 N. Main St.
Kanab, Utah 84741

Millard County Clerk
765 S. Highway 99
Fillmore, Utah 84631

Morgan County Clerk
48 W. Young St.
Morgan, Utah 84050

Piute County Clerk
21 N. Main St.
Junction, Utah 84740

Rich County Clerk
20 S. Main St.
Randolph, Utah 84064

Salt Lake County Clerk
610 S. 200 E.
Salt Lake City, Utah 84111

San Juan County Clerk
117 S. Main St.
Monticello, Utah 84535

Sanpete County Clerk
160 N. Main
Manti, Utah 84642-1266

Sevier County Clerk
250 N. Main
Richfield, Utah
84701-2158

Summit County Clerk
P.O. Box 128
Coalville, Utah 84017

Tooele County Clerk
47 South Main
Tooele, Utah 84074

Uintah County Clerk
147 E. Main St.
Vernal, Utah 84078

Utah County Clerk
589 S. State St.
Provo, Utah 84606

Wasatch County Clerk
25 N. Main St.
Heber City, Utah 84032

**Washington County
Clerk**
197 East Tabernacle St.
St. George, Utah 84770

Wayne County Clerk
18 South Main
Loa, Utah 84747

Weber County Clerk
2549 Washington Blvd,
Suite 320
Ogden, Utah 84401

VERMONT
http://www.state.vt.us/

Addison County Clerk
5 Court St.
Middlebury, Vermont
05753-1405

Bennington County Clerk
207 South St.
Bennington, Vermont
05201

Caledonia County Clerk
27 Main St.
St. Johnsbury, Vermont
05819-2637

Chittenden County Clerk
175 Main St.
Burlington, Vermont
05401-8310

Essex County Clerk
Courthouse
Guildhall, Vermont 05905

Franklin County Clerk
Church St.
St. Albans, Vermont 05478

Grand Isle County Clerk
P.O. Box 7
North Hero, Vermont
05474-0007

Lamoille County Clerk
P.O. Box 303
Hyde Park, Vermont
05655-0303

Orange County Clerk
Courthouse
Chelsea, Vermont 05038

Orleans County Clerk
P.O. Box 787
Newport, Vermont
05855-0787

Rutland County Clerk
83 Center St.
Rutland, Vermont
05701-4017

**Washington
County Clerk**
P.O. Box 426
Montpelier, Vermont
05602-0426

Windham County Clerk
P.O. Box 207
Newfane, Vermont
05345-0207

Windsor County Clerk
12 The Green
Woodstock, Vermont
05091-1212

VIRGINIA
http://www.state.va.us/

Accomack County Clerk
Courthouse
Accomack, Virginia 23301

Albemarle County Clerk
401 McIntire Rd.
Charlottesville, Virginia
22901-4579

Alleghany County Clerk
Main Street
Covington, Virginia 24426

Amelia County Clerk
Courthouse
Amelia Court House,
Virginia 23002

Amherst County Clerk
100 E. St.
Amherst, Virginia 24521

Appomattox
County Clerk
P.O. Box 672
Appomattox, Virginia
24522-0672

Arlington County Clerk
1400 N. Courthouse Rd.
Arlington, Virginia
22201-2622

Augusta County Clerk
6 East Johnson St.
Staunton, Virginia 24401-4301

Bath County Clerk
P.O. Box 180
Warm Springs, Virginia
24484-0180

Bedford County Clerk
201 East Main St.
Bedford, Virginia 24623

Bland County Clerk
P.O. Box 295
Bland, Virginia 24315-0295

Botetourt County Clerk
P.O. Box 219
Fincastle, Virginia 24090

Brunswick County Clerk
P.O. Box 399
Lawrenceville, Virginia
23868-0399

Buchanan County Clerk
P.O. Box 950
Grundy, Virginia
24614-0950

Buckingham
County Clerk
P.O. Box 252
Buckingham, Virginia
23921-0252

Campbell County Clerk
P.O. Box 7
Rustburg, Virginia 24588

Caroline County Clerk
Courthouse
Bowling Green, Virginia
22427

Carrol County Clerk
P.O. Box 515
Hillsville, Virginia
24343-0515

Charles County Clerk
P.O. Box 128
Charles City, Virginia
23030-0128

Charlotte County Clerk
P.O. Box 38
Charlotte Court House,
Virginia 23923

Chesterfield
County Clerk
P.O. Box 40
Chesterfield, Virginia
23832-0040

City of Alexandria
County Clerk
301 King St.
Alexandria, Virginia 22313

City of Fredericksburg
County Clerk
P.O. Box 7447
Fredericksburg, Virginia
22404-7447

City of Martinsville
County Clerk
P.O. Box 1112
Martinsville, Virginia
24114

City of Petersburg
County Clerk
Union and Tabb St.
Petersburg, Virginia 23803

City of Richmond
Vital Records
109 Governor St.
Richmond, Virginia 23219

City of Roanoke Vital
Records
515 8th St. SW
Richmond, Virginia
24016-3529

City of Salem
County Clerk
P.O. Box 869
Salem, Virginia
24153-0869

City of Virginia Beach
County Clerk
Municipal Center,
Building 1
Virginia Beach, Virginia
23456

Clarke County Clerk
P.O. Box 189
Berryville, Virginia
22611-0189

Craig County Clerk
P.O. Box 185
New Castle, Virginia 24127

Culpeper County Clerk
Courthouse
Culpeper, Virginia 22701

Cumberland
County Clerk
P.O. Box 77
Cumberland, Virginia
23040-0077

Dickenson County Clerk
P.O. Box 190
Clintwood, Virginia 24228

Dinwiddie County Clerk
14103 Boydton Plank Rd.
Dinwiddie, Virginia
23841-2511

Emporia County Clerk
201 N. Main Street
Emporia, Virginia 23817

Essex County Clerk
P.O. Box 445
Tappahannock, Virginia
22560-0445

Fairfax County Clerk
4110 Chain Bridge Rd.
Fairfax, Virginia 22030

Fauquier County Clerk
40 Culpeper St.
Warrenton, Virginia 22186

Floyd County Clerk
Courthouse
Floyd, Virginia 24091

Fluvanna County Clerk
Courthouse
Palmyra, Virginia 22963

Franklin County Clerk
Courthouse Building
Rocky Mount, Virginia
24151

Frederick County Clerk
5 North Kent St.
Winchester, Virginia 22601

Giles County Clerk
120 North Main St.
Pearisburg, Virginia
24134-1625

Gloucester County Clerk
P.O. Box 329
Gloucester, Virginia 23061-0329

Goochland County Clerk
P.O. Box 10
Goochland, Virginia
23063-0010

Grayson County Clerk
129 Davis St.
Independence, Virginia
24348-9602

Greene County Clerk
P.O. Box 386
Stanardsville, Virginia
22973-0386

Greensville County Clerk
337 S. Main St.
Emporia, Virginia
23847-2027

Halifax County Clerk
P.O. Box 786
Halifax, Virginia
24558-0786

Hanover County Clerk
Courthouse
Hanover, Virginia 23069

**Henrico (East) County
Health Dept.**
3810 Nine Mile Rd.
Richmond, Virginia 23223

**Henrico (West) County
Health Dept.**
8600 Dixon Powers Dr.
Richmond, Virginia 23273

Henry County Clerk
Courthouse
Martinsville, Virginia
24114

Highland County Clerk
P.O. Box 190
Monterey, Virginia 24465

**Isle of Wight
County Clerk**
Courthouse
Isle of Wight, Virginia
23397

James County Clerk
114 Stanley Dr.
Williamsburg, Virginia
23185-2538

**King and Queen
County Clerk**
Courthouse
King and Queen
Courthouse, Virginia 23085

**King George County
Clerk**
P.O. Box 105
King George, Virginia
22485

**King William
County Clerk**
P.O. Box 215
King William, Virginia
23086

Lancaster County Clerk
P.O. Box 125
Lancaster, Virginia 22503

Lee County Clerk
Courthouse
Jonesville, Virginia 24263

Loudoun County Clerk
P.O. Box 550
Leesburg, Virginia
22075-0550

Louisa County Clerk
P.O. Box 160
Louisa, Virginia
23093-0160

Lunenburg County Clerk
Courthouse
Lunenburg, Virginia 23952

Madison County Clerk
Main St.
Madison, Virginia 22727

Mathews County Clerk
Court St.
Mathews, Virginia 23109

**Mecklenburg
County Clerk**
P.O. Box 307
Boydton, Virginia
23917-0207

Middlesex County Clerk
Courthouse
Saluda, Virginia 23149

**Montgomery
County Clerk**
P.O. Box 6126
Christiansburg, Virginia
24068-6126

Nelson County Clerk
Courthouse
Lovingston, Virginia 22949

New Kent County Clerk
P.O. Box 98
New Kent, Virginia
23124-0050

**Northampton
County Clerk**
Courthouse
Eastville, Virginia 23347

**Northumberland
County Clerk**
Courthouse
Heathsville, Virginia 22473

Nottoway County Clerk
Courthouse
Nottoway, Virginia 23955

Orange County Clerk
P.O. Box 230
Orange, Virginia 22960

Page County Clerk
101 South Court St.
Luray, Virginia 22835-1224

Patrick County Clerk
P.O. Box 148
Stuart, Virginia 24171-0148

Pittsylvania County Clerk
P.O. Box 31
Chatham, Virginia
24531-0031

Powhatan County Clerk
3834 Old Buckingham Rd.
Powhatan, Virginia
23139-7019

**Prince Edward
County Clerk**
P.O. Box 304
Farmville, Virginia
23901-0304

**Prince George
County Clerk**
P.O. Box 68
Prince George, Virginia
23875-0068

**Prince William
County Clerk**
P.O. Box 191
Prince William, Virginia
22192

Pulaski County Clerk
Third St.
Pulaski, Virginia 24301

**Rappahannock
County Clerk**
P.O. Box 116
Washington, Virginia
22747-0116

Richmond County Clerk
Court St.
Warsaw, Virginia 22572

Roanoke County Clerk
P.O. Box 1126
Salem, Virginia
24153-1126

Rockbridge County Clerk
Courthouse Square
Lexington, Virginia 24450

**Rockingham
County Clerk**
Circuit Court Square
Harrisonburg, Virginia
22801

Russell County Clerk
P.O. Box 435
Lebanon, Virginia 24266

Scott County Clerk
P.O. Box 665
Gate City, Virginia
24251-0665

**Shenandoah
County Clerk**
P.O. Box 406
Woodstock, Virginia
22664-0406

Smyth County Clerk
P.O. Box 1025
Marion, Virginia
24354-1025

**Southampton
County Clerk**
Courthouse
Courtland, Virginia 23837

**Spotsylvania
County Clerk**
P.O. Box 99
Spotsylvania, Virginia
22553-0099

Stafford County Clerk
P.O. Box 339
Stafford, Virginia
22554-0339

Suffolk County Clerk
441 Market St.
Suffolk, Virginia
23434-5237

Surry County Clerk
P.O. Box 65
Surry, Virginia 23883-0065

Sussex County Clerk
P.O. Box 1337
Sussex, Virginia
23884-0337

Tazewell County Clerk
P.O. Box 958
Tazewell, Virginia 24651

Warren County Clerk
1 East Main St.
Front Royal, Virginia
22630

**Washington
County Clerk**
111 North Court St.
Abingdon, Virginia 24210

**Westmoreland
County Clerk**
P.O. Box 467
Montross, Virginia
22520-0467

Wise County Clerk
P.O. Box 570
Wise, Virginia 24293-0570

Wythe County Clerk
P.O. Box 440
Wytheville, Virginia
24382-0440

York County Clerk
P.O. Box 532
Yorktown, Virginia
23690-0532

WASHINGTON
http://www.state.va.us/

Adams County Clerk
210 West Broadway
Ritzville, Washington
99169-1860

Asotin County Clerk
135 2nd St.
Asotin, Washington 99402

Benton County Clerk
P.O. Box 190
Prosser, Washington
99350-0190

Chelan County Clerk
P.O. Box 3025
Wenatchee, Washington
98801-0403

Clallam County Clerk
223 East 4th St.
Port Angeles, Washington
98362-3098

Clark County Clerk
1200 Franklin St.
Vancouver, Washington
98660-2872

Columbia County Clerk
341 East Main St.
Dayton, Washington
99328-1361

Cowlitz County Clerk
312 SW First St.
Kelso, Washington
98626-1724

Douglas County Clerk
P.O. Box 516
Waterville, Washington
98858-0516

Ferry County Clerk
P.O. Box 498
Republic, Washington
99166-0498

Franklin County Clerk
1016 N. Fourth Ave.
Pasco, Washington
99301-3706

Garfield County Clerk
P.O. Box 915
Pomeroy, Washington
99347-0915

Grant County Clerk
P.O. Box 37
Ephrata, Washington
98823-0037

**Grays Harbor
County Clerk**
102 W. Broadway, Rm. 203
Montesano, Washington
98563

Island County Clerk
P.O. Box 1317
Coupeville, Washington
98239-1317

Jefferson County Clerk
P.O. Box 1220
Port Townsend,
Washington 98368

King County Clerk
500 4th Ave. Admin Bldg,
Rm. 214
Seattle, Washington 98104

Kitsap County Clerk
614 Division St.
Port Orchard, Washington
98366-4614

Kittitas County Clerk
205 West Fifth Ave.
Ellensburg, Washington
98926-2887

Klickitat County Clerk
205 South Columbus
Goldendale, Washington
98620-9286

Lewis County Clerk
344 West Main
Chehalis, Washington
98532-1922

Lincoln County Clerk
450 Logan St.
Davenport, Washington
99122-9501

Mason County Clerk
Fourth and Alder
Shelton, Washington 98584

Okanogan County Clerk
P.O. Box 72
Okanogan, Washington
98840-0072

Pacific County Clerk
P.O. Box 67
South Bend, Washington
98586-0067

**Pend Oreille
County Clerk**
P.O. Box 5000
Newport, Washington
99156-5000

Pierce County Clerk
3629 South D St.
Tacoma, Washington 98408

San Juan County Clerk
Courthouse
Friday Harbor, Washington
98250

Skagit County Clerk
P.O. Box 837
Mt. Vernon, Washington
98273-0837

Skamania County Clerk
P.O. Box 790
Stevenson, Washington
98648-0790

Snohomish County Clerk
3000 Rockefeller
Everett, Washington 98201

Spokane County Clerk
1101 W. College Ave.
Spokane, Washington
99210

Stevens County Auditor
215 South Oak St.
Colville, Washington 99114

Thurston County Clerk
2000 Lakeridge SW
Olympia, Washington
98502-6045

**Wahkiakum
County Clerk**
P.O. Box 116
Cathlamet, Washington
98612-0116

**Walla Walla County
Clerk**
315 West Main St.
Walla Walla, Washington
99362-2838

Whatcom County Clerk
311 Grand Ave.
Bellingham, Washington
98225-4038

Whitman County Clerk
P.O. Box 390
Colfax, Washington
99111-0390

Yakima County Clerk
Second and East B St.
Yakima, Washington 98901

WEST VIRGINIA
http://www.state.wv.us/

Barbour County Clerk
P.O. Box 310
Philippi, West Virginia
26416-0310

Berkeley County Clerk
100 West King St.
Martinsburg, West Virginia
25401-3210

Boone County Clerk
Boone County Courthouse
Madison, West Virginia
25130

Braxton County Clerk
P.O. Box 486
Sutton, West Virginia
26601-0486

Brooke County Clerk
632 Main St.
Wellsburg, West Virginia
26070

Cabell County Clerk
Courthouse
Huntington, West Virginia
25701

Calhoun County Clerk
P.O. Box 230
Grantsville, West Virginia
26147

Clay County Clerk
P.O. Box 190
Clay, West Virginia 25043

Doddridge County Clerk
118 East Court St.
West Union, West Virginia
26456

Fayette County Clerk
Courthouse
Fayetteville, West Virginia
25840

Gilmer County Clerk
Courthouse
Glenville, West Virginia
26351

Grant County Clerk
5 Highland Ave.
Petersburg, West Virginia
26847-1705

Greenbrier County Clerk
P.O. Box 506
Lewisburg, West Virginia
24901-0506

Hampshire County Clerk
Courthouse
Romney, West Virginia
26757

Hancock County Clerk
P.O. Box 367
New Cumberland,
West Virginia 26047

Hardy County Clerk
P.O. Box 540
Moorefield, West Virginia
26836-0540

Harrison County Clerk
301 West Main
Clarksburg, West Virginia
26301-2909

Jackson County Clerk
Courthouse
Ripley, West Virginia
25271

Jefferson County Clerk
Courthouse
Charles Town,
West Virginia 25414

Kanawha County Clerk
P.O. Box 3226
Charleston, West Virginia
25332-3226

Lewis County Clerk
P.O. Box 87
Weston, West Virginia
26452-0087

Lincoln County Clerk
Courthouse
Hamlin, West Virginia
25523

Logan County Clerk
Courthouse
Logan, West Virginia
25601

Marion County Clerk
Courthouse
Fairmont, West Virginia
26554

Marshall County Clerk
P.O. Box 459
Moundsville, West Virginia
26041-0459

Mason County Clerk
Courthouse
Point Pleasant,
West Virginia 25550

Mcdowell County Clerk
P.O. Box 967
Welch, West Virginia
24801-0967

Mercer County Clerk
Courthouse Square
Princeton, West Virginia
24740

Mineral County Clerk
150 Armstrong St.
Keyser, West Virginia
26726-0250

Mingo County Clerk
P.O. Box 1197
Williamson, West Virginia
25661-1197

**Monongalia
County Clerk**
Courthouse
Morgantown, West Virginia
26505

Monroe County Clerk
Courthouse
Union, West Virginia
24983

Morgan County Clerk
Fairfax St.
Berkeley Springs,
West Virginia 25411

Nicholas County Clerk
Courthouse
Summersville,
West Virginia 26651

Ohio County Clerk
1500 Chapline St., Rm. 205
Wheeling, West Virginia
26003-3553

Pendleton County Clerk
Courthouse
Franklin, West Virginia
26807

Pleasants County Clerk
Courthouse
St. Marys, West Virginia
26170

Pocahontas County Clerk
900C Tenth Ave.
Marlinton, West Virginia
24954-1333

Preston County Clerk
101 West Main
Kingwood, West Virginia
26537-1121

Putnam County Clerk
P.O. Box 508
Winfield, West Virginia
25213-0508

Raleigh County Clerk
Courthouse
Beckley, West Virginia
25801

Randolph County Clerk
Courthouse
Elkins, West Virginia
26241

Ritchie County Clerk
115 East Main St.
Harrisville, West Virginia
26362

Roane County Clerk
P.O. Box 69
Spencer, West Virginia
25276

Summers County Clerk
P.O. Box 97
Hinton, West Virginia
25951-0097

Taylor County Clerk
Courthouse
Grafton, West Virginia
26354

Tucker County Clerk
Courthouse
Parsons, West Virginia
26287

Tyler County Clerk
P.O. Box 66
Middlebourne,
West Virginia 26149-0066

Upshur County Clerk
Courthouse
Buckhannon, West Virginia
26201

Wayne County Clerk
Courthouse
Wayne, West Virginia
25570

Webster County Clerk
Courthouse
Webster Springs,
West Virginia 26268

Wetzel County Clerk
P.O. Box 156
New Martinsville,
West Virginia 26155-0156

Wirt County Clerk
P.O. Box 53
Elizabeth, West Virginia
26143-0053

Wood County Clerk
Courthouse
Parkersburg, West Virginia
26101

Wyoming County Clerk
P.O. Box 309
Pineville, West Virginia
24874-0309

WISCONSIN
http://www.state.wi.us/

Adams County Clerk
402 N. Main St.
Friendship, Wisconsin
53934-9375

Ashland County Clerk
201 Main St. W.
Ashland, Wisconsin
54806-1652

Barron County Clerk
330 E. LaSalle Ave.
Barron, Wisconsin
54812-1540

Bayfield County Clerk
117 E. 5th St.
Washburn, Wisconsin
54891-9464

Brown County Clerk
305 E. Walnut St.
Green Bay, Wisconsin
54301-5027

Buffalo County Clerk
407 S. 2nd St.
Alma, Wisconsin 54610

Burnett County Clerk
7410 County Rd K #103
Siren, Wisconsin 54872

Calumet County Clerk
206 Court St.
Chilton, Wisconsin
53014-1127

Chippewa County Clerk
711 N. Bridge St.
Chippewa Falls, Wisconsin
54729

Clark County Clerk
P.O. Box 384
Neillsville, Wisconsin
54456

Columbia County Clerk
400 Dewitt St.
Portage, Wisconsin 53821

Crawford County Clerk
220 N. Beaumont Rd.
Prairie Du Chien,
Wisconsin 53821

Dane County Clerk
P.O. Box 1438
Madison, Wisconsin 53701

Dodge County Clerk
127 E. Oak St.
Juneau, Wisconsin 53039

Door County Clerk
421 Nebraska St.
Sturgeon Bay, Wisconsin
54235

Douglas County Clerk
1313 Belknap St.
Superior, Wisconsin 54880

Dunn County Clerk
800 Wilson Ave.
Menomonie, Wisconsin
54751

Eau Claire County Clerk
721 Oxford Ave.
Eau Claire, Wisconsin
54703-5481

Florence County Clerk
501 Lake Ave.
Florence, Wisconsin 54121

**Fond du Lac
County Clerk**
160 S. Macy St.
Fond du Lac, Wisconsin
54936

Forest County Clerk
200 E. Madison St.
Crandon, Wisconsin
54520-1415

Grant County Clerk
130 West Maple St.
Lancaster, Wisconsin
53813-1625

Green County Clerk
1016 16th Ave.
Monroe, Wisconsin
53566-1702

Green Lake County Clerk
492 Hill St.
Green Lake, Wisconsin
54941

Iowa County Clerk
222 North Iowa St.
Dodgeville, Wisconsin
53533-1557

Iron County Clerk
300 Taconite St.
Hurley, Wisconsin
54534-1546

Jackson County Clerk
307 Main St.
Black River Falls,
Wisconsin 54615-1756

Jefferson County Clerk
320 Main St.
Jefferson, Wisconsin 53549

Juneau County Clerk
220 E. State St.
Mauston, Wisconsin
53948-1398

Kenosha County Clerk
1010 56th St.
Kenosha, Wisconsin
53140-3738

Kewaunee County Clerk
613 Dodge St.
Kewaunee, Wisconsin
54216-1322

LaCrosse County Clerk
400 4th St. N.
LaCrosse, Wisconsin
54601-3227

Lafayette County Clerk
626 Main St.
Darlington, Wisconsin
53530-1397

Langlade County Clerk
800 Clairmont St.
Antigo, Wisconsin
54409-1947

Lincoln County Clerk
1110 East Main St.
Merrill, Wisconsin
54452-2554

Manitowoc County Clerk
1010 S. 8th St.
Manitowoc, Wisconsin
54221

Marathon County Clerk
500 Forest St.
Wausau, Wisconsin 54403

Marinette County Clerk
1926 Hall Ave.
Marinette, Wisconsin
54143-1717

Marquette County Clerk
77 W. Park St.
Montello, Wisconsin 53949

Menominee County Clerk
Courthouse Lane
Keshena, Wisconsin 54135

Milwaukee County Clerk
Courthouse Annex
907 N. 10th St.
Milwaukee, Wisconsin
53233

Monroe County Clerk
202 South K St., Rm. 2
Sparta, Wisconsin
54656-2187

Oconto County Clerk
301 Washington St.
Oconto, Wisconsin 54153

Oneida County Clerk
1 Courthouse Square
Rhinelander, Wisconsin
54501

Outagamie County Clerk
410 South Walnut St.
Appleton, Wisconsin
54911-5936

Ozaukee County Clerk
121 West Main St.
Port Washington,
Wisconsin 53074-1813

Pepin County Clerk
740 7th Ave. W.
Durand, Wisconsin
54736-1635

Pierce County Clerk
414 W. Main St.
Ellsworth, Wisconsin
54011-0119

Polk County Clerk
100 Polk County Plaza
Balsam Lake, Wisconsin
54810-9071

Portage County Clerk
1516 Church St.
Stevens Point, Wisconsin
54481-3501

Price County Clerk
104 S. Eyder Ave. #205
Phillips, Wisconsin
54555-1342

Racine County Clerk
730 Wisconsin Ave.
Racine, Wisconsin
53403-1238

Richland County Clerk
181 W. Seminary St.
Richland Center, Wisconsin
53581-2356

Rock County Clerk
51 South Main St.
Janesville, Wisconsin
53545-3951

Rusk County Clerk
311 Miner Ave. E.
Ladysmith, Wisconsin
54848-1862

Sauk County Clerk
505 Broadway St.
Baraboo, Wisconsin
53913-2401

Sawyer County Clerk
P.O. Box 273
Hayward, Wisconsin
54843-0273

Shawano County Clerk
311 N. Main St.
Shawano, Wisconsin
54166-2145

Sheboygan County Clerk
615 N. 6th St.
Sheboygan, Wisconsin
53081-4612

St. Croix County Clerk
1101 Carmichael Rd.
Hudson, Wisconsin
54016-7708

Taylor County Clerk
224 S. 2nd St.
Medford, Wisconsin
54451-1811

**Trempealeau
County Clerk**
36245 Main St.
Whitehall, Wisconsin
54773

Vernon County Clerk
400 Court House Square St.
Viroqua, Wisconsin
54665-1555

Vilas County Clerk
P.O. Box 369
Eagle River, Wisconsin
54521-0369

Walworth County Clerk
100 W. Walworth St.
Elkhorn, Wisconsin
53121-1769

Washburn County Clerk
10 West 4th Ave.
Shell Lake, Wisconsin
54871

**Washington
County Clerk**
432 E. Washington St.
West Bend, Wisconsin
53095-2530

Waukesha County Clerk
1320 Pewaukee Rd.
Waukesha, Wisconsin
53188-3870

Waupaca County Clerk
109 South Main
Waupaca, Wisconsin 54981

Waushara County Clerk
209 S. Saint Marie
Wautoma, Wisconsin
54982

Winnebago County Clerk
415 Jackson St.
Oshkosh, Wisconsin
54901-4751

Wood County Clerk
400 Market St.
Wisconsin Rapids,
Wisconsin 54494-4868

WYOMING

http://www.state.wy.us/

Albany County Clerk
Courthouse
Laramie, Wyoming
82070-3836

Big Horn County Clerk
Courthouse
Basin, Wyoming 82410

Campbell County Clerk
500 South Gillette Ave.
Gillette, Wyoming
82716-4239

Carbon County Clerk
Fifth and Spruce
Rawlins, Wyoming 82301

Converse County Clerk
P.O. Box 990
Douglas, Wyoming
82633-0990

Crook County Clerk
P.O. Box 37
Sundance, Wyoming
82729-0037

Fremont County Clerk
P.O. Box CC
Lander, Wyoming 82520

Goshen County Clerk
P.O. Box 160
Torrington, Wyoming
82240

Hot Springs County Clerk
Courthouse
Thermopolis, Wyoming
82443-2729

Johnson County Clerk
76 North Main
Buffalo, Wyoming
82834-1847

Laramie County Clerk
1902 Carey Ave.
Cheyenne, Wyoming 82001

Lincoln County Clerk
Courthouse
Kemmerer, Wyoming
83101-3141

Natrona County Clerk
200 North Center
Casper, Wyoming
82601-1949

Niobrara County Clerk
P.O. Box 420
Lusk, Wyoming 82225

Park County Clerk
P.O. Box 160
Cody, Wyoming
82414-0160

Platte County Clerk
P.O. Box 728
Wheatland, Wyoming
82201-0728

Sheridan County Clerk
224 S. Main St.
Sheridan, Wyoming
82801-4855

Sublette County Clerk
21 South Tyler St.
Pinedale, Wyoming 82941

Sweetwater County Clerk
P.O. Box 730
Green River, Wyoming
82935-0730

Teton County Clerk
P.O. Box 1727
Jackson, Wyoming
83001-1727

Uinta County Clerk
225 Ninth St.
Evanston, Wyoming
82930-3415

Washakie County Clerk
P.O. Box 260
Worland, Wyoming
82401-0260

Weston County Clerk
1 West Main
Newcastle, Wyoming
82701-2106

✍ ✍ ✍

Another Book from Joseph Culligan

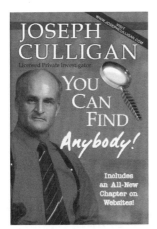

$29.95 • Hardcover
ISBN: 1-58872-000-4
**Available from your local
bookstore or library, or
from Jodere Group, Inc.**

It's true! You can . . .

. . . use the **United States Postal Service's** own policy to give you a street
address on certain **post office boxes** so that you can find anybody!

. . . have the address of every **hunting and fishing license department** in all 50
states so you can find anybody!

. . . have the address of every **bankruptcy court in all 50 states** so you can find
anybody!

. . . have the address of every **Armed Forces records department** so you can
find anybody!

. . . have the address to order **birth, death, marriage, and divorce records** in all
50 states so you can find anybody!

. . . have the address of every **corporation department in all 50 states** so you
can find anybody!

. . . have the address of **all the United States Government National Archives'
offices** so you can find anybody!

. . . have the **Web addresses of city, county, state, and federal government
departments and agencies** so you can find anybody!

. . . use the **government's own Child Support Enforcement Agencies** so you
can find anybody!

. . . have the address of every **state police agency** in all 50 states so you can find
anybody!

. . . use the same company private investigators and other professionals use to find
someone's **Social Security Number,** to run **Social Security Number
Address Update Reports,** and many other reports so you can find anybody!

And much, much more!

*Includes little-known search techniques that
have been used to reunite people on many national TV programs.*

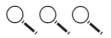

Joseph Culligan Investigative Camp Exclusive Weekend Programs

Be one of the select few to spend a weekend with Joe Culligan and his colleagues as they share all of their professional secrets. Joe Culligan's Investigative Camps are open to a very limited number of people and will be held in some of the most beautiful hotels in the world. Come learn the tricks of the trade from one of the most sought-after P.I.'s in the world.

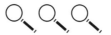

Joe Culligan Investigative Camp

You will learn:

- how to perform surveillance and place concealed cameras;

- forensic locksmithing, including thumbprint and retina scans;

- how to obtain and use high-tech spy equipment (it's not justfor the CIA anymore);

- secrets from the best computer wizards around;

- how to create your own lock-picking tools . . .

. . . and many more of Joseph Culligan's exclusive secrets!

For more information, visit
www.josephculligan.com or **www.Jodere.com**.

OTHER JODERE GROUP TITLES

BOOKS

Crossing Over, by John Edward

The Game, by Sarano Kelley

What If God Were the Sun? a novel by John Edward

When Your Moment Comes, by Dan Pallotta

You Can Find Anybody!
by Joseph Culligan, Licensed Private Investigator

❧   ❧   ❧

AUDIO PROGRAMS

Crossing Over, an abridged audio book by John Edward

Heaven on Earth, by Gary Quinn (audio and CD)

What If God Were the Sun? an abridged audio book by John Edward

The Dark Side of the Light Chasers,
an abridged audio book by Debbie Ford

❧   ❧   ❧

All of the above are available at your local bookstore,
by calling **Jodere Group, Inc., at (800) 569-1002,**
or by contacting the Jodere Group distributor:
Hay House, Inc., at (760) 431-7695 or (800) 654-5126

NOTES

NOTES

NOTES

NOTES

NOTES

NOTES

NOTES

≈ ≈ ≈

We hope you enjoyed this Jodere Group book.
If you would like additional information
about Jodere Group, Inc., please contact:

JODERE
GROUP

Jodere Group, Inc.
P.O. Box 910147
San Diego, CA 92191-0147
(800) 569-1002
(858) 638-8170 (fax)
www.jodere.com

Distributed in the United States by:

Hay House, Inc.
P.O. Box 5100
Carlsbad, CA 92018-5100
(760) 431-7695 or (800) 654-5126
(760) 431-6948 (fax) or (800) 650-5115 (fax)
www.hayhouse.com

≈ ≈ ≈